GW00721926

™

How to access your on-line resources

Kaplan Financial students will have a MyKaplan account and these extra resources will be available to you online. You do not need to register again, as this process was completed when you enrolled. If you are having problems accessing online materials, please ask your course administrator.

If you are not studying with Kaplan and did not purchase your book via a Kaplan website, to unlock your extra online resources please go to www.en-gage.co.uk (even if you have set up an account and registered books previously). You will then need to enter the ISBN number (on the title page and back cover) and the unique pass key number contained in the scratch panel below to gain access.

You will also be required to enter additional information during this process to set up or confirm your account details.

If you purchased through the Kaplan Publishing website you will automatically receive an e-mail invitation to register your details and gain access to your content. If you do not receive the e-mail or book content, please contact Kaplan Publishing.

Your code and information

This code can only be used once for the registration of one book online. This registration and your online content will expire when the final sittings for the examinations covered by this book have taken place. Please allow one hour from the time you submit your book details for us to process your request.

Please scratch the film to access your unique code.

Please be aware that this code is case-sensitive and you will need to include the dashes within the passcode, but not when entering the ISBN.

PUBLISHING

CIMA

Subject E3

Strategic Management

Study Text

KAPLAN PUBLISHING'S STATEMENT OF PRINCIPLES

LINGUISTIC DIVERSITY, EQUALITY AND INCLUSION

We are committed to diversity, equality and inclusion and strive to deliver content that all users can relate to.

We are here to make a difference to the success of every learner.

Clarity, accessibility and ease of use for our learners are key to our approach.

We will use contemporary examples that are rich, engaging and representative of a diverse workplace.

We will include a representative mix of race and gender at the various levels of seniority within the businesses in our examples to support all our learners in aspiring to achieve their potential within their chosen careers.

Roles played by characters in our examples will demonstrate richness and diversity by the use of different names, backgrounds, ethnicity and gender, with a mix of sexuality, relationships and beliefs where these are relevant to the syllabus.

It must always be obvious who is being referred to in each stage of any example so that we do not detract from clarity and ease of use for each of our learners.

We will actively seek feedback from our learners on our approach and keep our policy under continuous review. If you would like to provide any feedback on our linguistic approach, please use this form (you will need to enter the link below into your browser).

https://docs.google.com/forms/d/1YNo3A16mtXGTDIFJzgJhcu377QA4Q4ihUgfYvVKclF8/edit

We will seek to devise simple measures that can be used by independent assessors to randomly check our success in the implementation of our Linguistic Equality, Diversity and Inclusion Policy.

Published by: Kaplan Publishing UK

Unit 2 The Business Centre, Molly Millars Lane, Wokingham, Berkshire RG41 2QZ

Acknowledgements

We are grateful to the CIMA for permission to reproduce past examination questions. The answers to CIMA Exams have been prepared by Kaplan Publishing, except in the case of the CIMA November 2010 and subsequent CIMA Exam answers where the official CIMA answers have been reproduced. Questions from past live assessments have been included by kind permission of CIMA,

British Library Cataloguing in Publication Data

A catalogue record for this book is available from the British Library.

ISBN: 978-1-83996-238-7

Printed and bound in Great Britain

Contents

Introduction

How to use the Materials

These official CIMA learning materials have been carefully designed to make your learning experience as easy as possible and to give you the best chances of success in your objective tests.

The product range contains a number of features to help you in the study process. They include:

- a detailed explanation of all syllabus areas

- extensive 'practical' materials

- generous question practice, together with full solutions.

This Study Text has been designed with the needs of home study and distance learning candidates in mind. Such students require very full coverage of the syllabus topics, and also the facility to undertake extensive question practice. However, the Study Text is also ideal for fully taught courses.

The main body of the text is divided into a number of chapters, each of which is organised on the following pattern:

- **Detailed learning outcomes.** These describe the knowledge expected after your studies of the chapter are complete. You should assimilate these before beginning detailed work on the chapter, so that you can appreciate where your studies are leading.

- **Step-by-step topic coverage.** This is the heart of each chapter, containing detailed explanatory text supported where appropriate by worked examples and exercises. You should work carefully through this section, ensuring that you understand the material being explained and can tackle the examples and exercises successfully. Remember that in many cases knowledge is cumulative: if you fail to digest earlier material thoroughly, you may struggle to understand later chapters.

- **Activities.** Some chapters are illustrated by more practical elements, such as comments and questions designed to stimulate discussion.

- **Question practice.** The text contains three styles of question:

    - Exam-style objective test questions (OTQs).

    - 'Integration' questions – these test your ability to understand topics within a wider context. This is particularly important with calculations where OTQs may focus on just one element but an integration question tackles the full calculation, just as you would be expected to do in the workplace.

–   'Case' style questions – these test your ability to analyse and discuss issues in greater depth, particularly focusing on scenarios that are less clear cut than in the objective tests, and thus provide excellent practice for developing the skills needed for success in the Strategic Level Case Study Examination.

- **Solutions.** Avoid the temptation merely to 'audit' the solutions provided. It is an illusion to think that this provides the same benefits as you would gain from a serious attempt of your own. However, if you are struggling to get started on a question you should read the introductory guidance provided at the beginning of the solution, where provided, and then make your own attempt before referring back to the full solution.

If you work conscientiously through this Official CIMA Study Text according to the guidelines above you will be giving yourself an excellent chance of success in your objective tests. Good luck with your studies!

Quality and accuracy are of the utmost importance to us so if you spot an error in any of our products, please send an email to mykaplanreporting@kaplan.com with full details, or follow the link to the feedback form in MyKaplan.

Our Quality Co-ordinator will work with our technical team to verify the error and take action to ensure it is corrected in future editions.

Icon explanations

 Definition – These sections explain important areas of knowledge which must be understood and reproduced in an assessment environment.

 Key point – Identifies topics which are key to success and are often examined.

 Supplementary reading – These sections will help to provide a deeper understanding of core areas. The supplementary reading is **NOT** optional reading. It is vital to provide you with the breadth of knowledge you will need to address the wide range of topics within your syllabus that could feature in an assessment question. **Reference to this text is vital when self-studying.**

 Test your understanding – Following key points and definitions are exercises which give the opportunity to assess the understanding of these core areas.

 Illustration – To help develop an understanding of particular topics. The illustrative examples are useful in preparing for the Test your understanding exercises.

Study technique

Passing exams is partly a matter of intellectual ability, but however accomplished you are in that respect you can improve your chances significantly by the use of appropriate study and revision techniques. In this section we briefly outline some tips for effective study during the earlier stages of your approach to the objective tests. We also mention some techniques that you will find useful at the revision stage.

Planning

To begin with, formal planning is essential to get the best return from the time you spend studying. Estimate how much time in total you are going to need for each subject you are studying. Remember that you need to allow time for revision as well as for initial study of the material.

With your study material before you, decide which chapters you are going to study in each week, and which weeks you will devote to revision and final question practice.

Prepare a written schedule summarising the above and stick to it!

It is essential to know your syllabus. As your studies progress you will become more familiar with how long it takes to cover topics in sufficient depth. Your timetable may need to be adapted to allocate enough time for the whole syllabus.

Students are advised to refer to the examination blueprints (see page P.13 for further information) and the CIMA website, www.cimaglobal.com, to ensure they are up-to-date.

The amount of space allocated to a topic in the Study Text is not a very good guide as to how long it will take you. The syllabus weighting is the better guide as to how long you should spend on a syllabus topic.

Tips for effective studying

(1) Aim to find a quiet and undisturbed location for your study, and plan as far as possible to use the same period of time each day. Getting into a routine helps to avoid wasting time. Make sure that you have all the materials you need before you begin so as to minimise interruptions.

(2) Store all your materials in one place, so that you do not waste time searching for items every time you want to begin studying. If you have to pack everything away after each study period, keep your study materials in a box, or even a suitcase, which will not be disturbed until the next time.

(3) Limit distractions. To make the most effective use of your study periods you should be able to apply total concentration, so turn off all entertainment equipment, set your phones to message mode, and put up your 'do not disturb' sign.

(4) Your timetable will tell you which topic to study. However, before diving in and becoming engrossed in the finer points, make sure you have an overall picture of all the areas that need to be covered by the end of that session. After an hour, allow yourself a short break and move away from your Study Text. With experience, you will learn to assess the pace you need to work at. Each study session should focus on component learning outcomes – the basis for all questions.

(5) Work carefully through a chapter, making notes as you go. When you have covered a suitable amount of material, vary the pattern by attempting a practice question. When you have finished your attempt, make notes of any mistakes you made, or any areas that you failed to cover or covered more briefly. Be aware that all component learning outcomes will be tested in each examination.

(6) Make notes as you study, and discover the techniques that work best for you. Your notes may be in the form of lists, bullet points, diagrams, summaries, 'mind maps', or the written word, but remember that you will need to refer back to them at a later date, so they must be intelligible. If you are on a taught course, make sure you highlight any issues you would like to follow up with your lecturer.

(7) Organise your notes. Make sure that all your notes, calculations etc. can be effectively filed and easily retrieved later.

Progression

There are two elements of progression that we can measure: how quickly students move through individual topics within a subject; and how quickly they move from one course to the next. We know that there is an optimum for both, but it can vary from subject to subject and from student to student. However, using data and our experience of student performance over many years, we can make some generalisations.

A fixed period of study set out at the start of a course with key milestones is important. This can be within a subject, for example 'I will finish this topic by 30 June', or for overall achievement, such as 'I want to be qualified by the end of next year'.

Your qualification is cumulative, as earlier papers provide a foundation for your subsequent studies, so do not allow there to be too big a gap between one subject and another. For example, E3 *Strategic management* builds on your knowledge of digital ecosystems and management of performance and projects from E2 *Managing performance*.

We know that exams encourage techniques that lead to some degree of short term retention, the result being that you will simply forget much of what you have already learned unless it is refreshed (look up Ebbinghaus Forgetting Curve for more details on this). This makes it more difficult as you move from one subject to another: not only will you have to learn the new subject, you will also have to relearn all the underpinning knowledge as well. This is very inefficient and slows down your overall progression which makes it more likely you may not succeed at all.

Also, it is important to realise that the Strategic Case Study (SCS) tests knowledge of all subjects within the Strategic level. Please note that candidates will need to return to this E3 material when studying for SCS as it forms a significant part of the SCS syllabus content.

In addition, delaying your studies slows your path to qualification which can have negative impacts on your career, postponing the opportunity to apply for higher level positions and therefore higher pay.

You can use the following diagram showing the whole structure of your qualification to help you keep track of your progress. Make sure you seek appropriate advice if you are unsure about your progression through the qualification.

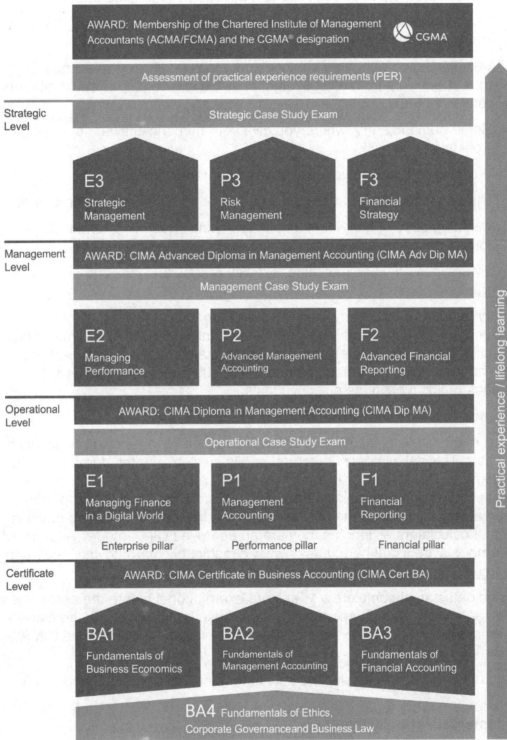

Reproduced with permission from CIMA

Objective test

Objective test questions require you to choose or provide a response to a question whose correct answer is predetermined.

The most common types of objective test question you will see are:

- Multiple choice, where you have to choose the correct answer(s) from a list of possible answers. This could either be numbers or text.

- Multiple choice with more choices and answers, for example, choosing two correct answers from a list of eight possible answers. This could either be numbers or text.

- Single numeric entry, where you give your numeric answer, for example, profit is $10,000.

- Multiple entry, where you give several numeric answers.

- True/false questions, where you state whether a statement is true or false.

- Matching pairs of text, for example, matching a technical term with the correct definition.

- Other types could be matching text with graphs and labelling graphs/diagrams.

In every chapter of this Study Text we have introduced these types of questions, but obviously we have had to label answers A, B, C etc. rather than using click boxes. For convenience, we have retained quite a few questions where an initial scenario leads to a number of sub-questions. There will be no questions of this type in the objective tests.

Guidance re CIMA on-screen calculator

As part of the CIMA objective test software, candidates are now provided with a calculator. This calculator is on-screen and is available for the duration of the assessment. The calculator is available in each of the objective tests and is accessed by clicking the calculator button in the top left hand corner of the screen at any time during the assessment. Candidates are permitted to utilise personal calculators as long as they are an approved CIMA model. Authorised CIMA models are listed here: https://www.cimaglobal.com/Studying/study-and-resources/.

All candidates must complete a 15-minute exam tutorial before the assessment begins and will have the opportunity to familiarise themselves with the calculator and practise using it. The exam tutorial is also available online via the CIMA website.

Candidates may practise using the calculator by accessing the online exam tutorial.

Fundamentals of objective tests

The objective tests are 90-minute assessments comprising 60 compulsory questions, with one or more parts. There will be no choice and all questions should be attempted. All elements of a question must be answered correctly for the question to be marked correctly. All questions are equally weighted.

CIMA syllabus 2019 – Structure of subjects and learning outcomes

Details regarding the content of the new CIMA syllabus can be located within the CIMA 2019 professional syllabus document.

Each subject within the syllabus is divided into a number of broad syllabus topics. The topics contain one or more lead learning outcomes, related component learning outcomes and indicative knowledge content.

A learning outcome has two main purposes:

(a)   To define the skill or ability that a well prepared candidate should be able to exhibit in the examination.

(b)   To demonstrate the approach likely to be taken in examination questions.

The learning outcomes are part of a hierarchy of learning objectives. The verbs used at the beginning of each learning outcome relate to a specific learning objective, e.g.

Calculate the break-even point, profit target, margin of safety and profit/volume ratio for a single product or service.

The verb '**calculate**' indicates a level three learning objective. The following tables list the verbs that appear in the syllabus learning outcomes and examination questions.

The examination blueprints and representative task statements

CIMA have also published examination blueprints giving learners clear expectations regarding what is expected of them.

The blueprint is structured as follows:

- Exam content sections (reflecting the syllabus document)
- Lead and component outcomes (reflecting the syllabus document)
- Representative task statements.

A representative task statement is a plain English description of what a CIMA finance professional should know and be able to do.

The content and skill level determine the language and verbs used in the representative task.

CIMA will test up to the level of the task statement in the objective tests (an objective test question on a particular topic could be set at a lower level than the task statement in the blueprint).

The format of the objective test blueprints follows that of the published syllabus for the 2019 CIMA Professional Qualification.

Weightings for content sections are also included in the individual subject blueprints.

CIMA VERB HIERARCHY

CIMA place great importance on the definition of verbs in structuring objective tests. It is therefore crucial that you understand the verbs in order to appreciate the depth and breadth of a topic and the level of skill required. The objective tests will focus on levels one, two and three of the CIMA hierarchy of verbs. However, they will also test levels four and five, especially at the management and strategic levels.

Skill level	Verbs used	Definition
Level 5 **Evaluation** How you are expected to use your learning to evaluate, make decisions or recommendations	Advise	Counsel, inform or notify
	Assess	Evaluate or estimate the nature, ability or quality of
	Evaluate	Appraise or assess the value of
	Recommend	Propose a course of action
	Review	Assess and evaluate in order, to change if necessary
Level 4 **Analysis** How you are expected to analyse the detail of what you have learned	Align	Arrange in an orderly way
	Analyse	Examine in detail the structure of
	Communicate	Share or exchange information
	Compare and contrast	Show the similarities and/or differences between
	Develop	Grow and expand a concept
	Discuss	Examine in detail by argument
	Examine	Inspect thoroughly
	Interpret	Translate into intelligible or familiar terms
	Monitor	Observe and check the progress of
	Prioritise	Place in order of priority or sequence for action
	Produce	Create or bring into existence
Level 3 **Application** How you are expected to apply your knowledge	Apply	Put to practical use
	Calculate	Ascertain or reckon mathematically
	Conduct	Organise and carry out
	Demonstrate	Prove with certainty or exhibit by practical means
	Prepare	Make or get ready for use
	Reconcile	Make or prove consistent/compatible

Skill level	Verbs used	Definition
Level 2 **Comprehension** What you are expected to understand	Describe	Communicate the key features of
	Distinguish	Highlight the differences between
	Explain	Make clear or intelligible/state the meaning or purpose of
	Identify	Recognise, establish or select after consideration
	Illustrate	Use an example to describe or explain something
Level 1 **Knowledge** What you are expected to know	List	Make a list of
	State	Express, fully or clearly, the details/facts of
	Define	Give the exact meaning of
	Outline	Give a summary of

Information concerning formulae and tables will be provided via the CIMA website, www.cimaglobal.com.

SYLLABUS GRIDS

E3: Strategic Management

Formulate strategy and create conditions for successful implementation

Content weighting

Content area	Weighting
A The strategy process	15%
B Analysing the organisational ecosystem	20%
C Generating strategic options	15%
D Making strategic choices	15%
E Strategic control	20%
F Digital strategy	15%
	100%

Lead outcome	Component outcome	Study Text Chapter
E3A: The strategy process		
1 Explain the purpose of strategy.	a Define strategy	1
	b Explain the purpose of strategy	1,2
2 Discuss the types and levels of strategy.	a Discuss types of strategy	1
	b Discuss levels of strategy	1
3 Outline the strategy process.	Apply the following:	
	a Outline the rational and emergent processes of arriving at strategy	4
E3B: Analysing the organisational ecosystem		
1 Analyse the elements of the ecosystem.	Analyse:	
	a Markets and competition	2,4,7
	b Society and regulation.	4
2 Discuss drivers of change in the ecosystem.	Discuss the following drivers of change:	
	a Institutional and systemic	4
	b Social	4
	c Market	4
	d Technology	4
	e Sustainability	4
3 Discuss the impact of the ecosystem on organisational strategy.	a Discuss the impact of strategic networks and platforms on organisational strategy	5
	b Conduct stakeholder analysis in networks	3,5

Lead outcome	Component outcome	Study Text Chapter
E3C: Generating strategic options		
1 Discuss the context of generating options.	Discuss:	
	a The role of governance and ethics in the strategy process	2,3
	b The purpose, vision and values of the organisation and their impact on strategy	2
2 Discuss how to generate and develop options.	Discuss how to:	
	a Frame key strategic questions	8
	b Diagnose organisation's starting position	8
	c Forecast potential organisational operating ecosystem	7
	d Use various frameworks to generate options	7,9
E3D: Making strategic choices		
1 Evaluating options.	a Develop criteria for evaluation	8
	b Evaluate options against criteria	8
	c Recommend appropriate options	8
2 Produce strategy by the integration of choices into coherent strategy.	Conduct:	
	a Value analysis	6
	b Portfolio analysis	8

Lead outcome	Component outcome	Study Text Chapter
E3E: Strategic control		
1 Develop strategic performance management system.	a Develop detailed action plans	9
	b Communicate action plans	9
	c Monitor implementation	9
	d Align incentives to performance	9
2 Advise on resource allocation to support strategy implementation.	a Advise on resource availability	6
	b Align resource allocation to strategic choices	8
3 Recommend change management techniques and methodologies.	a Assess impact of strategy on organisation	10
	b Recommend change management strategies	10
	c Discuss the role of the leader in managing change	11
E3F: Digital strategy		
1 Describe the governance of digital transformation.	a Describe the roles and responsibilities of the board and executive leadership in digital strategy	13
2 Analyse digital transformation.	Analyse:	
	a Digital technologies	12
	b Digital enterprise	12
3 Discuss the various elements of digital strategies.	Discuss:	
	a Economics of digitisation	13
	b Digital ecosystems	13
	c Digital consumption	13
	d Data and metrics	13
	e Leadership and culture	13

The strategy process

Chapter learning objectives

Lead	Component
A1: The purpose of strategy.	(a) Define strategy.
	(b) The purpose of strategy.
A2: Discuss the types and levels of strategy.	(a) Types of strategy.
	(b) The levels of strategy.
A3: Outline the strategy process.	(a) Outline the rational and emergent processes of arriving at strategy.

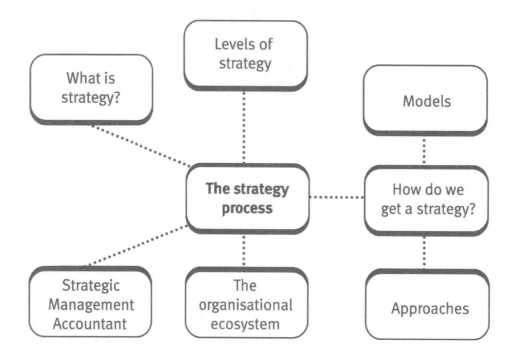

🔑 1 Introduction – the organisational ecosystem

The E3 syllabus, as its title suggests, looks at how organisations are managed from a strategic perspective. Much of this paper is therefore about understanding what is meant by the term strategy and the different processes that a management team might go through to formulate and implement an appropriate strategy.

It should be accepted from the outset that there is no 'one size fits all' strategy that is appropriate for all organisations; what will work for, say, a global oil company is likely to be very different for a manufacturer of consumer electronics.

Fundamental to recognising what will work for a particular organisation is understanding the **ecosystem** in which it exists.

What is meant by the term 'ecosystem'?

An organisation's ecosystem is made up of a network of organisations – including customers, suppliers, distributors, competitors, government agencies etc. – involved in the delivery of a product or service. This can be via either cooperation (e.g. customers and suppliers) or competition.

The idea is that all components of an ecosystem impact on each other, creating a relationship that is constantly evolving and within which each organisation must be flexible and adaptable to survive. The term ecosystem was first used in the 1930s in a botanic context; a community of organisms (for example, plants and insects) interact with each other and their environments (such as air, water, sunshine, the earth). In order to survive and thrive, these organisms compete and collaborate with each other on available resources, evolve together, and adapt jointly to external disruptions.

The same concept was then used in the 1990s to look at the business world. In his article "Predators and Prey: A New Ecology of Competition", the strategist James Moore identified similarities between the commercial and botanical worlds. He argued that organisations operating in the increasingly connected world of commerce should not be viewed as single companies in an industry; instead they should be seen as members of a business ecosystem with participants spanning across multiple industries.

Advances in technology and the increasing degree of globalisation have made people question the best ways in which to do business. The concept of a business ecosystem is thought to help organisations consider how to succeed in an environment which is changing constantly and at great speed.

Illustration 1 – The Apple ecosystem

Apple exists in a highly complex business ecosystem, made up of many participants. Examples would include:

Software developers – both those employed by the company and those who are not e.g. developers of apps which are then marketed via the App Store.

Suppliers – of components, organisations that assemble the product, of accessories (e.g. Belkin is an approved manufacturer of Apple accessories).

Retailers – not just employees in Apple Stores, but also approved 3rd party retailers.

Competitors – organisations such as Microsoft and Samsung, which are constantly innovating and therefore forcing Apple to do the same.

Customers – both individuals and also corporate customers.

Learning institutions – such as universities, that develop potential employees with the necessary skills.

Governments – e.g. much of Apple's product is sourced from China. Any trade wars between the US and China will inevitably impact Apple.

Legislators – those who formulate the law, which impacts not just on Apple but also other organisations e.g. privacy laws and Facebook.

This list is not exhaustive; there are many other elements of Apple's ecosystem!

In this chapter we look at the process of strategy formulation. This is fundamental to your understanding of the E3 syllabus as a whole. However, before we look at how strategies are created, we will first look at what we mean by the word 'strategy'.

2   The purpose of strategy

Strategy can be defined in a number of different ways, including:

 'A course of action, including the specification of resources required, to achieve a specific objective.'

CIMA official terminology

'Strategy is the direction and scope of an organisation over the long term: which achieves advantage for the organisation through its configuration of resources within a changing environment, to meet the needs of markets and to fulfil stakeholder expectations.'

Johnson, Scholes and Whittington (Exploring corporate strategy)

Essentially strategy involves setting the future plans of the organisation, but it requires a comprehensive understanding of the organisation's:

- resources (such as cash, assets and employees)

- ecosystem i.e. its environmental factors (such as markets, political and economic issues, customers and competitors)

- stakeholders (anyone with an interest in the business, such as shareholders, staff, customers, government, etc) and what they expect of the organisation.

This will allow organisations to decide how they are going to achieve a sustainable competitive advantage in the market(s) they operate within.

 The characteristics of strategic decisions

In their book 'Exploring Corporate Strategy', Johnson, Scholes and Whittington outline the characteristics of strategic decisions. They discuss the following areas:

- Strategic decisions are likely to be affected by the scope of an organisation's activities, because the scope concerns the way the management conceives the organisation's boundaries. It is to do with what they want the organisation to be like and be about.

- Strategy involves the matching of the activities of an organisation to its ecosystem.

- Strategy must also match the activities of an organisation to its resource capability. It is not just about being aware of the environmental threats and opportunities but about matching the organisational resources to these threats and opportunities.

- Strategies need to be considered in terms of the extent to which resources can be obtained, allocated and controlled to develop a strategy for the future.

- Operational decisions will be affected by strategic decisions because they will set off waves of lesser decisions.

- As well as the environmental forces and the resource availability, the strategy of an organisation will be affected by the expectations and values of those who have power within and around the organisation.

- Strategic decisions are apt to affect the long-term direction of the organisation.

In his book 'Competitive Strategy', Michael Porter put it this way:

'The essence of formulating competitive strategy is relating a company to its environment.'

 Advantages and disadvantages of deliberate long-term planning

Advantages of adopting a long-term planning approach include:

- **Forces managers to look ahead** – formal planning methodologies require managers to identify changes in the organisation's circumstances and look at ways to deal with them. This will help to ensure that the organisation stays relevant in its market and survives in the long term.

- **Improved control** – the organisation is forced to identify a mission and objectives. This will be communicated to management, meaning that they know what targets they are working towards/being assessed against. This will also improve goal congruence.

- **Identifies key risks** – by undertaking detailed analysis, management can identify key external and internal risks and create contingency plans to deal with these.

- **Encourages creativity** – management will have to generate ideas for the organisation, meaning that it can benefit from their experience and ability to innovate.

Disadvantages of formal, long-term planning include:

- **Setting corporate objectives** – it may be difficult for the organisation to create an overall mission and objectives. This is often due to the contradictory needs of key stakeholders. For example, maximising profit for shareholders may require restructuring to the organisation that causes employee redundancy. Dealing with stakeholder conflict will be dealt with in chapter 2.

- **Short-term pressures** – The pressures on management are often for short-term results. It can therefore be difficult to motivate managers by setting long-term strategies when short-term problems can consume their entire working day.

- **Difficulties in forecasting accurately** – it may be hard to identify long-term trends in the market – especially in fast-moving industries such as computing. This may make it difficult to create a strategy that is effective for the organisation over several years.

- **Bounded rationality** – the internal and external analysis undertaken as part of long-term strategic planning is often incomplete. This means that any strategies developed by the organisation based on this incomplete analysis may be ineffective.

- **Rigidity** – Once a long-term plan is created, managers often believe it should be followed at all costs – even if it is clearly no longer in the best interests of the organisation. This can also lead to the long-term strategy stifling initiative as managers refuse to act 'outside the plan'.

- **Cost** – the strategic planning process can be costly, involving the use of specialists, sometimes a specialist department, and taking up management time.

- **Management distrust** – the strategic planning process involves the use of management accounting techniques, including forecasting, modelling, cost analysis and operational research. This may be unfamiliar to some managers, leading to resistance. It is worth noting that many academics mistrust these models – not just managers!

3 Levels of strategy

Strategy can be broken down into three different levels.

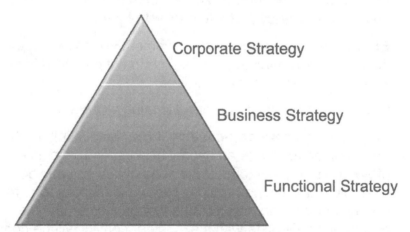

Corporate (or strategic) level

This is the highest level of strategy within the organisation and examines the strategies **for the organisation as a whole**. In particular it focuses on which businesses and markets the organisation should operate within.

Corporate strategy is therefore often concerned with issues such as:

- acquisitions, disposals and diversification
- entering new industries
- leaving existing industries.

Business (or management) level

Having selected a market, the organisation must develop a plan to be successful in that market. Business strategy therefore looks at **how the organisation can compete successfully in the individual markets** that it chooses to operate within.

Business strategy is concerned with issues such as:

- achieve advantage over competitors
- meet the needs of key customers
- avoid competitive disadvantage.

Corporate strategy affects the organisation as a whole, but business strategy will focus upon **strategic business units (SBUs).** An SBU is a unit within an organisation for which there is an external market for products distinct from other units.

Functional (or operational) level

This level of strategy is concerned with how the component parts of the organisation in terms of resources, people and processes are pulled together to form a strategic architecture which will effectively deliver the overall strategic direction. It looks at the **day to day management strategies of the organisation**.

Operational strategy is concerned with:

- human resource strategy
- marketing strategy
- information systems and technology strategy
- operations strategy.

These could be unique to the SBU and benefit from being individually focused or the corporate unit may seek to centralise them and so benefit from synergy.

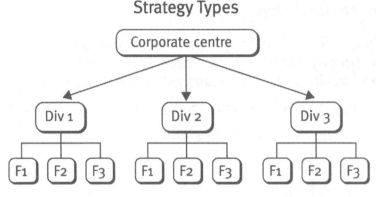

Strategy Types

✓ One corporate strategy

✓ Three business strategies

✓ A choice for functional strategies

Remember that all three levels are linked. A corporate or business level strategy is only going to succeed if it is supported by appropriate operational strategies.

For instance, a hotel chain may have a high level strategy of 'excellence in customer care', but the success or failure of this will depend on the staff who clean the rooms and cook the meals, etc. Therefore the day to day activities **must** be focused on achieving the corporate level strategy.

It is worth mentioning that formulating the strategy is the easy part. Actually implementing it is the difficult part. Premiership football clubs in the UK will all have strategies in place to win their league. Only one will actually do so!

 Illustration 2 – Levels of planning

Gap is an international clothing retailer. Classification of different levels of planning could be as follows.

Strategic

- Should another range of shops be established to target a different segment of the market? (Gap opened Banana Republic, a more up-market chain to do just that.)

- Should the company raise more share capital to enable the expansion?

Business

- Which geographical markets should the new range of shops open in?

- How often should inventories be changed to ensure the business keeps up with changing fashions?

- What prices should be charged in the new stores relative to rivals?

Operational

- How will suitable premises be found and fitted out for the new range of shops?

- Which staff should be hired for the new stores?

- Which IT systems need to be installed in the stores?

Gap's strategic decision to create the Banana Republic chain had to be supported by new business and operational level strategies. For example, poor business strategies for Banana Republic (such as pricing goods too high relative to rivals) would have led to the failure of the new stores. Likewise, poor operational strategies (such as poor training for employees in the new stores) would have damaged Banana Republic's brand and ruined Gap's overall strategic level strategy.

Whichever approach is chosen, remember that many different types of organisation will need a strategy. This will include companies (large and small), unincorporated businesses, multinational organisations, not-for-profit organisations such as charities, schools and hospitals, etc.

Anywhere that is likely to have a management accountant is likely to need a strategy. Remember that the exam itself will be based on any of these types of organisation. Be prepared for a wide range of scenarios!

4 Types of strategy

Having an appropriate strategy is seen as vital to the future success of most organisations. So how does an organisation create a strategy?

There are a number of different models that can be adopted. None can be considered to be the 'best' approach – it simply depends on which one each organisation feels is the most appropriate for their needs.

4.1 The rational model

The rational model is a logical, step-by-step approach. It requires the organisation to analyse its existing circumstances, generate possible strategies, select the best one(s) and then implement them.

The rational model follows a series of set stages as shown in the diagram below:

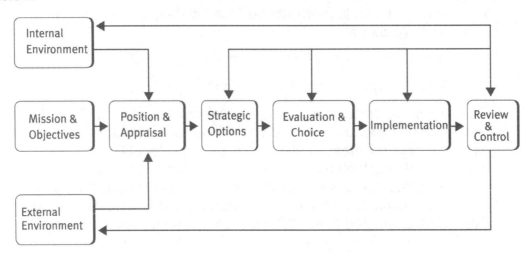

Johnson, Scholes and Whittington took the stages from the rational model and grouped them into three main stages:

Strategic analysis

- External analysis to identify opportunities and threats
- Internal analysis to identify strengths and weaknesses
- Stakeholder analysis to identify key objectives and to assess power and interest of different groups
- Gap analysis to identify the difference between desired and expected performance.

Strategic choice

- Strategies are required to 'close the gap'
- Competitive strategy – for each business unit
- Directions for growth – which markets/products should be invested in
- Whether expansion should be achieved by organic growth, acquisition or some form of joint arrangement.

Strategic implementation

- Formulation of detailed plans and budgets
- Target setting for KPIs
- Monitoring and control.

Illustration 3 – The rational model

H plc is a company with a chain of high-street stores selling CDs and DVDs across country V. It has posted significant losses in the last three financial years and wishes to create a strategy using the rational model.

Mission and objectives

In this stage, H will decide on what it needs to accomplish. For this business, it may consider its mission to be a 'turnaround' of the organisation's fortunes.

While this gives an overall direction to the organisation, it will also need to convert this into specific objectives, or targets. These may include (for example) a return to profitability, a reduction of costs by fifteen percent and a rise in sales by three percent over the next five years.

H can use these objectives to assess when it has achieved its mission of turning the business around.

Position and appraisal

This stage will require H to undertake a detailed analysis of its situation. It needs to understand its operations and external environment before it can suggest how to achieve its mission.

H will examine its internal environment – for example the quality and number of its stores, the ability and motivation of its staff and its cash balances. It will also examine its external environment – noting the shift in the market towards online downloading of music and films, rather than the purchase of DVDs and CDs.

H will also examine its stakeholders at this point to try and understand what they expect from the company. For example, what do H's shareholders want? Are they willing to invest more money into the company? What do H's customers expect from H and how powerful are they in determining H's overall strategic direction?

Strategic options

Once H has gained an understanding of its position (and why it is making significant losses), it can suggest possible strategic options that would help it achieve its mission.

For example, it could consider offering online downloads to customers as well as selling through its traditional stores. Alternatively it could continue selling via its stores, but dispose of any that are unprofitable. There are likely to be a number of different options that H could consider.

Evaluation and choice

Based on H's position analysis, H will pick the strategic option that best fits its circumstances. For example, it may lack the cash and skills to create a new online download site, meaning that it simply chooses to dispose of any unprofitable stores.

Implementation

H undertakes the chosen strategy. This involves choosing and closing any stores identified as underperforming as well as dealing with any unexpected problems (such as the reaction of staff unions).

Review and control

Once H's new strategy has been implemented it can go back to its initial mission and objectives. Has the store closure led to a return to profits, a reduction in costs by fifteen percent and a rise in sales by three percent? If not, H will need to decide on a new strategy to accomplish these goals.

Illustration 4 – The JSW approach

A full-price airline in considering setting up a 'no-frills', low-fare subsidiary. The strategic planning process, according to JSW, would include the following elements:

Strategic analysis: Competitor action, oil price forecasts, passenger volume forecasts, availability of cheap landing rights, public concern for environmental damage, effect on the main brand.

Strategic choices: Which routes to launch? Set up a subsidiary from scratch or buy an existing low-cost airline? Which planes to use? Which on-board services to offer?

Strategic implementation: Setup of new subsidiary. Staff recruitment and training. Acquisition of aircraft and obtaining of landing slots.

Test your understanding 1

Which THREE of the following are stages in the rational model of strategic development?

A   Implementation

B   Strategic analysis

C   Mission and objectives

D   Review and control

E   Strategic planning

F   Operational strategy

4.2 The emergent approach – Mintzberg

 Strategies are not always formally planned. In reality, strategies may evolve in response to unexpected events that impact on the organisation. **Mintzberg referred to these as emergent strategies.**

Mintzberg argued that in a changing environment, the rational model is often too slow and quickly becomes outdated. As an alternative, Mintzberg suggested that in reality, an emergent approach to strategy development occurs, whereby strategy tends to evolve rather than result from a logical, formal process. An emergent approach is evolving, continuous and incremental.

A strategy may be tried and developed as it is implemented. If it fails a different approach will be taken. It is likely to be more short term than the traditional process. To attempt to rely on emergent strategies in the longer term requires a culture of innovation where new ideas are readily forthcoming.

In effect the timing, order and distinctions between analysis, choice and implementation become blurred in emergent approaches. For this reason the analysis/choice/implementation identified earlier approach is sometimes shown as a triangle rather than a straight line in the emergent approach.

Note that the emergent approach does not necessarily mean that the organisation does not have a formal plan for the future. However to be successful it will need to be able to amend this strategy for unexpected events.

 Illustration 5 – The emergent model

The emergent model

Pfizer, a multinational pharmaceutical company, developed a drug known as Sildenafil in an attempt to deal with high blood pressure in patients.

The drug was ultimately unsuccessful, but patients in the test groups reported an interesting side-effect. Pfizer sold the drug as Viagra and started a new multi-billion dollar market.

4.3 Logical incrementalism

This approach suggests that strategy tends to be a small-scale extension of past policy, rather than radical change.

Incrementalism (initially developed by **Lindblom**) does not believe that the rational model of decision-making is sensible and suggests that, in the real world, it is rarely used. This is because:

- Strategy is not usually decided by autonomous strategic planning teams that have time to impartially sift all the information and possible options before deciding on the optimal solution.

- Instead, managers have to sift through the options themselves. Due to time and knowledge constraints (also known as **bounded rationality**), this means that they usually only choose between relatively few options.

- This typically leads to strategy being small scale extensions of past policy – in other words, managers try to make small changes to what they know has worked well in the past.

This approach to strategy has a number of advantages over the rational model. In particular it is often more acceptable to stakeholders as consultation, compromise and accommodation are built into the process. In addition, it is less of a cultural shift for the organisation to adopt an incremental approach to strategy as the organisation will not be trying to implement major shifts in its activities.

However, incrementalism may mean that the organisation has no overall long-term plan, causing it to suffer from strategic drift, eventually leading to it being unable to meet the needs of its customers. In addition, it could mean that the organisation fails to make major changes if needed.

Test your understanding 2

Which ONE of the following statements are consistent with incrementalism?

A   Strategy tends to be small-scale extensions of past policies

B   No formal planning should be undertaken – the business should simply react to events as they occur

C   Strategy development should follow a series of logical stages

D   Detailed internal and external analysis should be undertaken before deciding on the future strategy of the organisation

4.4   Freewheeling opportunism

Freewheeling opportunism suggests that organisations should avoid formal planning and instead simply take advantage of opportunities as they arise.

The main justification for this is that formal planning takes too long and is too constraining – especially for organisations in fast-changing industries, such as pharmaceuticals and technology development. It may also suit any experienced managers who happen to dislike planning.

Problems with a lack of formal planning

Freewheeling opportunists dislike formal planning. However, there are a number of practical risks involved with this approach.

- **Failure to identify risks** – the business is not being forced to look ahead. This means that it may fail to identify key risks, which means that it will not have contingency plans in place to deal with these, should they arise.

- **Strategic drift** – the organisation does not have an overall plan for the future, meaning that it may be difficult for it to effectively compete in its market in the long term.

- **Difficulty in raising finance** – investors typically like to know what plans the organisation has for the future. If the company does not have a formal plan, it may be difficult to convince shareholders and banks (amongst others) that the company is a worthwhile investment.

- **Management skill** – freewheeling opportunists require managers that are highly skilled at understanding and reacting to the changing market. Less able or experienced managers will find this a difficult approach to use.

Test your understanding 3

T plc is an electronics manufacturer, which has recently created a detailed strategic review of its operations, as well as its external environment. T identified that it had significant skills with regards to the manufacture of electronic displays and launched a range of flat screen televisions. Unfortunately, its new product range, while praised by reviewers, failed to sell well to the public. T therefore abandoned its original strategy and took advantage of an offer by HHH, another electronics manufacturer, to make screens for HHH's popular mobile smartphones.

Which ONE approach to strategy is closest to that adopted by T when accepting HHH's offer?

A   Emergent

B   Rational

C   Incrementalist

D   Opportunism

4.5 Which approach to strategy should we adopt?

We have identified four different approaches to developing a strategy. While we have already mentioned that there is no 'correct' approach, it is important that you can justify which one would be the most appropriate for a particular organisation to adopt.

We can consider the four approaches as a spectrum:

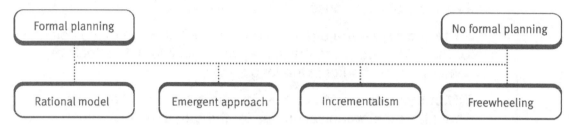

More formal planning approaches, such as the rational model (and to a degree the emergent model) tend to suit organisations which:

- exist in relatively stable industries, meaning there is sufficient time to undertake detailed strategic analysis

- have relatively inexperienced managers, as the formal planning approach helps to ensure they are familiar with the organisation as well as providing a series of guidelines they can follow to help them develop a strategy.

More informal approaches, such as freewheeling opportunism (and to a degree incrementalism) tend to suit organisations which:

- are in dynamic, fast changing industries where there is little time to undertake formal strategic analysis

- have experienced, innovative managers who are able to quickly identify and react to changes in the organisation and its environment

- do not need to raise significant external finance (external investors typically prefer a formal planning approach).

Note that incrementalism is unlikely to be suitable for new organisations as they have no past strategies upon which they can base their future policy.

Test your understanding 4

K is a small organisation which makes plastic toys. The company was very recently formed by Mr V. Mr V is a skilled entrepreneur with many years of experience in the industry.

The toy industry is incredibly fast-changing, with new innovations being developed regularly. In addition, tastes and trends change regularly, meaning that sales of toys can drop quickly as they fall out of fashion.

Mr V is aware that K will often require radically new strategies in order to keep up with these changes.

Which ONE of the following approaches to strategic development would be most appropriate for K to adopt?

A   Incrementalism

B   Rational

C   Emergent

D   Freewheeling

Test your understanding 5 – HAA – (Case Style)

You are Ali, a management accountant working for HAA plc – a computer games company that operates in country F. You have just found the following note from your manager on your desk:

NOTE

Hi Ali,

As I'm sure you're aware, HAA is planning to expand abroad, into the European market. To support this, we have undertaken a detailed review of our existing operations and the European market. This has been used to produce a three-year budget and operational plan for our proposed European operations.

The European electronics market has always been seen as a difficult market for new entrants. This is due to the fast-moving, innovative nature of the companies currently operating there. HAA has a high spend on research and development and our directors feel that the company is well placed to compete with European games manufacturers.

I'm meeting with the directors in fifteen minutes so I need you to make some brief notes for me evaluating our current approach to strategic planning. Can you suggest any more appropriate approaches we should consider?

Thanks

Required:

Draft a response to your manager, as requested.

(15 minutes)

Strategic planning for not-for-profit organisations (NFPs)

Strategic planning

Many of the organisations in exam questions will be profit-seeking businesses. However, some may involve charities, councils, schools, hospitals and other organisations where profit is not the main objective. With such a 'NFP' a discussion of objectives is likely to be problematic for the following reasons:

- It is more likely to have multiple objectives. A large teaching hospital may want to give the best quality care and treat as many patients as possible and train new doctors and research new techniques. Conflict is inevitable.

  This is not just an issue for NFPs, profit-seeking organisations also have multiple stakeholders with conflicting demands.

- It will be more difficult to measure objectives. How can one measure whether a school is educating pupils well? Performance in exams? Percentage going on to university? Percentage getting jobs? Percentage staying out of prison once they leave?

- There may be a more equal balance of power between stakeholders. In a company, the shareholders hold ultimate power. If they do not use it, the directors generally get their way. In a school, the balance of power may be more even (or even undefined) between parents, governors, the headmaster and the local education authority.

- The people receiving the service are not necessarily those paying for it. The Government and local NHS trusts determine a hospital's funding, not the patients. Consequently there may be pressure to perform well in national league tables at the expense of other objectives.

In spite of these problems, NFPs are still likely to need strategies. In the UK, for example, many public sector organisations have to produce strategic plans for between one and five years ahead as this is a Government requirement.

One of the reasons for this is that the public sector is required to hit certain targets and key performance indicators (KPIs), which are set by central government. In a company these targets and KPIs are used to ensure that the business is competitive. For a public sector organisation, they are used by the government to exert control over the activities of the organisation and to ensure that the government's funding is being used appropriately.

The 3Es

Public sector organisations and charities often have difficulty in using traditional private-sector-based approaches to objective setting since they do not make a profit by which their success or failure can be measured. One way to address this problem is to use the following approach.

The 'three **E**s approach' of the Audit Commission:

- **Economy** looks solely at the level of inputs, e.g. did the hospital spend more or less on drugs this year? Or on nurses' wages?

- **Efficiency** looks at the link between outputs and inputs (the internal processes approach). The 'internal processes approach' looks at how well inputs have been used to achieve outputs – it is a measure of efficiency. For example, what was the average cost per patient treated? What was the average spend per bed over the period? What was the bed occupancy rate that this achieved?

- **Effectiveness** looks at the outputs (the goal approach). The 'goal approach' looks at the ultimate objectives of the organisation, i.e. it looks at output measures. For example, for an NHS hospital, have the waiting lists been reduced? Have mortality rates gone down? How many patients have been treated?

The best picture of the success of an organisation is obtained by using all of the above approaches and by examining both financial and non-financial issues. Think about effectiveness meaning 'doing the right things' and efficiency 'about doing things right'.

Illustration 6 – The 3Es

Consider O – a large teaching hospital based in a major city which is funded by the Central Government. O may want to analyse its value for money using the 3Es in the following ways:

Economy:

O is given an annual budget by the Central Government. Economy is likely to look at whether this budget has been met. Has O spent more overall than expected? Has more or less been spent on drugs or wages than predicted? These would help O measure if it has been economical with the use of its funds.

Efficiency:

How well have O's inputs been used to generate its desired outputs? This looks at O's internal processes and could include measures such as the average cost per patient, average spend per hospital bed, or the spend per student in the period.

Effectiveness:

This looks solely at the outputs of O's operations. For example, has O had a higher or lower mortality rate than expected? What percentage of students have qualified or passed exams? How long is the patient waiting list at O?

Test your understanding 6

H College is a government funded provider of education to several thousand students in country G. It aims to ensure that at least 75% of all exams sat by its students are passed.

In the last year, it achieved a pass rate of 75% on its exams (the same as the previous year). The head of the college claimed that this was in spite of the government limiting H College's budget rise to 3%, which meant that H College was unable to provide the level of service it had in previous years. Inflation in the economy of country G is 2%.

The government's official auditor has discovered that the cost per student has risen by 5% in H College over the last year, due to internal problems in operations.

H College is expected to offer value for money (VFM). Which ONE aspect of VFM has H College managed to achieve over the last year?

A   Efficiency

B   Economy

C   Effectiveness

D   Ethical behaviour

5 Perspectives to strategic planning

While each aspect of strategic planning is important, firms may prioritise the perspectives in different ways:

5.1 A traditional approach – stakeholders

The traditional approach starts by looking at stakeholders and their objectives (e.g. increase EPS by 5% per annum). The emphasis is then on formulating plans to achieve these objectives.

Objectives are very important but this approach is often flawed in so far as objectives are often set in isolation from market considerations and are thus unrealistic.

However, this approach can be particularly useful for not-for-profit organisations where a discussion of mission and objectives is often key.

5.2   A 'market-led' or 'positioning' approach

The more modern 'positioning' approach starts with an analysis of markets and competitors' actions before objectives are set and strategies developed.

The essence of strategic planning is then to ensure that the firm has a good 'fit' with its environment. If markets are expected to change, then the firm needs to change too. The idea is to be able to predict changes sufficiently far in advance to control change rather than always having to react to it.

The main problem with the positioning approach lies in predicting the future. Some markets are so volatile that it is impossible to estimate further ahead than the immediate short term.

5.3   A 'resource-based' or 'competence-led' approach

Many firms who have found anticipating the environment to be difficult have switched to a competence or resource-based approach, where the emphasis of strategy is to look at what the firm is good at – its core competences.

Ideally these correlate to the areas that the firm has to be good at in order to succeed in its chosen markets (critical success factors or CSFs – see chapter 5 for more detail on this area) and are also difficult for competitors to copy.

 Test your understanding 7

J Ltd is a company which offers home television repairs to customers. It has an excellent reputation for customer service and good quality workmanship. J feels that this has given it a competitive advantage in the market.

J is considering launching a car maintenance and repair service. It feels that its excellent reputation is likely to make such a move successful.

Which ONE of the following approaches to strategic planning is J adopting?

A   A positioning approach

B   A traditional stakeholder approach

C   A resource-led approach

D   A corporate approach

Test your understanding 8 – GYU – (Case Style)

You have just received an email from your manager.

To: A

From: A. B Jones

Date: 17/05/XX

Subject: GYU

Hi A,

You may not have heard of GYU – they are a new client of ours. GYU is a large company which manufactures mobile phone handsets. This is an extremely competitive market and GYU has recently been struggling to keep up with other companies in its sector. This is due to the fast-paced nature of the market. New handsets with increasingly complex features are constantly being launched by competitors and the directors of GYU are concerned that the range of handsets manufactured by the company are beginning to look dated.

This has caused a sharp fall in GYU's cash balances and in response, for the first time in its history, GYU has had to cut its dividend. The fall, which was around 10%, was met with an angry response by shareholders and GYU's share price has fallen significantly since the announcement.

While GYU's position appears weak, it is still seen as a market leader in the production of mobile handset software. While the reviews of its handsets are no longer entirely favourable, most customers agree that the software on the mobile phones is significantly superior to that produced by any of GYU's competitors.

I'm about to have a meeting with GYU's directors for the first time and I think they will ask me to advise them about the three different approaches to strategy that GYU could use and which is the most appropriate for their business. I'd like you to email me back in the next fifteen minutes and tell me your thoughts on these matters.

Required:

Reply to the manager as requested.

(15 minutes)

6   The role of the management accountant

It is important to appreciate the role of management accountants within the process of developing strategy. Normally this will involve providing information to aid in strategic planning and decision-making.

Strategic management accounting

Strategic management accounting is a 'form of management accounting in which emphasis is placed on information which relates to factors external to the entity, as well as non-financial information and internally generated information'.

CIMA Official Terminology

This indicates some key differences between **strategic** and **traditional** management accountants.

External focus

Traditional management accountants tend to focus on internal company issues. This is because their role is, amongst other things, to:

- aid in the creation of operational strategies for the business

- safeguard company assets – both tangible and intangible

- measure and report both financial and non–financial performance to managers

- ensure efficient use of assets and resources.

Strategic management accountants must provide information to help managers make key strategic decisions. This requires a stronger external focus – especially regarding the behaviour of competitors, customers and suppliers. Indeed, the strategic management accountant will need to consider all aspects of the ecosystem in which their organisation operates; the activities of business partners will also need to be carefully monitored.

This information will be vital to allow the business to understand the market it is operating in, which is a fundamental part of strategic planning.

Forward-looking

A large part of a traditional management accountant's role is to do with the measurement of historic performance of a business and its divisions.

Strategic management accountants need to be more forward-looking. This is because they will be analysing strategies that the business will employ in the future, rather than looking back at past performance.

Information provided by strategic management accountants

The information provided by strategic management accountants (SMAs) will include:

- **competitor analysis** – identification of competitors and detailed analysis of their activities

- **customer profitability** – which customers are the most important?

- **pricing decision** – forecasting of customer behaviour as well as competitor responses may help the business to decide on product pricing

- **portfolio analysis** – identification of key products and the strategies that should be adopted for each

- **corporate decision support** – this could include helping managers to decide whether or not to launch new products or enter/leave new markets

- **customer profitability analysis** – the SMA can help the business to identify which of its customers are most profitable and which may be costing the business money.

- **evaluation of brand value** – SMAs can help assess the value of an organisation's brand name, which may be useful when considering acquisitions and disposals of businesses or strategic business units

- **strategic information for acquisitions**, disposals and mergers – the SMA can help to assess what value such actions could have for an organisation

- **investment in strategic management systems** – SMAs can help management assess the need for and value of investment in new information technology and systems. For example, establishing and managing use of technology such as cloud computing or blockchain as part of the organisational ecosystem.

A comparison of the information produced by strategic and traditional management accountants may be useful:

Traditional management accountants:	Strategic management accountants:
Cost structure	Competitor cost structure
Product costs	Competitor product costs
Market share	Relative market share
Profitability	Relative profitability
Price margins	Competitor price margins

Value of strategic management information

The information produced by strategic management accountants will help the business in a number of ways, including:

- more effective strategic planning

- increased awareness of the business and its environment

- increased control over business performance

- better decision-making.

Test your understanding 9
Which ONE of the following statements is consistent with the role of a typical strategic management accountant?

A   They focus primarily on the provision of information about internal company issues to management.

B   The information they provide to management is typically forward-looking.

C   Their primary focus is on the provision of financial information to management.

D   They typically focus on the production of the organisation's financial statements.

7   Summary

By the end of this chapter, you should be able to discuss:

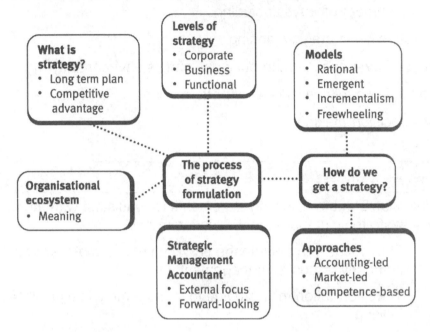

Test your understanding answers

Test your understanding 1

The correct answers are A, C and D.

Test your understanding 2

The correct answer is A

B relates to freewheeling opportunism.

C and D relate to the rational model.

Test your understanding 3

The correct answer is A

T has created a formal strategy after extensive analysis of its position. While this is consistent with the rational model, T has subsequently abandoned this and reacted to unforeseen events – i.e. the failure of its product to sell well.

This willingness to adapt to events as they occur is consistent with the emergent approach.

Note that incrementalism would involve small scale extensions to past strategies. HHH's proposal is significantly different to its original strategy, so this does not appear to be the case.

HHH is still basing its actions, at least in part, on a formally designed original strategy. This would indicate that it is not following an opportunistic approach.

Test your understanding 4

The correct answer is D

The pace of change in the market would tend to indicate that formal planning is not viable. This would suggest that the rational and emergent models are less useful. Incrementalism suggests that future strategies are small scale extensions of what has worked in the past. Again, this is clearly not appropriate given the need for radically new strategies highlighted in the scenario.

Test your understanding 5 – HAA – (Case Style)

Meeting notes

Current approach to strategy

HAA is currently using the rational model to develop its strategies. This involves taking a logical, step-by-step approach. HAA has clearly done this by undertaking such detailed planning, including strategic analysis of the market and the production of detailed operating plans.

The key advantage of such an approach to HAA is the level of understanding it will give them in the new market. They are currently not used to operating in the European market, so the initial strategic analysis they have performed will be invaluable. It will give them a picture of the their own capabilities as well as the European market they will be entering.

However, the European market is fast-moving, both due to its nature (high-tech) and the level of innovation by competitors. HAA will have to be prepared to quickly change its approach to deal with unexpected developments in the market. If the company produces a detailed operational plan, this may stifle the innovation that is required.

In addition, given the lack of experience that HAA has in the European market, any detailed forecasts it produces may prove to be unreliable. This may cause it to make inaccurate decisions based on flawed market predictions.

Alternative approaches to strategy for HAA

HAA could adopt the **emergent model**. While this would still involve some initial formal planning, these plans would merely be a starting point for the European operations. They will be continuously reviewed and updated as the games market changes, improving HAA's chances of success in the fast-moving market.

Alternatively HAA could choose the **freewheeling opportunism** approach to strategy. This would involve not producing a formal strategy – instead merely taking advantage of opportunities as they arise. The more rapidly the market evolves, the more applicable this approach may be, although it is considered too high risk for many managers.

Test your understanding 6

The correct answer is C

Effectiveness looks at the outputs of the organisation. As H has achieved its goal of a 75% pass rate, it has been effective.

Economy looks at the level of inputs – in this case, inputs have risen by 3% in the year (above inflation), but the efficiency with which H has used these inputs has fallen significantly. These factors would indicate a lack of efficiency and economy.

Test your understanding 7

The correct answer is C

J has identified a key resource or capability – its strong reputation. It is now looking for new ways to capitalise on this.

Test your understanding 8 – GYU – (Case Style)

There are three main approaches to strategic planning that GYU could take.

Traditional

This would involve GYU examining its key stakeholders and developing objectives that will meet their needs. The two key stakeholders in the scenario are GYU's customers and shareholders. The shareholders are clearly upset with the reduction in their dividend and will expect GYU to reverse this in coming years. The customers will be looking for handsets with more features and that are less 'dated'.

Unfortunately, while these are important objectives, they may be difficult for GYU to accomplish in the short term. Given the poor level of its finances, it may struggle to either increase dividends or invest enough in research and development to update its product line.

Market-led

This will involve the examination of GYU's competitors and market. Doing so should help GYU to ensure that it is competitive in what is a very fast-paced market.

While this appears to have been a weakness of GYU's to date (given the fact that it seems to have fallen so far behind many of its competitors), it may be inherently difficult in the mobile phone handset market. As the market is changing so rapidly, it may be difficult for GYU to accurately predict future trends and create appropriate strategies.

Resource-based

This involves GYU focusing its business strategies on areas that it is good at. For GYU its key area of skill is in the production of mobile handset software. It is acknowledged to be the market leader in this area and it appears to be very important to customers. Any future strategies should therefore be based around leveraging this area of skill.

For example, if it feels unable to produce handsets that are competitive, GYU could consider focusing on producing software which could then be licensed on other manufacturer's handsets. If this is a big enough market, this could help GYU to turn its business around.

Conclusion

Based on the information provided, the resource–based approach is likely to be best for GYU.

Test your understanding 9

The correct answer is B

Strategic management accountants tend to focus on information that is both internal and external, financial and non-financial information, and forward-looking. This will help management to make the best strategic decisions possible by having all relevant information to hand. Note that strategic management accountants would not usually focus on the production of the financial statements of the organisation – this role would usually be filled by financial accountants.

Generating strategic options: Mission, vision, values and stakeholders

Chapter learning objectives

Lead	Component
A1: Explain the purpose of strategy	(b) Explain the purpose of strategy
B1: Analyse the elements of the ecosystem	(a) Markets and competition
B3: Discuss the impact of the ecosystem on organisational strategy	(a) Discuss the impact of strategic networks and platforms on organisational strategy
	(b) Conduct stakeholder analysis in networks
C1: Discuss the context of generating options	(b) Purpose, vision and values of organisation and their impact on strategy

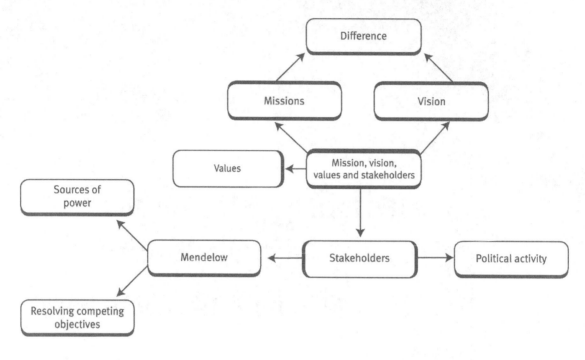

1 Mission

Missions

A mission is:

The 'fundamental objective(s) of an entity expressed in general terms'.

(CIMA Official Terminology)

The mission therefore is the **basic purpose of the organisation** and tries to identify the reason it exists. Ultimately the strategies of the organisation should be designed to support the accomplishment of this mission.

It is important that the organisation is able to communicate its mission both internally and externally, which requires the creation of a mission statement.

'The mission says why you do what you do, not the means by which you do it.'

Peter Drucker

Mission statements

A mission statement is:

A 'published statement, apparently of the entity's fundamental objective(s). This may or may not summarise the true mission of the entity'.

(CIMA Official Terminology)

Essentially, the mission statement is a **statement in writing that outlines the organisation's mission and summarises the reasoning and values that underpin its operations**.

There is no 'correct' format for the mission statement and it will vary in style and length for each organisation. However, typically it is a short, punchy (and hopefully memorable) explanation of the reason the organisation exists.

Illustration 1 – Examples of missions

We are a global family with a proud heritage passionately committed to providing personal mobility for people all around the world.

(Ford Motor Company)

Our Mission is:

- To refresh the world in mind, body and spirit.
- To inspire moments of optimism through our brands and actions.
- To create value and make a difference everywhere we engage.

(Coca Cola)

To create lasting solutions to poverty, hunger and social injustice.

(Oxfam)

Google's mission is to organise the world's information and make it universally accessible and useful.

(Google)

Characteristics of mission statements

There are a number of fundamental questions that an organisation will need to address in its search for its purpose and mission. According to Drucker, these are:

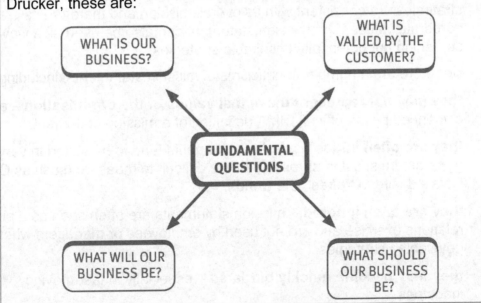

> Mission statements will therefore typically have some or all of the following characteristics:
>
> - usually a brief statement of no more than a page in length (often much shorter)
>
> - very general statement of entity culture
>
> - states the aims (or purposes) of the organisation
>
> - states the business areas in which the organisation intends to operate
>
> - open-ended (not stated in quantifiable terms)
>
> - does not include commercial terms, such as profit
>
> - not time-assigned
>
> - forms a basis of communication to the people inside the organisation and to people outside the organisation
>
> - used to formulate goal statements, objectives and short-term targets
>
> - guides the direction of the entity's strategy and as such is part of management information.

Mission statements fulfil a number of purposes:

- **to communicate to all the stakeholder groups** – everyone involved in the organisation will be made aware of its mission and should therefore know what to expect from the organisation.

- **to help develop a desired corporate culture** – by communicating core values, policies and expected standards of behaviour to key groups, such as employees.

- **to assist in strategic planning** – the organisation should ensure that its strategies are consistent with its overall mission and therefore its corporate values. The mission statement can also be used as a way of screening out potentially unsuitable strategies.

However there are a number of criticisms of mission statements, including:

- **they may not represent the actual values of the organisation** – as evidenced by the official CIMA definition of a mission statement.

- **they are often vague** – mission statements tend to be stated in very general terms, using phrases that are difficult to measure (such as Coca-Cola's desire to 'refresh the world').

- **they are often ignored** – mission statements are often seen as a public relations exercise and are not used by employees or managers when developing strategies.

- **they may become quickly outdated** – especially in fast-moving industries.

The process of creating a mission statement

The process of writing a mission statement

Mission statements are normally drafted by the senior managers or directors of the organisation, as they are uniquely positioned to understand the needs and aims of the business at a high level.

Usually the first step in creating a mission statement is to analyse the stakeholders of the organisation – customers, shareholders and employees (amongst others). More detail on this stage can be found later in this chapter.

The directors of the company should identify the needs and aims of these stakeholders. They can then attempt to create a mission statement that reflects these aims and that shows how the organisation wants to relate to the stakeholders.

A draft mission statement can then be written and distributed to key stakeholders for review. Any feedback can be built into the final mission statement, which can then be published and widely distributed to as many interested parties as possible.

The life span of a mission statement

There are no set rules on how long a mission statement will be appropriate for an organisation. It should be reviewed periodically to ensure it still reflects the company's environment.

If the market or key stakeholders have changed since the mission statement was written, then it may no longer be appropriate.

Illustration 2 – Yahoo

Yahoo – an internet search based company – had a mission statement in the early 2000s which identified that it wanted to be 'the most essential global internet service for consumers and businesses'.

However, by 2007 Yahoo was beginning to struggle due to the rise of major competitors such as Google, whose mission statement was 'to organise the world's information and make it universally accessible and useful.' Yahoo felt that its existing mission statement did not show stakeholders how it was different to these rivals.

It therefore made its mission statement more specific, changing it to reflect that it wanted to 'connect people to their passions, their communities and the world's knowledge'.

This attempted to show the difference between the two companies. Yahoo wished to position itself in the entertainment market, rather than merely providing information like Google.

As time moved on, Yahoo identified more about its target markets and the need to connect not only with users and their desire for more personalised service, but also their advertisers and key sources of revenue. By 2012, their mission statement had developed further into:

'Yahoo! is the premier digital media company. Yahoo! creates deeply personal digital experiences that keep more than half a billion people connected to what matters most to them, across devices and around the globe. That's how we deliver your world, your way. And Yahoo!'s unique combination of Science + Art + Scale connects advertisers to the consumers who build their businesses.

Test your understanding 1

JJJ Ltd's mission statement is 'to offer fantastic service to all customers'. The mission statement has recently been created by senior management but has not been widely circulated to anyone else. The CEO of JJJ has stated that all of the high-level strategies created by the organisation need to be measured against this mission.

Which ONE of the following benefits is JJJ most likely to see from its new mission statement in the short term?

A   Rapid change in JJJ's corporate culture to a focus on quality

B   Improved awareness amongst stakeholders of JJJ's goals

C   Improved strategic decision-making

D   Improved image to customers

Test your understanding 2 – (Integration question)

The mission statement of C plc is "to provide our customers with a top quality product at a fair price".

Required:

Evaluate the usefulness of this mission statement.

(5 minutes)

2   Vision statements

Vision statements are often confused with mission statements, but the two are subtly different.

While a mission statement defines the present purpose and state of an organisation, the vision statement identifies the ideal position that the company wants to reach within the medium to long-term. It is, essentially, the **longer term aspirations** of the organisation.

Illustration 3 – Examples of vision statements

A just world without poverty.

(Oxfam)

Our vision is a world without Alzheimer's.

(Alzheimer's Association)

To make people happy.

(Disney)

To become the world's leading consumer company for automotive products and services.

(Ford Motor Company)

Vision statements help give a longer term direction to the organisation's strategies and are designed to help staff make decisions and behave in a way that helps move the company towards its ideal long-term position.

Unfortunately, they have many of the same drawbacks as mission statements.

Illustration 4 – mission or vision?

The main difference between vision and mission is illustrated by the statements produced by Microsoft:

Mission statement:

To help people and businesses throughout the world realise their full potential.

Vision statement:

A personal computer in every home running Microsoft software.

This shows that the mission statement focuses on the company's present operations. The vision shows the ideal state that the company wishes to achieve in the future.

3 Values

The values of the organisation describe the core ethics or principles which the organisation will abide by, no matter what circumstances it might find itself in. The values will help drive the behaviour of the business, and guide the actions of management, employees and other stakeholders, such as suppliers.

Appropriate values that are clearly stated and adhered to serve a number of purposes for the organisation:

- **to guide staff behaviour** – everyone involved in the organisation will be expected to share and exhibit its values, resulting in suitable strategic and operational decisions being made.

- **to demonstrate integrity and accountability to external stakeholders** – by stating a commitment to set levels of behaviour, failing to adhere will naturally result in steps being taken against the business.

- **set the organisation apart from its competitors** – a proven adherence to stated values can be a source of competitive advantage should competitors fail to display the same expected standards of behaviour.

- **Reduce the risk of inappropriate behaviour from staff** – particularly if the consequences of failing to act in an expected manner are made widely known.

- **Set the culture of the organisation.**

The values set out by the organisation will depend on its industry and circumstances. For example, an academic institution such as a university (and therefore not a business driven by profit) may well place great value on freedom of thought, the value of research, or intellectual rigour. On the other hand, a listed telecoms company may adopt values such as network reliability, customer service, and returns to shareholders.

Illustration 5 – adidas Group values

The adidas Group publishes the following extracts under the governance section on its website:

For the adidas Group, corporate responsibility is rooted in its values:

Performance. Passion. Integrity. Diversity.

These values come from sport and sport is the soul of the adidas Group. It is what links our past and our present. It is what orients us towards the future.

Our values help us to create brands that our customers believe in, and a company our stakeholders can trust. Corporate responsibility has many facets and permeates all parts and operations of the company. For the adidas Group, operating responsibly means:

- Improving working conditions in our suppliers' factories

- Reducing the environmental impacts of our operations and in our supply chain

- Caring for the welfare and development of our employees

- Making a positive difference to people in the communities where we operate.

4 Objectives

A mission is an open-ended statement of the firm's purpose and strategy. Objectives are more specific and seek to translate the mission into a series of mileposts for the organisation to follow.

To be useful for motivation, evaluation and control purposes, objectives should be SMART:

- **S**pecific – clear statement, easy to understand
- **M**easurable – to enable control and communication down the organisation
- **A**ttainable – it is pointless setting unachievable objectives
- **R**elevant – appropriate to the mission and stakeholders
- **T**imed – have a time period for achievement.

Key issues

In the same way that an organisation's overall strategic plans need to be translated into a hierarchy of lower level tactical and operational plans, there will be a hierarchy of objectives where the mission statement is translated into detailed strategic, tactical and operational objectives and targets.

Typical issues this gives rise to are as follows:

- Objectives drive action, so it is important that goal congruence is achieved and the agreed objectives do drive the desired strategy.

- It can be difficult (although necessary) to prioritise multiple, often conflicting objectives.

- This is made more complex when some objectives are hard to quantify (e.g. environmental impact).

- There will be a mixture of financial and non-financial objectives.

- There is always the danger of short-termism.

- Objectives will vary across stakeholder groups and a strategy may satisfy some groups but not others.

Primary and secondary objectives

Organisations will typically set themselves different types of objective, with some being more important than others.

 Primary objectives (also known as corporate objectives) are the major, overriding objectives of the organisation. They can be financial or non-financial but relate to the organisation as a whole and, typically, the needs of its stakeholders.

 Secondary objectives directly relate to the various strategies that the organisation needs to adopt in order to meet its primary objective.

For instance, a company may set itself a primary objective of growing returns for its shareholders. It will then need to implement a number of strategies to help it achieve this – each strategy having its own 'secondary' objective. These secondary objectives could (for example) be an increase in customer satisfaction, increased sales growth, reduced wastage, or the launch of a number of innovative new products.

If the company can achieve these secondary objectives then it will be closer to meeting its primary objective of growing shareholder returns.

Long and short-term objectives

Objectives can either be long or short-term in nature. Short-term objectives typically focus on what the organisation wishes to accomplish over the coming year or so. Short-term objectives should be designed to help the organisation work towards achieving its longer term goals.

For example, a small retailer may have a long-term objective to grow its turnover by 25% within five years' time. This will need to be supported by a number of short-term objectives, such as a need to grow sales by 5% over the next financial year, or move to larger premises within the next six months.

If resources are scarce (or simply badly planned by management), then short-term and long-term objectives may be in conflict. For example, an organisation may set aggressive short-term profit targets for the coming year for its managers. This could lead to managers making decisions that meet the short term profit objectives but which compromise the long-term success of the organisation, such as:

- Reduced research and development investment, thereby reducing the organisation's ability to innovate and continue to meet its customer needs in the future.

- Reducing investment in the organisation's brand (such as cutting advertising costs), which may lead to loss of customers in the longer term.

- Delaying or cancelling capital investment (such as new production facilities or retail space) which may reduce the ability of the organisation to grow in the future.

- Reducing expenditure on staff motivation and training which may lead to higher staff turnover in future, as well as reduction in service quality offered to customers causing a fall in goodwill.

Management therefore must be careful when setting short-term and long-term objectives. In reality, there may have to be a trade-off between the two, but they should not be in direct conflict with each other.

Test your understanding 3

Which ONE of the following is **NOT** a required feature of an objective?

A   Measurable

B   Strategic

C   Timed

D   Attainable

Test your understanding 4

Q Ltd is owned by three shareholders. They have stated their desire to improve the profitability of the company and thereby increase their dividends.

Q Ltd has created a number of objectives to respond to its shareholders' needs. One of these is to 'delight its customers and the world at large with our products by the end of the next financial year'.

One of Q's managers has suggested that this does not meet all of the criteria for an objective.

Which ONE of the following criteria IS being met by Q's objective?

A   Measurable

B   Relevant

C   Attainable

D   Timed

Test your understanding 5 – JAA – (Case style)

JAA plc is a publisher of both fiction and non–fiction books, a market in which it faces significant competition.

It has recently published a new mission statement:

'JAA will continue to grow and innovate as an organisation, while acting in a socially responsible way.'

For a future meeting of the Board of Directors, the Marketing Director has been asked to prepare a presentation to discuss this in more detail. She has asked you to help her by suggesting objectives that could be used to help the company achieve its missions of 'growth' and 'innovation'.

The Marketing Director has suggested that the only objective for 'social responsibility' will be the happiness of the workforce.

> **Required:**
>
> Recommend, with reasons, TWO possible objectives each for BOTH growth and innovation for JAA, as requested by the Marketing Director.
>
> Comment on her proposed objective for social responsibility and recommend, with reasons, an alternative.
>
> **(10 minutes)**

Not-for-profit organisation (NFP) objectives

While we often look at organisations that seek to make a profit, there are many organisations for whom this is not the primary objective. These include:

- government departments and agencies

- trade unions

- schools

- charities (e.g. Oxfam, Red Cross)

- mutual associations (e.g. building societies).

Rather than seeking to make a profit, these organisations will try to satisfy particular needs of their members or the sections of society they have been set up to benefit.

Illustration – the Chartered Institute of Management Accountants

The objectives of the Institute are (amongst other things):

- To promote and develop the science of Management Accountancy and to foster and maintain investigations into and research into the best means and methods of developing and applying such science...'

- '...by means of examination and other methods of assessment to test the skill and knowledge of persons desiring to enter the profession.'

The services provided by many NFPs are limited only by the funds they have available. This means they normally aim to:

- raise as much money as possible

- spend this money as effectively as possible on the target group (with the minimum of administration costs).

Setting formal objectives can be difficult for NFPs. This is often due to the wide range of possible stakeholders as well as the fact the stakeholders who provide the funds may be different to the stakeholders who benefit from the NFP's activities (e.g. a charity). This gives much more power to the providers of finance and their objectives may not be the same as the NFP's.

5   Stakeholders

Mission and objectives need to be developed with two sets of interests in mind:

(1)   the interests of those who have to carry them out – typically managers and staff

(2)   the interests of those who focus on the outcome – such as shareholders, customers, suppliers, etc.

Together these groups are known as **stakeholders**, 'those persons and organisations that have an interest in the strategy of the organisation.'

(CIMA Official Terminology)

Given the range of differing interests that these stakeholders will have in the organisation, it is not surprising to find that the mission may take several months of negotiation before it is finalised. The key aspect is that the organisation must take its stakeholders into account when formulating its mission and objectives.

The mission-setting process can be a useful basis for getting the stakeholder groups to communicate their ideas and then be able to appreciate other viewpoints.

Stakeholder groups, and strategic networks and platforms

Before looking at stakeholders in more detail, it should be appreciated that most businesses no longer consider strategy in isolation, and that strategy is best developed by considering the strategic networks and platforms that the organisation operates within.

A **strategic network** can be defined as a collection of different organisations that are separate in legal terms but which work collectively to try to achieve long term strategic advantage. This might be via formal arrangements such as a joint venture, or a simple agreement to share information on an informal basis. The idea is that organisations can perform better if they work together, rather than simply working in isolation. For any organisation, the other members of its strategic network should be seen as a form of stakeholder.

The **strategic platform** is the means by which the transfer of goods or services between provider and consumer can take place. Historically, this has been more physical in nature; for example, a publisher might encourage a new book to be reviewed in a magazine or newspaper, and the consumer would then go to a bookshop in a shopping centre in order to make the purchase.

The modern day format of a strategic platform might be a digital platform, but the principles are still the same; a platform business model is developed that encompasses providers, suppliers, consumers and employees to create or exchange goods, services and social interaction. Others might integrate with other organisations' digital platforms. Regardless of the set-up, the strategy must integrate and consider all of the key stakeholders within the network and platform.

Strategic networks and platforms will be considered more fully in chapter 5, and the concept of **digital** strategic networks and platforms will be developed in more detail in chapters 12 and 13.

Stakeholder groups and their differing needs

It is worth noting that stakeholders are not only interested in the organisation's mission statement. In fact, they are far more interested in the strategies which the organisation is undertaking as it is these strategies that are likely to impact upon the different stakeholder groups. It is this influence and interest which organisations need to carefully manage.

In order to consider its stakeholders when developing strategies, the organisation must first identify who its stakeholders are and what they want or expect.

A large company, for example, could have a wide range of stakeholders, including:

Stakeholder:	Objectives:
Internal stakeholders	
Managers and employees	Career development, pay, job security, enjoyable jobs.
External stakeholders	
Government and regulatory agencies	Compliance with relevant laws and regulations, collection of taxation.
Civil society (including Non-Government Organisations (charities, pressure groups), civic clubs, trade unions, public groups, social and sports clubs, co-operatives, environmental groups, professional associations, consumer organisations and media)	Varied – could include: Pollution controls, health of public, human or member rights.
Industry associations	Member rights, compliance with industry rules and practises.

Connected stakeholders	
Shareholders	Profit, share price and dividends.
Customers	Low prices, good quality products, good service.
Financiers	Interest payments, security, meeting loan agreement terms.
Suppliers	Assured demand, fair prices paid, payments made on time.

As you can identify from the table above, some stakeholder objectives are likely to directly conflict with one another. Examples of conflict include:

- shareholders want higher profits, employees want better pay and working conditions

- customers want may want 24/7 service, while employees want working arrangements which fit into their personal lifestyles and home and family arrangements

- customers want high quality and low prices, shareholders want high profits

- suppliers want prompt payment, lenders want overdraft limits adhered to.

This means that it may be impossible for an organisation to satisfy the needs of all of its stakeholders. It must therefore find a way to prioritise its stakeholders, which is normally done by analysing their level of power and interest in the organisation.

 The more power and interest, the greater the involvement in setting the mission and strategy.

 Actors (Braithwaite and Drahos)

It is worth mentioning Braithwaite and Drahos to consider the full range of 'actors' who may have an influence on the way an organisation conducts its business.

- **Organisations of states:** Organisations formed by groups of states that meet and employ staff to explore common agendas (e.g. the WTO, the EU).

- **States**: Organised political communities with governments and geographical boundaries recognised by international law (e.g. Sweden).

- **Organisations formed by firms** and/or business organisations with common agendas, such as Chambers of Commerce.

- **Corporations**: Organisations formed by actors who invest in them as commercial vehicles (e.g. Ford, British Telecom).

- **Non-Governmental Organisations (NGOs):** Organisations (excluding business organisations) that explore common agendas. They can be international (e.g. Consumers International) or national (e.g. British Standards Institute).

- **Mass publics**: Large audiences of citizens who express together a common concern about an issue.

- **Knowledge based (epistemic) communities:** These consist of state, business and NGO representatives who meet sporadically and share a common discourse based on shared knowledge – sometimes technical knowledge requiring professional training; CIMA is an example.

The last three groups may be collectively termed civil society. Civil society includes, among others, nongovernment organisations; people's organisations; civic clubs; trade unions; gender, cultural, and religious groups; charities; social and sports clubs; cooperatives; environmental groups; professional associations; academic and policy institutions; consumers/consumer organisations and the media.

6 Mendelow's power/interest matrix

Mendelow's matrix is a model which can be used to prioritise stakeholders and decide how to deal with each of them. It does this by examining their level of power (how much control they have over the organisation) with their level of interest (how likely the stakeholder is to try and exercise their power over the organisation).

Stakeholder Mapping: The Power Interest Matrix

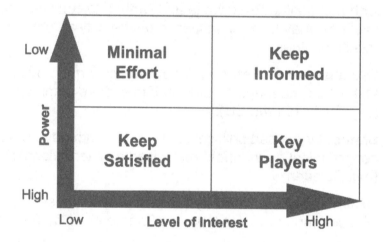

Sources of stakeholder power

Typically, stakeholder power can come from a number of sources:

- **Positional power:** This arises because of an individual's position in the organisational hierarchy and is reflected in their formal authority and reputation. Directors, for example, will usually be powerful because of their rank in the organisation.

- **Resource power:** This arises because an individual can control, obtain or create resources or other items of value. For instance, a unionised workforce will be powerful as they control the key labour resource in the business.

- **System power:** This arises because a stakeholder has high visibility or political access and relevance to a particular situation. A director who is closely connected to a major shareholder is likely to have significant power within the organisation.

- **Expert power:** This arises where an individual has information, knowledge or expertise that is important to the organisation. Skilled employees, for example, will normally have more power than unskilled employees as they have skills that are important to the business and they are harder to replace.

- **Personal power:** This arises because an individual has good communication skills and reputation and (usually) is well liked within the organisation. A popular director is likely to have more power in an organisation, as staff will be willing to follow his or her instructions.

Applying Mendelow's matrix

- **Minimal effort**

  Their low level of interest and power makes these stakeholders open to influence. They are more likely than others to accept what they are told and follow instructions.

- **Keep informed**

  These stakeholders are likely to have high levels of interest in the strategy but lack sufficient power to influence it. Management needs to convince opponents to the strategy that the plans are justified; otherwise these stakeholders will try to gain power by joining with parties with high power but low interest.

- **Keep satisfied**

  The key here is to keep these stakeholders satisfied to avoid them gaining interest and moving to the "key players" box. This could involve reassuring them of the outcomes of the strategy well in advance.

- **Key players**

  These stakeholders are potentially the most influential stakeholders in the strategic planning process. Their participation in the planning process is vital. Management, therefore, needs to communicate plans to them and then discuss implementation issues.

Managing the relationship with stakeholder groups

Powerful stakeholder groups must have confidence in the management team of the organisation. The organisation should ensure therefore that adequate management systems are in place. Some suggestions:

- Allocate organisational responsibility for the process of stakeholder management along with a budget.

- Use a team to manage stakeholders and decide on appropriate management techniques – ensuring a broad range of opinion and expertise.

- Establish and order the objectives of the organisation. Identify the areas for potential conflict and target resources into those areas.

- Frequent face-to-face meetings with the key player and keep satisfied groups.

- Communication processes for the keep informed and minimal effort groups – possibly via public Q&A sessions.

- Periodic formal reporting to stakeholders including, for example, the use of a website for 'frequently asked questions'.

It is worth remembering that this is complicated by the fact that individuals may be part of more than one stakeholder group at any point in time. For example, factory workers can also be members of the local community or even elected local government officials. This can mean that there are conflicts between their interests and objectives regarding a particular decision that the company is about to make.

Test your understanding 6
According to Mendelow, which ONE of the following methods should be adopted to manage a stakeholder with high power and low interest?
A   Keep informed
B   Key players
C   Keep satisfied
D   Minimal effort

Test your understanding 7

Country N is split into a number of regions, each with their own local government. The local government (LG) is given funding by the central government of country N, though LG officials are elected by local residents every four years. Resident turnout at local elections is high and local elections often result in a number of changes to LG officials.

LG budget is spent on a large number of local issues, such as transport and education for the region – issues that have a significant effect on the lives of local residents. The central government of country N has ultimate control over the amount of money that LG receives. However, central government rarely intervenes in LG affairs unless there is evidence of mismanagement of funds.

One LG has recently undertaken stakeholder analysis using Mendelow's matrix and identified local residents and central government as two of these stakeholder groups.

Which ONE of the following methods would be appropriate for each of these stakeholders?

	Local residents	Central government
A	Keep satisfied	Key players
B	Key players	Keep satisfied
C	Keep informed	Key players
D	Key players	Keep informed

Test your understanding 8 – AYL – (Case style)

You are Joe, a strategic management account at AYL, which operates the only public hospital within a small city in country U. All of its income is provided by the central government. However, due to a recent economic downturn, the central government is urgently looking for ways to save money. It has therefore decided to significantly cut AYL's budget for the coming period.

The management of AYL have therefore been looking at ways of reducing their expenditure while attempting to minimise the impact on the services provided to the public. They are planning to freeze pay for the semi-skilled nurses working at the hospital.

Your manager has left you the following note:

Note

Hi Joe,

Our proposed pay freeze has prompted significant opposition from nurses. Nurses are not heavily unionised, but the remaining staff members in the hospital, such as doctors, are all members of the same union. There are no plans to cut the number of remaining staff jobs in the hospital, or to freeze the wages of anyone other than the nurses.

Can you please write me some briefing notes identify the key stakeholders that the managers will need to consider? Using Mendelow's matrix, recommend what approach the managers of AYL should take in relation to each one. I know what Mendelow's matrix looks like, so please don't draw it in your briefing note.

Required:

Draft the briefing notes as requested by the manager.

(15 minutes)

 Resolving competing stakeholder objectives

Cyert and March suggest four ways to resolve conflicting stakeholder objectives.

- **Satisficing** involves negotiations between key stakeholders to arrive at an acceptable compromise.

- **Sequential attention** is when management focus on stakeholder needs in turn. For example, staff may receive a pay rise with the clear implication that it will not be their 'turn' again for a few years and so they should not expect any further increases.

- **Side payments** are where a stakeholder's primary objectives cannot be met so they are compensated in some other way. For example, a local community may object to a new factory being built on a site that will cause pollution, noise and extra traffic. The firm concerned may continue to build the factory but try to appease the community by also building local sports facilities.

- **Exercise of power** is when a deadlock is resolved by a senior figure forcing through a decision simply based on the power they possess.

Test your understanding 9

L runs a small business which sells second hand motor vehicles. She did not offer a pay rise to her staff last year, stating that she had not earned sufficient profits to be able to do so. However, she promised that she would offer a pay rise this year – regardless of whether a significant profit was made or not.

Which ONE of Cyert and March's stakeholder conflict resolution strategies is L adopting?

A   Sequential attention

B   Satisficing

C   Exercise of power

D   Side payments

Stakeholder alliances

As outlined above, organisations do not exist in isolation and can be affected by a wide variety of stakeholders. Some of these stakeholders can become important allies, helping the organisation to achieve its goals.

Stakeholder analysis

Not all stakeholders will make useful allies for the organisation. Using Mendelow's matrix will help the organisation determine the most important stakeholders and the ones that would be sensible to consider as potential allies.

For example, a company may wish to focus on major shareholders, as well as significant customers and suppliers, as these groups are likely to have a high degree of interest and power – making them more useful as allies.

Matching needs

A strategic alliance will only work if it benefits both parties. Once the organisation has located potential partners, it needs to research what their aims are, as well as considering how they could link with its own and support its own aims.

For example, if a manufacturing company knows that a government wishes to attract more jobs to a given region, it may suggest opening a factory in the region in exchange for subsidies.

Creation of the alliance

Once the organisation has identified the benefits of an alliance, it will be in a position to negotiate the terms with the desired partner. The alliance will need to be monitored on an ongoing basis to ensure that both parties are achieving the benefits they wanted.

Illustration 6 – Stakeholder alliances

Alliances can form between any organisations with matching interests.

Microsoft and Dell are an example of this. Dell is one of the world's largest manufacturers of personal computers and Microsoft writes the operating system used by the majority of these computers.

The two companies work together to ensure that the technological development of Dell's computers (i.e. memory and processor speed) keeps pace with Microsoft's software.

This arrangement benefits both organisations as it maximises the functionality of their products and provides their mutual customers with the best possible experience.

Test your understanding 10 – WRL – (Case style)

You are an accountant working in HHH – an accounts consultancy firm. You have received the following email from one of HHH's senior partners:

To: M. Williams

From: A. Scott

Date: 10/05/20XX

Subject: WRL meeting this afternoon

As you are probably aware, we are meeting with the managers of WRL later this afternoon to discuss several key issues, and I need you to do some research for me. I need a report in 45 minutes that covers the following:

(i)   Categorise, according to Mendelow's matrix, any three of the stakeholder groups of WRL with respect to the decision about the disposal of the polluted water. You should explain what the power and interests of the three stakeholder groups you have categorised are likely to be.

Note: I don't want you to draw the Mendelow matrix.

(ii)   Advise the Board of WRL of the actions it should take to resolve the problem of its stakeholders' competing objectives.

(iii)   Discuss the extent to which WRL's mission statement is consistent with its plan to put the polluted water in the lake.

To help you with this, I've attached a copy of our background analysis of WRL and its current situation. Please read it carefully and email me back within the next 45 minutes so I have time to prepare before the meeting.

Thanks

A. Scott

Attachment 1 – Background to WRL

WRL is a multi-national gold mining company. Its mission statement explains that 'WRL exists to make the maximum possible profit for its shareholders whilst causing the least damage to the environment. WRL will, at all times, be a good corporate citizen'.

In 2017 WRL was granted a licence to mine for gold by the national government of Stravia, a small country whose economy is mainly based on agriculture. The national government of Stravia was very keen to develop its economy and saw gold mining as an important aspect of this. The area where WRL was granted the licence is very remote and has no towns or cities nearby. There are small villages near the site of the gold mine. One of the conditions of the licence is that WRL would employ local people wherever possible, which it has done. WRL is entitled under the terms of the licence to dispose of the waste from the gold mining wherever is convenient for it.

The terms of the licence granted a payment by WRL to the national government of Stravia, payable in US dollars, which in 2019 totalled $50 million. This is a significant amount of foreign exchange for Stravia's economy. Similar levels of payment by WRL to the national government are likely to continue annually for the foreseeable future. The mine has operated profitably since it began.

WRL's mine is in an area controlled by the Eastern state government. The Eastern state government was not involved in the negotiations to bring WRL to Stravia and is not entitled to any payment from WRL. However, Stravia's national government granted the Eastern state government $1 million in 2019 from the payments which it received from WRL.

The Eastern state government discovered that WRL's proposed mining techniques use a great deal of water which becomes polluted. The cheapest way for WRL to dispose of this polluted water is to dispose of it in a lake near the mine and it intends to do this.

The Eastern state government feared that if the polluted water was disposed of in the lake this would kill all the aquatic life in the lake and have a long-lasting adverse effect on the lake and the surrounding area. Therefore, the Eastern state government took legal action against WRL in the Eastern state courts to prevent the disposal of the polluted water in the lake.

During the court action, WRL argued that if it was not allowed to dispose of the polluted water in the lake its mining operations in Stravia would become uneconomic and the mine would have to close. A small number of WRL's shareholders argued that it was better to close the mine than to pollute the lake.

The state courts granted the Eastern state government's request to prevent WRL disposing of the polluted water in the lake. However, upon appeal to the National Supreme Court, WRL has been granted permission to pump the polluted water into the lake as its licence imposes no restrictions.

Required:

Send the email as requested by the partner.

(45 minutes)

7 Non-market stakeholders

When businesses consider their stakeholders, they typically focus on the needs of those groups that help them directly gain competitive advantage, such as customers, suppliers and competitors – who collectively form the organisation's 'market environment', and who are part of its strategic network. In reality, however, competitive advantage can be built or lost outside of this market environment.

 Non-market strategy refers to an organisation's relationship and interactions with its 'non-market' environment – such as:

- governments
- regulators
- charities
- pressure groups
- the media
- the public at large.

Essentially non-market strategy sees the organisation as having social and political considerations, rather than simply economic concerns.

For example, governments can have a major impact on an organisation through their policies, such as through the setting or removal of subsidies or licenses to operate, employee legislation, environmental regulation and taxation policies.

Energy utility companies are under intense pressure from many governments (and the regulators that they have set up to monitor the energy industry) to not only provide affordable energy for their customers, but also to offer acceptable customer service levels and improve their environmental footprint. Failure on the behalf of the energy companies to meet these targets could lead to fines, other penalties, or even closure in extreme circumstances.

It is therefore vital that an organisation constantly scans its environment to identify these non-market issues in advance and hopefully create appropriate strategies to deal with them. Models such as PEST analysis (which we will examine in more detail in chapter 4) are vital tools to help with this.

However, it is easy for an organisation to feel that they must simply accept and try to manage non-market issues as they arise. In reality, organisations may wish to try and actually influence non-market issues. For instance, rather than simply waiting for governments to pass new laws, organisations may wish to influence political decision making – a process referred to as **corporate political activity**.

Porter's view on the influence of government

The influence of government on an industry

Porter identifies seven ways in which a government can affect the structure of an industry.

- Capacity expansion. The government can take actions to encourage firms or an industry as a whole to increase or cut capacity. Examples include capital allowances to encourage investment in equipment; regional incentives to encourage firms to locate new capacity in a particular area, and incentives to attract investment from overseas firms. The government is also (directly or indirectly) a supplier of infrastructure such as roads and railways, and this may influence expansion in a particular area.

- Demand. The government is a major customer of business in all areas of life and can influence demand by buying more or less. It can also influence demand by legislative measures. The tax system for cars is a good example: a change in the tax relief available for different engine sizes has a direct effect on the car manufacturers' product and the relative numbers of each type produced. Regulations and controls in an industry will affect the growth and profits of the industry, for example minimum product quality standards.

- Divestment and exit. A firm may wish to sell off a business to a foreign competitor or close it down, but the government might prevent this action because it is not in the public interest (there could be examples in health, defence, transport, education, agriculture and so on).

- Emerging industries may be controlled by the government. For instance, governments may control numbers of licences to create networks for next-generation mobile phones.

- Entry barriers. Government policy may restrict investment or competition or make it harder by use of quotas and tariffs for overseas firms. This kind of protectionism is generally frowned upon by the World Trade Organisation, but there may be political and economic circumstances in which it becomes necessary.

- Competition policy. Governments might devise policies which are deliberately intended to keep an industry fragmented, preventing one or two producers from having too much market share.

- New product adoption. Governments regulate the adoption of new products (e.g. new drugs) in some industries. They may go so far as to ban the use of a new product if it is not considered safe (a new form of transport, say). Policies may influence the rate of adoption of new products, e.g. the UK Government 'switched off' the analogue television networks in 2012, effectively forcing users to buy digital, cable or satellite services.

Illustration 7 – non-market strategy in action

Toyota Prius

Toyota is the market leader in the production and sale of hybrid cars. In the US it successfully lobbied the California state government to allow drivers of its flagship Prius hybrid model use car lanes which were reserved for vehicles with two or more passengers – even if the Prius contained no passengers. It also convinced the state government to allow Prius owners to park for free in public owned car parks.

This lobbying required little investment from Toyota, but significantly boosted their green credentials, as well as giving their cars a competitive advantage in the market place. However, this was accomplished through their interactions with the government, meaning that this is an example of a non-market strategy.

Novartis

Non-market strategies do not have to only relate to political issues. Non-market strategy also looks at an organisation's interactions with wider society.

Novartis is a leading pharmaceutical company which tried for a number of years to gain a patent for one of its anti-cancer drugs (Glivec) in India. India denied a patent, stating that the drug was not a sufficient improvement over existing anti-cancer drugs to warrant a patent. As well as engaging in a high profile court case over the issue, Novartis also offered its new drug to needy Indian patients at a drastically reduced price, as part of its 'corporate citizenship' programmes. This helped to build its brand, improve its image with the wider public and thereby undermine its critics. As such, this is another example of a non-market strategy.

Corporate political activity

 Corporate political activity (CPA) is the involvement by an organisation in the political process, with the aim of obtaining certain policy preferences.

CPA can take many forms, including:

- **Lobbying** – this can involve members of the organisation (or hired professional lobbyists) putting their case to government officials such as ministers, MPs or civil servants, in an attempt to win their support.

- **Directorships** – the business may give MPs or retired senior civil servants non-executive directorships, in the hope that they will take an interest in legislation that affects the business and will exercise their influence.

- **Influencing public opinion** – the business may attempt to change public perception on a key issue through advertising, media or even gathering petitions. The business will hope that public feeling will affect the legislative agenda.

- **Donations** – the business may fund individual candidates or whole political parties as a way of influencing future legislation.

- **Associations** – an organisation may try to act upon the government collectively through the creation of an association with other interested parties. In theory this collective action should have more influence on governmental policy than each company acting alone. In the UK examples of this within the business world include:

  - the Confederation of British Industry (CBI), representing the private business sector

  - the Institute of Directors (IOD)

  - the Federation of Small Businesses (FSB).

- **Legal action** – if an organisation believes that a proposed or enacted law is unfair, they may take direct action through the courts for its repeal.

Corporate political activity and ethics

Several of the methods that organisations can use as part of their corporate political activities (CPA) may raise ethical concerns. For example:

- donations to candidates or political parties could be seen as bribery, which would be highly unethical

- offering directorships to MPs or retired civil servants in order to gain favourable votes on relevant legislation could equally be seen as a form of bribery

- advertising campaigns, petitions or legal action could be seen as a way of large, well-resourced organisations bringing unfair pressure on the public or government on certain issues, simply for their own profit.

It is therefore very important that organisations consider what actions to take as part of their CPA. Organisations therefore need to carefully consider:

- relevant law (i.e. anti-bribery legislation) AND

- professional ethics (such as the CIMA code of ethics discussed in chapter 3)

when deciding on a strategy.

Test your understanding 11

K is a large, multinational manufacturer of food and drink products. It has manufacturing facilities in five countries, but it sells in almost ninety countries around the world – typically through local supermarkets.

Which of the following options are examples of non-market strategy for K? Select ALL that apply.

A   K participates in an annual charity fund-raising day in country H to help meet its corporate social responsibility duties

B   K has centralised its purchasing function, allowing it to improve its ability to get quantity discounts from suppliers

C   K has recently started an online petition in country G against proposed new restrictive health and safety laws

D   K's stores in country B have joined a trade association to help improve planning restrictions for retail stores

E   K has cut the prices of its goods by fifteen percent in country K in order to attract new shoppers

8 Summary

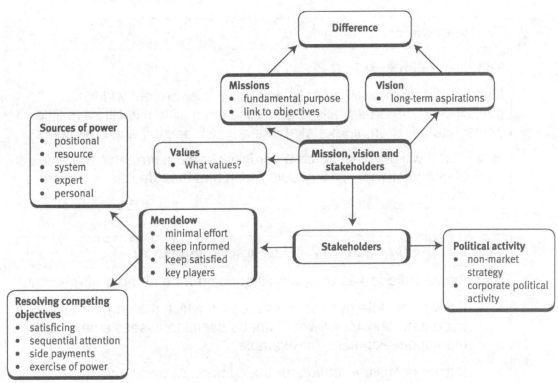

Test your understanding answers

Test your understanding 1

The correct answer is C

Mission statements will be of limited use if they are not widely publicised. If the Board fails to advertise the mission, it will have little immediate effect on other stakeholders, such as staff and customers.

However, it will give the Board a yardstick to measure their strategies against going forward. This should mean that their decisions are more consistent.

Test your understanding 2 – (Integration question)

This can be criticised as a mission statement for a number of reasons.

- It does not state the business areas in which the company intends to operate. As such it would not be useful to assess a strategy of market development, for example.

- It does not give a reason for the company's existence. In particular, the statement fails to give any indication why the company will be better than its competitors in what it does.

- It appears to focus on customer requirements only, and has nothing to say about other stakeholder groups, particularly employees and shareholders. It does not actually define who its customers are or who it wants its customers to be.

- It is dull. Short mission statements should be inspiring.

- It communicates nothing about the firm's values to employees.

- The terms 'top quality' and 'fair price' are unclear in their meaning. It is not clear what is meant by 'quality', nor what 'fair' is in terms of price. Assuming that it will be expensive to achieve top quality, how high might a fair price be? Does it mean fair to the customer or fair to the shareholders? Taken at face value there is a danger the company could make a loss!

In defence of the statement it does highlight the need to meet customer expectations in order to be successful.

On balance, however, the mission statement will fail to inspire employees, determine culture or assist strategic planning.

Test your understanding 3

The correct answer is B

Objectives should be SMART – specific, measurable, attainable, relevant and timed.

Test your understanding 4

The correct answer is D

The objective asks for the company to 'delight' customers – which is not easy to measure. The chances of the company delighting its customers and the rest of the world seem low – especially by the end of the next financial year – suggesting that it is not attainable. It is also not directly relevant to the shareholders needs of raising profits and dividends.

The only aspect of an objective that is present is that there is a time limit built in.

Test your understanding 5 – JAA – (Case style)

Possible objectives for JAA could include:

Growth

JAA could set itself an objective to increase its **sales volume** – either in terms of the additional number of books it wishes to sell, or in terms of the percentage increase it wishes to see compared to its current sales volume.

The company could also consider setting itself an objective relating to its **market share.** As it operates in a highly competitive market, JAA may wish to set itself an objective to achieve a set percentage share of the total market for fiction and non-fiction books.

Innovation

To achieve this objective, JAA could set itself objectives relating to the **number of new books launched** each year. By bringing more new books to market than its competitors, it may be able to increase its market share and put pressure on other publishers.

JAA could also set objectives relating to the **number of new ways of selling its products** that it utilises. This could involve selling its books online, as electronic downloads or through tablet computers and electronic readers.

Marketing director's suggestion

The marketing director has suggested that the happiness of employees could be used as the sole objective for social responsibility. While it is correct that an employer who has good social responsibility should see an increase in staff happiness, this will not make a good objective on its own.

Firstly, social responsibility extends beyond how the company treats its employees. To get a full picture, the company needs to examine how its actions are impacting on other stakeholders and the wider environment.

In addition, employee happiness in itself is not directly measurable, meaning it cannot be a good objective. The marketing director needs to be more specific. For example, she could measure the staff turnover to get an indication of how staff feel about the company.

Test your understanding 6

The correct answer is C

By definition.

Test your understanding 7

The correct answer is B

Local residents are highly affected by the LG's decisions and are willing to exert significant power (as evidenced by the high turnout at elections). This would indicate high power and high interest, making them key players.

Central government also seems to have high power as they control the funding to the LG. However, they rarely get involved in LG operations unless there is evidence of mismanagement. This would suggest they should be kept satisfied.

Test your understanding 8 – AYL – (Case style)

Nurses

Given the proposals to cut or freeze their pay in the coming period, nurses will have **high interest** in the proposals.

However, they are not unionised. This would tend to indicate a lower **level of power** as they lack a clear ability to co-ordinate strike action and could be relatively easy to replace due to their relatively low level of skill.

Under Mendelow's matrix, nurses should therefore be **kept informed**.

The management of AYL need to try and convince them of the need for the pay freeze in order for the hospital to continue to function. This may, however, be difficult to do. This may lead to the nurses attempting to gain power by unionising and joining with the other workers in AYL, or alternatively lobbying the government.

Patients

If the proposed pay cuts are implemented, patients are unlikely to see a significant change in their level of care. This will give them a **low level of interest**.

In addition, while patients may collectively have an influence on the elected national government, there is no indication that patients have any kind of organisation, indicating a **low level of power**.

Mendelow's matrix would therefore suggest that the managers of AYL should adopt a **minimal effort** approach with regards to patients in this area. They are likely to accept what the management tell them as long as it does not affect their level of care. Should it do so, they may become more interested.

Other members of hospital staff

As it stands, there is no evidence that any other types of hospital staff will be affected by the pay cuts. Given the fact that the nurses are not part of the main union that represents the other members of staff, it is likely that they will have **low interest**.

However, should they choose to take an interest, the remaining members of staff will probably have **high power**. They are unionised and include key members of staff (skilled doctors). This means that any strike action could be extremely damaging to the hospital.

As such, the managers of AYL should adopt an approach of **keeping them satisfied**. By reassuring other workers that their circumstances are not affected by the cuts, AYL may be able to prevent them taking an active interest in the proposals.

> **Central government**
>
> The government ultimately controls the budget for the hospital. This gives it **high power**.
>
> In addition, it is currently looking for ways to reduce its expenditure, so it has **high interest** in the success of AYL's proposals.
>
> AYL have no choice but to adopt a **key players** approach. They need to fully communicate their plans to the central government and ensure they are happy with the proposals. If the central government recommends changes to the proposed cuts, AYL's managers would be wise to accept them.

Test your understanding 9

The correct answer is A

Last year, L focused on giving herself a sufficient return. This year, she is making other stakeholders (her staff) a priority.

Test your understanding 10 – WRL – (Case style)

To: A. Scott

From: M. Williams

Date: 10/05/20XX

Subject: Re: WRL Meeting this afternoon

Please find below my analysis of the points you wished me to examine for WRL. Please let me know if you wish to discuss any of these points in more detail.

Kind regards

A. Scott

(i) **Categorisation of three stakeholder groups in WRL**

Eastern State Government/Local residents – High Interest, Low power (keep informed)

The Eastern state government, representing the local population of the area around the mine has proven it has high levels of interest in the project.

On a positive note, the mine will provide local employment as well as a payment from the central government of $1m. However, it will also have a significant adverse effect on the local environment, which has caused the state government to take legal action against WRL.

The Eastern state government seems to have low levels of power. It was not part of the negotiations and it appears that after its unsuccessful legal action against WRL it has no further power to prevent the mine from going ahead.

Central Stravian government – Low Interest, High Power (keep satisfied)

The central government seems to have been unconcerned with possible effects on the environment as they have not built any controls into the licence with WRL. After the initial negotiations were concluded, the central government seems to have taken relatively little interest in the problems that have arisen with the project.

Should they decide to take an active interest in the future, however, they would undoubtedly have significant power over the project and could ultimately decide to close it down.

The Central government's interest may increase if the impact on the environment is a concern for local residents – meaning that it is possible they may become key players in the future.

WRL Shareholders – Low Interest, High Power (keep satisfied)

RL's shareholders ultimately own the company and therefore they have significant control over its actions. Should a significant number of shareholders become unhappy with the operations in Stravia, it would put pressure on the company to withdraw.

In addition, as the investors in the company, they will also have a great deal of interest in WRL providing them with sufficient return on their investment. However, only a small number of shareholders have indicated any concern over the potential pollution of the lake in Stravia. The majority seem uninterested in the pollution, as long as their returns are sufficient.

(ii) **Advice on the actions needed to resolve competing stakeholder objectives**

The key conflict here is between the needs of the bulk of WRL's shareholders to make a profit and the concerns of the Eastern state government and a small minority of shareholders over pollution in the surrounding area. Unfortunately, this conflict is not easily resolved.

Reduction of environmental impact – One possible method is to investigate ways of treating the polluted water before it is pumped into the lake. While this may be more expensive, it may allow a compromise position to be found whereby the damage to the lake is minimised but the project is still economically viable for WRL.

Publicity – Failing this, WRL may need to attempt a damage-limitation exercise. This could involve the publicising of the positive effects of the mine on the local economy and residents. The Eastern state government presumably represents the needs of the residents, so highlighting the benefits of the new mine may go a long way towards calming their fears.

Withdrawal – Alternatively, given WRL's insistence on being a good corporate citizen, it could opt to pull out of Stravia completely and look for alternative investments that will not pollute the environment to such a degree.

It is unclear whether many alternatives are available for WRL to pursue. If not, this may not be acceptable to shareholders, who for the most part seem to support the Stravian mine. There may also be financial penalties for WRL withdrawing from its agreement with the central government.

WRL could use the model proposed by Cyert & March, who examined possible ways to deal with stakeholder conflict. These include:

- Satisficing – this would involve keeping the most powerful stakeholders happy – presumably in WRL's case, this would be its shareholders.

- Sequential attention – this involves WRL taking turns prioritising stakeholders' needs. This would be unlikely to be useful in this scenario due to the conflicting nature of the stakeholders needs.

- Side payments – if WRL is unable to deal with the Eastern State Government's needs, it could look at other ways of compensating them. Perhaps offering additional payments would appease the local government.

- Exercise of power – ultimately if, as in this case, no agreement can be reached, the most powerful stakeholders can exercise their influence and force a settlement.

Conclusion – It should be noted that ultimately there may be no way to completely resolve this stakeholder conflict. In these cases, stakeholder analysis would indicate the need to side with the most powerful groups – the 'key players' – who in this case would be the shareholders.

(iii) **Discussion of the extent to which WRL's mission statement is consistent with its plan to pollute the lake.**

WRL's mission statement breaks down into three key statements. The proposed strategy in Stravia should be analysed to see whether it conforms to these.

To make the maximum possible profit for its shareholders

WRL obviously feels that this project is profitable for investors. After negotiations with the local government it has decided to proceed and feels it will only become uneconomic if the waste water has to be disposed of in an environmentally friendly way.

Causing the least damage to the environment

WRL would appear to not be meeting this requirement due to the damage about to be done to the lake and local environment. However, given the vague nature of the mission statement, WRL may argue this is the least possible damage to the environment, given the nature of their business. The damage to the lake could be seen as the least damage they can do whilst still meeting their other goal of maximising investor returns.

Be a good corporate citizen

Again, the answer to whether WRL is meeting this part of its mission statement is more complex than it might initially appear.

Certainly the effect on the local environment of the polluted water would not be consistent with good corporate citizenship.

However, it could be argued that WRL is also providing significant investment in the local area – with jobs for local workers as well as the $1m pay-out that the Eastern state government received.

Contributing to the local economy could be seen as meeting the requirement for good corporate citizenship.

Test your understanding 11

The correct answers are A, C and D

Remember that non-market activities will not relate to stakeholders such as suppliers (option B) and customers (option E). A, C and D all relate to activities that relate to society (option A) or political issues (options C and D), which would form part of a non-market strategy.

The role of governance and ethics in the strategy process

Chapter learning objectives

Lead		Component	
B3:	Discuss the impact of the ecosystem on organisational strategy	(b)	Conduct stakeholder analysis in networks.
C1:	Discuss the context of generating options	(a)	The role of governance and ethics in the strategy process.

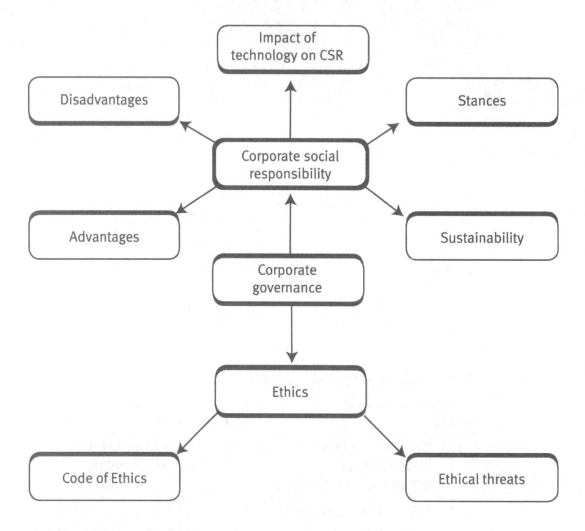

1   What is corporate governance?

The **Cadbury Report 1992** provides a useful definition:

- 'the system by which companies are directed and controlled'.

An expansion might include:

- 'in the interests of shareholders' highlighting the agency issue involved

- 'and in relation to those beyond the company boundaries' or

- and stakeholders' suggesting a much broader definition that brings in concerns over social responsibility.

To include these final elements is to recognise the need for organisations to be accountable to someone or something.

 Governance could therefore be described as:

- **'the system by which companies are directed and controlled in the interests of shareholders and other stakeholders'.**

Coverage of governance

Companies are directed and controlled from inside and outside the company. Good governance requires the following to be considered:

Direction from within:

- the nature and structure of those who set direction, the board of directors

- the need to monitor major forces through risk analysis

- the need to control operations: internal control.

Control from outside:

- the need to be knowledgeable about the regulatory framework that defines codes of best practice, compliance and legal statute

- the wider view of corporate position in the world through social responsibility and ethical decisions.

 2 The business case for governance

Providing a business case for governance is important in order to enlist management support. Corporate governance is claimed to bring the following benefits:

- It is suggested that strengthening the control structure of a business increases accountability of management and maximises sustainable wealth creation.

- Institutional investors believe that better financial performance is achieved through better management, and better managers pay attention to governance, hence the company is more attractive to such investors.

- The above points may cause the share price to rise – which can be referred to as the "governance dividend" (i.e. the benefit that shareholders receive from good corporate governance).

- Additionally, a socially responsible company may be more attractive to customers and investors hence revenues and share price may rise (a "social responsibility dividend").

The hard point to prove is how far this business case extends and what the returns actually are.

3 Purpose and objectives of corporate governance

Corporate governance has both purposes and objectives.

For the private sector:

- The basic purpose of corporate governance is to monitor those parties within a company which control the resources owned by investors.

- The primary objective of sound corporate governance is to contribute to improved corporate performance and accountability in creating long term shareholder value.

For the public and not for profit sectors:

Often objectives within these organisations are more complex and conflicting.

Organisations are often appraised according to the "value for money" (VFM) that they generate.

Value for money may be defined as performance of an activity to simultaneously achieve economy, efficiency and effectiveness.

This means maximising benefits for the lowest cost and has three constituent elements:

- Economy – a measure of inputs to achieve a certain service or level of service.

- Effectiveness – a measure of outputs, i.e. services/facilities.

- Efficiency – the optimum of economy and effectiveness, i.e. the measure of outputs over inputs.

```
┌─────────────────────────┐
│  CORPORATE GOVERNANCE   │
└─────────────────────────┘
```

PURPOSES

Primary:

Monitor those parties within a company who control the resources owned by investors.

Supporting:

- Ensure there is a suitable balance of power on the board of directors.
- Ensure executive directors are remunerated fairly.
- Make the board of directors responsible for monitoring and managing risk.
- Ensure the external auditors remain independent and free from the influence of the company.
- Address other issues, e.g. business ethics, corporate social responsibility (CSR), and protection of 'whistleblowers'.

OBJECTIVES

Primary:

Contribute to improved corporate performance and accountability in creating long-term shareholder value.

Supporting:

- Control the controllers by increasing the amount of reporting and disclosure to all stakeholders.
- Increase level of confidence and transparency in company activities for all investors (existing and potential) and thus promote growth.
- Ensure that the company is run in a legal and ethical manner.
- Build in control at the top that will 'cascade' down the organisation.

 4 Key concepts of governance

The foundation to governance is the action of the individual. These actions are guided by a person's moral stance.

Characteristics which are important in the development of an appropriate moral stance include the following:

Fairness

- A sense of equality in dealing with internal stakeholders.

- A sense of even-handedness in dealing with external stakeholders.

- An ability to reach an equitable judgement in a given ethical situation.

Openness/transparency

- One of the underlying principles of corporate governance, it is one of the 'building blocks' that underpin a sound system of governance.

- In particular, transparency is required in the agency relationship that exists between directors and investors. In terms of definition, transparency means openness (say, of discussions), clarity, lack of withholding of relevant information unless necessary.

- It has a default position of information provision rather than concealment.

Innovation

- Innovation occurs when a firm "transforms knowledge and ideas into new products, processes and systems for the benefit of the firm and its stakeholders."

- In the context of corporate governance, this covers innovation and experimentation in reporting, allowing the business to move away from rigid compliance, and towards the better communication of its individual value creation story for its providers of financial capital.

- Ultimately, innovation improves a firm's reporting performance to the benefit of investors and consumers.

- Much of the knowledge from which innovation stems is tacit and "local," meaning that such knowledge is unique to the company and the environment in which the knowledge arises.

- In addition, the capacity of a firm to integrate external knowledge is crucial for successful innovation.

Scepticism

- Scepticism (often referred to as professional scepticism) is an attitude which includes a questioning mind, being alert to conditions which may indicate possible misstatement due to error or fraud. This is to provide a critical assessment of evidence.

- For example, The UK Corporate Governance Code provisions advocate for non-executives to apply scepticism in order to challenge and scrutinise management effectively.

Independence

- Independence from personal influence of senior management for non-executive directors (NEDs).

- Independence of the board from operational involvement.

- Independence of directorships from overt personal motivation since the organisation should be run for the benefit of its owners.

- A quality possessed by individuals and refers to the avoidance of being unduly influenced by a vested interest.

- This freedom enables a more objective position to be taken on issues compared to those who consider vested interests or other loyalties.

Probity/honesty

- Honesty in financial/positional reporting.

- Perception of honesty of the finance team from internal and external stakeholders.

- A foundation ethical stance in both principles – and rules-based systems.

Illustration 1 – Tesco

In 2014 a whistle blower in the finance team at Tesco alerted management to a possible overstatement of profits. This has been produced through recognising transactions with suppliers in the wrong accounting period, and was a response to pressure to show improved performance following increased competitive threats from discount retailers such as Aldi and Lidl.

Tesco lost approximately 50% of its market value that year.

In response, the new Tesco CEO wrote a letter to all suppliers, stating:

"I expect Tesco to act with integrity and transparency at all times.

Our values are what we stand for and we will live those values in all that we do for Tesco. It is in times of challenge that our values are tested, and I want to reassure you that we will live our values fully at this challenging time.

Our relationships with suppliers are critical. They form the bedrock of the service we provide to our customers."

Responsibility

- Willingness to accept liability for the outcome of governance decisions.

- Clarity in the definition of roles and responsibilities for action.

- Conscientious business and personal behaviour.

Accountability

- The obligation of an individual or organisation to account for its actions and activities.

- Accounting for business position as a result of acceptance of responsibility.

- Providing clarity in communication channels with internal and external stakeholders.

- Development and maintenance of risk management and control systems.

Reputation

- Developing and sustaining personal reputation through other moral virtues.

- Developing and sustaining the moral stance of the organisation and the industry in which it operates.

Illustration 2 – BP Chief Executive

Lord Browne resigned from his position as CEO of oil giant BP in May 2007 due to media stories regarding his private life.

His resignation was to save BP from embarrassment after a newspaper had won a court battle to print details of his private life. Lord Browne apologised for statements made in court regarding a four year relationship with Jeff Chevalier that he described as being 'untruthful' (he had actually lied, this relationship had existed).

Due to this 'untruthfulness' Lord Browne gave up a formidable distinguished 41 year career with BP, and did the honourable thing by resigning as the damage to his reputation would have impacted adversely on BP.

Judgement

- The ability to reach and communicate meaningful conclusions.

- The ability to weigh up numerous issues and give each due consideration.

- The development of a balanced and evaluated approach to making business decisions and personal relationships covering intellectual and moral aspects.

- To make decisions in the best interests of the organisation.

Integrity

- A steadfast adherence to strict ethical standards despite any other pressures to act otherwise.

- Integrity describes the personal ethical position of the highest standards of professionalism and probity.

- It is an underlying and underpinning principle of corporate governance and it is required that all those representing shareholder interests in agency relationships both possess and exercise absolute integrity at all times.

5 How does corporate governance impact organisational strategy?

Corporate governance is very important to help maximise the effectiveness of an organisation's strategy. This is for a number of reasons.

- Corporate governance works to ensure that no individual can dominate the board of directors (by ensuring the CEO and Chairman roles are separated as well as the presence of independent non-executive directors). This helps to ensure that no-one is powerful enough to force through inappropriate or ineffective strategy. The non-executive directors should be able to impartially assess whether a proposed strategy is in the best interests of the organisation.

- Corporate governance should help to improve the diversity of the board of directors. This allows the board to identify a wide range of possible strategies, as well as analyse them from a variety of different viewpoints.

- Adequate internal audit and control systems should ensure that the board has accurate information about the current operations of the company. This will enable them to develop more effective strategies for the organisation. In addition, strong internal control increases the chance that the organisation will be able to implement its strategies successfully.

- Having good corporate governance is attractive to investors. This will make it easier for the organisation to raise the funding necessary to invest in the new strategies that they have identified.

It is therefore extremely important that companies consider corporate governance principles if they wish to develop and implement successful strategies. The increasing emphasis on corporate governance has naturally lead to more scrutiny of the sense of business ethics which is displayed by an organisation (this is examined in more detail later in this chapter).

It has also lead people to question the overall impact an organisation has on the world, and a subsequent increasing demand that this should be as positive as possible. This leads us to examine the subject of corporate social responsibility.

Test your understanding 1
Which ONE of the following is NOT a strategic aim of corporate governance?

A   To reduce costs within the organisation

B   To increase the organisation's transparency to stakeholders

C   To improve investor confidence in the organisation

D   To ensure that the organisation abides by relevant laws and acts ethically

Test your understanding 2 – ADF – (Case Study)

You are the Finance Director of ADF – a large national firm that retails clothes direct to the public through a chain of 250 high-street stores in country F. You have just received the following email from the Managing Director (MD), Carlos Smith:

To: Anne Accountant

From: Carlos Smith

Date: 1/5/20XX

Subject: Review of corporate governance arrangements

Hi Anne,

As you may be aware, we are currently reviewing our corporate governance arrangements within the company after some of our investors expressed concerns. I felt that you would be the right person to ask about this as I'm aware you've studied this topic.

You're probably aware that ADF's executive directors are all employees who have worked their way up through the company. Half of the board is made up of non–executive directors.

If you remember, the Chairman of the board is a retired director of a major electrical retailer. All of the other non–executive directors are personal friends of his and were appointed on his recommendation.

As you know, only one member of the board is female. All the directors are from country F and between the ages of 45 and 55.

The company does have a small internal audit department but this is understaffed. The Head of Internal Audit has stated several times that the work undertaken on ADF's stores is minimal and that a number of stores have never been visited by internal audit.

As we discussed at the Board meeting last week, the company is concerned that its current market is saturated and is looking to expand abroad into neighbouring countries, though the Chairman has expressed concern over this as he feels it is too risky.

I'd be grateful if you could identify any weaknesses in our corporate governance. Please could you explain how each weakness will affect the company strategically. I'm meeting a few other Board members to discuss this in 20 minutes, so I be grateful if you could give this some urgent attention.

Thanks

Carlos

Required:

Draft a reply to Carlos, as requested.

(20 minutes)

6 What is corporate social responsibility?

In the modern world, it is seen as being increasingly important to consider how organisations manage their business processes to have an overall positive impact on society.

It is worth noting that corporate social responsibility (CSR) is distinct from ethics. Business ethics comprise principles and standards that govern behaviour in the world of business.

It should also be appreciated that CSR is now more and more integrated into corporate governance practices. Both focus on ethics in business practices and responsiveness to stakeholders. Both result in improved image of the business and affect performance. There is therefore a very clear link between CSR and corporate governance.

 CSR, however, refers to a **firm's obligation to maximise its positive impacts upon stakeholders while minimising the negative effects**.

The extent to which the organisation fulfils the economic, legal, ethical and charitable responsibilities placed on it by its stakeholders will determine to what extent it is seen as having good CSR.

The problem is that there is no one definition or theory of CSR.

Consider the following points. Is it socially responsible to:

- Experiment on animals?
- Use 'fracking' to access natural gas reserves?
- Build a new high speed rail network such as HS2 through countryside?
- Pay high salaries to senior executives?

Different individuals will have different views on each of these issues.

As far as possible, managers have to take account of a range of differing viewpoints when deciding on their strategies. In addition, there is always the need to balance a company's responsibility to society with its responsibility to earn financial returns for its investors.

Illustration 3 – corporate social responsibility issues

Nikon is a well-known multinational company that specialises in the manufacture of cameras and other photographic and visual equipment. The company's corporate social responsibility (CSR) statement (extracts of which are shown below) highlights a number of key examples of issues that companies need to consider when thinking about CSR.

Nikon CSR charter (extracts)

Sound corporate activities

The Nikon Group endeavours to comply with international regulations, related laws, and internal rules, exercise sound and fair corporate practices, earn the trust of stakeholders such as customers, shareholders, employees, business partners, and society. The Group will maintain constructive relationships with administrative bodies, remaining politically neutral and complying with laws, and will not engage in relationships with individuals or groups that threaten social order or safety.

Provision of valuable goods and services for society

The Nikon Group will provide valuable products and services with superior quality and safety to society, endeavouring to increase the satisfaction and trust of our customers and contributing to the healthy development of society.

Respect for human beings

The Nikon Group will respect diversity and individual human rights and provide a healthy and safe working environment in which all persons receive fair treatment without discrimination. It will also oppose enforced labour and child labour and respect fundamental human rights as well as workers' rights.

Protection of the natural environment

The Nikon Group will proactively engage in environmental efforts and work to protect the natural environment, as these are common issues for all of mankind.

Responsibility to society as a corporate citizen

The Nikon Group will carry out corporate activities that take into account the cultures and practices of each country and region and proactively engage in activities that contribute to society as a good corporate citizen.

Socially responsible behaviour within the supply chain

The Nikon Group will encourage socially responsible behaviour within its supply chain.

Transparent operating activities

The Nikon Group will communicate extensively with customers, shareholders, employees, business partners, and society and disclose business information in a timely and fair manner. It will also conduct reliable financial reporting through accurate accounting processes.

Responsibility of top management

Top management and employees in managerial positions within each department must understand that they play an essential role in fulfilling the spirit of this Charter and thus, in addition to leading by example, they must ensure that this information is disseminated to everyone in the Group and all related parties.

Arguments against CSR

It can be argued that companies should not pursue corporate social responsibility. Milton Friedman argues that:

'The business of business is business.'

This means that the primary purpose of a business is to try and earn a profit. In a company, for instance, the managers have been employed in order to earn the owners of the business a return on their investment.

As such, it is a manager's duty to act in a way that maximises shareholder wealth, while conforming to all relevant laws and customs. If a manager does anything that is not directly related to wealth maximisation, he is failing in his responsibilities to the owners and therefore acting unethically.

For example, it can be argued that it is not right for a manager to donate any company funds to charity. The manager should instead work to maximise the return to the owner. If the owner wishes to make donations to charity, he can do so out of his earnings from the business.

In addition, it can be argued that maximising the wealth of business owners is, in itself, socially responsible. This is because:

- Increased returns will lead to increased tax payments made to the state. These can then be passed on to 'worthy causes'.

- A high proportion of company shares are owned by pension funds. This means that any gains will go to help provide pensions to individuals who may well be disadvantaged.

Don't forget that there may also be practical reasons why a business chooses not to pursue CSR. These can include:

- Increased cost of sourcing materials from ethical sources (e.g. Fairtrade products or free-range eggs).

- Having to turn away business from customers considered to be unethical (e.g. an 'ethical' bank may choose not to invest in a company that manufactures weapons).

- The management time that can be taken up by CSR planning and implementation.

Arguments for CSR

Not everyone agrees with Friedman's statements. There are a number of reasons why many businesses feel that CSR is a vital part of their strategy. These include:

- A key part of running a successful business is the ability to offer customers and consumers what they need. One of those needs is often a requirement for socially responsible behaviour from the organisation.

  Basically, **having good CSR can attract customers!** This can be because good CSR tends to enhance a company's reputation and therefore its brand. It can also be used a basis for differentiation in the market place – given the choice, many customers will prefer to trade with a company they feel is ethical.

- Good CSR is likely to involve good working conditions for employees, allowing the business to **attract a higher calibre of staff**.

- Avoiding discrimination against workers is likely to give the company **access to a wider human resource base**.

- Avoiding pollution will tend to save companies in the long run – many governments are now **fining or increasing taxes of more polluting businesses**.

- Sponsorship and charitable donations are tax deductible, improve staff morale and can be seen as a **form of advertising**.

Ultimately, having good CSR can **increase the financial value of the business**. Remember that the value of the business will be the present value of its perceived future cash flows discounted at its risk-adjusted cost of capital.

- Good CSR will reduce the risk of adverse environmental reactions against the company. Anything that reduces risk should lower the risk adjusted cost of capital, increasing the value of the company.

- A socially responsible business will be allowed to operate for longer in society. This will mean that there will be more years of cash flows in the future. This would also increase the value of the company.

7 Approaches to corporate social responsibility

If an organisation wishes to consider how it should approach corporate social responsibility, there are a number of models that it can use to help it.

Carroll's corporate social responsibility model

Carroll (The Pyramid of Corporate Social Responsibility: Toward the Moral Management of Organizational Stakeholders), devised a four-part model of CSR:

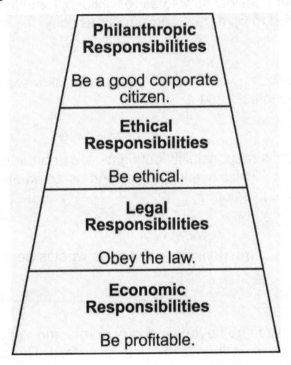

True CSR requires satisfying all four parts consecutively.

Economic responsibility – be profitable

- This is the fundamental level – all other levels rest on this.
- Shareholders demand a reasonable return.
- Employees want safe and fairly paid jobs.
- Customers demand quality at a fair price.

Legal responsibility – obey the law

- The law is a baseline for operating within society.
- It is an accepted rule book for company operations.

Ethical responsibility – do what is right and fair

- This relates to doing what is right, just and fair.
- Actions taken in this area provide a reaffirmation of social legitimacy.
- This is naturally beyond the previous two levels.

Philanthropic responsibility – be a good corporate citizen

- Relates to discretionary behaviour to improve the lives of others.

- Charitable donations and recreational facilities.

- Sponsoring the arts and sports events.

The different parts will help the management of an organisation to understand the various obligations that society expects from them.

Carroll suggests four possible strategies (or philosophies) that the organisation can adopt with regard to corporate social responsibility.

Reaction

The corporation denies any responsibility for social issues, arguing that it is not to blame or required to act.

Defence

The corporation admits responsibility but fights it, doing the very least that seems to be required. Typically this is only done as an attempt to defend the organisation's current position.

Accommodation

The corporation accepts responsibility and does what is demanded of it by relevant groups.

Proaction

The corporation seeks to go beyond industry norms and anticipates future expectations by doing more than is currently expected. The organisation attempts to improve society.

Illustration 4 – Carroll's philosophies in action

Q is a large, multinational company which manufactures a popular carbonated soft drink – Yu. Yu is one of the leading soft drinks in country H and accounts for around 75% of Q's profits. In recent months it has been reported in the international press that one of the flavourings in Yu has been linked to an increased risk of cancer, though at much higher levels than those found in Yu. This has led to Yu being criticised by pressure groups, who have already complained about Yu's high sugar content which they claim is not healthy for Q's customers (though Yu's sales continue to rise). The Government of country H has not stated that they will ban the ingredient, though it has indicated concern over rising levels of obesity in the local population.

Q's management could consider adopting any of Carroll's four corporate social responsibility philosophies with regards to Yu.

Reaction

Q denies that there is any problem with Yu whatsoever. Its managers release a statement arguing that there is clearly no health risk associated with consumption of Yu by customers as the government has not made the product illegal. Q then ignores the issue and makes no changes to Yu's recipe.

Defence

Q's management accepts that there is a potential risk from the high sugar content and the flavouring identified by the international press. It therefore places additional health information on the bottle about the calorie content of the drink, along with a 'suggested amount' that should be consumed each day. It argues that this suggested consumption level would also reduce any risk to the consumer of the flavouring identified in the international press.

The pressure groups claim this is insufficient as most consumers do not read the label on soft drinks they consume.

Accommodation

Q's managers form a focus group made up of consumers, government health officials and pressure group representatives to discuss their concerns. After lengthy discussions to ensure it fully understands their needs, Q lowers the sugar content of Yu and replaces it with natural low-calorie sweeteners to reduce the calorie content but without altering the taste of the product. It also changes the recipe to eliminate the need for the flavouring in question to ensure the government and consumer confidence is maintained.

Proaction

Q undertakes detailed analysis of its product and the impact of all the ingredients it uses on consumer health. Unlike its competitors, Q significantly reduces the level of sugar in Yu, as well as eliminating all artificial additives in an attempt to reduce any negative health impact of consuming Yu.

Test your understanding 3

L operates a popular chain of gyms. As well as standard exercise equipment, L's gyms also have personal trainers that work with clients for an extra monthly fee (the personal trainer earns 25% of this, with L keeping the remainder). L also has cafes in each of its gyms, which serve food and drink to gym members.

L is aware that some customers feel that they are not seeing any benefit from attending its gyms or seeing a personal trainer. One customer recently complained that 'L's cafes offer food that is high in fat and salt, meaning customers that eat there will get little benefit from their earlier workout. L's personal trainers also have an incentive to ensure that clients make slow process so that they can continue to earn revenue from the client for as long as possible.'

L has decided to use Carroll's corporate social philosophies model to decide how to react to these issues.

Which of the following approaches are most consistent with an accommodation strategy? Select all that apply.

A   If the service offered to customers does not breach any local laws, no further action needs to be taken by L

B   Admit that the service being offered to customers is not appropriate or socially responsible

C   Add nutritional information to the menu in the cafe to provide more information to customers

D   Redesign personal trainer pay in order to remove any incentive to ensure clients make slow progress

E   Introduce a healthier menu for customers in the cafe

8   Sustainability

One aspect of CSR that is also becoming increasingly important is sustainability.

Sustainability is the use of resources in such a way that they do not compromise the needs of future generations. It also involves not polluting the environment at a rate faster than they can be absorbed.

There are many examples of this. For example, some logging companies plant a tree for every one they fell.

Other companies try to make their products easy to recycle, helping to ensure that materials are reused rather than wasted. The computer manufacturer Apple has used this as part of its marketing approach for some years. (http://www.apple.com/recycling/)

The reason that sustainability is so important for many businesses is that acting in a sustainable manner not only helps look after the environment and the wider community, but it strengthens the business and helps ensure its long-term survival.

It is worth noting that sustainability is increasingly being seen as important within the public sector. Ensuring that goods and services procured by the public sector are sustainable can help meet environmental goals across government, save considerable amounts of public money; and help support innovation and economic growth. This will involve taking account of a wide range of costs, such as pollution impacts, carbon emissions and waste disposal.

The difficulty for many businesses is that many companies focus on short term gains, rather than the long-term sustainability of the business and its environment. This is often evident in businesses that offer senior managers bonuses based on short-term or annual performance.

However, it should be noted that sustainability can lead to cost savings for an organisation in the short term. For example, an organisation that reduces packaging on its products may have a positive impact on the environment by generating less waste, but it will also reduce its costs, thereby improving profits.

9 Incorporating sustainability and CSR into strategy

CIMA itself has been heavily involved in identifying and discussing the implications of sustainability for the business. To this end, in 2010 they published a research article discussing this.

The article came to six key conclusions:

- Strong ethical principles that go beyond upholding the law can add great value to a brand, whereas failure to do the right thing can cause social, economic and environmental damage, undermining a company's long–term prospects in the process.

- Once they have adopted an ethical approach, companies will often find there are bottom-line benefits from demonstrating high ethical standards.

- The ethical tone comes from the top.

- High-quality management information on social, environmental and ethical performance is vital for monitoring the environmental and social impacts of a company and for compiling connected reports showing how effective its governance arrangements are.

- Corporate communications and reporting on sustainability need to do more than just pay lip service to the green agenda. They need to provide hard evidence of the positive impact on society, the environment and the strategic returns for the business, and how any negative effects are being addressed.

- Management accountants have a particular ethical responsibility to promote an ethics-based culture that doesn't permit practises such as bribery.

Illustration 5 – Corporate social responsibility in action

Corporate social responsibility is seen as vital for many organisations. One company that is often hailed as a leader in this area is Ben & Jerry's – a US based manufacturer of ice-cream, frozen yoghurt and sorbet. The company has stated that 'business has a responsibility to the community and the environment'.

Ben & Jerry's CSR has included the following:

- Fair Trade ingredients – this ensures that suppliers of many of the company's raw materials enjoy safe working conditions, reasonable work hours and are paid fairly.

- Ethically sourced supplies – as well as a commitment to Fair Trade, the company also ensures, where possible, that it sources ingredients from suppliers who share its values. For example, Ben & Jerry's has historically sourced free-range eggs and sustainably produced dairy for its products.

- Community work – the company has engaged with communities to improve sustainability. Ben & Jerry's Vermont Dairy Farm Sustainability Project was launched in 1999 and sought to develop practical methods for dairy farms to reduce nitrogen and phosphorous run-off in order to prove water quality and overall sustainability.

- Corporate philanthropy – the company donates a portion of its pre-tax profits to corporate philanthropy via, in part, the Ben & Jerry's Foundation.

Further CIMA information on sustainability

In December 2010, CIMA collaborated with the AICPA and CICA in a report entitled 'Evolution of corporate sustainability practices'.

Some key issues that this report raised include:

General

Business sustainability is about ensuring that organisations implement strategies that contribute to long–term success. Organisations that act in a sustainable manner not only help to maintain the well–being of the planet and people, they also create businesses that will survive and thrive in the long run.

The accounting profession can play an important role in this. Accountants can serve as leading agents for change by applying their skills and competencies to develop sustainability strategies, facilitate effective implementation, accurate measurement and credible business reporting.

Why do businesses have sustainability plans?

According to research conducted by CIMA, the key reasons include:

- **Compliance** – the need to comply with laws and regulations.

- **Reputational risk** – companies are concerned with how stakeholders will view them if they fail to act in a sustainable manner.

- **Cost-cutting and efficiency** – acting in a sustainable manner (for example becoming more energy-efficient) can help to reduce business expenditure. This is especially valuable for smaller companies.

Ten elements of organisational sustainability

The following areas are considered crucial to the successful embedding of sustainability within an organisation. It is worth noting that the accounting function will be useful in a number of these areas.

Strategy and oversight

- Board and senior management commitment.

- Understanding and analysing the key sustainability drivers for the organisation.

- Integrating the key sustainability drivers into the organisation's strategy.

Execution and alignment

- Ensuring that sustainability is the responsibility of everyone within the organisation (not just a specific department).

- Breaking down the sustainability targets and objectives for the organisation as a whole into targets and objectives which are meaningful for individual subsidiaries, divisions and departments.

- Processes that enable sustainability issues to be taken into account clearly and consistently in day-to-day decision-making.

- Extensive and effective sustainability training.

Performance and reporting

- Including sustainability targets and objectives in performance appraisal.

- Champions to promote sustainability and celebrate success.

- Monitoring and reporting sustainability performance.

Test your understanding 4 – Router – (Case style)

You are A. North – and you have recently been provided with the following letter from one of your company's major clients, Router plc (a major mining company).

Letter from Router plc

H.West

21 Epp Way

Helway

Helland

HDH 67TY

Dear Mr North,

Router plc has an opportunity to mine for gold in a remote and sparsely populated area. The mining process proposed in this instance would remove all vegetation from the land concerned. After mining has finished, there will remain substantial lakes of poisonous water which will remain toxic for a hundred years.

The mining process is profitable, given the current high world value of gold. However, if the company were to reinstate the mined land, the process would be extremely unprofitable. The company has received permission from the government to carry out the mining. The few local residents are opposed to the mining.

As you know, our mission statement says that we will 'endeavour to make the maximum possible profit for our shareholders while recognising our wider responsibility to society'.

Several investors have raised concerns regarding our mission statement, suggesting that it is 'contradictory'. I would appreciate your thoughts on this.

We are aware that our decision relating to the above gold mining opportunity could potentially cause a conflict between our objectives. We would be grateful for your advice on how we can deal with strategies that cause such a conflict.

Finally, could you please outline the ethical issues surrounding the proposed gold mining operations for our consideration.

Thank you for your help and we look forward to your urgent response.

Kind regards

H. West

Required:

Draft a response to the above letter.

(45 minutes)

10 The impact of technologies on CSR

The rapid development in technologies has had a significant impact on CSR in a number of ways, from how stakeholders get access to information to the level of detail that they can see. Impacts have been witnessed in the following areas:

- **Quicker scrutiny** – stakeholders are updated in real-time on the actions of organisations, leading to quicker scrutiny of those actions. Connected networks and the widespread use of mobile devices mean that that users expect to receive information more quickly, and thus respond more quickly as information is released. Public scrutiny has therefore been accelerated.

- **Greater stakeholder engagement** – whereas the annual CSR report used to be the main medium by which organisations engaged with stakeholders, there is now much more diversity in communications channels – social media, interactive infographics, virtual reality etc. This has led to increased stakeholder engagement.

- **More integrated CSR practices** – organisations are better placed to provide data on the whole of their supply chains, meaning that stakeholders get a bigger picture of the ecosystem as a whole, rather than just one individual component of that ecosystem.

- **Improved measurement** – the use of technologies such as Big Data analytics, blockchain and artificial intelligence means that more meaningful data can be gathered and interpreted about an organisation's CSR practices. This in turn leads to greater accuracy in assessing CSR impact and performance against metrics.

- **Increased openness in the ecosystem** – the result of all the above is that there is a greater expectation of openness and transparency from all who make up an organisational ecosystem, which should (in theory) result in more acceptable CSR behaviour being displayed.

11 Corporate code of ethics

Corporate ethics relates to the application of ethical values to business behaviour.

- It encompasses many areas ranging from board strategies to how companies negotiate with their suppliers.

- It goes beyond legal requirements and is to some extent therefore discretionary.

- Many companies provide details of their ethical approach in a corporate and social responsibility report.

- Key areas included in a code of corporate ethics:

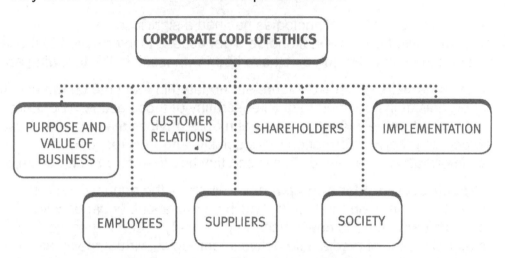

Areas covered by Corporate Ethics	
Key area	Explanation
The purpose and values of the business	This provides the reason for the organisation's existence. Key areas in the purpose or mission statement of the company will include: the products or services to be provided, the financial objectives of the company, and the role of the business in society as seen by the company itself.
Employees	There must be information on how the business relates to its employees. Employees have rights and they must not be seen simply as a means of producing goods/services. The company will therefore have policies on: • working conditions • recruitment • development and training • rewards • health, safety and security • equal opportunities • retirement • redundancy • discrimination • use of company assets by employees, and • any other areas required by statute or thought appropriate by the company.

Customer relations	The company has a responsibility to produce quality goods/services for customers at a reasonable price (taking into account the fact that the company needs to make some profit). Customer faith in the company and its products must be established and built up over time. Key areas for the company to invest in include: <ul><li>product quality</li><li>fair pricing</li><li>after sales service.</li></ul>
Shareholders or other providers of money	Shareholders are investors in the company – they therefore expect an appropriate and proper return on the money they have invested. The company therefore must commit to: <ul><li>providing a proper return on shareholder investment</li><li>providing timely and accurate information to shareholders on the company's historical achievements and future prospects.</li></ul> Shareholders will normally be involved to a greater or lesser extent with the decision making in the company under the principles of good corporate governance.
Suppliers	Suppliers provide goods and services for a company. They will usually attempt to provide those goods and services to an appropriate quality in a timely fashion. The company will therefore normally: <ul><li>attempt to settle invoices promptly</li><li>co-operate with suppliers to maintain and improve the quality of inputs</li><li>not use or accept bribery or excess hospitality as a means of securing contracts with suppliers</li><li>attempt to select suppliers based on some ethical criteria such as support of 'fair trade' principles or not using child labour in manufacture.</li></ul>

Society or the wider community	The company is located within society, which implies some social and corporate responsibility to that society. Many companies produce a CSR report as a means of communicating this relationship to third parties. Explained in the CSR report will be features of the company's activities including: • how it complies with the law • obligations to protect, preserve and improve the environment • involvement in local affairs, including specific staff involvement • policy on donations to educational and charitable institutions.

Ethical stances (Johnson, Scholes and Whittington)

Johnson, Scholes and Whittington (Exploring corporate strategy) define an ethical stance as:

 'The extent to which an organisation will exceed its minimum obligations to stakeholders.'

There are four possible ethical stances:

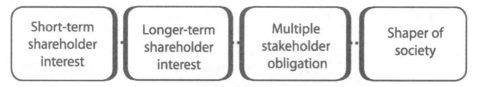

Short-term shareholder interest — Longer-term shareholder interest — Multiple stakeholder obligation — Shaper of society

Short-term shareholder interest (STSI)

This ethical stance has a short-term focus in that it aims to maximise profits in the financial year. Organisations with this ethical stance believe that it is the role of governments to set the legal minimum standard, and anything delivered above this would be to the detriment of their taxpayers.

Longer-term shareholder interest (LTSI)

This ethical stance takes broadly the same approach as the short-term shareholder interest except that it takes a longer-term view. Hence it may be appropriate to incur additional cost now so as to achieve higher returns in the future. An example could be a public service donating some funds to a charity in the belief that it will save the taxpayer the costs associated with providing the entire service should the charity cease to work. Hence this ethical stance is aware of other stakeholders and their impact on long-term profit or cost.

Multiple stakeholder obligation (MSO)

This ethical stance accepts that the organisation exists for more than simply making a profit, or providing services at a minimal cost to taxpayers. It takes the view that all organisations have a role to play in society and so they must take account of all the stakeholders' interests. Hence they explicitly involve other stakeholders, and believe that they have a purpose beyond the financial.

Shaper of society

This ethical stance is ideologically driven and sees its vision as being the focus for all its actions. Financial and other stakeholders' interests are secondary to the overriding purpose of the organisation.

Test your understanding 5

J runs a business which sells flowers from a small shop. He ensures that all of his flowers are sourced from ethically responsible suppliers, even though this is not legally required. While these flowers are more expensive to purchase, he feels that his ethical approach differentiates him from his rivals and allows him to charge a premium price.

Which ONE of Johnson, Scholes and Whittington's ethical stances is J adopting?

A   Shaper of society

B   Multiple stakeholder obligation

C   Longer-term shareholder interest

D   Short-term shareholder interest

---

12   Fundamental ethical principles

Professionals need to follow the following fundamental ethical principles:

- Integrity

- Objectivity

- Professional competence and due care

- Confidentiality

- Professional behaviour.

Fundamental ethical principles

Integrity

Integrity implies fair dealing and truthfulness.

Members are also required not to be associated with any form of communication or report where the information is considered to be:

- materially false or to contain misleading statements

- provided recklessly

- incomplete such that the report or communication becomes misleading by this omission.

Objectivity

Accountants need to ensure that their business/professional judgement is not compromised because of bias or conflict of interest.

However, there are many situations where objectivity can be compromised, so a full list cannot be provided. Accountants are warned to always ensure that their objectivity is intact in any business/ professional relationship.

Professional competence and due care

There are two main considerations under this heading:

(1) Accountants are required to have the necessary professional knowledge and skill to carry out work for clients.

(2) Accountants must follow applicable technical and professional standards when providing professional services.

Appropriate levels of professional competence must first be attained and then maintained. Maintenance implies keeping up to date with business and professional developments, and in many institutes completion of an annual return confirming that continued professional development (CPD) requirements have been met.

Where provision of a professional service has inherent limitations (e.g. reliance on client information) then the client must be made aware of this.

Confidentiality

The principle of confidentiality implies two key considerations for accountants:

(1) Information obtained in a business relationship is not disclosed outside the firm unless there is a proper and specific authority or unless there is a professional right or duty to disclose.

(2) Confidential information acquired during the provision of professional services is not used to personal advantage.

The need to maintain confidentiality is normally extended to cover the accountants' social environment, information about prospective clients and employers, and where business relationships have terminated. Basically there must always be a reason for disclosure before confidential information is provided to a third party.

The main reasons for disclosure are when:

(1) it is permitted by law and authorised by the client

(2) it is required by law, e.g. during legal proceedings or disclosing information regarding infringements of law

(3) there is professional duty or right to disclose (when not barred by law), e.g. provision of information to the professional institute or compliance with ethical requirements.

Ethical considerations on disclosure

The accountant needs to consider the extent to which third parties may be adversely affected by any disclosure.

The amount of uncertainty inherent in the situation may affect the extent of disclosure – more uncertainty may mean disclosure is limited or not made at all.

The accountant needs to ensure that disclosure is made to the correct person or persons.

Professional behaviour

Accountants must comply with all relevant laws and regulations.

There is also a test whereby actions suggested by a third party which would bring discredit to the profession should also be avoided.

An accountant is required to treat all people contacted in a professional capacity with courtesy and consideration. Similarly, any marketing activities should not bring the profession into disrepute.

Test your understanding 6

Under the CIMA Code of Ethics, members are not allowed to be associated with any 'materially false or misleading statements'.

Which ONE of the fundamental ethical principles does this statement relate to?

A   Integrity

B   Professional competence

C   Objectivity

D   Professional behaviour

> ### Test your understanding 7 – (Integration question)
>
> **Explain why each of the following actions appears to be in conflict with fundamental ethical principles.**
>
> (1) An advertisement for a firm of accountants states that their audit services are cheaper and more comprehensive than a rival firm.
>
> (2) An accountant prepares a set of accounts prior to undertaking the audit of those accounts.
>
> (3) A director discusses an impending share issue with colleagues at a golf club dinner.
>
> (4) The finance director attempts to complete the company's taxation computation following the acquisition of some foreign subsidiaries.
>
> (5) A financial accountant confirms that a report on his company is correct, even though the report omits to mention some important liabilities.
>
> (6) You believe your colleague has asked you to include what you believe to be misleading information in your forecast.
>
> (7) Your analysis of a strategic proposal suggests that profitability will be improved by making 30 people redundant.
>
> (8) You can outsource your manufacturing to a country where labour costs are much lower.
>
> (9) Your country is allowed, legally, to dump its waste into a river. This will kill all aquatic life along a 50-mile stretch.

Resolving ethical conflicts

The code is clear that the professional accountant should respond to an ethical conflict. Inaction or silence may well be a further breach of the code.

Ethical conflicts can be resolved as follows:

(1) Gather all relevant facts.

(2) Establish ethical issues involved.

(3) Refer to relevant fundamental principles.

(4) Follow established internal procedures.

(5) Investigate alternative courses of action.

(6) Consult with appropriate persons within the firm.

(7) Obtain advice from professional institutes.

(8) If the matter is still unresolved, consider withdrawing from the engagement team/assignment/role.

Additional resources

For more examples of real-life ethical dilemmas and their recommended solutions, see the CIMA website.

http://www.cimaglobal.com/Professional-ethics/Ethics/Responsible-business/Ethical-dilemma/Case-studies/

 Test your understanding 8 – (Integration question)

Explain your response to the following ethical threats.

(1) Your employer asks you to suggest to a junior manager that they will receive a large bonus for working overtime on a project to hide liabilities from the financial statements.

(2) In selecting employees for a new division, you are advised to unfairly discriminate against one section of the workforce.

(3) You have been asked to prepare the management accounts for a subsidiary located in South America in accordance with specific requirements of that jurisdiction. In response to your comment that you do not understand the accounting requirements of that jurisdiction, your supervisor states 'no problem, no one will notice a few thousand dollars' error anyway'.

 Test your understanding 9 – ABC – (Case style)

One of your colleagues, a junior accountant at ABC Ltd has sent you the following email:

Email

To: J. Bank F

From: A. Halifax

Date: 15/06/XX

Subject: Professional ethics

Hi J,

I was hoping you could give me some advice!

The IT Director of ABC Ltd asked me undertake a cost-benefit analysis of a proposed new IT system. The IT Director will use this analysis to try and convince the Board of Directors of ABC that they should invest in the new system.

As part of my analysis, I found that the new system will not run properly on ABC's existing computers. This means that ABC would have to replace the majority of their desktop computers and servers, leading to an excess of costs over benefits.

The IT Director has suggested that I downplay the costs of replacing the IT infrastructure as he was sure that he 'could find a work-around' that would allow the existing computers to use the new software, though he was currently uncertain how this would be accomplished.

The IT Director has told me that he 'expects' the cost-benefit analysis to show a favourable result for the new system and has indicated that my future promotion prospects may depend on this being the case.

Could you email me back right away and explain the CIMA fundamental ethical principles that I would be breaching if I agree to the IT Director's request. I need to know before I decide on the appropriate course of action.

Thanks for your help!

A

Required:

Reply to the email as requested.

(15 minutes)

Ethical threats and safeguards

Ethical threat	Safeguard
Conflict between requirements of the employer and the fundamental principles For example, acting contrary to laws or regulations or against professional or technical standards.	Obtaining advice from the employer, professional organisation or professional advisor. • The employer providing a formal dispute resolution process. • Legal advice.
Preparation and reporting on information Accountants need to prepare/report on information fairly, objectively and honestly. However, the accountant may be pressurised to provide misleading information.	• Consultation with superiors in the employing company. • Consultation with those charged with governance. • Consultation with the relevant professional body.

Having sufficient expertise Accountants need to be honest in stating their level of expertise – and not mislead employers by implying they have more expertise than they actually possess. Threats that may result in lack of expertise include time pressure to carry out duties, being provided with inadequate information or having insufficient experience.	• Obtaining additional advice/training. • Negotiating more time for duties. • Obtaining assistance from someone with relevant expertise.
Financial interests Situations where an accountant or close family member has financial interests in the employing company. Examples include the accountant being paid a bonus based on the financial statement results which he/she is preparing, or holding share options in the company.	• Remuneration being determined by other members of management. • Disclosure of relevant interests to those charged with governance. • Consultation with superiors or relevant professional body.
Inducements – receiving offers Refers to incentives being offered to encourage unethical behaviour. Inducements may include gifts, hospitality, preferential treatment or inappropriate appeals to loyalty. Objectivity and/or confidentiality may be threatened by such inducements.	• Do not accept the inducement! • Inform relevant third parties such as senior management and professional association (normally after taking legal advice).
Inducements – giving offers Refers to accountants being pressurised to provide inducements to junior members of staff to influence a decision or obtain confidential information.	• Do not offer the inducement! If necessary, follow the conflict resolution process.

Confidential information	• Disclose information in compliance with relevant statutory requirements, e.g. money laundering regulations.
Accountants should keep information about their employing company confidential unless there is a right or obligation to disclose, or they have received authorisation from the client.	
However, the accountant may be under pressure to disclose this information as a result of compliance with legal processes such as anti-money laundering/ terrorism – in this situation there is a conflict between confidentiality and the need for disclosure.	
Whistleblowing	Follow the disclosure provisions of the employer, e.g. report to those responsible for governance. Otherwise disclosure should be based on assessment of: legal obligations, whether members of the public will be adversely affected, gravity of the matter, likelihood of repetition, reliability of the information, reasons why employer does not want to disclose.
Situations where the accountant needs to consider disclosing information, where ethical rules have been broken by the client.	

Test your understanding 10

The management accountant of L plc has recently discovered that the company is about to launch a major new product which is expected to cause a huge increase in company profits. He has therefore purchased a number of shares in L plc, as he expects the share price to rise significantly when the new product is launched.

Which TWO of the CIMA fundamental ethical principles is the management accountant likely to be in breach of?

A   Objectivity

B   Integrity

C   Professional behaviour

D   Confidentiality

E   Professional competence

F   Honesty

Test your understanding 11

The CEO of G Ltd has stated at a recent board meeting that 'the company has a responsibility to consider the needs of a wide range of stakeholders and ensure that we minimise any negative impacts that G Ltd has upon them.'

Which ONE of the following best describes the concept referred to by the CEO of G Ltd?

A   Ethics

B   Stakeholder management

C   Non-market strategy

D   Corporate social responsibility

13 Summary

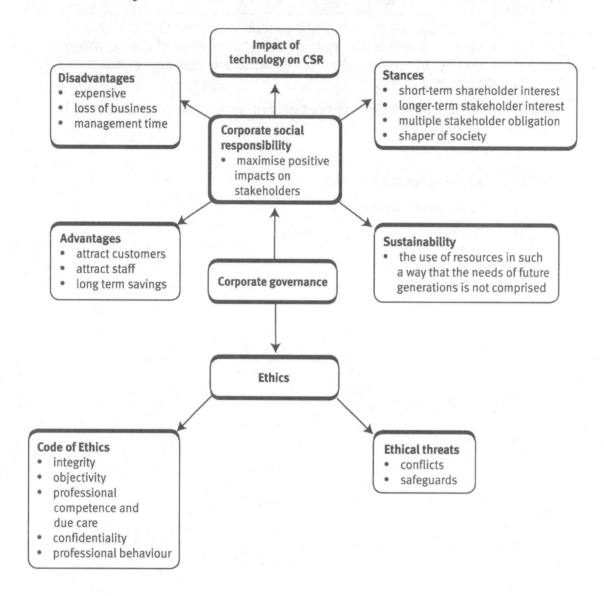

Test your understanding answers

Test your understanding 1

The correct answer is A

Corporate governance is not designed to reduce organisational costs. It may, in fact, have the opposite effect due to the management time and additional staff required by corporate governance codes.

Test your understanding 2 – ADF – (Case Study)

To: Carlos Smith

From: Anne Accountant

Date: 1/5/20XX

Subject: Review of corporate governance arrangements

Dear Mr Smith,

Thank you for your email. I have looked through the information you provided and have identified the following weaknesses:

Lack of diversity of the board of directors

Most of the directors in ADF are older men from country F. There is only one woman on the board.

Having a diverse board can ensure that the company has a wide range of experience to draw on when making decisions.

For example, ADF wants to expand abroad. By having directors from other countries or with experience of these foreign markets, the company would be far better placed to achieve this growth.

Lack of independence of non–executive directors

All the non–executive directors are linked to the Chairman. This makes it unlikely that they will act impartially. They are likely to vote along with the Chairman.

This could lead them to reject acceptable projects, such as the proposed foreign expansion, merely because the Chairman disapproves.

Weak internal audit

The fact that the directors allow ADF to have such an inadequate internal audit function indicates an alarming lack of control. If they are unable to rely fully on the accounts produced, they may find it difficult to implement sensible strategies in the future.

Overall

The ultimate goal of corporate governance is to provide investors with increased confidence in the company and increase the transparency of the board's decisions.

Should investors feel that ADF has poor corporate governance, it can damage ADF's reputation with investors. This may harm its share price and make it harder for the company to raise much needed finance in the future – which is likely to be important if it is planning overseas expansion.

I hope this helps. If you need any further information, please let me know.

Kind regards

Anne

Test your understanding 3

The correct answers are B, D and E

A would match a 'reaction' strategy where L denies any wrongdoing and does nothing to deal with customer concerns. C most closely matches a defence strategy, where the gym chain does as little as possible to deal with customer concerns. There is no solution to the problem, simply a small effort towards keeping customers quiet.

An accommodation strategy occurs when the corporation accepts responsibility for the identified problems (as in option B) and then does what is demanded by its stakeholders (i.e. prevent personal trainers from behaving unethically, as well as improving the menu in the restaurant).

Test your understanding 4 – Router – (Case style)

A. North

Business Advice Ltd

122 Left Way

Helland

HYY GT65

Dear Mr West,

Thank you for your recent letter. I have pleasure in enclosing our thoughts on each of your queries below.

Conflicting mission statement

The mission statement that Router plc has published states that the firm aims to make the 'maximum possible profit'. It is quite common for objectives of this kind to be included in mission statements.

In addition, the 'wider responsibilities to society' are recognised. This company objective is difficult to measure and there will be instances where this conflicts with the maximisation of profit. The gold-mining project provides a perfect example of this. It is expected to be profitable, but also result in the loss of vegetation and the creation of poisonous lakes for the one hundred years.

While the business could attempt to repair the local environment, doing so would make the mine unprofitable, leading to a loss of value to Router's shareholders.

However, it could be argued that in the long run, being socially responsible could increase the wealth of Router's shareholders. Router needs the government to grant it licences in order to mine for gold and shareholders to continue investing in it. If it develops a reputation as a 'dirty' firm, both stakeholders may change their minds. This would cause a loss of profits and a drop in the share price. This would of course mean a fall in shareholder wealth.

Dealing with conflicting objectives

As identified above, Router's objectives may conflict with each other. Methods of dealing with this include:

(1) **Establish a hierarchy of objectives:** Prioritise objectives and score alternative projects against them. For Router, it may need to decide which is more important – its wider social responsibilities or its desire to maximise profits.

(2) **Satisficing:** Router could try to give each stakeholder group something of what it wants. In this case, it could proceed with the mine and then provide some small amount of environmental restitution so that some of the damage is repaired.

(3) **Sequential attention:** This involves giving each stakeholder group's interests consideration over time, though not necessarily for every project. The effect is to keep them on board. In this case the mine could be abandoned because the environmental costs are too great. However, the next project, with less environmental damage, will be adopted. Shareholders and environmentalists will both feel that something has been achieved.

(4) **Side payments:** These are compensatory payments to keep stakeholders content. Perhaps good quality housing could be provided for the labour force which could be left after the works had finished. This could be pointed to as some compensation for the environmental damage and population displacement.

The principal ethical issues in mining are:

(1) **The use of non-renewable resources:** The mining operation results in non-replaceable resources being extracted from the mine. This deprives both the present owners and future generations of the resources. Adequate compensation should be provided to the current owners and the resources extracted should not be wasted out of consideration for future generations.

(2) **The use of power in negotiations:** In the negotiations it is important that the profit motive does not lead to Router acting improperly and exploiting the present owner of the mining rights. Where the country is poor this is a particular concern.

(3) **The environmental damage:** Poisoning the land for a hundred years is clearly not a socially acceptable outcome. Router has an ethical duty to minimise the effect of this pollution by developing a plan to deal with the problem. This should be seen as the minimum the company should do.

(4) **Impacts on the life of local residents:** While they may benefit from the economic boost the mine provides to the region, it is likely that the pollution will also affect them. While there may only be a small number of local residents, this does not give Router the right to ignore their needs. They should explain the steps the company is going to take to minimise the effect on their local environment.

(5) **Safety of procedures:** Mining is an industry noted for its poor safety record. Router must ensure that strict safety guidelines are in place and that they are followed by the workforce. It should ensure these conform to best practises in its industry – even if this is more than the legal requirements in the country of operation.

I hope this answers your queries. If you wish to discuss these issues further, please do not hesitate to contact us.

Kind regards

A. North

Test your understanding 5

The correct answer is C

This approach is also known as 'enlightened self-interest'. J is going beyond regulations in an attempt to win customers in the longer term and stand out in his market.

J is showing no signs of considering the role he plays in society or his responsibility to wider stakeholders, suggesting that he is not operating as a shaper of society or under the multiple stakeholder objectives level.

Test your understanding 6

The correct answer is A

By definition.

Test your understanding 7 – (Integration question)

(1) Potential conflict with professional behaviour – audit services observe the same standards, therefore implying that a rival has lower standards suggests that a firm is not complying with professional standards.

(2) The accountant is likely to lose objectivity because errors in the accounts made during preparation may not be identified when those accounts are reviewed.

(3) As the information is likely to be confidential, discussing it in a public place is inappropriate.

(4) The accountant needs to ensure that knowledge of the foreign country's taxation regime is understood prior to completing the return, otherwise there is the possibility that the appropriate professional skill will not be available.

(5) There is an issue of integrity. The accountant should not allow the report to be released because it is known that the report is incorrect.

(6) This is an issue of integrity. Accountants must not be associated with any form of communication or report that they know to be either materially false or misleading.

(7) The reduction of the number of staff in an organisation in order to increase profit is not necessarily unethical. For example, if the business has an unnecessarily high number of employees, reducing this number may be appropriate. However, the accountant would need to ensure that the analysis was accurate, as it will impact on individual's livelihoods. If there is any uncertainty in the results, they may need to consider whether it should be disclosed. In addition, the accountant will need to be aware of the implications and should ensure that the decision-makers are made aware of the potential ethical considerations.

(8) Again, this is an operational decision. There are ethical concerns over the loss of current staff which the accountant should make the decision-maker aware of along with the potential adverse impact on the reputation of the company.

(9) Ethics involves avoiding negative impacts on the environment that the company operates in. Even though legal, the decision to dump pollution into a river is unethical due to the impact on marine life. Should an accountant be complicit in such an action, it is likely to bring the profession into disrepute.

Test your understanding 8 – (Integration question)

Threat 1

- Do not offer the inducement!

- If necessary, follow the conflict resolution process of the employer.

- Consider the impact of the financial statements being misrepresented.

Threat 2

- Obtaining advice from the employer, professional organisation or professional advisor.

- The employer providing a formal dispute resolution process.

- Legal advice.

Threat 3

- Obtaining additional advice/training.

- Negotiating more time for duties.

- Obtaining assistance from someone with relevant expertise.

Test your understanding 9 – ABC – (Case style)

Email

To: A. Halifax

From: J. Bank

Date: 15/06/XX

Subject: Re: Professional ethics

Hi A,

If you agree to the IT Director's demands, you will be in breach of several parts of the CIMA Code of Ethics.

Integrity

This requires members not to be associated with any form of communication or report where the information is materially false, provided recklessly or incomplete.

You have identified a potential problem with the proposed new system that would involve a large outflow of cash to upgrade ABC's infrastructure.

Following the IT Director's suggestion would involve you ignoring the issue without a firm idea of how it will be resolved (the IT Director is simply suggesting a vague 'work-around'). This means that the report will be incomplete and misleading to its users.

Objectivity

This requires accountants to ensure that their judgement is not compromised because of bias or conflict of interest.

You are only likely to agree to the IT Director's demands because failing to do so could jeopardise your career. This would clearly be acting in your own self-interest.

Professional competence and due care

This requires accountants to follow all applicable technical and professional standards when providing services.

You are aware that the cost-benefit analysis, when undertaken properly, shows an unfavourable result for the new IT system. Failing to use the correctly obtained result could be seen as a failure to meet professional and technical standards.

Professional behaviour

This principle requires accountants to avoid any activities that might bring the profession into disrepute.

If you are found to have knowingly misled the Board of Directors into buying a system that is not cost effective, it would clearly damage confidence in the accountancy profession as a whole.

I hope that helps! Let me know if you need any more information and I'll try to help.

A

Test your understanding 10

The correct answers are C and D

The accountant is in breach of confidentiality as he is using information for his own personal gain (regardless of whether he communicates this information to others). He also risks bringing the profession into disrepute (and could be in breach of insider dealing laws), which breaches professional behaviour.

There is no evidence that he is producing any reports or providing information relating to the new product, which would tend to suggest that integrity, objectivity and professional competence are not being breached.

Note that honesty (while being preferable!) is not a fundamental ethical principle.

Test your understanding 11

The correct answer is D

Note that sustainability is part of CSR – however the CEO appears to be referring to the wider concept of how the organisation looks after its social responsibility.

The organisational ecosystem: External environmental analysis

Chapter learning objectives

Lead	Component
A3: Outline the strategy process	(a) Outline the rational and emergent processes of arriving at strategy
B1: Analyse the elements of the ecosystem	(a) Markets and competition (b) Society and regulation
B2: Discuss the drivers of change in the ecosystem	(a-e) Institutional/systemic, social, market, technology and sustainability

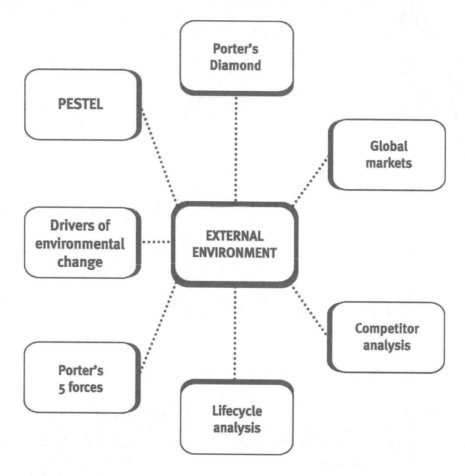

1   Introduction

As we have already seen in chapter 1, in order to formulate a suitable strategy, the organisation must first undertake a detailed appraisal of its ecosystem. Assuming that a rational approach is to be adopted part of such an appraisal will be to consider the ecosystem from both an external and internal point of view. This chapter looks at the external perspective; the organisation must understand what is happening in the outside world (its business environment) that could impact on its future strategies.

Chapter 6 will then take a look at the internal perspective.

There are a number of different models that can be used to help organisations undertake this analysis, each of which focus on a different part of its environment.

Purpose of environmental analysis

Why should an organisation bother to spend the time (and money) needed to undertake a complete environmental analysis? There are several key purposes, including:

- **Identification of threats and opportunities**

    Analysing its environment can help an organisation to identify potential problems it may have to face within its ecosystem (such as future changes in legislation that will affect its operations) as well as possible areas for growth and development that it may wish to take advantage of.

- **Assessment of competition**

  Environmental analysis involves, in part, the examination of the organisation's competitors. Understanding how rivals are acting in the ecosystem may help the organisation stay more competitive in the market.

- **Identification of strengths and weaknesses**

  Understanding its strengths and weaknesses will help the organisation to decide on appropriate strategies. These strategies may be to deal with its weaknesses or build on its strengths.

- **Meeting stakeholder needs**

  Environmental analysis will help the organisation gain a clear understanding of what its key stakeholders require from it. While shareholders are likely to want a high return on their investment, other stakeholders may have different demands on the organisation. These were explored in more detail in chapter 2.

2 Environmental analysis – the drivers of change

Before we look at models that help management to identify relevant issues when conducting an environmental analysis of the organisation's ecosystem, it is important to recognise that it is becoming increasing difficult to undertake. The reason for this is the increasing volatility and rate of change in the global market.

The business environment has become more volatile for a number of reasons, including:

- **Changing technology** is leading to the development of new products and services and/or altering how existing ones are delivered. For instance, the rise of online gaming has had a serious impact on companies such as Game and HMV in the UK, who both sell computer games on physical discs. Indeed, HMV went into administration for the second time in late 2018 because its business model of selling through fixed premises was no longer viable.

- Continuing weakness in the global economy has led to **unpredictable demand** in the market and made it more difficult for many organisations to access credit.

- Increasing **globalisation** of many markets means that organisations may be affected by issues in many different countries. A company like Ford, which trades globally, may be affected by issues in any of the countries it operates within. For example, continued uncertainty over Brexit in the UK led Ford to announce that it was reviewing its UK operations in January 2019.

- The **development of high-growth, emerging economies** – such as the 'BRIC' economies (Brazil, Russia, India and China) – means that organisations looking to expand may need to consider ways of tapping into these new markets. Investment in such economies can provide high returns if done in the right way and at the right time. However, there is no guarantee that a rate of growth in a particular economy can be maintained indefinitely.

  For example, between 2000 and 2012 Brazil's economy was officially one of the fastest growing in the world, with an average annual rate of growth in GDP of 5%. Then, between 2013 and 2017, the country officially slipped into recession.

- **Geopolitical impact,** such as the relations between countries brought about by political policy. For example, the protectionist stance adopted by President Trump in the early years of his administration lead to tariffs being imposed on foreign steel imported into the United States and a threatened trade war with China. A change of ruling party and/or leader might lead to a reversal of such policies.

- Changing **demographics** can naturally impact an ecosystem. This refers to the make-up of populations, both within particular countries and also globally.

Illustration 1 – World population growth

It is reckoned that the global population has grown from 3 billion people 50 years ago to around 7 billion today, caused (not surprisingly!) by birth rates far exceeding death rates, as medical science and standards of living improve to result in the average life-span increasing. It has also been projected that there will be as many as 9 or 10 billion people on the planet by 2050.

This has all sorts of consequences, from demand for food and water to energy and housing, education, healthcare and so on.

- Increasing levels of **customer empowerment**. Customers in many industries have become accustomed to having greater input into the product offering they receive, and the purchasing experience they enjoy. This has been due in large part to the use of digital technology, giving greater awareness of choice and also an expectation of instant fulfilment.

Illustration 2 – Amazon Prime Air

Amazon has announced that it should be able to deliver goods in urban areas to customers within 30 minutes of an order being placed via its future delivery system known as Amazon Prime Air. Delivery will be via drone. In theory, a customer could place an order whilst on the move, via their smartphone, and be home in time to take delivery just half an hour later.

- **Social change**. This refers to the way in which society behaves. For example, increasing levels of consumerism, greater awareness of social issues, such as a focus on business ethics or sustainability, change in activity levels (e.g. the number of foreign holidays taken a year – typically just one or possibly two foreign trips each year, but now considerably more than that, thanks to a demand for a better work-life balance and cheaper flights), greater diversity in our social make-up, etc.

- Rapid developments in **digital technology**. Traditional business models are being challenged and redeveloped as the opportunities of new digital technologies are recognised and are being introduced into organisations and their ecosystems.

  More details on this and examples can be found later in chapter 12.

- Increasing levels of **automation** are redefining the way in which businesses operate. Perhaps the classic example is to look at the motor vehicle industry, where modern production lines consist of a series of sophisticated robots carrying out the work that was once performed by people. However, manufacturing is not the only industry sector that is experiencing automation; it can occur just as much in the service and other sectors.

Illustration 3 – Café X

Based in San Francisco, Café X has adapted the traditional coffee bar model employed by other operators such as Starbucks and Costa by introducing robot baristas.

Instead of being welcomed by a member of staff when they walk into the coffee bar, customers place their order either via an app on their smartphone or at an on-site kiosk. The order is then processed by a robotic arm which brews and prepares the coffee for pick up.

The entrepreneurs behind Café X claim a number of benefits, in addition to reduced costs:

- Reduced waiting time for the customer (so-called 'millennials' are not prepared to wait in queues for long) – it is reckoned a robot is capable of making 120 cups of coffee per hour.

- Greater order accuracy i.e. customers get exactly what they have ordered.

- Product consistency i.e. each medium sized skinny latte made by the robot is exactly the same as the last.

- Data is captured about customer preferences which can then be used for marketing purposes.

- Increasing awareness of **sustainability** issues and demands from customers that organisations address those concerns.

  Sustainability was considered in detail in chapter 3; as was examined there, sustainability isn't merely about issues such as recycling and looking after the environment, it is more wide-reaching than that.

Illustration 4 – Aldi

In the UK Aldi has committed to paying staff more than the minimum living wage that is required by law. This is because the company believes the legal pay level set by the government is not sufficient to enjoy a reasonable standard of living and risks keeping people trapped in poverty.

Understanding these drivers of change should allow the organisation to appreciate the different risks and opportunities that each can present.

For example, investing in **automation**, as has been seen in the example at Café X above, can result in greater operating efficiency and more being known about each customer's preferences, which can lead to improved profitability. The driver of change therefore represents an opportunity.

However, investment costs might be expensive, and payback could take some considerable time. What if an alternative procedure were to be invented that is even more efficient or beneficial to the business, created by a rival, within a short time of the investment occurring? It is possible that the innovator would not be able to afford further investment so soon.

Also, it might be argued that a more automated ordering system will not appeal to as many customers as hoped. For those in a rush, perhaps on the commute to work, it probably will do. But many people see a trip to a café as a chance to relax, to interact with people on a social basis, including with those serving the drinks; automation will eliminate this experience, and so negate a main reason for going to the café in the first place.

Each of these drivers for change must be seen as sources of both **opportunity** and **risk** to the business.

Furthermore, all of these drivers of change mean that an organisation's environment will be changing all the time. This may lead to environmental analysis quickly becoming outdated.

It is therefore important that companies consider undertaking environmental analysis on a regular basis.

Illustration 5 – Jaguar Land Rover (JLR)

In September 2014 JLR flew a helicopter over Tower Bridge in London with a car slung beneath it. This was to publicise the company's ambitions for the future (the plan was to build 1m cars a year by 2020) and to show that the company was in very good health.

In January 2019, the company announced plans to make over 4,500 job cuts in the UK (around 10% of its workforce) in response to changes in its markets. 3 particular factors were identified as causing the change in strategy:

- The clampdown on diesel-powered cars

- The slowing rate of growth in one of its core markets, China

- The continuing uncertainty over the UK's future relationships with the European Union caused by its pending departure from that trade bloc (or "Brexit")'.

3 PESTEL analysis

Exam focus

- PESTEL analyses the **general macro-environment**, identifying key drivers of change and hence sources of risk.

- Particularly good at identifying whether a market is growing/declining and why.

- Can also be used to generate ideas for a position analysis (SWOT) – identifying opportunities and threats.

Model

P   Political

E   Economic

S   Social

T   Technological

E   Environmental

L   Legal

Look for factors on local, industry, national and global levels, both now and in the future.

Generic examples of ideas that are relevant under each heading are:

Political	Social
• Change of government	• Demography
• New political initiatives	• Culture & lifestyle
• Political union	• Education
• War	• Income
• Tax	• Consumerism
• Global political moves	
Economic	**Technological**
• Interest rates	• Rate of development & transfer
• Exchange rates	• Innovation
• Inflation	• Obsolescence
• Unemployment	• Changing cost base
• Balance of payments	
• Business cycle	
Legal	**Environmental**
• Health and safety legislation	• Pollution
• Consumer laws	• Wastage
• Data protection laws	• Climate and climate change
• Accounting regulations	
• New laws	

Criticisms of PESTEL analysis

PESTEL analysis is an excellent way of gaining an understanding of the main environmental issues that may affect the organisation, but it does have a number of drawbacks, including:

- The issues identified by a formal PESTEL analysis may quickly become irrelevant. This is particularly a problem in fast-moving industries, such as computing or mobile phones.

- The PESTEL analysis process is prone to bias. Different managers may have different ideas on what the important issues are that need to be included in the analysis.

- The PESTEL may be incomplete. It can be difficult (or impossible) for managers to correctly identify and understand every environmental issue that might affect the organisation in the future. This problem is sometimes referred to as 'bounded rationality'.

Test your understanding 1

Y is a retailer of clothes in country H.

Which THREE of the following issues would most likely be identified under the 'social' heading of PESTEL analysis carried out for Y?

A   Unemployment levels in country H

B   Change of government

C   Education levels

D   Changing fashions

E   Changing tax regimes

F   Increased use of automation in production

G   Shift in customer attitudes towards ethical consumerism

Test your understanding 2

H is a company that manufactures toys. Its core business has stayed constant for many years, allowing H to make reasonable profits. H's managers have an excellent knowledge of the market and wider industry, having worked in H for many years, though the company has not undertaken formal external analysis for many years. One of H's managers has been asked to undertake a PESTEL analysis for the business. Before he started, he has stated that he feels that the only possible threat to the organisation is changes to the national and international economy.

Which ONE of the following problems with PESTEL analysis is most likely to arise for H?

A   Issues becoming outdated before the analysis can used

B   Bounded rationality

C   Bias in the issues chosen to be included in the analysis

D   Failure to identify all environmental issues for the organisation

4   Porter's Five Forces analysis

Exam focus

- Five forces examines an organisation's **industry**.

- Just because an industry is large and/or growing, high profits do not necessarily follow. The five forces determine profit potential, both for the industry as a whole and for individual firms/SBUs.

- Strong collective forces give low profitability overall.

- An individual firm can earn better margins than competitors if it can deal more effectively with key forces.

- The model can also be useful to generate ideas for a position analysis – especially threats.

Model

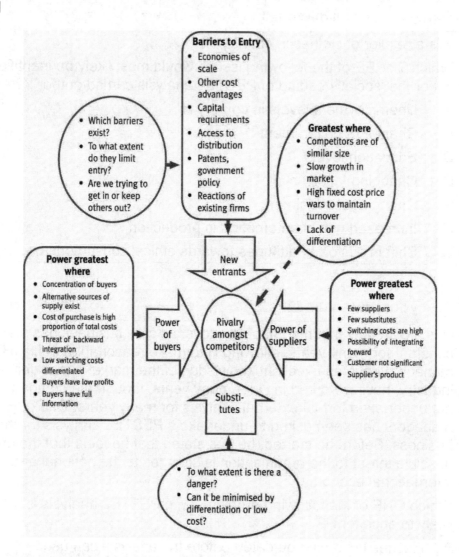

📖 **Explanation of Porter's 5 Forces**

(1) Threat of new entrants

This will depend upon the extent to which there are **barriers to entry**.

Establish:

–   which barriers exist

–   the extent to which they are likely to prevent entry

–   the organisation's position – is it trying to prevent or attempt entry?

Barriers may include:

Economies of scale

The scale of operation allows economies of scale to be reaped which new entrants may not be able to match, e.g. UK supermarkets with bulk purchasing, the computer industry and the steel industry.

Capital requirement for entry

This could be high for capital intensive industries such as chemicals, power and mining but low for high-street retailers who would be able to lease premises. Pharmaceutical industry has large R&D costs and long lead times.

Access to distribution channels

For decades brewing firms have invested in bars and pubs which has guaranteed distribution of their product and made it difficult for competitors to break into the marketplace. Effectively the new entrant is prevented from reaching the customer.

Cost advantages independent of size

Access to cheaper labour or raw materials. Well-established companies know the market well and have the confidence of the major buyers along with the established architecture which serves the market.

Expected retaliation

If you expect a competitor to retaliate on your entry then this may act as a deterrent to enter the market – they may enter a price war and drive down margins in response to your entry.

Legislation

Legal conditions may exist for entry, e.g. licences and personal guarantees, telecommunications and financial services.

Differentiation

Branding and/or high quality may create customer loyalty and inelastic demand for their product, which may take longer to break down for the new entrant.

Switching costs

Customers may have to invest in the trading relationship via contractual arrangements or an investment in IT. To switch supplier would entail substantial costs and therefore the new entrant would have a challenge on their hands.

(2) **Bargaining power of buyers**

This is likely to be high when there is a concentration of buyers, particularly if the volume purchases of the buyers are high, e.g. grocery retailing.

This is likely to be further accentuated when the selling industry comprises a large number of small firms and the product is standard with little or no switching costs involved.

(3) **Bargaining power of suppliers**

Close linkages to the preceding section. Supplier power is likely to be high when:

- the input is important to the buying company

- the supplier industry is dominated by a few suppliers who have secure market positions and are not subject to competitive pressure

- supplier products are branded or involve switching costs

- supplier customers are highly fragmented with little buying power.

(4) **Threat of substitutes**

Substitutes can render products obsolete and can be direct or indirect. They can be based on actual products or uses, e.g. a Ferrari or a Fiat Punto; a car or a bicycle.

There can also be substitution based on income or even doing without, e.g. new furniture or a holiday; giving up smoking.

The availability of substitutes can place a limit on price and change the basis of the product. Consideration must be given to the ease with which consumers can switch to substitutes along with the perceived value that consumer groups would place on the products. At the same time, evaluation of potential actions to build customer loyalty should be undertaken. For example, advertising to build brand image.

(5) **Competitive rivalry**

Some markets are more competitive than others. In highly competitive markets companies regularly monitor competitors. It can be intense or remote and tends to depend upon historical development.

Factors affecting level of rivalry:

- The extent to which competitors are in balance – roughly equal-sized firms in terms of market share or finances – often leads to highly competitive marketplaces.

- Stage of the life cycle. During market growth stages all companies grow naturally, whilst in mature markets growth can only be obtained at the expense of someone else.

- High storage costs may lead to cost-cutting to improve turnover which in turn increases the rivalry.

- Extra capacity comes in large increments which means price cutting may follow to fill capacity.

- Difficulty in differentiating products leaves the basis for competition on price or augmented product.

- High exit barriers mean that some companies must stay in the market.

Conclusion

A desirable circumstance would be a situation where there are weak suppliers and buyers, few substitutes with high barriers to entry and little rivalry.

Criticisms of Porter's 5 Forces model

Over the last three decades business has focused on one fundamental idea – the pursuit of sustainable competitive advantage. While the idea of competition is not new, Michael Porter expanded the concept from competing with rivals to incorporating the struggle for power between the firm and five competitive forces. Porter argued that each of these forces can reduce overall industry profitability and the individual firm's share of that profit – their 'profit potential' – because they can influence prices, costs and the level of investment required.

Not everyone agrees with Porter – some would argue that the idea of satisfying customer needs should not be abandoned in favour of a view that sees customers either as direct competitors or as means to the firm's end. Customers are not objects whose reason for being is to be fought over by competitors seeking 'sustainable competitive advantage'. Porter's model might thus distract managers from seeing customers as potential partners.

Other limitations include the following:

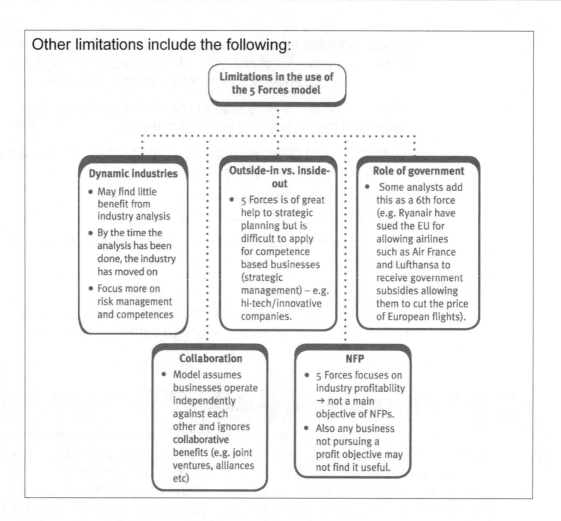

Test your understanding 3

WWW Ltd is a large company that sells paint and wallpaper through homeware retailers in Country X. WWW has several major competitors, each of whom is a similar size to WWW and offers a similar range of products. Due to the generic nature of the products they produce, WWW is unable to secure patents on any of their products.

WWW sells its goods via several retailers, including BBB, which has a 52% share of the paint and wallpaper retail market in Country X. WWW has a one-year rolling contract with BBB to stock their products, though BBB is considering launching its own brand range of paint and wallpaper in the near future. WWW is uncertain of how this will affect their sales agreement with BBB.

Which ONE of the following statements relating to Porter's Five Forces model is correct in relation to WWW's industry?

A   It has high barriers to entry

B   It has high supplier bargaining power

C   It has high buyer bargaining power

D   It has a high threat of substitutes

Test your understanding 4

Under Porter's five forces model, which ONE of the following would be evidence of HIGH supplier power?

A   Customers are relatively small compared to the supplier

B   Low probability of forward integration by suppliers

C   Large numbers of suppliers

D   Supplier's product is not differentiated

Test your understanding 5 – Hawk – (Case style)

Hawk Leathers Ltd ("Hawk") is a company based in the UK that employs around 60 people in the manufacture and sale of leather jackets, jeans, one- and two-piece suits and gloves. These are aimed primarily at motorcyclists, although a few items are sold as fashion garments.

Hawk sells 65% of its output to large retail chains such as Motorcycle City and Carnells, exports 25% to the USA and Japan, and sells the remaining 10% to individuals who contact the company directly. The latter group of customers specify their requirements for a made-to-measure suit (they are often professional racers whose suits must be approved by the authorities, such as the Auto Cycle Union). The large retailers insist on low margins and are very slow to settle their debts.

There are around a dozen companies in the UK who make similar products to Hawk, plus very many other companies who compete with much lower prices and inferior quality. Hawk's typical selling price for a one-piece suit is £1,000, whereas the low quality rivals' suits retail at around £400. As Hawk say in their literature "if you hit the tarmac, there's no substitute for a second skin from Hawk". Synthetic materials are waterproof, unlike leather, but do not currently offer sufficient protection in an accident.

Sales of leathers in the UK are growing rapidly, mainly due to a resurgence of biking from more mature riders of large, powerful machines. Such riders are often wealthy and have family and financial commitments. Currently Hawk, and its rivals for quality leathers are finding it hard to keep up with demand. However, government policy and EU emissions controls are likely to limit motorcycle performance, and some experts predict that these regulations will cause sales of large motorcycles to level off.

Whilst supplies of leather from Asia, Scandinavia and the UK are plentiful, a key problem is recruiting and training machinists to stitch and line the garments. Hawk has been able to invest in modern machinery to help production but the process is still labour intensive. Hawk has found that the expertise, reputation and skilled labour needed to succeed in the industry takes years to build up.

Although the industry is fairly traditional, there are some new developments such as a website for individual customers to browse and specify requirements, and new colours such as metallics for leathers, and a small but growing demand from non-bikers who are interested in 'recreational' and 'club wear' items.

The Managing Director of Hawk has sent you the following note:

Note

Hi N,

I'm currently heading up an internal strategy group who are looking into Hawk's external position. Could you please analyse the issues facing Hawk's industry using a PESTEL analysis for me. I also need you to evaluate the strength of each competitive pressure facing Hawk, using Porter's five forces model.

If you could draw on your knowledge of the company and its situation, that would be great. I only need a couple of points under each heading.

If you could send me a copy of your analysis in about forty-five minutes that would be fantastic.

Thanks

MD

Required:

Undertake the analysis requested by the MD.

(45 minutes)

5 Industry life cycle analysis

The life-cycle model suggests that both individual products and services, as well as entire industries, move through a number of different stages in their lives. Understanding this for our organisation can be a useful analysis tool and can help to suggest which strategies the organisation needs to adopt in order to compete successfully.

This model can therefore be used to look at the **industry as a whole** that the organisation operates in, or can be used to assess **individual products or divisions** within the organisation.

Industry/Product life cycle

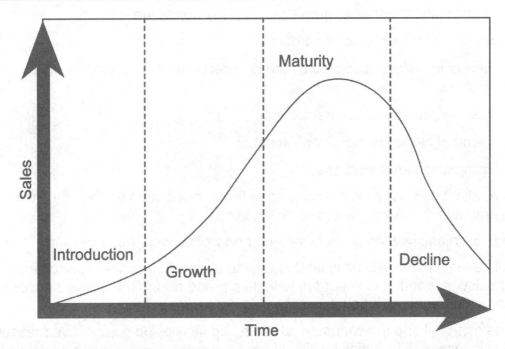

The model can be used to predict competitive conditions and identify key issues for management in corporate appraisals and strategic choices.

Introduction stage

The product is new to the market at this stage. Key points are:

- it will be purchased by 'innovators'
- high launch and marketing costs are likely
- production volumes will be low and product cost will be high
- buyers are unsophisticated
- competition is little if any.

Price elasticity of demand will influence the pricing strategy.

- **Price skimming** is appropriate when the product is known to have a price-inelastic demand.

- **Penetration pricing** is appropriate where the demand is thought to be price-elastic and when gaining market share is seen as more important than fast recovery of development costs.

'Pioneer companies', who are the first to the market with a particular product, are usually forced to sell the concept. These early promotions will help competitor companies who enter later with 'me too' versions of the product concept.

Early entry is risky as heavy requirement for cash and product idea may fail BUT early entry allows the prospect of establishing market share and developing first mover advantage.

Growth stage

During this stage the market grows rapidly. Key points are:

- sales for the market as a whole increase

- new competitors, attracted by the prospects, enter to challenge the 'pioneer'

- new segments may be developed

- demand becomes more sophisticated

- competition levels increase.

The market becomes profitable and cash flows increase to recover the initial investment in development and launch costs.

There are many new consumers with no preference who they buy from.

It will become more difficult in later stages to persuade people to switch from their existing brand. It is important to build a brand during this stage if possible to ease the traumas at the later stages via defensive strategy.

Prices often fall due to economies of scale and increasing competitive pressure, and evidence of differentiation will become apparent, e.g. branding develops.

Maturity stage

During this stage market growth slows or even halts. Key points are:

- fully sophisticated demand

- high levels of competition

- price becomes more sensitive

- demand reaches saturation. The only way to increase market share is to gain business from competitors or from 'late adopters' or 'laggards'

- it would be desirable to have a high market share at this stage or to have successfully developed a niche

- large market share changes can be difficult to achieve at this stage and most companies would concentrate on defensive strategies to protect their current position and compete hard for the new customers coming into the marketplace

- over time the company must be vigilant to detect and anticipate changes in the market and be ready to undertake product or market modifications with a view to lengthening the life.

Decline

During this stage the number of customers falls. Key points are:

- competition reduces as players leave

- price falls to attract business as sophisticated customers expect cheap prices

- slow 'harvesting' must be balanced with straight divestment

- investment kept to a minimum to take up any market share that may be left by departing competitors

- there may be profitable niches remaining after industrial death.

Considerations

- Offer a range of products at various stages of the life cycle – mature products will fund the development of new products

- competencies need to change – at the early stages, creativity and innovation are key whilst at later stages efficiencies and low costs become important

- life cycles are difficult to predict, can change quickly and will vary from one product to another. Turning points are very hard to predict

- management anticipation of decline can cause decline! Reduction in investment and advertising can cause the appropriate market response

- SWOT varies across the life cycle

- strategies will need to change as the organisation progresses through the life cycle.

For example, the market for calculators started with scientists and engineers and then moved to business before moving to higher education students. Finally the market moved to include schoolchildren, which proved to be the largest segment of all. A pioneer wishing to stay the course would experience radical change as they move from the organisational markets to the mass consumer version.

Summary of industry life cycle

	Intro	Growth	Maturity	Decline
Sales	Low	Rapidly rising	Peak	Declining
Costs per customer	High cost	Average	Low	Low
Profits	Negative	Rising	High	Falling
Customers	Innovators	Early adopters	Middle majority	Laggards
Competitors	Few	Growing number	Stable number beginning to decline	Declining number
Objectives	Create product awareness & trial	Maximise market share	Maximise profit whilst defending market share	Reduce expenditure & 'milk the brand'

Marketing strategies

	Intro	Growth	Maturity	Decline
Product	Offer basic product	Offer product extensions, service & warranty	Diversify brands & models	Phase out weak items
Price	Cost plus	Price penetration	Price matching	Price cutting
Promotion	Build product awareness amongst early adopters & dealers	Build awareness & interest in mass market	Stress brand differences & benefits	Reduce to level to maintain hard core loyalty
Place	Limited	Growing	Maximum	Limited

Usefulness of the life cycle model

Management within the organisation can benefit from the use of the life cycle model in a number of ways, including:

- **Improved strategic planning**

  Using the product life cycle helps organisations with their strategic planning. For example, the organisation will realise that the demand for a product typically does not last forever. It can therefore put in place contingency plans to deal with this – for example ensuring the development and launch of new products on a periodic basis. Knowing that it will need to replace even successful products at some point in the future can therefore lead to a more innovative organisational focus.

- **Improved budgeting**

  The life cycle model indicates when products should generate or use cash throughout their lives. Understanding which stage each product in the organisation's portfolio has reached (and will reach in the future) can help the organisation to estimate its future cash flow needs.

- **Proactive approach**

  Rather than sitting waiting for the decline of a product to begin, the life cycle model allows companies to take a more proactive approach to boosting sales and profits during each stage. For example, if the organisation identifies that a product is moving into decline, it can look at ways of maximising returns by, for example, cutting prices or redesigning the product.

Test your understanding 6

F plc sells a product known as the YYU500. The YYU500 has seen sales growth of around 1% for the last two years, after strong growth in the previous five years. This is due to new products entering the market in competition with the YYU500.

F is therefore considering cutting its prices to be in line with its major rivals. It hopes that this will help it to maintain its market share. Market research indicates that this will now cause a significant increase in the level of sales, even though in previous years price cuts have had little effect on demand.

F is also planning to launch a promotional campaign to highlight the benefits of the YYU500 against its rival products.

Which stage of the product life cycle does the YYU500 appear to have reached?

A   Growth

B   Decline

C   Maturity

D   Introduction

Test your understanding 7

AJJ Ltd has identified that all three of its main products are at the maturity phase of the product life cycle. Which ONE of the following is AJJ likely to be experiencing due to this?

A   High, but declining sales

B   Growing numbers of competitors

C   Product diversification and differentiation strategies

D   Adoption of price skimming strategies

Test your understanding 8 – (Case style)

You have recently been appointed to the European strategy steering group at PTP Electronics, the holding company for a number of subsidiary companies making household name consumer electronic products. Four products were discussed at the recent meeting. All appear to be profitable, and some large retail outlets sell the whole range of PTP products in their stores.

- High Definition Digital recorders – the market has been expanding very quickly since its launch four years ago and PTP has a very small share compared to Sony and Panasonic.

- Home cinema systems – sales are levelling off as people switch to soundbars and playbars. PTP's brands have been a market leader since the early 2000s.

- Conventional plasma and LED colour television monitors – demand for plasma/LED TVs is declining as customers and manufacturers turn to newer technologies. PTP has recently built a new factory in Holland to produce high definition televisions (HDTV) in both 4K and 8k format. Consequently it has not pushed sales of conventional TVs.

- 4K and 8K televisions – although expensive, PTP sees these as a huge future market with the increase in digital broadcasting. It is the market leader in this field although sales in volume terms are not rising as fast as had been hoped. Launch was two years ago.

You have been asked by the Chairman of the steering group to make a presentation to the rest of the steering group. She has asked that you use the product lifecycle model to identify and comment on the lifecycle position of each product type, with reasons. She also wishes you to evaluate the balance of PTP's product portfolio as a whole. The presentation should advise PTP's directors of one idea that you feel may help improve the portfolio balance.

Required:

Draft notes that you will use to help you make your presentation to the rest of the group as outlined by the Chairman.

(30 minutes)

6 Competitor analysis (competitor intelligence)

This can be defined as a set of activities which examines the comparative position of competing enterprises within a given strategic sector. It seeks to:

- provide an understanding of the company's competitive advantage/disadvantage relative to its competitor's positions

- help generate insights into competitors strategies – past, present and potential

- give an informed basis for developing future strategies to sustain/establish advantages over competitors.

Grant highlights three purposes:

- to forecast competitors' future strategies and decisions

- to predict competitors' likely reactions to a firm's strategic initiatives

- to determine how competitor **behaviour** can be influenced to make it more favourable for the organisation.

A framework for competitor analysis

Step 1: identify competitors

- **Brand competitors** sell similar products to the same customers we serve, e.g. Coke and Pepsi.

- **Industry competitors** sell similar products but in different segments, e.g. BA and EasyJet.

- **Form competitors** sell products that satisfy the same need as ours though technically very different, e.g. speedboat and sports car.

- **Generic competitors** compete for the same income, e.g. home improvements and golf clubs.

Step 2: analyse competitors

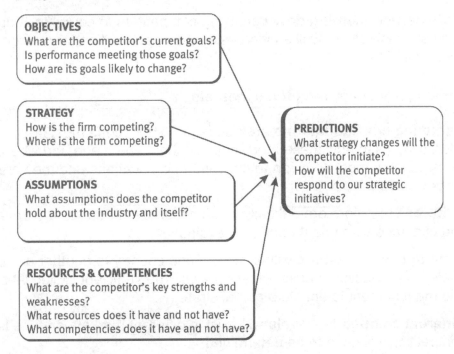

Step 3: develop competitor response profiles

- **Laid back:** Does not respond

- **Selective:** Reacts to attack in only selected markets

- **Tiger:** Always responds aggressively

- **Stochastic:** No predictable pattern exists.

7 The nature of global competition

It was identified in section 2 of this chapter that increasing globalisation is one of the drivers of change in the organisational ecosystem; this section looks at some of the details as to why there is increased international trade.

Why enter foreign markets

- **pressure** from shareholders to increase their return on capital employed

- **saturated** domestic markets making home expansion difficult

- **opportunities** as emerging markets arise with increases in economic income and spending power. Advances in technology, such as the internet and cloud computing, means recognising and exploiting such opportunities becomes more viable

- **trade barriers coming down** enabling competitors to compete in our domestic markets as well as increasing the opportunities for our company overseas.

Risks arising from entering global markets

- **Marketing mix adaptations** are needed and questions must be addressed as to how these modifications should be made and when. Consideration must be given to the cultural implications and the potential costs involved.

- **Cultures vary** more dramatically when national boundaries are traversed and cultural environment needs full evaluation.

- **Varying cost structures** will exist from one country to another as will the quality of production factors – there may not be sufficient skilled labour and management to enable a global strategy.

- **Different competitive levels** will exist in different markets and the level of competition will need to be determined.

- **Exchange rate volatility** requires the deployment of control systems to protect the company.

- **Different economic situations** will alter the demand for the product and the availability of factors of production.

- **Political involvement** as governments will seek to be involved in decisions. Careful planning will be needed to ensure that no conflict arises or, if likely, the allocation of responsibility to a suitably qualified individual.

- **Political situation** should be considered with regard to war, terrorism and government stability. What are the risks to our personnel and our organisation?

- **Entry requirements?** What do we have to do to get in? Is it legal and ethical?

Benefits of entering global markets

- **Economies of scale** are possible as research and development can now be spread over wider production volumes. Bulk-buying discounts may be available as the volume of our purchases and our reputation increases.

- **Management opportunity** is increased and this may prove motivational to certain types of managers whilst at the same time allowing those managers to experience a wider range of cultural situations.

- This in turn allows the **challenge to the traditional home cultural** perspective. Items can be viewed from a different perspective with cultural benchmarks being developed.

- **Cheaper sources of raw materials** and labour may allow the development of a competitive advantage which could be sustainable for a period of time.

- **Market development** as the emerging markets bring a whole new range of consumers who will be embarking on their 'first buy' and so may not be as 'fussy' as consumers in a saturated market.

- **Risk reduction** via portfolio spread will arise when different markets are combined into a portfolio.

- **Political sponsorship** will be possible as national governments, keen to boost or maintain home employment, offer attractive packages to global companies to invest in that country.

- **Political power** becomes possible as the company grows in size and is seen to be contributing to wealth creation as opposed to exploitation of the nation concerned.

8   Competitive advantage of nations – Porter's Diamond

This model suggests reasons why some nations are more competitive than others and why some industries within nations are more competitive than others. This can be used in a number of different ways:

- The organisation can understand what, if any, factors have caused it to be successful in its current country or countries of operation.

- The model can be used by the organisation to assess whether a particular country is suitable for expansion into.

- Governments can identify how to adjust their policies in order to attract or strengthen certain industries.

Porter identified four key factors (or dimensions) that determine the relative attractiveness of different countries to a particular industry.

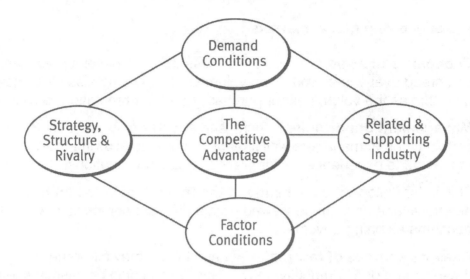

Factor conditions – supply side

A supply of production factors that convey advantage. They provide initial advantage which is then subsequently built upon to develop more advanced factors. Basic factors are unsustainable as they are easily copied (unskilled labour) whilst advanced factors can convey the advantage as they are less easy to emulate (scientific expertise).

They include human, physical, knowledge, capital and infrastructure, for example:

*   linguistic ability of the Swiss has provided advantage in the banking industry

*   financial expertise within the UK.

You can use the national identity as the basis for a brand, e.g. New Zealand lamb.

Demand conditions – demand side

Sophisticated home demand can lead to the company developing significant advantages in the global marketplace. Demanding consumers set high standards for products whilst past experience of the product's progress through the life cycle in the home market can provide valuable input to new strategic initiatives.

*   Japanese customers have high expectations of their electrical products, which forces producers to provide a technically superior product for the global marketplace. They are so used to dealing with sophisticated customers that when they come across unsophisticated markets, they excel way beyond the competition.

Related and supporting industry – the value chain and system

Advantage conveyed by the availability of superior supplier industries, e.g. Italy has a substantial leatherwear industry which is supported by leather-working plants and top fashion and design companies.

Strategy, structure and rivalry – the competition element

Different nations have different approaches to business in terms of structure and the intensity of rivalry that can take place. If a company is used to dealing with strong competition then it will have experience of rivals' attacks and so will be better able to fight them off.

Domestic rivalry can keep the organisations 'lean and mean' so that when they go out into the global marketplace they can compete more successfully with the less capable foreign competition, e.g. Nokia and Finland's approach to the regulation of telecoms.

Governments can promote this rivalry via policy.

Other events

Porter points out that countries can produce world-class firms due to two further factors:

- **The role of government** – subsidies, legislation and education can all impact on the other four elements of the diamond to the benefit of the industrial base of the country.

- **The role of chance events** – wars, civil unrest, chance discoveries and others can also change the four elements of the diamond unpredictably.

A business will initially choose to enter markets in those countries where the above conditions are most favourable. This involves considering the attractiveness of the markets and the barriers to entry that may exist. Strong position audit is needed to assess our company's strategic capability in these new segments.

Research is critical before entering a foreign market. Then on a regular basis, more research is needed as well as the setting up of systems to ensure that it is continually updated and monitored.

Criticisms of Porter's Diamond model

The following criticisms are made of Porter's Diamond model:

- Porter developed the model by looking at ten developed countries. The model thus only really applies to developed economies.

- Porter argues that inbound foreign direct investment does not increase domestic competition significantly because domestic firms lack the capability to defend their own markets and face a process of market-share erosion and decline. However, there seems to be little empirical evidence to support that claim.

- The Porter model does not adequately address the role of multi-national corporations. There seems to be ample evidence that the diamond is influenced by factors outside the home country.

- Porter's analysis focused on manufacturers, banks and management consultancy firms. Some have questioned its relevance to service-based companies such as McDonalds.

- Porter's focus is on the domestic country rather than which foreign markets have been targeted. A careful choice of target is essential to ensure that the firm has the competences required for success.

- Not all firms from a given country are successful, suggesting that corporate management is more important than geographical location.

Test your understanding 9

B is an airline, which operates in a number of different countries around the world. It is currently considering entry into country G, but is concerned that there are not enough skilled workers in country G for their needs.

Insert the missing TWO words into the sentence below:

According to Porter's Diamond model, country G lacks a key _____ and therefore may not be an appropriate expansion target for B.

Test your understanding 10

AHH is a supermarket chain which is considering expansion into country L. It has decided to analyse the decision using Porter's Diamond.

Consider the following lists of issues relating to the AHH's expansion as well as the dimensions of Porter's Diamond.

	Issue		Dimension
A	Lack of farmers required for fresh produce	**1**	Demand conditions
B	A range of existing supermarkets serving a large number of customers	**2**	Strategy, structure and rivalry
C	Lack of available land to build supermarkets	**3**	Factor conditions
D	AHH currently operates in highly competitive markets	**4**	Related and supporting industry

Show which issue relates to each dimension by pairing the appropriate letter and number (e.g. A1, B4, etc).

Test your understanding 11 – (Integration question)

Australia has a long-established wine industry, but in the 1970s it decided to expand exports to Europe and the USA, since growth was becoming limited in domestic markets.

Australian producers had benefitted from strong domestic demand, and had produced excellent results by cultivating grape varieties imported from Europe, combined with innovative techniques such as cool fermentation in stainless steel containers. Producers had achieved success in a wide range of wines including red, white, sparkling, dry and sweet.

Although many producers started out as independent small businesses, major listed groups such as Penfolds had consolidated many of these small producers into well-known labels.

Required:

(a) Discuss two reasons why Australian wine producers decided to enter foreign markets, and two risks arising.

(b) By giving one example of each element, use Porter's Diamond to evaluate the degree of competitive advantage achieved by the Australian wine industry.

9 Summary

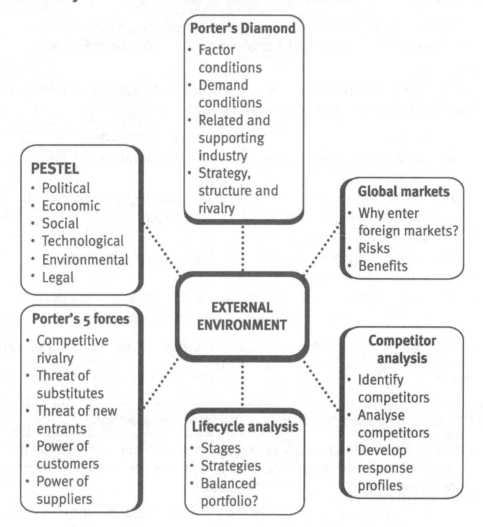

Test your understanding answers

Test your understanding 1

The correct answers are C, D and G

A is economic, B and E are political, while F is technological.

Test your understanding 2

The correct answer is C

The company seems to be in a stable, fairly slow-moving industry, so A is less likely to be an issue. B and D are the same issue (just stated differently) – the scenario mentioned that management had a deep knowledge of the market, reducing the risk of bounded rationality.

However, as can be seen from the scenario, the manager in charge of undertaking the PESTEL analysis already has definite ideas about what is important, which could lead to bias creeping into his work.

Test your understanding 3

The correct answer is C

Barriers to entry appear to be low. Given the lack of patents and its distributor's plans to enter the market, WWW should be worried about the threat of new entrants.

Supplier power is unknown. No information is provided about WWW's suppliers – its retail partner is a customer.

Customer power seems to be high – BBB has alternative wallpaper and paint suppliers it could choose to stock and seems keen to, potentially, replace WWW's products with its own in the short to mid-term.

Substitutes are not mentioned in the scenario. BBB will turn into a rival to WWW if it enters the market.

Test your understanding 4

The correct answer is A

If the customer is relatively small, the supplier is likely to have more power in their relationship as it does not rely on the customer for a large proportion of its sales.

The other three options would all suggest low supplier power – if suppliers are unlikely to take over the business (low chance of forward integration), there are many of them for the business to choose from, or it easy to switch to other suppliers due to a lack of differentiation in their products, the customer enjoy higher power over the supplier.

Test your understanding 5 – Hawk – (Case style)

PEST analysis

Political factors

Government/EU regulation that could damage motorcycle sales is an issue for the whole industry. If there is a clamp down it might seriously threaten sales. Hawk might consider setting up a lobby group with other manufacturers.

Economic factors

The recession in the UK economy (and foreign markets) is likely to result in lower disposable incomes for what is often a luxury purchase. Hawk may well find a major dip in sales as the recession continues.

The weakening pound is making exports to the USA and Europe easier, but is increasing the import costs of leather. There is little Hawk can do about that, so it is likely to seek new global markets such as the BRIC economies (Brazil, Russia, India and China).

Social factors

There has been a growth in demand from mature riders ("born-again bikers"). Have companies such as Hawk done any research to assess the life of this trend? How effective is Hawk's marketing at reaching this potentially important market segment?

More emphasis on safety of riders who often have family; this is a boost for the industry and Hawk's customers are likely to be responsible bikers.

Technological factors

Relevant issues include website ordering and metallic paints but neither of these is especially important. However, Hawk and others should be aware of new ideas that could help with their processes.

Environmental factors

Care will need to be taken with how dyes etc. are dealt with as part of the manufacturing process, as the level of scrutiny on how manufacturing companies impact on the environment increases.

Legal

Approval from the ACU is vital for Hawk's racing suits. Whilst this will require regular inspections, it is important for credibility amongst customers. It may be seen as an endorsement of quality for the entire range (the so-called "halo effect").

Porter's five forces

Threat of new entrants

The threat of new entrants is reasonably high from overseas rivals but is limited by existing entry barriers. These include recruiting skilled staff, close associations with racing teams, established relationships with major retailers and brand reputation.

Bargaining power of customers

The power of customers depends on which customers are being considered. For individual customers it is low because they will be loyal to the brand and are not buying in bulk.

However, for the large retailers there is higher power that arises from the volumes purchased. Retail chains will exercise this power in terms of designs, lead times, prices paid and credit period taken. Hawk need to meet these needs or risk losing major customers to existing/new competition.

It will also be high for the professional racing teams. Having Hawk's products associated with top class racing teams is imperative to maintain the quality of its brand in the marketplace. Suits must be made to a high quality and exactly to customer specification/compliance with the Auto Cycle Union's requirements.

Bargaining power of suppliers

The power of suppliers is generally low, because leather and machinery are readily available. (Note: It may be that supply of leather of the required quality for professional suits is limited, in which case the power would be higher.)

However, supplies of skilled labour are limited and Hawk may find it has to pay high wages.

Threat of substitutes

Hawk believes that the threat from substitutes is low and states that only leather can offer the required degree of abrasion resistance. Clearly this must be kept under review as newer fabrics and technologies may change this perception.

The threat of substitute products/fabrics may be higher in the fashion lines, although this does not yet constitute a major proportion of Hawk's turnover.

Competitive rivalry

Rivalry is considered to be low. Those "rivals" that offer cheap leathers are not really rivals at all, because serious bikers will not contemplate such offerings.

Furthermore, sales are rising so quickly that all players are working at near capacity without the need to take customers from one another.

Summary

The key risk areas for Hawk do not come from within the industry as, with the exception of the power of larger retailers, competitive forces are low. However, there are major issues that impact the industry as a whole in respect of the current economic climate and government policy.

(**Tutorial note:** each point within the models has been explained and assessed for its importance. Finally key points must be highlighted in order to then formulate or appraise strategy.)

Test your understanding 6

The correct answer is C

The seeming saturation of the market and the increase in competition would suggest the product is at the maturity stage. This stage typically sees the volume of product sales become more sensitive to selling price changes.

Test your understanding 7

The correct answer is C

A would indicate products that are in decline. B would tend to occur during growth, while D would usually be part of the introduction/growth phase of the product life cycle.

Test your understanding 8 – (Case style)

Presentation notes:

(**Tutorial note:** it is relatively straightforward to classify the individual products/SBUs but make sure you justify your choice. The higher skills element is in looking at the bigger picture to evaluate the overall portfolio balance.)

The market for high definition digital recorders is still expanding and hence is in the growth phase. PTP really must try to boost its presence in this crucial market area (see below), or risk being left behind by rivals.

Sales of home cinema systems are static, indicating a market that is mature and possibly saturated. This is a problem given PTP's historical dependence on this product stream. The risk is that profits will soon decline or disappear if retailers lose interest in this product group.

The market for conventional plasma and LED televisions is in decline, suggesting that PTP should focus instead on 4K and 8K televisions – the growth area.

Despite being a market leader, PTP's sales of 4K and 8K televisions are only rising modestly suggesting that the industry (or at least PTP's products) are still in late introduction or early growth stages. PTP believes that this segment is going to be huge, so will need to invest heavily in marketing and product development to ensure it can capitalise on the high growth when it arises.

Overall portfolio evaluation

The balance of a portfolio can be assessed against a range of criteria including cash flow, growth, risk and investment required. This can be achieved to some extent by having products at different stages throughout the lifecycle. While PTP has products at different stages within the lifecycle, the main problems with its portfolio are:

- Conventional plasma and LED TVs are facing decline but PTP does not have any new products in the development stage to replace them.

- The overall portfolio may require a net investment of cash in the future. Home cinema systems may be strong cash generators but both high definition digital recorders and HDTVs require investment to benefit from future growth.

Suggestions for re-balancing the portfolio include:

- Invest to develop soundbars and playbars. PTP might offer a guaranteed trade-in value for old units if customers purchase a new soundbar.

- Switch production away from the old factory to the new one in Holland, perhaps selling the old site and using the proceeds for an acquisition of a home entertainment-focused business.

Test your understanding 9

The correct answer is FACTOR CONDITIONS

The business is missing a key factor that would enable it to operate in the target country.

Test your understanding 10

The correct answers are: A4, B1, C3, D2

A4 – Lack of farming indicates a missing related industry for a supermarket.

B1 – Large numbers of existing supermarkets could indicate that there is insufficient spare demand for AHH to win if it wishes to expand into country L.

C3 – The lack of land is a specific missing factor that AHH also needs in order to successfully expand into country L.

D2 – AHH's success in other competitive markets may indicate that it has the necessary strategy and structure to deal with the competition in country L.

Test your understanding 11 – (Integration question)

Why enter export markets?

Australian producers would have been under pressure to increase profits since some are effectively listed companies. Furthermore, it is likely that domestic markets had become saturated. There must be a limited consumption in Australia, therefore producers' attention would turn to export volumes. They would have spotted an opportunity to target growth markets in the UK and Europe.

Likely risks

One risk would have been culture and tradition. For example, wine drinking in the UK was far less common than it is today, and the risk would have been non-acceptance by a UK market.

Equally, the French are very protective of their own wines and reluctant to stock those from other countries. National bias would be a major barrier to overcome in some wine-drinking countries.

Another risk would be financial – namely exchange rate fluctuations and costs involved in transporting a product that is over 85% water for thousands of miles.

Porter's Diamond

Factor conditions would include the availability of land, the favourable climate, and the skill of Australian winemakers (so impressive that they have exported their talents back to European producers – the so-called "flying winemakers"). These would combine to give a strong advantage to Australia, because few rival countries possess such a favourable mix.

Demand conditions are also strong; Australia has an alcohol tolerant culture, and domestic consumers would have set high standards. However, this would also apply to countries such as France, so this factor may have given Australia a medium-level advantage overall.

Related and supporting industries will be strong since Australia is a modern, developed industrial nation. This will confer a medium-level advantage compared to Western-European countries and the USA, but a strong one compared to, say, Chile. Australian firms may also have had an advantage as they could have invested in newer technologies while rivals in France would have been committed to traditional methods.

Strategy structure and rivalry would be favourable, since there is a properly developed stock market, and reasonably intense local rivalry. This would give a strong advantage compared to developing economies such as Argentina and Bulgaria. It would also give a strong advantage compared to countries with old-fashioned rules about wine, such as France (these rules often prevent true competition).

Strategic networks and platforms

Chapter learning objectives

Lead	Component
B3: Discuss the impact of the ecosystem on organisational strategy	(a) Discuss the impact of strategic networks and platforms on organisational strategy
	(b) Conduct stakeholder analysis in networks

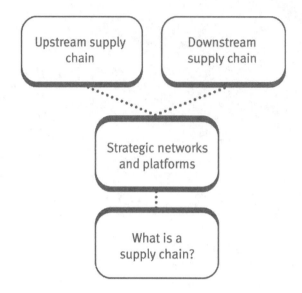

1 Introduction

Customers and suppliers are often key stakeholder groups in an organisational ecosystem. One framework that we have already met – Mendelow's power/interest matrix – and another that you have probably seen before in earlier studies, and which was revisited in chapter 4 – Porter's five forces model – are useful for assessing the power of customers and suppliers and suggesting suitable strategies for dealing with them.

In this chapter we will consider in more detail the idea of strategic networks and platforms. This concept was first introduced in chapter 2, in which the following definitions were laid out:

A **strategic network** can be defined as a collection of different organisations that are separate in legal terms but which work collectively to try to achieve long term strategic advantage. This might be via formal arrangements such as a joint venture, or a simple agreement to share information on an informal basis. The idea is that organisations can perform better if they work together, rather than simply working in isolation. For any organisation, the other members of its strategic network should be seen as a form of stakeholder.

The **strategic platform** is the means by which the transfer of goods or services between provider and consumer can take place. Historically, this has been more physical in nature; for example, a publisher might encourage a new book to be reviewed in a magazine or newspaper, and the consumer would then go to a bookshop in a shopping centre in order to make the purchase.

The modern day format of a strategic platform might be a digital platform, but the principles are still the same; a platform business model is developed that encompasses providers, suppliers, consumers and employees to create or exchange goods, services and social interaction. Others might integrate with other organisations' digital platforms. Regardless of the set-up, the strategy must integrate and consider all of the key stakeholders within the network and platform.

So, central to understanding this chapter is the idea that some of the organisation's key stakeholders are partners within its strategic networks.

Furthermore, the key partners within the strategic network are often customers and suppliers who work together using some sort of platform to create value.

In this chapter the practicalities of managing the relationships with suppliers and customers within the organisational ecosystem is considered. In particular the role of technologies in supply chain management is analysed in detail.

2 What is a supply chain?

 A supply chain encompasses all activities and information flows necessary for the transformation of goods from the origin of the raw material to when the product is finally consumed or discarded.

This typically involves distribution of the product from the supplier to the manufacturer to the retailer and then on to the final consumer. Each link in the supply chain (i.e. the supplier, or the consumer) is known as a node.

Transactions between the business and its suppliers are referred to as its 'upstream' supply chain. Transactions between the business and its customers are referred to as 'downstream supply chain'.

 Businesses are no longer able to just consider their immediate customers and immediate suppliers. This is because problems anywhere in the organisation's ecosystem can have a significant impact on the business.

---

e.g | **Illustration 1 – The supply chain**

Imagine a (simplified) supply chain for a large, national baker who makes and sells bread through a chain of supermarkets.

Farmer → Mill → Wholesaler → Baker → Supermarket → Consumer

The baker makes bread with wheat. This means that the supply chain starts with the farmers who grow the wheat – the original creator of the resource. The farmers then sell this wheat to mills, who convert the wheat into flour. The flour is then purchased by wholesalers who sell the flour in bulk to larger companies, such as our baker. The baker makes the loaves of bread and sells it onto the supermarkets, who sell the bread onto the end consumers (customers).

Management of the supply chain means that the baker needs to be aware of the activities and needs of each part (or node) of the supply chain – from the farmer to the end consumer.

The baker's upstream supply chain includes farmers, mills and wholesalers, while its downstream supply chain is made up of supermarkets and consumers.

So the network that forms the organisational ecosystem of the baker is comprised of many components in both the upstream and downstream supply chains.

> Note that problems in any part of the supply chain can affect the baker. For example, if farmers switch from growing wheat to other, more profitable crops then it will lead to a scarcity of flour on the market, pushing the baker's costs up. If the end consumers start to dislike the types of bread that the baker is selling (for example if the market shifts away from white bread to brown or granary breads) then this will affect how many of the baker's products will be stocked by the supermarkets.
>
> As such, even though the baker may not directly transact with the consumer and the farmers, it is still affected by them as they are part of its supply chain.

It is worth noting that managing the supply chain and moving materials and products from node to node includes activities such as:

- production planning
- purchasing
- materials management
- distribution
- customer service
- forecasting.

While each firm can be competitive through improvements to its internal practices, ultimately the ability to do business effectively depends on the efficient functioning of the entire supply chain. This requires the business to seriously consider how to most effectively monitor and control its entire supply network.

Illustration 2 – Supply chain management (SCM)

A wholesaler's inability to adequately maintain inventory control or respond to sudden changes in demand for stock may mean that a retailer cannot meet final consumer demand. Conversely, poor sales data from retailers may result in inadequate forecasting of manufacturing requirements.

Types of supply chain – push and pull

In the traditional supply chain model, the raw material suppliers are at one end of the supply chain.

- They are connected to manufacturers and distributors, who are in turn connected to a retailer and the end-customer.
- Although customers are the source of the profits, they are at the end of the chain in the 'push' model.

Driven by e-commerce's capabilities to empower clients, many companies are moving from the traditional 'push' business model, where manufacturers, suppliers, distributors and marketers have most of the power, to a customer-driven 'pull' model.

This new business model is less product-centric and more directly focused on the individual consumer – a more marketing-oriented approach.

- In the pull model, customers use electronic connections to pull whatever they need out of the system. For example, using a platform such as cloud computing allows customers to liaise with suppliers in real time.

- Electronic connectivity in the supply chain network gives end customers the opportunity to give direction to suppliers, for example about the precise specifications of the products they want.

- Ultimately, customers have a direct voice in the functioning of the supply chain.

E-commerce creates a much more efficient supply chain that benefits both customers and manufacturers. Companies can better serve customer needs, carry fewer inventories, and send products to market more quickly.

Illustration 3 – Supply chain management (SCM)

Several personal computer manufacturers allow users to order over the internet and to customise their machines (for example Lenovo and Dell). PCs are then made to customers' orders.

This is an example of a **pull** supply chain, where the product is not produced until the customer requests it. It is then created to fit their specific needs.

Test your understanding 1

V retails toy cars. He manufactures the product in batches of one thousand and then visits various independent toy shops, trying to convince them to stock them on their shelves.

This is an example of a _____ supply chain.

Required:

Insert the word missing in the above sentence.

> **Test your understanding 2**
>
> When managing a supply chain, a business may wish to ensure that every part of the chain has sufficient cash and/or profits.
>
> Which ONE of the following reasons would best explain this?
>
> A   To ensure ongoing supply and demand for the business's products
>
> B   To ensure that the business has sufficient information on all parts of its supply chain
>
> C   To ensure quality throughout the overall supply chain
>
> D   To ensure maximum collaboration throughout the chain

3   Upstream supply chain management

As mentioned above, it is crucial for an organisation to monitor and control its entire supply chain. In this section, we will examine some of the methods a company could use to look after its upstream supply chain – i.e. its chain of suppliers.

3.1 Managing supplier relationships

There are a number of general issues that an organisation needs to consider in relation to its suppliers.

Overall supplier strategy

A supply strategy is likely to take account of matters such as the following.

*   Sources

    What sources are available and where are they located? Are suppliers' businesses larger or smaller than the buying organisation (this affects bargaining power). Will different suppliers need to be used in different parts of the world?

*   Number of suppliers

    If there is only a single source of supply this may bring the advantage of bulk purchase discounts, but the organisation may prefer to have several or multiple suppliers to avoid the risk of failed deliveries and to prevent a single supplier from getting either too powerful or/and complacent.

*   Cost, quality and speed of delivery

    These factors are closely interrelated and the strategy will probably need to make compromises to achieve the right balance.

- Make or buy and outsourcing

  The outsourcing decision is effectively the same as the strategy of vertical integration discussed in chapter 7 "Strategic analysis and choice". The decision will depend on the above factors and whether or not the firm has the required competences and resources to bring the supply in-house.

Factors to consider when choosing suppliers

- What does the company charge?
- Does it offer discounts or other incentives?
- Can it deliver the required quality of product or service (for example is it ISO 9001 certified)?
- Is the supplier willing to customise orders or handle other special needs?
- How will it ship its products, and how much will that cost?
- How quickly will orders be delivered?
- Will delivery quantities be accurate?
- How will the supplier handle returns or other problems?
- Is technical support available, if required?
- How will the supplier manage the account?
- Do they have adequate technology?
- Are they financially secure? Credit reports can help here.
- Are they reliable? Can references be obtained?
- What credit period is offered?

Antagonism or partnership?

In the past the supply chain was typically defined by **antagonistic** relationships.

- The purchasing function sought out the lowest-price suppliers, often through a process of tendering, the use of 'power' and the constant switching of supply sources to prevent getting too close to any individual source.

- Supplier contracts featured heavy penalty clauses and were drawn up in a spirit of general mistrust of all external providers.

- The knowledge and skills of the supplier could not be exploited effectively: information was deliberately withheld in case the supplier used it to gain power during price negotiations.

Hence no single supplier ever knew enough about the ultimate customer to suggest ways of improving the cost-effectiveness of the trading relationship, for instance buying additional manufacturing capacity or investing in quality improvement activities.

It is now recognised that management of supplier networks is based upon **partnership** – collaboration and offers benefits to an organisation's suppliers as well as to the organisation itself. By working together organisations can make a much better job of satisfying the requirements of their end market, and thus both can increase their market share.

- Organisations seek to enter into partnerships with key customers and suppliers so as to better understand how to provide value and customer service.

- Organisations' product design processes include discussions that involve both customers and suppliers. By opening up design departments and supply problems to selected suppliers a synergy results, generating new ideas, solutions, and new innovative products.

- To enhance the nature of collaboration the organisation may reward suppliers with long-term sole sourcing agreements in return for a greater level of support to the business and a commitment to ongoing improvements of materials, deliveries and relationships.

Service level agreements

Service level agreements should include the following factors:

- A detailed explanation of exactly what service the supplier is offering to provide.

- The targets/benchmarks to be used and the consequences of failing to meet them.

- Expected response time to technical queries.

- The expected time to recover the operations in the event of a disaster such as a systems crash, terrorist attack, etc.

- The procedure for dealing with complaints.

- The information and reporting procedures to be adopted.

- The procedures for cancelling the contract.

3.2 The use of technologies in managing the upstream supply chain network

The key activities of upstream SCM are procurement and upstream logistics. Much of the modern approach to managing such areas of the organisational ecosystem will be via technologies.

What is e-procurement?

The term 'procurement' covers all the activities needed to obtain items from a supplier: the whole purchases cycle.

E-procurement is therefore used to describe the electronic methods used in every stage of the procurement process, from the identification of the organisation's requirements through to payment.

E-sourcing, e-purchasing and e-payment

E-procurement is the term used to describe the electronic methods used in every stage of the procurement process, from identification of requirement through to payment. It can be broken down into the stages of e-sourcing, e-purchasing and e-payment.

E-sourcing covers electronic methods for finding new suppliers and establishing contracts.

Not only can e-sourcing save administrative time and money, it can enable companies to discover new suppliers and to source more easily from other countries.

Issuing electronic invitations to tender and requests for quotations reduces:

- administration overheads

- potentially costly errors, as the re-keying of information is minimised

- the time to respond.

E-purchasing covers product selection and ordering.

Buying and selling online streamlines procurement and reduces overheads through spending less on administration time and cutting down on bureaucracy. E-purchasing transfers effort from a central ordering department to those who need the products. Features of an e-purchasing system include:

- electronic catalogues for core/standard items

- recurring requisitions/shopping lists for regularly purchased items.

The standard shopping lists form the basis of regular orders and the lists can have items added or deleted for each specific order

- electronic purchase orders despatched automatically through an extranet to suppliers

- detailed management information reporting capabilities.

Improvements in customer service can result from being able to place and track orders at any time of day. An e-catalogue is an electronic version of a supplier's paper catalogue including product name, description, an illustration, balance in hand and so on. User expectations have increased dramatically in recent years as a result of their personal experiences of shopping on the internet. Well-designed websites and web interfaces are essential to offer good functionality so as to maintain user satisfaction.

E-payment includes tools such as electronic invoicing and electronic funds transfers. Again, e-payment can make the payment processes more efficient for both the purchaser and supplier, reducing costs and errors that can occur as a result of information being transferred manually from and into their respective accounting systems. These efficiency savings can result in cost reductions to be shared by both parties.

E-procurement gives rise to a number of specific applications that the organisation can use to manage its upstream supply chain. These include:

- EDI (electronic data interchange) – this involves the organisation linking its systems to those of its suppliers, allowing for faster and more efficient paperless ordering. This can improve the speed and accuracy in the fulfilment of orders.

- Use of the Internet – the organisation can use the Internet to shop around to ensure that they are using the most reliable, cost effective suppliers.

- Disintermediation – the organisation may be able to buy its supplies online directly from an earlier stage in the supply chain (e.g. from a wholesaler rather than a retailer), which could help the business to save money.

Benefits and drawbacks of e-procurement

The benefits of e-procurement

The more of the procurement process that can be automated, the better, as there will be considerable financial benefits.

- Labour costs will be greatly reduced.

- Inventory holding costs will be reduced. Not only should overstocking be less likely, but if orders are cheap to place and process, they can be placed much more frequently, so average inventories can be lower.

- Production and sales should be higher as there will be fewer stock- outs because of more accurate monitoring of demand and greater ordering accuracy.

- The firm may benefit from a much wider choice of suppliers rather than relying on local ones.

- Greater financial transparency and accountability.

- Greater control over inventories.

- Quicker ordering, making it easier to operate lean or JIT manufacturing systems.

- There are also considerable benefits to the suppliers concerned, such as reduced ordering costs, reduced paperwork and improved cash flow, that should strengthen the relationship between the firm and its suppliers.

Potential risks of e-procurement

There are some risks associated with e-procurement. These are:

- technology risks. There is a risk that the system (whether software or hardware) will not function correctly. There are risks that it might not interface properly with the organisation's system. There are very high risks that it will not communicate properly with a wide range of supplier systems

- organisational risks. Staff might be reluctant to accept the new procurement methods

- no cost savings realised. As with all IS/IT projects, it is very difficult to predict all the benefits that can arise. Tangible benefits (such as might arise if fewer staff have to be employed) are relatively easy to forecast. However, intangible benefits (such as better customer service giving rise to an improved reputation) are very difficult to estimate with any accuracy.

Other uses of technologies within the upstream supply chain

- Communication – email and other IT-based communication allow for more rapid communication with all parts of the upstream supply chain.

- Information gathering – gathering and processing information on the upstream supply chain that may impact on the organisation is easier thanks to the Internet.

- Extranets – this allows the organisation to grant suppliers access to information that can help enable aid collaboration (such as co-ordination of production and inventory levels) as well as joint development of products.

- Big data – collecting and interrogating data on those involved in the upstream supply chain network can help organisations to manage better the product offering and thereby differentiate themselves in the market.

Illustration 4 – Tesco and Big Data

Tesco makes use of Big Data to monitor weather forecasts and feed information back to suppliers of likely requirements for the immediate future.

By using historical buying patterns from customers and expected weather trends, Tesco expects to be reasonably accurate in what it predicts consumers in specific locations will be looking to purchase. It then feeds this information back to suppliers so that they can ensure that the right products are in the right locations at the right time.

For example, if a particularly cold spell of weather is soon to be followed by warmer temperatures, Tesco suppliers will ensure that this location is properly supplied with foodstuffs such as meat for a barbecue. This means not only increased trade for suppliers, but will also help ensure that Tesco customers have a better chance of seeing what they are looking for in a Tesco store compared to other food retailers.

- Blockchain – the use of blockchain technology can create much greater confidence over the entire supply chain, as the data relating to transactions is more secure and cannot be altered by just one party in isolation.

Illustration 5 – Soil Association

The Soil Association has looked to introduce a process whereby customers are able to identify how food has gone from the original producer to the shelf in a shop with complete confidence over the accuracy of data provided.

The foodstuffs that have received organic certification can be traced back through the supply chain; shoppers will be able to see information including the certification validity documentation, the criteria that have been met by the product to earn the organic certification, a map of the food's journey, and even pictures of the farm from which it was originally sourced.

The blockchain technology, having greater security, means consumers can be confident over the accuracy of food labelling, country of origin, 'food miles' etc., as such information cannot have been tampered with at any point in the overall supply.

- Cloud computing – liaising with upstream suppliers via the use of cloud computing has the benefits of greater speed in information flow and also added security. For example, adding new suppliers to the network, or new inventory lines to different locations, becomes an easier administrative exercise, thereby saving time and money.

Test your understanding 3 – (Integration question)

XL Travel are a tour operator based in the capital city of country S. They run weekly trips to the seaside resort of Black Rock (around 140km away) for four–day visits (typically from Friday to Monday).

The tours are very popular, especially with people aged over 65 (who make up over 90% of XL's customers). The company has traded profitably for many years on the back of premium pricing. However, recently profits have started to fall, coinciding with a minority of complaints from regular users. Some users feel that the quality of the trips have fallen and are not up to previous high standards. Other users feel that, whilst XL itself has invested (with attractive new offices, better marketing, more staff and easier booking systems) this investment has gone on the wrong areas.

XL has built up a large cash surplus for further investment. One of the ways it is considering using this cash is to invest in and improve its supply chain.

Required:

What are likely to be the elements of XL's upstream supply chain? Give some examples of what areas XL could aim to change?

(20 minutes)

4 Downstream supply chain management

As mentioned earlier in this chapter, downstream supply chain management refers to the need for the organisation to manage its transactions and relationships with its customer network and consumers of its products and services.

This can be undertaken in a number of different ways.

4.1 Analysis of customers and their behaviour

In order to be able to effectively manage the organisation's customers, it is vital that their needs and behaviour are analysed and understood. This will help the organisation to improve its service levels (and the product range it offers) in order to better meet customer needs.

Customer analysis and behaviour – industrial markets

Customer behaviour

Here are the main features of industrial buyers:

Motivation

An industrial buyer is motivated to satisfy the needs of the organisation rather than his or her individual needs. Often, purchases are repeat orders when the stock of items has fallen below a certain level and thus the buying motive is clear, i.e. avoiding nil stocks. With significant one-off purchases, the motivation will be the achievement of the organisation's goals or targets. Thus a profit target may mean the buyer placing an emphasis on cost minimisation. A growth target expressed in terms of sales motivates a purchase that will promote that goal.

The influence of the individual or group

An industrial purchase may be made by an individual or group. The individual or group is buying on behalf of the organisation but the buying decision may be influenced by the behavioural complexion of the individual or group responsible. The behavioural complexion will be influenced by the same influences on consumer buyers already discussed.

General organisational influences

Each organisation will have its own procedures and decision-making processes when purchases are made. Large centrally controlled organisations will often have centralised purchasing through a purchasing department. The purchase decisions will tend to be formal with established purchasing procedures. In small organisations there will not be a purchasing department. Purchasing decisions will tend to be made on a personal basis by persons who have other functions as well in the organisation. Personal relationships between the supplier and the buyer will often be very important.

Reciprocal buying

A feature in many industrial markets is the purchase of goods by organisation A from organisation B only on condition that organisation B purchases from organisation A.

Purchasing procedures

An industrial buyer appraises a potential purchase in a more formal way than a consumer buyer. Written quotations, written tenders and legal contracts with performance specifications may be involved. The form of payment may be more involved and may include negotiations on credit terms, leasing or barter arrangements.

Size of purchases

Purchases by an industrial buyer will tend to be on a much larger scale.

Derived demand

Demand for industrial products is generally derived from consumer demands. For example, when consumers demand more motor cars, the demand for steel, glass, components and so on will increase in the industrial sector. Industrial strategists have to know what markets the demand for their products is derived from, and monitor this market as well as their own. This may sound obvious, but when the firm is selling through intermediaries, or in overseas markets, there may be very little contact with users and end-users.

When industrialists predict a downturn in consumer markets, they will often cut back on production in the short run. This, of course, has the effect of lowering demand in the consumer markets through its effect on employment and wages, and is part of the trade cycle process discussed earlier.

Customer analysis – Industrial segmentation

- **Geographic:** The basis for sales-force organisation.

- **Purchasing characteristics:** The classification of customer companies by their average order size, the frequency with which they order, etc.

- **Benefit: Industrial** purchasers have different benefit expectations from consumers. They may be oriented towards reliability, durability, versatility, safety, serviceability, or ease of operation. They are always concerned with value for money.

- **Company type:** Industrial customers can be segmented according to the type of business they are, i.e. what they offer for sale. The range of products and services used in an industry will not vary too much from one company to another. A manufacturer considering marketing to a particular type of company would be well advised to list all potential customers in that area of business.

- **Company size:** It is frequently useful to analyse marketing opportunities in terms of company size. A company supplying canteen foods would investigate size in terms of numbers of employees. Processed parts suppliers are interested in production rate, and cutting lubricants suppliers would segment by numbers of machine tools.

Customer analysis and behaviour – consumer markets

Customer behaviour

It is critical in consumer markets to understand **why** buyers purchase an organisation's goods or services. This will enable an organisation to identify critical success factors (CSFs) in markets.

Critical success factors refer to things that the company needs to do well in order to compete in its market and attract customers. For example, a supermarket may need to be cheaper, or stock a better range of products than its rivals in order to successfully compete.

Customer behaviour analysis will also see if they organisation has the required core competences to meet those CSFs and, hence, to determine an appropriate strategy.

Traditional views of marketing tend to assume that people purchase according to the value-for-money that they obtain. The customer considers the functional efficiency of the alternative products, and arrives at a decision by comparing this with the price. This set of beliefs is demonstrably inadequate in explaining consumer behaviour.

Cognitive dissonance

Dissonance is said to exist when an individual's attitudes and behaviour are inconsistent. One kind of dissonance is the regret that may be felt when a purchaser has bought a product, but subsequently feels that an alternative would have been preferable. In these circumstances, that customer will not repurchase immediately, but will switch brands. It is the job of the marketing team to persuade the potential customer that the product will satisfy his or her needs, and to ensure that the product itself will not induce dissonant attitudes.

Personality and product choice

Products, and their brand names, tend to acquire attributes in the mind of the potential customer; indeed, this is one of the primary functions of branding. When considering goods or services for a purchase, customers will invariably select those that have an image consistent with their own personality and aspirations.

Influence of other people

When people make purchase decisions, they reflect the values of their social and cultural environment. Often the form of products and services for sale has been determined by that environment. Among the more obvious influences are those of family and of reference groups.

The family is often important in engendering brand purchasing habits in grocery lines, although it also has a far broader influence in forming tastes in its younger members.

Customer analysis – consumer segmentation

Psychological

Consumers can be divided into groups sharing common psychological characteristics. One group may be described as security-oriented, another as ego-centred and so on. These categories are useful in the creation of advertising messages.

A recent trend is to combine psychological and socio-demographic characteristics to give a more complete profile of customer groups. Appropriately called lifestyle segmentation by one of the companies originating the method, this kind of segmentation uses individuals to represent groups that form a significant proportion of the consumer market. These individuals are defined in terms of sex, age, income, job, product preferences, social attitudes and political views.

Purchasing characteristics

Customers may be segmented by the volume they buy (heavy user, medium user, light user, non-user). They may be segmented by the outlet type they use, or by the pack size bought. These variables, and many others, are useful in planning production and distribution and in developing promotion policy.

Demographic

Customers are defined in terms of age, sex, socio-economic class, country of origin, or family status. The most widely used forms of demographic segmentation in the UK are the socio-economic classification based on class (A, B, C1, C2 , D and E) and the life cycle model (Bachelor, Newly married couple, Full nest 1, Full nest 2, Full nest 3, Empty nest 1, Empty nest 2).

Geographic

Markets are frequently split into regions for sales and distribution purposes. Many consumer goods manufacturers break down sales by television advertising regions.

Benefit

Customers have different expectations of a product. Some people buy detergents for whiteness, others want economy, and yet others stain removal.

It can be seen that, within the same product class, different brands offer different perceived benefits. An understanding of customers' benefits sought enables the manufacturer to create a range of products each aimed precisely at a particular benefit.

Customer analysis – use of technologies

In the digital era, technologies offer organisations greater scope for understanding the possible opportunities for marketing to customers in the downstream supply chain network. Examples include:

Use of social media

The extent to which content is disseminated to other users across social platforms can be assessed by the organisation. This can be assessed by means of variables such as the number of retweets on Twitter, or the shared likes on Facebook. Products or marketing campaigns which do not achieve high results in such variables can be changed or removed from the business portfolio.

Big Data

Just as with the upstream supply chain network, data can be collected and interrogated on those in the downstream supply chain network to result in a product or service offering that matches greater the demands of customers and consumers.

Illustration 6 – Time Warner and Big Data

Time Warner is using Big Data to track which types of media customers are watching and when. This can help to manage bandwidth and therefore optimise the customer experience. The company also uses sophisticated systems to integrate public data such as voter registration and property records with local viewing figures. This enables targeted marketing campaigns by Time Warner's advertising clients.

4.2 Marketing

A key aspect of managing the downstream supply chain is to ensure effective marketing. This will help to attract customers and improve the image of the organisation with consumers.

There are a number of possible approaches that can be used to help the organisation accomplish this.

The six markets model (Payne)

This model helps the organisation understand **who it needs to market to**. The six markets model advocates that an organisation has six key markets, not just the traditional customer market. Marketing activity should be extended to build and manage relationships in all these areas.

- Customer markets

  The final destination for the product. This ability to reach the customer in a highly competitive environment depends on other parties or relationships.

- Referral markets

  This is the institution or person who refers the customer to the supplier. A bank refers customers to providers of insurance services. The Automobile Association (AA) refers members to a bank or hire purchase company.

- Supplier markets

  Partnerships with suppliers have replaced old adversarial relationships. A supermarket sets up a JIT arrangement with a supplier for short-life articles, such as ready-made salads, in order to retain customer interest in an instant healthy food product.

- Recruitment markets

  A service provider such as PriceWaterhouseCoopers depends on quality staff to deliver quality service. Such an organisation will build up a relationship with careers advisers, professional bodies and others to supply the necessary human resources.

- Influence markets

  Influence marketing used to be called public relations – a new low fat spread depends upon the sponsorship of a body that promotes healthy eating (Weightwatchers).

- Internal markets

  This concept is not dissimilar to the concept of internal quality management. Every department has a customer provider relationship with others. The UK corporate lending market recognises that the supplier of banking services (transaction processing) supports the manager of the client account (the relationship manager).

Relationship marketing

This examines the overall approach to marketing that the organisation can adopt. Should it focus on maximising one-off sales, or focus on long-term customer retention? This is a critical issue for many businesses.

Customers can be lost by a number of factors:

- unhelpful staff
- poor quality of service
- inappropriate prices
- lack of customer care.

The concept of relationship marketing has been defined as the technique of maintaining and exploiting the firm's customer base as a means of developing new business opportunities.

Traditional marketing	Relationship marketing
• concentrates on products	• concentrates on retention and loyalty
• little knowledge of customer	• considerable customer commitment
• product quality a key issue	• considerable customer contact
• little effort on customer retention	• emphasis on quality service
• focus on single sale	• focus on building long-term relationships
• focus on product features	• importance of customer benefits

4.3 Customer acquisition

Methods of acquiring customers can be split between traditional off-line techniques (e.g. advertising, direct mail, sponsorship, etc.) and rapidly-evolving on-line techniques (e-marketing). Examples of e-marketing are:

Search engine marketing

- Search engine optimisation – improving the position of a company in search engine listings for key terms or phrases. For example, increasing the number of inbound links to a page through 'link building' can improve the ranking with Google.

- Pay per click (PPC) – an advert is displayed by search engines as a 'sponsored link' when particular phrases are entered. The advertiser typically pays a fee to the search engine each time the advert is clicked.

- Trusted feed – database-driven sites such as travel, shopping and auctions are very difficult to optimise for search engines and consequently haven't enjoyed much visibility in the free listings. Trusted Feed works by allowing a 'trusted' third party, usually a search engine marketing company, to 'feed' a website's entire online inventory directly into the search engine's own database, bypassing the usual submission process.

Online PR

- Media alerting services – using online media and journalists for press releases.

- Portal representation – portals are websites that act as gateways to information and services. They typically contain search engines and directories.

- Businesses blogs (effectively online journals) can be used to showcase the expertise of its employees.

- Community C2C portals (effectively the e-equivalent of a village notice board) – e.g. an oil company could set up a discussion forum on its website to facilitate discussion on issues including pollution.

- Social media – platforms such as Facebook and Twitter are often used to get news about the organisation into the public domain and to respond to stories in which it features.

Online partnerships

- Link-building – reciprocal links can be created by having quality content and linking to other sites with quality content. The objective is that they will then link to your site.

- Affiliate marketing – a commission-based arrangement where an e-retailer pays sites that link to it for sales. For example, hundreds of thousands of sites direct customers to Amazon to buy the books or CDs that they have mentioned on their pages.

- Sponsorship – web surfers are more likely to trust the integrity of a firm sponsoring a website than those who use straight advertising.

- Co-branding – a lower cost form of sponsorship where products are labelled with two brand names. For example, as well as including details about their cars, the website Subaru.com also includes immediate co-branded insurance quotes with Liberty Mutual Insurance and pages devoted to outdoor lifestyles developed with LL Bean.

- Aggregators – these are comparison sites allowing customers to compare different product features and prices. For example, moneysupermarket.com allows analysis of financial services products. Clearly a mortgage lender would want their products included in such comparisons.

Interactive adverts

- Banners – banners are simply advertisements on websites with a click through facility so customers can surf to the advertiser's website.

- Rich-media – many web users have become immune to conventional banner ads so firms have tried increasingly to make their ads more noticeable through the use of animation, larger formats, overlays, etc. For example, an animated ad for Barclays banking services will appear on some business start-up sites.

- Some ads are more interactive and will change depending on user mouse movements, for example generating a slide show.

Opt-in e-mail

It is estimated that 80% of all e-mails are spam or viruses. Despite this, e-mail marketing can still deliver good response rates. One survey found only 10% of e-mails were not delivered (e.g. due to spam filters), 30% were opened and 8% resulted in 'clickthroughs'. Options for e-mail include the following.

- Cold, rented lists – here the retailer buys an e-mail list from a provider such as Experian.

- Co-branded e-mail – for example, your bank sends you an e-mail advertising a mobile phone.

- 3rd party newsletters – the retailer advertises itself in a 3rd party's newsletter.

- House list e-mails – lists built up in-house from previous customers, for example.

Viral marketing

- Viral marketing is where e-mail or social media platforms such as Facebook or Twitter are used to transmit a promotional message from one person to another.

- Ideally the viral ad should be a clever idea, a game or a shocking idea that is compulsive viewing so people send it to their friends.

Test your understanding 4

Which ONE of the following statements are consistent with the concept of transaction marketing?

A   Focus on product quality

B   Emphasis on quality of service

C   Focus on retention and loyalty

D   Investment in customer management

Test your understanding 5

WOT is an organisation based in country F that reviews and recommends electrical and other products to consumers. WOT has around 4 million subscribers in country F, who will typically only buy the products that WOT has highly rated.

JJH is an electronics manufacturer based in country F. According to Payne's six markets model, which ONE of JJH's key markets is WOT classified within?

A   Referral

B   Customer

C   Supplier

D   Influence

Test your understanding 6

Which THREE of the following are methods of acquiring customers?

A   Electronic data interchange

B   Social media marketing

C   Search engine optimisation

D   Personalisation and customisation

E   Extranet access

F   Interactive advertisements

4.4 Managing the ongoing relationship with customers

Management of the downstream supply chain for many businesses involves the need to identify their major customers and look for ways to keep them satisfied – ensuring that they do not switch to rival suppliers – as well as trying to identify if more sales can be made to the customer (customer extension).

Customer relationship management

Customer relationship management (CRM) consists of the processes a company uses to track and organise its contacts with its current and prospective customers, with particular emphasis on software-based approaches.

 CRM is defined as a culture, possibly supported by appropriate information systems, where emphasis is placed on the interfaces between the entity and its customers. Knowledge is shared within the entity to ensure that the customer receives a consistently high service level.

CIMA official terminology

This 'customer focused' approach, which will involve building a strong relationship with the customer as well as gathering, storing and sharing information across the organisation, will likely improve customer loyalty. This has historically been achieved through the use of databases and other specific CRM software, but in the digital era much greater use is being made of technologies such as cloud computing and big data.

It is usually argued that retaining existing customers is cheaper that trying to win new customers, so CRM systems may well help the organisation to achieve higher profits.

Marketing audits

The marketing audit is a particular form of position audit which focuses on the products of the firm and the relationship it has with customers.

It helps to not only give the company a deeper understanding of the wider organisational ecosystem market it operates in, but also the strategies it will need to implement in order to gain competitive advantage. Its position within that ecosystem and its unique selling points will help to decide the appropriate marketing strategy to adopt.

The normal stages in a marketing audit include:

(1) **Define the market.** This involves the firm describing the products or services it wishes to offer in the market, as well as the key characteristics of the market itself. These could include size, growth rate and the strategies most likely to succeed in it.

(2) **Determine performance differentials.** The purpose here is to look for segments of the market that are currently not being fulfilled and which may provide an entry-point for the business (or a rival). For example, Subway exploited a niche in the fast-food market by attracting health conscious consumers who were not having their needs met by existing suppliers.

(3) **Profile the strategies of competitors.** This involves 'getting to know your enemy'. Major competitors should be identified, along with a profile of their products, services and style of competitive strategy. The firm's own strategy can then be compared against those of its competitors.

(4) **Determine the strategic planning structure.** This involves deciding how the strategic marketing effort is to be organised, including the assignment of staff and the goals and objectives of the marketing department.

 Customer satisfaction and retention

Key to retention is understanding and delivering the drivers of customer satisfaction as satisfaction drives loyalty and loyalty drives profitability.

The 'SERVQUAL' approach to service quality developed by Parasuraman et al focuses on the following factors.

Tangibles

- The 'tangibles' heading considers the appearance of physical facilities, equipment, personnel and communications.

- For online quality, the appearance and appeal of websites, and the social media presence and usage, will determine to what extent customers will consider their interaction with the organisation useful and engaging. Customers will revisit websites that they find appealing and interact with the organisation more if its social media presence serves a purpose for them.

- This can include factors such as structural and graphic design, quality of content, ease of use, speed to upload and frequency of update. For example, in the newspaper industry the speed of delivery and ease of use of their social media feeds and instant updates are critical. Multi-media content, such as graphics and videos, will also be an important element of the customer experience.

Reliability

- Reliability is the ability to provide a promised service dependably and accurately and is usually the most important of the different aspects being discussed here.

- For online service quality, reliability is mainly concerned with how easy it is to connect to the website and social media platforms. Specially developed apps for smartphones that are free of glitches can enhance the consumer experience, as well as being an increased source of information about the organisation.

- Reliability will also be assessed on the basis of the content and how accurate it is – the phrase 'fake news' has become an everyday part of the English language!

- If websites are inaccessible some of the time and/or e-mails are bounced back, then customers will lose confidence in the retailer.

- Equally, given the increasing usage of many customers (particularly those who have grown up during the digital era, the so-called 'millennials') to interact with organisations using Facebook, Instagram, Twitter or the like, it is vital that these channels be available and updated at all times.

Responsiveness

- Responsiveness looks at the willingness of a firm to help customers and provide prompt service.

- In the context of e-business, excessive delays can cause customers to 'bail-out' of websites and/or transactions and go elsewhere.

- This could relate to how long it takes for e-mails to be answered or even how long it takes for information to be downloaded to a user's browser.

- Equally, a failure to respond to a tweet could be interpreted as lack of concern at a customer issue. Twitter feeds will need to be monitored around the clock.

Assurance

- Assurance is the knowledge and courtesy of employees and their ability to inspire trust and confidence.

- For an online retailer, assurance looks at two issues – the quality of responses and the privacy/security of customer information.

- Quality of response includes competence, credibility and courtesy and could involve looking at whether replies to e-mails are automatic or personalised and whether questions have been answered satisfactorily.

- Again, the issue of fake news on social media could be seen as an assurance issue.

Empathy

- Empathy considers the caring, individualised attention a firm gives its customers.

- Most people would assume that empathy can only occur through personal human contact but it can be achieved to some degree through personalising websites and e-mail.

- Key here is whether customers feel understood. For example, being recommended products that they would never dream of buying can erode empathy.

Techniques for retaining customers

Given the above consideration of service quality, firms use the following e-techniques to try to retain customers.

- Personalisation – delivering individualised content through web-pages or e-mail. For example, portals such as Yahoo! enable users to configure their home pages to give them the information they are most interested in.

- Mass customisation – delivering customised content to groups of users through web-pages or e-mail. For example, Amazon may recommend a particular book based on what other customers in a particular segment have been buying.

- Extranets – for example, Dell Computers uses an extranet to provide additional services to its 'Dell Premier' customers.

- Opt-in e-mail – asking customers whether they wish to receive further offers.

- Online communities – firms can set up communities where customers create the content. These could be focussed on purpose (e.g. Autotrader is for people buying/selling cars), positions (e.g. the social media site Pinterest), interest (e.g. Football365) or profession. Despite the potential for criticism of a company's products on a community, firms will understand where service quality can be improved, gain a better understanding of customer needs and be in a position to answer criticism.

- Customisation of social media content that feeds through to your profile. For example, if you look at a website with a view to, say, buy clothes, you suddenly find that that same retailer's details now appear when you next look at Facebook. Or, in a wider context, you look online at a ski holiday and then start to see adverts for ski accessories, such as goggles or gloves, without having actively searched for such products.

Illustration 7 – North Face

Faced with the problem of correctly satisfying customer demand for outdoor clothing, North Face have invested in artificial intelligence to try to deliver a better and more personalised customer experience. This is particularly important for an online transaction, given that the customer does not have an assistant to ask – will this clothing be appropriate for certain hiking conditions or locations, for example.

The customer is asked where they are going, what time of year and what sort of activities they will be doing. A personalised response is then given that takes into account likely weather conditions and the characteristics of the landscape in that particular part of the world; the customer is directed to products that are most suited to their needs.

Customer extension

Customer extension has the objective of increasing the lifetime value of a customer and typically involves the following.

- 'Re-sell' similar products to previous sales.

- 'Cross sell' closely related products.

- 'Up sell' more expensive products.

- For example, having bought a book from Amazon you could be contacted with offers of other books, DVDs or DVD players.

- Reactivate customers who have not bought anything for some time.

Key to these is propensity modelling.

Propensity modelling

Propensity modelling involves evaluating customer behaviour and then making recommendations to them for future products. For example, if you have bought products from Amazon, then each time you log on there will be a recommendation of other products you may be interested in.

This can involve the following.

- Create automatic product relationships – e.g. through monitoring which products are typically bought together.

- Using trigger words or phrases – e.g. 'customers who bought …also bought…'.

- Offering related products at checkout – e.g. batteries for electronic goods.

Once again, technologies such as artificial intelligence and big data analytics can make propensity modelling much more effective and produce a speedier outcome.

4.5 The use of technologies in downstream supply chain management

Technologies can be used in a number of ways within the downstream supply chain, including:

- **Electronic Data Interchange (EDI)** – the business can link its sales system to the purchasing system of its major customers, increasing the speed and efficiency of placing orders. This can act as a tie-in/switching cost as it is likely to make it harder for the customer to leave and move to a rival supplier, as this would lead to expense and disruption.

- **Cloud computing** – the business may be able to keep customers updated in real time on important matters such as inventory levels and the fulfilment status of orders.

- **E-commerce** – the business may be able to sell online to customers, allowing it to expand its customer base and brand awareness.

- **Intelligence gathering** – online customer transactions can be monitored, helping the business to understand their needs and work to meet them. Online surveys and questionnaires will allow the business to quickly and efficiently ask for customer opinions and feedback. This can all be used to improve the quality of the business's marketing using Big Data analytics.

- **Communication** – email and other IT systems have been used for many years in ways that allow the organisation to keep in touch with its customers, keeping them informed about order progress, or new products and services they may be interested in. In the digital era these technologies are still relevant, and are being supplemented or replaced by use of social media, blogs, and web communities.

- **User communities** – the users of some complex products, such as software, set up user communities where members help each other and where pressure on the product supplier can be organised. Strong user communities are valued by their members and the organisation would be wise to look at the comments and queries on the bulletin boards. For example, adverse comments on a review site such as Tripadvisor can have disastrous effects on future revenues, as many customers will be swayed in their choice of restaurant or hotel by what people who have visited before have posted.

The use of intranets and extranets

One key way that an organisation can use IT to improve its downstream supply chain management is through the use of intranets and extranets.

An intranet is a private network within a single company using Internet standards to enable employees to share information using e-mail and web publishing.

An extranet is formed by extending an intranet beyond a company to customers, suppliers and other collaborators.

The benefits of using an extranet are as follows:

- **Information sharing in a secure environment**

  For example, the advertising agency Saatchi allows customers to view draft advertising material during a project.

- **Cost reduction**

  Savings can arise from need fewer people in the ordering process and the elimination of the need to re-key information from paper documents.

- **Order processing and distribution**

  For example, a customer's point of sales terminals can be linked to a supplier's delivery system, ensuring prompt replenishment of goods sold. This results in fewer lost sales due to stock-outs and lower inventory holding.

- **Improved customer service**

  Customer service can be improved through easier/quicker access to information, increased accuracy and consistency of information and quicker response times. Together these build customer confidence and may result in increased revenue.

The effects of technologies on the structure of the downstream supply chain

There are three main ways in which technologies can affect an organisation's relationship with its customers:

Disintermediation – in this process intermediate organisations (middlemen) can be taken out of the supply chain. Intermediaries include distributors, wholesalers and agents. The business can therefore sell its product or service direct to the end consumer, rather than selling via a middleman who takes a share of the profits.

For example, musicians can sell their music directly through their own websites rather than being produced and sold through a record company. Games console manufacturers have started selling games that can be downloaded straight to the console, cutting out games retailers and allowing the manufacturer to earn a higher share of the profits from the sale.

The process of **reintermediation** is also found, where the business creates a new intermediary into the downstream supply chain.

In the UK, Confused.com was set up by Admiral (a group of companies that offer various types of insurance) to help users pick between insurance providers for their car and home insurance policies. Admiral therefore introduced a new intermediary into the supply chain as customers now went through the comparison site before purchasing a policy from an insurance company.

Countermediation is where established firms create their own new intermediaries to compete with established intermediaries.

The launch of Confused.com was followed by the creation of several rival comparison sites, including Comparethemarket.com, which was set up by BGL – another UK insurance group.

Illustration 8 – Downstream SCM

An example of disintermediation is seen in the travel industry where travel agents have been cut out of many transactions as the public can book directly with hotels, airlines and rail companies.

The travel industry also gives an example of reintermediation. Companies like lastminute.com and expedia.com are like new travel agents, presenting a wide choice of products and services.

An example of countermediation is Opodo.com, set up by a collaboration of European airlines to encourage customers to book flights directly with them rather than using cost-comparison intermediaries such as lastminute.com.

Test your understanding 7

Z plc offers car insurance to its customers. The car insurance industry is large and made up of hundreds of different rivals, all offering similar insurance products.

One of Z's rivals, M, has recently created a new website that allows consumers to compare quotes quickly and easily from the majority of the car insurance companies in the market.

While not every customer chooses M from the list of quotes they are given, M receives commission from every policy sold through its site.

Z wishes to respond to this change in the market by creating its own comparison website.

Z's planned strategy is an example of which ONE of the following?

A   Intermediation

B   Disintermediation

C   Reintermediation

D   Countermediation

Test your understanding 8 – DRB – (Case style)

DRB Electronic Services operates in a high labour cost environment in Western Europe and imports electronic products from the Republic of Korea. It re-brands and re-packages them as DRB products and then sells them to business and domestic customers in the local geographical region. Its only current source of supply is ISAS electronics based in a factory on the outskirts of Seoul, the capital of the Republic of Korea. DRB regularly places orders for ISAS products through the ISAS web-site and pays for them by credit card. As soon as the payment is confirmed ISAS automatically e-mails DRB a confirmation of order, an order reference number and likely shipping date. When the order is actually despatched, ISAS send DRB a notice of despatch e-mail and a container reference number. ISAS currently organises all the shipping of the products. The products are sent in containers and then trans-shipped to EIF, the logistics company used by ISAS to distribute its products. EIF then delivers the products to the DRB factory. Once they arrive, they are quality inspected and products that pass the inspection are re-branded as DRB products (by adding appropriate logos) and packaged in specially fabricated DRB boxes. These products are then stored ready for sale. All customer sales are from stock. Products that fail the inspection are returned to ISAS.

Currently 60% of sales are made to domestic customers and 40% to business customers. Most domestic customers pick up their products from DRB and set them up themselves. In contrast, most business customers ask DRB to set up the electronic equipment at their offices, for which DRB makes a small charge. DRB currently advertises its products in local and regional newspapers. DRB also has a web site which provides product details. Potential customers can enquire about the specification and availability of products through an e-mail facility in the web site. DRB then e-mails an appropriate response directly to the person making the enquiry. Payment for products cannot currently be made through the web site.

Feedback from existing customers suggests that they particularly value the installation and support offered by the company. The company employs specialist technicians who (for a fee) will install equipment in both homes and offices. They will also come out and troubleshoot problems with equipment that is still under warranty. DRB also offer a helpline and a back to base facility for customers whose products are out of warranty. Feedback from current customers suggests that this support is highly valued. One commented that 'it contrasts favourably with your large customers who offer support through impersonal off-shore call centres and a time-consuming returns policy'. Customers can also pay for technicians to come on-site to sort out problems with out-of-warranty equipment.

Dilip Masood, the owner of DRB, has sent you the following email:

To: J. Kooper

From: D. Masood

Date: 17/06/XX

Subject: Supply chain management

Hi J,

I'm sure you're aware that DRB is planning to increase our product range and market share. We plan to grow from our current turnover of £5m per annum to £12m per annum in two years time. I believe that DRB must change its business model if it is to achieve this growth. I believe that these changes will also have to tackle problems associated with:

- Missing, or potentially missing shipments. Shipments can only be tracked through contacting the shipment account holder, ISAS, and on occasions they have been reluctant or unable to help. The trans-shipment to EIF has also caused problems and this has usually been identified as the point where goods have been lost. ISAS does not appear to be able to reliably track the relationship between the container shipment and the Waybills used in the EIF system.

- The likely delivery dates of orders, the progress of orders and the progress of shipments is poorly specified and monitored. Hence deliveries are relatively unpredictable and this can cause congestion problems in the delivery bay.

I also recognise that growth will mean that the company has to sell more products outside its region and the technical installation and support so valued by local customers will be difficult to maintain. I am determined that DRB will continue to import only fully configured products. I am not interested in importing components and assembling them. DRB will also not build or invest in assembly plants overseas or commit to a long-term contract with one supplier.

Bearing this in mind, I would be grateful for your thoughts on a number of key issues.

Firstly, I need you to draw the primary activities of DRB on a value chain. Please comment on the significance of each of these activities and the value that they offer to customers.

Explain how DRB might re-structure its upstream supply chain to achieve the growth required by DRB and to tackle the problems that I have identified.

Also, please explain how DRB might re-structure its downstream supply chain to achieve the growth required.

I need some briefing notes on this in the next 45 minutes as I am about to go into a meeting with our business advisors.

I look forward to your reply.

Kind regards

Dilip

Required:

Draft the briefing notes as requested by Dilip.

(45 minutes)

5   Summary

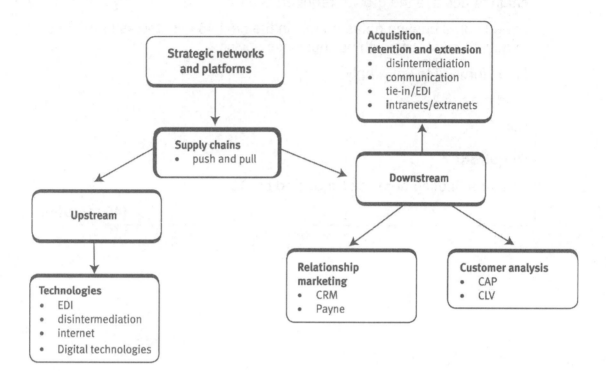

Test your understanding answers

Test your understanding 1

The correct answer is PUSH

V makes his products without reference to customers and then attempts to 'push' them onto his clients.

Test your understanding 2

The correct answer is A

Customers and consumers need to have sufficient cash to buy the product, while suppliers need to have enough cash/profit to want to make the components the business uses to make its products.

Ensuring every link in the supply chain has sufficient cash is therefore an important part of ensuring supply and demand for the business's products.

Test your understanding 3 – (Integration question)

The key elements of XL's upstream supply chain are likely to include:

- travel providers (such as bus, train or airline companies)

- accommodation providers

- local food producers and restaurants

- attractions, activity and excursion providers.

While it could also be widened to consider other suppliers, such as local bars and local infrastructure providers (amongst others), supply chain management is likely to focus on the key elements of the supply chain outlined above.

A key function of the supply chain is to ensure that the chain contains the correct value system to support XL's competitive advantage. As some customers are beginning to complain, there is growing evidence that it may no longer be doing so.

As such, XL should begin by communicating with a selection of customers (not just those who are complaining) to determine what they would like from their tour and how they feel things could be improved.

XL can then use this information to provide suppliers with areas that they will need to focus on to improve the customer experience.

For example, XL could examine the accommodation it offers. It could consider issues such as location, ease of access, appearance, staffing and facilities.

For travel providers, XL may wish to examine the safety measures, the ease of check-in, luggage facilities and in-journey refreshments and facilities.

Should there be any problem areas for customers that a supplier is either unwilling or unable to change, XL could consider attempting to switch to an alternative supplier.

Test your understanding 4

The correct answer is A

Transaction marketing focuses on the product, rather than the customer or service provided.

Test your understanding 5

The correct answer is D

A referral market occurs when someone refers a consumer to an organisation's products. An insurance broker would be an example of this – the broker is actively referring consumers to certain insurance company products and therefore is part of the insurance company's referral market.

WOT is simply rating and recommending products. This would suggest an influence market, as they are simply endorsing certain products.

Test your understanding 6

The correct answers are B, C and F

The others are methods of retaining or extending existing customers.

Test your understanding 7

The correct answer is D

M's website is an example of reintermediation. By setting up an equivalent comparison site of its own, Z is countermediating.

Test your understanding 8 – DRB – (Case style)

Briefing notes

(a) A simple value chain of the primary activities of DRB is shown below.

Handling and storing inbound fully configured equipment Quality inspection	Rebranding Of products Repackaging Of products	Customer collection Technician delivery and installation	Local advertising Web-based enquiries	Onsite technical support Back to base support
Inbound logistics	**Operations**	**Outbound logistics**	**Marketing and sales**	**Service**

Comments about value might include:

Inbound logistics: Excellent quality assurance is required in inbound logistics. This is essential for pre-configured equipment where customers have high expectations of reliability. As well as contributing to customer satisfaction, high quality also reduces service costs.

Operations: This is a relatively small component in the DRB value chain and actually adds little value to the customer. It is also being undertaken in a relatively high cost country. DRB might wish to re-visit the current arrangement.

Outbound logistics: Customer feedback shows that this is greatly valued. Products can be picked up from stock and delivery and installation is provided if required. Most of the company's larger competitors cannot offer this service. However, it is unlikely that this value can be retained when DRB begins to increasingly supply outside the geographical region it is in.

Marketing and sales: This is very low-key at DRB and will have to be developed if the company is to deliver the proposed growth. The limited functionality of the website offers little value to customers.

Service: Customer feedback shows that this is greatly valued. Most of the company's competitors cannot offer this level of service. They offer support from off-shore call centres and a returns policy that is both time consuming to undertake and slow in rectification. However, it is unlikely that this value can be retained when DRB begins to increasingly supply outside the geographical region it is in.

(b) DRB has already gained efficiencies by procuring products through the supplier's website. However, the website has restricted functionality. When DRB places the order it is not informed of the expected delivery date until it receives the confirmation e-mail from ISAS. It is also unable to track the status of their order and so it is only when it receives a despatch email from ISAS that it knows that it is on its way. Because DRB is not the owner of the shipment, it is unable to track the delivery and so the physical arrival of the goods cannot be easily predicted. On occasions where shipments have appeared to have been lost, DRB has had to ask ISAS to track the shipment and report on its status. This has not been very satisfactory and the problem has been exacerbated by having two shippers involved. ISAS has not been able to reliably track the transhipment of goods from their shipper to EIF, the logistics company used to distribute their products in the country. Some shipments have been lost and it is time-consuming to track and follow-up shipments which are causing concern. Finally, because DRB has no long term contract with ISAS, it has to pay when it places the order through a credit card transaction on the ISAS website.

DRB has stated that it wishes to continue importing fully configured products. It is not interested in importing components and assembling them. It also does not wish to build or invest in assembly plants in other countries. However, it may wish to consider the following changes to its upstream supply chain:

- Seek to identify a wider range of suppliers and so trade through other sell-side websites. Clearly there are costs associated with this. Suppliers have to be identified and evaluated and financial and trading arrangements have to be established. However, it removes the risk of single-sourcing and other suppliers may have better systems in place to support order and delivery tracking.

- Seek to identify suppliers who are willing and able to re-brand and package their products with DRB material at the production plant. This should reduce DRB costs as this is currently undertaken in a country where wage rates are high.

- Re-consider the decision not to negotiate long-term contracts with suppliers (including ISAS) and so explore the possibility of more favourable payment terms. DRB has avoided long-term contracts up to now. It may also not be possible to enter into such contracts if DRB begins to trade with a number of suppliers.

- Seek to identify suppliers (including ISAS) who are able to provide information about delivery dates prior to purchase and who are able to provide internet-based order tracking systems to their customers. This should allow much better planning.

- Consider replacing the two supplier shippers with a contracted logistics company which will collect the goods from the supplier and transport the goods directly to DRB. This should reduce physical transhipment problems and allow seamless monitoring of the progress of the order from despatch to arrival. It will also allow DRB to plan for the arrival of goods and to schedule its re-packaging.

DRB might also wish to consider two other procurement models; buy-side and the independent marketplace.

In the buy-side model DRB would use its website to invite potential suppliers to bid for contract requirements posted on the site. This places the onus on suppliers to spend time completing details and making commitments. It should also attract a much wider range of suppliers than would have been possible through DRB searching sell-side sites for potential suppliers. Unfortunately, it is unlikely that DRB is large enough to host such a model. However, it may wish to prototype it to see if it is viable and whether it uncovers potential suppliers who have not been found in sell-side websites searches.

In the independent marketplace model, DRB places its requirements on an intermediary website. These are essentially B2B electronic marketplaces which allow, on the one hand, potential customers to search products being offered by suppliers and, on the other hand, customers to place their requirements and be contacted by potential suppliers. Such marketplaces promise greater supplier choice with reduced costs. They also provide an opportunity for aggregation where smaller organisations (such as DRB) can get together with companies that have the same requirement to place larger orders to gain cheaper prices and better purchasing terms. It is also likely that such marketplaces will increasingly offer algorithms that automatically match customers and suppliers, so reducing the search costs associated with the sell-side model. The independent marketplace model may be a useful approach for DRB. Many of the suppliers participating in these marketplaces are electronics companies.

(c) DRB's downstream supply chain is also very simple at the moment It has a website that shows information about DRB products. Customers can make enquiries about the specification and availability of these products through an e-mail facility. Conventional marketing is undertaken through local advertising and buyers either collect their products or they are delivered and installed by a specialist group of technicians. DRB could tune its downstream supply chain by using many of the approaches mentioned in the previous section.

For example:

– Developing the website so that it not only shows products but also product availability. Customers would be able to place orders and pay for them securely over the website. The site could be integrated with a logistics system so that orders and deliveries can be tracked by the customer. DRB must recognise that most of its competitors already have such systems. However, DRB will have to put a similar system in place to be able to support its growth plans.

– Participating in independent marketplace websites as a supplier. DRB may also be able to exploit aggregation by combining with other suppliers in consortia to bid for large contracts.

– DRB may also consider participating in B2C marketplaces such as eBay. Many organisations use this as their route to market for commodity products.

DRB may also wish to consider replacing its sales from stock approach with sales from order. In the current approach, DRB purchases products in advance and re-packages and stores these products before selling them to customers. This leads to very quick order fulfilment but high storage and financing costs. These costs will become greater if the planned growth occurs. DRB may wish to consider offering products on its website at a discount but with specified delivery terms. This would allow the company to supply to order rather than supply from stock.

Resources and value creation within the organisational ecosystem

Chapter learning objectives

Lead	Component
E2: Advise on resource allocation to support strategy implementation	(a) Advise on resource availability
D2: Produce strategy by the integration of choices into coherent strategy	(a) Value analysis

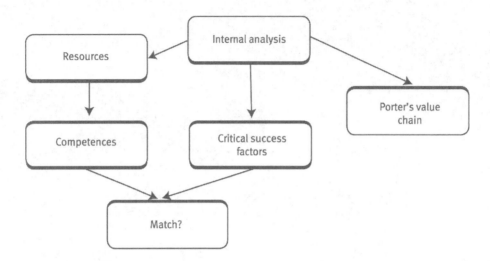

1   Introduction

The last two chapters identified the key external issues that an organisation would need to consider in its ecosystem when deciding upon an appropriate strategy.

In this chapter we will look at how an organisation examines itself – the resources it has, the skills, and how it can create value – which will be fundamental to its overall strategic analysis and choice. There is little to be gained in identifying a strategy that might address the external issues facing the organisational ecosystem if the business does not have the resources or capabilities to make that strategy work.

The process of internal analysis typically involves the following stages:

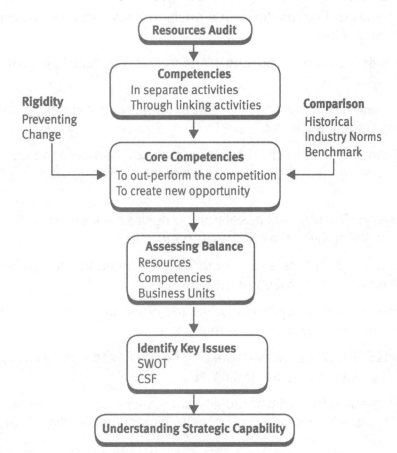

We will now look at these stages in more detail.

 Internal analysis is a crucial part of developing a strategy. It helps the organisation to identify what it is capable of – what skills and assets it possesses. Understanding this will help the organisation identify which strategies it is capable of implementing.

2   Resource audit

 The resources audit identifies the resources that are available to an organisation and seeks to start the process of identifying competencies.

It attempts to assess the relative strength of the resource base – the quantity of resources available, the nature of those resources and the extent to which those resources are unique and difficult to imitate.

One model in particular may help managers undertaking a resource audit locate these key factors.

M's model

This model suggests that the items in a position audit can be categorised into factors beginning with 'M':

- **Manpower (human resources):** The human assets of the firm, their skills and morale.

- **Money:** The company's cash position, gearing, investment plans, short and long term finance, etc.

- **Management:** The quality, expertise and experience of the top team. Is the firm well managed and does is have the skills and vision needed to progress?

- **Machinery:** The physical assets of the business, their flexibility, relative costs and the quality of what they produce.

- **Markets:** The products and the markets the company currently operates in. The quality and position of the products.

- **Materials:** The relationship between the company and its suppliers. Cost, quality and future availability of materials.

- **Methods:** The processes adopted by the business – outsourcing, JIT, AI, use of Big Data, cloud computing etc.

- **Management information:** Quality and timeliness of information provided to managers. Can include Big Data. Will impact on quality of decisions made.

- **Make-up:** The culture and structure of the organisation. Also, branding and other intangibles.

This is not an exhaustive list to memorise. Instead it is a memory aid to help the resource auditor to identify all the key resources that are central to a business' success.

Resources can alternatively be grouped under four headings:

- **physical or operational resources**

- **human resources**

- **financial resources**

- **intangibles.**

The key is to know what you have available to you and how this will help you in any strategic initiative. At the same time the organisation needs to know what it is lacking and how things may change in the future. Shortage of resources will often constrain strategic initiative.

Note that the audit should also include resources that can be accessed by the organisation, not just legally owned. Some strategically important resources may exist, such as a network of contacts or customers or maybe via a strategic alliance or joint venture i.e. to consider the resources available in the wider organisational ecosystem.

Resources are needed to undertake a strategy. They will not ensure its ultimate success. For that, the resources will need to be combined together into competencies.

Test your understanding 1

H Ltd has a strong brand name. Which ONE of the following resource classifications would this be included within?

A   Markets

B   Make-up

C   Methods

D   MIS

3   Competences

Resources are combined together to achieve a competence.

 A competence is a group of abilities, resources or skills that enable the organisation to act effectively.

There are two key types of competence that you need to be aware of:

- **Core competences** – these are things that you are able to do that are difficult for your competitors to emulate. They form the basis of competitive advantage and are referred to by Johnson and Scholes as **'the order winners'**.

- **Threshold competences** – these are things that you do well that simply enable you to compete in the market. They do not give competitive advantage – if they are not satisfied, you will not even be considered by the customer. They are referred to as **'the order qualifiers'**.

Illustration 1 – Coca–Cola

The Coca-Cola Corporation has, for many years, maintained a very strong position in the soft drinks market. Consider its flagship product, Coca-Cola. This has largely survived competition from supermarkets' own-brand colas. There is no great secret in how to make a reasonable imitation (though purists would argue that the imitations are not as good) and the resources needed are not demanding. The own-label colas sell at much lower prices, so how has Coca-Cola managed to keep its dominant position?

It has been argued that physical resources are often less important.

> These are likely to form the **threshold competences**. Coca-Cola has bottling plants, access to suitable water, and a formulation for its drink. However, its competitors also have these things. They do not give Coca-Cola a competitive edge.
>
> The reason Coca-Cola has managed to maintain its dominant position mainly lies in the non-physical or intangible resources, such as a very powerful brand. The **core competences** lie in managing the brand by producing memorable global advertising, global recognition, careful sponsorship and responding to customer requirements (diet/caffeine-free products).

Over time the core competence will become threshold as:

- cultures adjust and expectations develop

- customers and consumers become more sophisticated in terms of their needs and expectations

- competitors imitate our core competences.

Organisations need to ensure that they are continually monitoring their ecosystem to ensure that their core competences are still valid and that all thresholds are duly satisfied.

Remember, what is good today is not necessarily good tomorrow!

Illustration 2 – Changing competences

When Apple launched its iPhone in 2007, it had a number of features that gave it competitive advantage, including:

- full colour touch-screen interface

- use of premium materials

- aesthetically pleasing design

- user-friendly software interface

- linked to the strong Apple brand.

Today, rival mobile phone manufacturers have made many of these features standard in their products, meaning that they would no longer be considered 'order winners'. For example, most modern smartphones include touch-screen interfaces, strong design standards and premium materials. These 'core' features have thus become 'threshold' over time.

Competence audit

As well as the resource audit mentioned earlier in the chapter, the organisation may well undertake a **competence audit**. This will typically involve:

- analysis of what competences the organisation has, as well as how well resources are being deployed to create them.

- categorisation of competences as core or threshold. This will be done by looking at historic data, industry norms and benchmarking exercises (which will usually be undertaken by specialist teams).

> **Test your understanding 2**
>
> Insert the missing word into the following statement:
>
> _____ competences are those that help an organisation to achieve competitive advantage over its rivals.

4 Critical success factors

 Critical success factors (CSFs) are the limited number of areas in which results, if they are satisfactory, will ensure successful competitive performance for the business.

They are the vital areas where 'things must go right' and where the business must outperform its competitors.

It is important, therefore, that any assessment of resources, competences, strengths and weaknesses is done by reference to what we have to be good at.

For example, having the highest quality in the industry may be admirable but it misses the point if the market is driven by price wars and customers are only willing to pay low prices.

Examples of CSFs for major industries include:

- in the automobile industry – styling, an efficient dealer network, vehicle performance and fuel efficiency

- in the food manufacturing industry – new product development, good distribution channels, health aspects (e.g. low fat)

- in the supermarket industry – having the right product mix, competitive pricing.

The organisation's critical success factors should tie into their corporate objectives. For example, if a supermarket's objective is to grow its market share, it will need to ensure that understands what it must do in order to successfully implement this strategy (i.e. what its CSFs will be).

The problem with CSFs is that they are often vague. As mentioned above, a supermarket may have a CSF of having 'competitive pricing', but how would the company know whether its pricing is 'competitive' or not?

In order to deal with this, organisations will need to create ways of measuring whether their CSFs are being met. These measures are known as key performance indicators, or KPIs.

Test your understanding 3 – (Integration question)

What might a parcel delivery service such as DHL identify as two of its main critical success factors?

Illustration 3 – Mission, CSF and KPI

A, a major supermarket chain in the country O, has a **corporate mission to be 'the best value retailer in country O.'**

One of A's **critical success factors (CSFs) is that it needs to sell its goods for a lower price than its major rivals**. This will attract customers in the fiercely competitive country O supermarket industry, where many customers choose their supermarket based on price.

In order to measure this CSF, A has set itself a **key performance indicator (KPI) to keep its average selling price ten percent below that of its rivals. It monitors its rivals'** selling prices and amends its own prices on a daily basis to ensure that it achieves this KPI.

A can therefore be confident that if it meets its KPI, its major CSF will have been achieved. This will help it meet its overall mission.

Illustration 4 – Critical success factors

The following is an example of CSFs developed for a shipping terminal.

Critical success factor	Indicator	Mechanism for measurement
Customer satisfaction	• Complaints • Insurance claims • Losses of stock	• Complaints register • Correspondence • Internal audit
Maintenance of premises	• Repair costs	• Inspection
Efficient use of staff	• Time standards for loading and unloading	• Training schedules • Direct inspection

Test your understanding 4 – (Integration question)

Using the CSFs previously identified for a parcel delivery company such as DHL, explain how the company might measure their performance.

Sources of CSFs

Rockart claims that there are four sources for CSFs:

(1) The industry that the business is in – each has CSFs that are relevant to any company within it.

For example, the car industry must have as one of its CSFs 'compliance with pollution requirements regarding exhaust gases'.

(2) The company itself and its situation within the industry – e.g. its competitive strategy and its geographic location.

For example, a firm that has decided to compete on the basis of quality could have CSFs relating to identifying and delivering key product features that are valued by customers.

(3) The wider environment – e.g. the economy, the political factors and consumer trends in the country or countries that the organisation operates in.

For example, in a time of oil shortages 'energy supply availability' could be a critical success factor.

(4) Temporal organisational factors – these are areas of company activity that are unusually causing concern because they are unacceptable and need attention.

For example, a company with liquidity problems may place "short term cash management" as a CSF to ensure survival.

Test your understanding 5

H is a retailer of garden furniture. It has recently been told by its major shareholders that they wish to see a one-off increase in dividends from the company next year, meaning that H needs to improve its cash flow quickly.

According to Rockart, which ONE of the following sources of critical success factors (CSFs) is being described above?

A   The industry that H is in

B   Temporal organisational factors

C   The wider environment

D   The company and its position in the industry

Test your understanding 6 – GGG – (Case style)

You have recently been provided with the following document giving you some background to GGG – a company that you have applied to work for as a strategic management accountant.

Background document – GGG Trains

GGG operates trains across Country H. The train infrastructure (stations and tracks) are owned by the Government of Country H. GGG has a fifteen year franchising agreement with the Government which allows it to exclusively operate the trains across the entire national railway network. GGG is now seven years through its current franchise agreement.

While the franchise agreement is for fifteen years, it is reviewed annually by the Government. The Government wishes to maximise the number of residents of Country H that use the trains (as opposed to motor vehicles), as this will help Country H meet its international environmental targets for carbon emission reductions.

The road network in Country H is old and is often significantly congested. However, train passenger numbers are only growing slowly. A recent Government survey has suggested that this is because passengers still feel that GGG tickets are too expensive and that the services offered are usually overcrowded and often late. GGG's staff are felt to lack knowledge and are 'unhelpful' to customers.

The Government of Country H is threatening to strip GGG of its franchise unless it shows substantial improvement. GGG's managers have several initiatives planned to improve the issues highlighted by the survey, and are currently considering how they can measure whether these initiatives are being successful.

Required:

As part of your job application, you have been asked to suggest FOUR of the critical success factors that GGG's management might identify. For each critical success factor identify ONE key performance indicator that GGG could use to see if its initiatives are being effective. Justify your choices.

(20 minutes)

The link between CSFs and competences

Note that CSFs and competences are slightly different concepts.

- CSFs are what the organisation **needs** to be good at in order to compete in the market.

- Competences are what the organisation is good at.

It should, however, be clear that in order for an organisation to be successful, its competences and CSFs should be as closely aligned as possible – which is why regular analysis of both is so important. The organisation's strategy must look at ways of maximising the correlation between the two.

Test your understanding 7

HHH has stated that it wishes to ensure that it delivers 95% of goods to customers within 15 days of them placing an order.

Which ONE of the following is this an example of:

A   A mission

B   A key performance indicator

C   A critical success factor

D   A vision

Test your understanding 8

B Ltd has identified a critical success factor (CSF):

Have the best complaints handling department in the industry.

Which ONE of the following would be the most suitable key performance indicator for this CSF?

A   Increase customer happiness by 15%

B   Reduce the number of complaints received by 20%

C   Improve the effectiveness of training for complaints staff

D   Reduce the average time taken to deal with complaints by 15%

Test your understanding 9 – RCH – (Case style)

RCH, an international hotel group with a very strong brand image has recently taken over TDM, an educational institution based in Western Europe. RCH has a very good reputation for improving the profitability of its business units and prides itself on its customer focus. The CEO of RCH was recently quoted as saying 'Our success is built on happy customers: we give them what they want'. RCH continually conducts market and customer research and uses the results of these researches to inform both its operational and longer term strategies.

TDM is well-established and has always traded profitably. It offers a variety of courses including degrees both at Bachelor and Masters levels and courses aimed at professional qualifications. TDM has always concentrated on the quality of its courses and learning materials. TDM has never seen the need for market and customer research as it has always achieved its sales targets. Its students consistently achieve passes on a par with the national average. TDM has always had the largest market share in its sector even though new entrants continually enter the market. TDM has a good reputation and has not felt the need to invest significantly in marketing activities. In recent years, TDM has experienced an increasing rate of employee turnover.

RCH has developed a sophisticated set of Critical Success Factors which is integrated into its real-time information system. RCH's rationale for the take-over of TDM was the belief that it could export its customer focus and control system, based on Critical Success Factors, to TDM. RCH believed that this would transform TDM's performance and increase the wealth of RCH's shareholders.

Required:

(i)   Identify four Critical Success Factors which would be appropriate to use for TDM.

(ii)   Recommend, with reasons, two Key Performance Indicators to support each of the four Critical Success Factors you have identified.

(30 minutes)

5 Value drivers

 Value drivers are activities or features that enhance the perceived value of a product or service by customers and which therefore create value for the producer. Value drivers can be tangible or intangible.

For example, a high-street electronics retailer could have several value drivers, including:

- Product mix

- Convenient store locations

- Knowledgeable, friendly staff.

If these value drivers are present, it will attract customers to the retailer's stores and may help it achieve a competitive advantage over rivals.

Value drivers will be looked at in more detail in chapter 8 when we start to look at the concept of the organisational performance management system. For now, we need to consider how value drivers can be identified.

One of the main models that can be used to identify the value drivers of an organisation is Porter's Value Chain.

6 Porter's Value Chain

Porter's Value Chain

Support Activities					Primary Activities

Firm Infrastructure

Human Resource Management

Technology Development

Procurement

Inbound Logistics | Operations | Outbound Logistics | Marketing & Sales | Service

Margin

Margin

Primary Activities

This is a means by which the activities within and around the organisation are identified and then related to the assessment of competitive strength.

Resources are of no value unless they are deployed into activities that are organised into routines and systems. These should then ensure that products are produced which are valued by customers and consumers. Porter argued that an understanding of strategic capability must start with an identification of the separate value-adding activities.

Primary activities

These activities are involved in the physical creation of the product, its transfer to the buyer and any after-sales service. Porter divided them into five categories:

(1) **Inbound logistics** are activities concerned with receiving, storing and distributing the inputs to the product. They include materials handling, stock control and transport.

(2) **Operations** transform these various inputs into the final product – machining, packing, assembling, testing and control equipment.

(3) **Outbound logistics** relate to collecting, storing and distributing the product to buyers.

(4) **Marketing and sales** provide the means whereby consumers and customers are made aware of the product and transfer is facilitated. This would include sales administration, advertising, selling and so on.

(5) **Service** relates to those activities which enhance or maintain the value of a product such as installation, repair, training and after-sales service.

Support activities

Each of the primary activities are linked to support activities and these can be divided into four areas:

(1) **Infrastructure** refers to the systems of planning, finance, quality control, information management, etc. All are crucially important to an organisation's performance in primary activities. It also consists of the structures and routines that sustain the culture of the organisation.

(2) **Human resource management,** which involves all areas of the business and is involved in recruiting, managing, training, developing and rewarding people within the organisation.

(3) **Technology development** – all value activities have a technological content, even if it is just 'know how'. IT can affect product design or process and the way that materials and labour are dealt with. Big Data analytics can help identify how to sell more successfully to customers.

(4) **Procurement** refers to the processes for acquiring the various resource inputs to the primary activities – not the resources themselves. As such it occurs throughout the organisation.

Generally

The primary and secondary activities are designed to help create the organisation's margin by taking inputs and using them to produce outputs with greater value.

The value chain can be used to:

- give managers a deeper understanding of precisely what their organisation does

- identify the key processes within the business that add value to the end customer – strategies can then be created to enhance and protect these; and

- identify the processes that do not add value to the customer. These could then be eliminated, saving the organisation time and money.

The value system

Looks at linking the value chains of those in the wider organisational ecosystem – suppliers and customers – to that of the organisation.

Can add value by:

- Enhancing the supply – e.g. organic food for ready meals.

- Controlling of the retail process – e.g. car dealerships.

- Linking it all together to give advantage.

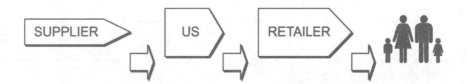

Illustration 5 – The Value Chain

Marks and Spencer plc compete in, amongst other areas, the food and grocery market. They have configured their value chain in order to offer customers a differentiated service.

FI	Central control of operations & credit services				
TD		Recipe research	Electronic point of sale	Customer research and testing	Itemised billing
HRD	Recruitment of mature staff	Client care training	Flexible staff to help with enquiries and packing		
P	Own label products	Prime retail positions		Adverts in quality press and poster sites	
	Dedicated refrigerated transport	In-store food halls Modern store design Dairy cabinets	Collect by car service	No price discounts	No quibble refunds
	IL	O	OL	M/S	S

Lidl also operates in the food and grocery market, but their value chain supports a cost–leadership approach.

Minimum head office costs				
Use of casual staff	De-skilled store ops	Dismissal for check-out error		
Branded and own-brand generics	Low-cost sites			Use of concessions
Bulk warehousing	Limited product range Price points Basic store design	Customers encouraged to use boxes Packing benches	Promotion of low prices Store manager decides stock	Nil

Test your understanding 10

Which THREE of the following are **primary** activities in Porter's value chain?

A   Service

B   Infrastructure

C   Procurement

D   Marketing and sales

E   Technology development

F   Procurement

G   Operations

Test your understanding 11

A manager at HG plc (which manufactures plasma televisions) has developed a new computerised system which will help the inventory control of finished units at HG's warehouse. She believes that this will reduce the time taken to ship these goods by around 25%.

Which ONE of the following primary activities with HG's value chain will the new system be directly improving?

A   Inbound logistics

B   Operations

C   Outbound logistics

D   Infrastructure

Test your understanding 12

H is an accountancy firm. It gathers data from its clients' systems and uses this to create a set of year end accounts. A recent internal analysis exercise has allowed H to create a list of its key internal activities. It now wishes to classify these activities using Porter's value chain.

	H's internal activities		Value chain activity
A	Creation of clients' year end accounts	1	Inbound logistics
B	Meeting with client to deliver and discuss year end accounts	2	Infrastructure
C	Central quality control systems to ensure accuracy of accounts	3	Outbound logistics
D	Receiving and storing data from client systems	4	Operations

Show which of H's internal activities relates to each value chain activity by pairing the appropriate letter and number (e.g. A1, B4, etc.).

Test your understanding 13 – Reggs – (Case style)

Background

Reggs is a long established bakers, based in country G. It specialises in selling pastries, cakes, sandwiches and basic tea and coffee, through a chain of high-street stores. It has grown rapidly over the last ten years and now operates more than 1,500 stores across the country.

Reggs marketing strategy is to focus on the low prices of its food, with heavy advertising in the free press and tabloids. It sells the majority of its products for less than its competitors – a strategy which has paid dividends as country G is suffering an extended period of poor economic growth.

To achieve these low prices, Reggs uses its purchasing power to source large amounts of good quality raw materials at low prices. These goods are transferred to a central warehouse. Reggs uses a sophisticated stock management system to track all materials and ensure that they are used before they perish.

The raw materials are then sent (using Reggs own fleet of delivery vans) to several regional bakeries, where G's products are part-baked. The part-baked products are then sent to the individual high-street stores, where they are completed. Much of this process is automated, enabling Reggs' to hire low-skilled workers. This automation has meant that Reggs feel that quality control is no longer necessary. The company does not keep track of customer complaints as these are normally dealt with by the in-store staff. No formal policies have been produced to guide employees when dealing with complaints.

The high-street stores are of a very basic design, with a large counter and racks of produce. There is no seating and, due to Reggs' popularity, there are often long queues filling the stores. Reggs' management is concerned that this may be putting off some potential customers from patronising the company. However, Reggs has not undertaken any significant customer research in some years as its managers have felt that its rapid growth indicates that there are no significant problems.

Reggs management are keen to expand the business further and are looking at their strategic options. One suggestion is to alter Reggs' traditional product range. Some lower priced items would be removed to make way for more expensive, luxury foods which will have a higher margin attached to them. These items would not travel well and would therefore need to be produced in the high-street stores. This would require moderately skilled workers.

Reggs feels that this may help to attract customers away from its competitors – such as coffee shops. These are significantly more expensive than Reggs, but have a much higher perceived quality of food and drink. Typically these competitors have well-designed, comfortable seating areas, enabling them to charge higher prices.

You are a management accountant working for Reggs. You report to the Operations Director, who has sent you the following email:

To: L. Ray

From: O. Flow

Date: 12/05/XX

Subject: Value chain

Hi L,

As you are aware, we have been considering making some changes to our operations (as we discussed the other day). I need you to undertake some analysis for me. Specifically, I would like you to analyse our primary activities of the value chain, identifying any weaknesses. Please identify how each activity enables our business to sell its goods at low prices. (I don't need a diagram of the value chain).

Could you also discuss the drawbacks of the strategy we are currently considering – relating to more expensive, luxury products. How far would the proposals impact on the existing value chain?

I am attending a meeting about this in forty-five minutes, so please email back by then with your thoughts.

Kind regards

O. Flow

Required:

Email the Operations Director as requested.

Benefits and criticisms of Porter's Value Chain

Proponents suggest that the value chain model has many benefits, including:

- It provides a generic framework to analyse both the behaviour of costs as well as the existing and potential sources of differentiation.

- Activities that are not adding value can be identified and addressed – for example, improved so they do add value or outsourced if this is not possible.

- It emphasises the importance of (re)grouping functions into activities to produce, market, deliver and support products, to think about relationships between activities and to link the value chain to the understanding of an organisation's competitive position.

- It makes it clear that an organisation is multifaceted and that its underlying activities need to be analysed to understand its overall competitive position.

- It is an attempt to overcome the limitations of portfolio planning in multidivisional organisations. Rather than assuming that SBUs should act independently, Porter used his Value Chain analysis to identify synergies or shared activities between them and to provide a tool to focus on the whole rather than on the parts.

The main criticisms of Porter's Value Chain model are as follows:

- It is more suited to a manufacturing environment and can be difficult to apply to a service provider.

- The Value Chain model was intended as a quantitative analysis. However, this is time consuming since it often requires recalibrating the accounting system to allocate costs to individual activities.

The value shop

The value shop is an alternative representation of a value chain for a professional services firm which was developed in 1998 by Stabell and Fjelstad.

A value shop is considered to be a workshop which mobilises resources to solve specific problems. This may involve repeating a generic set of activities until a satisfactory solution is reached. The shop model applies to many organisations, particularly those whose main purpose is to identify and exploit specific opportunities like designing a bespoke product.

The model has the same support activities as Porter's Value Chain but the primary activities are described differently. In the value shop they are:

- problem finding and acquisition

- problem solving

- choosing among solutions

- execution and control/evaluation.

The management in the value shop organisation therefore focuses on areas such as the assessment of problems and opportunities, the mobilisation of resources, project management, the delivery of solutions, the measurement of outcomes and also learning.

The value shop primary activities are arranged in a circle showing that they are cyclical, with an organisation often moving back and forth to develop or reject theories before reaching a conclusion.

Test your understanding 14

J wishes to link her inbound logistics activities to the outbound logistics operations of her suppliers in order to maximise efficiency.

Which of the following concepts is this referring to?

A   Value Shop

B   Value Driver

C   Value System

D   Value Linkage

Test your understanding 15 – Bowland – (Case style)

Bowland Carpets Ltd is a major producer of carpets within the UK. The company was taken over by its present parent company, Universal Carpet Inc., in 20X3. Universal Carpet is a giant, vertically-integrated carpet manufacturing and retailing business, based within the USA but with interests all over the world.

Bowland Carpets operates within the UK in various market segments, including the high-value contract and industrial carpeting area – hotels and office blocks, etc. – and in the domestic (household) market. Within the latter the choice is reasonably wide, ranging from luxury carpets down to the cheaper products. Industrial and contract carpets contribute 25% of Bowland Carpets' total annual turnover, which is currently $80 million. Up until 15 years ago the turnover of the company was growing at 8% per annum, but since 20X2 sales revenue has dropped by 5% per annum in real terms.

Bowland Carpets has traditionally been known as a producer of high-quality carpets, but at competitive prices. It has a powerful brand name, and it has been able to protect this by producing the cheaper, lower-quality products under a secondary brand name. It has also maintained a good relationship with the many carpet distributors throughout the UK, particularly the mainstream retail organisations.

The recent decline in carpet sales revenue, partly recession induced, has worried the US parent company. It has recognised that the increasing concentration within the European carpet manufacturing sector has led to aggressive competition within a low-growth industry. It does not believe that overseas sales growth by Bowland Carpets is an attractive proposition as this would compete with other Universal Carpet companies. It does, however, consider that vertical integration into retailing (as already practised within the USA) is a serious option. This would give the UK company increased control over its sales and reduce its exposure to competition. The president of the parent company has asked Jeremy Smiles, managing director of Bowland Carpets, to address this issue and provide guidance to the US board of directors. Funding does not appear to be a major issue at this time as the parent company has large cash reserves on its balance sheet.

You have been contacted by Jeremy Smiles, who has asked for briefing notes covering the following key issues:

(a)   To what extent do the distinctive competences of Bowland Carpets conform with the key success factors required for the proposed strategy change?

(b)   In an external environmental analysis concerning the proposed strategy shift what are likely to be the key external influences which could impact upon the Bowland Carpets decision?

Required:

Draft the briefing notes as requested.

(45 minutes)

Test your understanding 16 – (Integration question)

A university which derives most of its funds from the government provides undergraduate courses (leading to bachelor's degrees) and post-graduate courses (leading to master's degrees). Some of its funds come from contributions from student fees, consultancy work and research. In recent years the university has placed emphasis on recruiting lecturers who have achieved success in delivering good academic research. This has led to the university improving its reputation within its national academic community, and applications from prospective students for its courses have increased.

The university has good student support facilities in respect of a library which is well stocked with books and journals and up-to-date IT equipment. It also has a gymnasium and comprehensive sports facilities. Courses at the university are administered by well-qualified and trained non-teaching staff who provide non-academic (that is, not learning-related) support to the lecturers and students.

The university has had no difficulty in filling its courses to the level permitted by the government, but has experienced an increase in the number of students who have withdrawn from the first year of their courses after only a few months. An increasing number of students are also transferring from their three-year undergraduate courses to other courses within the university but many have left and gone to different universities. This increasing trend of student withdrawal is having a detrimental effect on the university's income as the government pays only for students who complete a full year of study.

You are the university's management accountant and have been asked by the Vice-Chancellor (who is the Chief Executive of the university) to review the withdrawal rate of students from the university's courses.

Required:

Apply Value Chain analysis to the university's activities, and advise the Vice-Chancellor how this analysis will help to determine why the rate of student withdrawal is increasing.

(30 minutes)

7   Summary

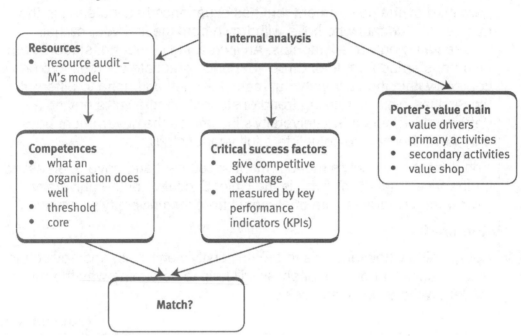

Test your understanding answers

Test your understanding 1

The correct answer is B

Make-up refers to the intangible resources of the organisation. Brand strength would be included here.

Test your understanding 2

The correct answer is CORE

Threshold competences are those that simply allow an organisation to compete with its rivals, but which do not give competitive advantage.

Test your understanding 3 – (Integration question)

The two main critical success factors would probably be:

- speedy collection from customers after their request for a parcel to be delivered

- rapid and reliable delivery.

Test your understanding 4 – (Integration question)

Their performance can be measured by establishing key performance indicators for each CSF and measuring actual achievements against them. For example:

- Collection from customers within three hours of receiving the order for orders received before 2.30 p.m. on a working day.

- Next-day delivery for 100% of parcels to destinations within the UK.

- Delivery within two days for 100% of parcels to destinations within Europe.

Test your understanding 5

The correct answer is B

There is a short-term need for the organisation to improve cash flow, indicating a temporal organisational issue.

Test your understanding 6 – GGG – (Case style)

There are a number of issues that the Government's survey has highlighted as areas of concern, which GGG should view as its critical success factors/objectives.

Growth in use of the railways

The Government wishes to **maximise the use of the railways in Country H**.

This would appear to be a key objective as it will help them to meet their international environmental targets and will reduce pressure on the road network.

A key performance measure here could be the annual percentage growth in passenger numbers. This will be a simple thing for GGG to measure and an area they can agree targets on with the Government.

Note that dealing with the other objectives (below) is likely to improve this area as well.

Value for money

The Government survey has indicated that the public views GGG's ticket prices as too high, which is putting them off travelling by train.

GGG therefore needs to find a way of **improving its perceived value for money if it wishes to grow passenger numbers**.

A key performance measure could be to ensure that the average ticket price is no more that the equivalent cost of travel by car or bus. This is likely to ensure that passengers see the train as a viable financial option.

Reduce overcrowding

The frequent overcrowding of the trains is a serious issue which causes discomfort for passengers and is limiting uptake of train travel.

GGG needs to **increase its capacity and reduce overcrowding if it wishes to attract customers**.

A key performance measure could be the average number of passengers having to stand per km of track. If GGG is able to put on more services (especially at peak times) this should fall, indicating reduced overcrowding.

Improve punctuality

Delays to the trains mean that passengers do not wish to travel as they cannot reliably guarantee that they will arrive at their destination on time.

Again, in order to attract customers, **GGG will need to improve the punctuality of its trains**.

The performance here could be measured by setting targets for the percentage of trains that arrive more than, say, five minutes after their stated arrival time. If this figure falls, GGG will be accomplishing its objective in this area.

Unhelpful staff

This is another area in which the Government survey has indicated problems – **GGG needs to improve on the level of service provided by its staff**.

Again this seems to be putting off potential customers (or at least reducing the likelihood of repeat business) and needs to be dealt with.

To measure whether this is being improved, GGG could set itself targets in areas such as a reduction in the number of complaints received about staff each year.

Alternatively, it could set targets on the average number of days of staff training per year, as improvements in this area are likely to improve the problem of unhelpful staff with poor knowledge of GGG's operations.

Note: The requirement only asks for FOUR critical success factors and ONE performance measure for each. Additional points have been added to this answer for completeness.

Test your understanding 7

The correct answer is B

This is an example of a measured target set by the organisation, suggesting that it is a KPI.

A mission, vision or CSF would be at a higher, more general level and would likely lack the specific measures set out in option B.

Test your understanding 8

The correct answer is D

A and C cannot easily be measured and therefore would not make suitable KPIs. B is not linked to the handling of complaints and therefore is not relevant to B's CSF.

D is measurable and, if achieved, would indicate that the CSF is being accomplished successfully.

Test your understanding 9

(i) **Identification of four CSFs appropriate for TDM**

Critical success factors for TDM may include:

– **Employee satisfaction** – given that TDM is in a service industry, staff are likely to be key to its products and high levels of staff turnover are a concern.

– **Course quality** – given the competitive nature of the market, it is vital that TDM continues to offer appropriate courses that will attract students.

– **Student satisfaction** – in order to be successful, TDM must ensure students are pleased with their courses. If not, they may move to alternative suppliers and may dissuade other students from using TDM.

– **Strong financial results** – after the takeover, TDM will need to make sufficient profits to maximise the wealth of RCH shareholders.

(ii) **Recommended key performance indicators**

TDM's performance can be measured by establishing key performance indicators for each CSF and measuring actual achievements against them.

Employee satisfaction

Number of staff leaving each period

This is the most direct measure of whether staff members are satisfied with their roles within the business. TDM is experiencing increasingly high staff turnover, which may mean they are losing valuable, skilled members of staff.

Sickness/absence per staff member per month

De-motivated or unhappy staff can tend to take more time off work due to sickness. TDM should monitor this as an indirect measure of staff satisfaction, especially as it is likely to cause disruption to courses.

Course quality

Pass rates compared to national average

TDM currently achieve exam pass rates that are comparable to the national average. Given the competitive nature of the market they operate in, this is likely to be something prospective students use as a way of choosing a tuition provider.

Number of students choosing not to complete the course compared to average

If a course is of poor quality (either poor materials or tuition), students may choose not to complete the course – either ceasing to study with TDM or moving onto an alternative course. If the number of students doing this is above average, it should be investigated and targets put in place to bring it down to average.

Student satisfaction

Percentage student approval rating

TDM could give students a questionnaire at the end of each course. This could ask them about how they rate the course, the tutor and the course material. This could be invaluable for identifying problem areas that the business needs to resolve. This would be likely to please RCH given their focus on customer research.

Percentage of students going on to further studies with TDM

TDM offers a range of courses, including degrees at both Bachelor and Masters level. If students feel that TDM have provided a good service, they will be more likely to take their studies further with the organisation.

Strong financial results

Market share

While TDM currently has the largest market share in its segment, large numbers of competitors are continually entering the market. If market share begins to fall, it will have a damaging effect on the profitability of the business.

Profit targets

Given that RCH has purchased TDM with the specific intention of increasing profitability, it is likely that they will have specific targets in mind for the business that TDM will need to work to achieve. For example, TDM may need to measure profit margins to ensure they meet the targets set by RCH.

Test your understanding 10

The correct answers are A, D and G

The other options are all secondary.

Test your understanding 11

The correct answer is C

Outbound logistics looks at management of finished goods as well as delivery to the customer.

Test your understanding 12

The correct answers are A4, B3, C2, D1

Remember that the value chain can be applied to service industries as well. In this case, the chain may show the acquisition and handling of data/information rather than raw materials.

In this case, the firm will receive information from its clients relating to their financial statements. This is inbound logistics (D1).

The firm will then use this information to create the clients' financial statements – the main operation of H. This gives us A4.

The prepared accounts will centrally quality checked prior to a client meeting. This is relates to the way the firm is organised and its systems, giving C2.

Finally, the accounts will be given to the client and discussed with them, forming H's outbound logistics – B3.

Test your understanding 13 – Reggs – (Case style)

Email

To: O.Flow

From: L. Ray

Date: 12/05/XX

Subject: Re: Value Chain

Dear O,

Porter's value chain helps to identify the activities within and around the organisation. These can then be used to help assess the organisation's competitive strength.

Primary activities

Inbound logistics

This relates to the receiving, storing and distributing the inputs to the product.

For Reggs, this involves the storage of raw materials in its central warehouse, followed by the transfer of these materials to the regional bakeries. This is particularly important for Reggs due to the perishable nature of its goods.

Reggs source "good quality" raw materials that are satisfying customer demand.

It is vital that materials are used promptly to ensure wastage is minimised in order to keep costs low and a sophisticated IT system helps to ensure this.

Operations

This examines the transformation of raw materials into the final product.

In Reggs, this occurs in two stages – firstly when the product is initially part-baked in the regional bakeries and secondly (after transport) when the baking is completed in the high-street stores. In both cases, the company automates as much as possible to keep costs low. This also ensures that employees do not need any specialised skills, keeping wage costs low.

A weakness here seems to be a lack of quality control. The assumption that automation means that there will not be any mistakes made seems worrying and there is a risk that problems may not be picked up, potentially damaging Reggs' reputation and overall brand.

Outbound logistics

This relates to the storing and distributing of products to customers. For Reggs, customers visit their 1,500 stores to buy food, meaning that outbound logistics is minimal. This stage of the value chain simply relates to making sales to customers in store.

This appears to be a major weakness for Reggs, who appear to be overwhelmed by the numbers of customers demanding their products, leading to long queues. While the level of demand is encouraging, long queues may be losing custom for Reggs, who may wish to look at ways of improving the efficiency with which customers are dealt with – although some research should be undertaken first to see whether this is a sufficient problem to warrant investment.

Marketing and sales

Reggs appears to be targeting the lower-end of the market by sourcing advertising in the free press and tabloids. This is consistent with its approach of stressing the low-cost aspect of its food. Given the economic conditions in country G, this appears to be a sensible approach.

The basic store design also reinforces the image that Reggs is a low-cost business, strengthening its market image.

Service

This looks at after-sales care for customers.

At present, this does not appear to be a significant area of concern for Reggs. Complaints are not monitored by the company, instead being left to low-skilled employees in store.

Again, this is consistent with the low-cost approach of the business, but does risk damaging Reggs' reputation in the event of any serious problems occurring and does not enable Reggs to use customer feedback in an effective way.

Overall

Reggs has a well-designed supply chain that allows for minimal wastage and maximum efficiency. It allows the business to gain competitive advantage by operating as a cost leader within its market. However, it lacks a positive approach to customer feedback.

Proposed strategy

If Reggs begins offering luxury items, it will have a significant impact on the value chain of the organisation.

- Reggs will need to procure higher quality materials – potentially requiring new suppliers. The luxury items will replace existing products, meaning that Reggs will be ordering less of its existing raw materials, which may undermine its economies of scale.

- Materials will have to be transported directly from the warehouse to the stores, where the luxury items will be made. This will increase the complexity and cost of Reggs' internal transport system.

- The manufacturing of the luxury goods will require moderately skilled workers. Reggs currently employs workers who have low levels of skills, as this keeps wages low. It will incur significant additional costs to hire new workers.

- The new luxury items do not match the current brand image of the company. Reggs has basic stores, little service and advertising that focuses on the low cost of the items. Offering luxury, high priced items does not match this cost leadership strategy. It may fail to attract customers and lead to Reggs becoming "stuck in the middle".

- Should the new luxury goods take off and allow Reggs to grow its customer base, it may cause additional pressure on the queuing systems of the stores. The staff already seem unable to cope with the volume of custom they have at peak periods. Reggs may wish to deal with this problem first, before trying to capture more customers.

There are also a number of other reasons why the Reggs proposals may not be a success.

- Reggs has failed to carry out any significant market research into either proposal. This means that the company risks proceeding with investments that may not be what customers want. At best this could waste money – at worst, Reggs could alienate its customer base.

- Reggs is also eliminating existing, presumably profitable, products to make way for the new luxury items. If these are unsuccessful, it may fail to increase its profits overall. Higher priced items may struggle due to the weaker economy in the country.

- It should also be noted that Reggs is assuming that they can compete with coffee shop chains by simply offering higher quality goods. In reality, there are likely to be other factors, such as the comfortable surroundings and atmosphere, as well as the coffee shop brand names, which may make it hard for Reggs to successfully attract their customers.

Overall, the business needs to undertake significant additional research in order to ensure that the proposal is worth both the disruption to the value chain and the potential brand image confusion that it may cause.

I hope this helps – if you need any further information, please let me know.

Kind regards

L.Ray

Test your understanding 14

The correct answer is C

By definition.

Test your understanding 15 – Bowland – (Case style)

Briefing notes

Bowland's competences

An organisation's **distinctive competences** are those things which an organisation does particularly well. They include the organisation's unique resources and capabilities as well as its strengths and its ability to overcome weaknesses. These competences can include aspects such as budgetary control, a strong technology base, a culture conducive to change and marketing skills.

Key success factors are those requirements which it is essential to have if one is to survive and prosper in a chosen industry/environment. These can include areas such as good service networks, up-to-date marketing intelligence and tight cost controls where margins are small.

It is not guaranteed that the distinctive competences and the key success factors are always in alignment. A company moving into the retail sector may have an excellent product research and development capability, but this alone will not help if it has no concept of service, or poorly sited retail outlets. It is critical to ensure that what the company excels at is what is needed to be successful in that particular area.

The **strengths of Bowland Carpets** include **strong brand names** which maintain integrity within the different market segments where the company operates. The company has a **balanced portfolio of customers** and the **range of products is equally balanced**, ensuring that any sectoral decline can be compensated for by growth in other markets. Other strengths which the company currently has include a **good relationship with distributors and strong support from a powerful parent company**. Some of its distinctive competences, such as a strong brand and a reasonable range of products, are critical in the proposed new environment, as will be the financial support of the parent company. However, there are some aspects which are cause for concern in the proposed new business environment.

The strength in the contract and industrial carpet segment will not be affected by the proposed vertical integration – sales tend to be through a direct sales force. The strong **relationship with distributors** will however be **jeopardised by the opening up of retail outlets**. Other retail chains will be unwilling to permit a rival to operate so freely, and therefore there will be a reluctance to stock Bowland's carpets. Unless Bowland Carpets can obtain wide retail market coverage to compensate for this potential problem, sales revenue will be adversely affected.

The **cost of developing extensive market coverage** will be enormous and whether it is in high-street outlets or specialist out-of-town centres the investment may be greater than the parent company has budgeted for. The company also has **no expertise in site appraisal and selection**. Although the newly structured value chain will generate greater control there is an associated **lack of flexibility** along with an **increase in the fixed cost base** of the business.

Another key success factor is the **need for expertise in retailing**. It may be that the UK company can import this from the USA but the culture of marketing household durables may not be transferable internationally. Bowland Carpets as the domestic company has no experience in this field.

A critical factor in successful retailing is the ability to provide a **comprehensive range of products**. Does Bowland Carpets have one? It is unlikely that the competitive carpet manufacturers will provide such a supply to one of their rivals.

It would, therefore, appear that there is no close conformity between the distinctive competences of Bowland Carpets and the key success factors required in the carpet retailing sector.

External environment

The **external environment** scan is an essential prerequisite prior to selecting a strategic option. It enables the company to identify and understand the key external and uncontrollable influences which will have an impact upon the company's strategy. The environment is increasingly turbulent and often hostile. Without this knowledge and appreciation the strategist will be operating in a minefield. The acquisition of the external information is obtained by scanning the environment continuously and monitoring key indicators, which should enable the company to position itself appropriately with respect to the external environment and the competition. The external scan should be structured around a PESTEL framework covering the following environments – social, legal, economic, political and technological. In addition it is also important to assess potential competitive reactions as part of the scanning process.

The environmental scan will influence the decision as to whether Bowland Carpets should concentrate on the UK or seek diversification elsewhere, either in products or markets. Possible factors are as follows:

- **Social issues:** Trends towards increasing car-centred shopping (superstores and out-of-town sites) or movements back to city-centre shopping: trends in fashion and furnishing – will carpets become a fashion item and result in greater replacement sales? Other factors of importance to Bowland include the rate of growth or decline in populations and changes in the age distribution of the population. In the UK there will be an increasing proportion of the national population over retirement age. In developing countries there are very large numbers of young people. Rising standards of living lead to increased demand for certain types of goods. This is why developing countries are attractive to markets.

- **Legal issues:** Laws in the UK differ from the US. They come from common law, parliamentary legislation and government regulations derived from it, and obligations under EU membership and other treaties. Legal factors that can influence decisions include aspects of employment law, e.g. minimum wage, laws to protect consumers and tax legislation. The monopoly/competition issues in this case are likely to be insignificant.

- **Economic issues:** An increased concentration for Bowland Carpets within the UK economy will depend upon future economic prospects, taxation policy (sales tax) and interest rates, income distribution and unemployment (influencing site location), trade barriers (cheap imports from Third World suppliers, or even low-cost tufted carpets from countries such as Belgium).

- **Political issues:** Government policy affects the whole economy and governments are responsible for enforcing and creating a stable framework in which business can be done. The quality of government policy is important in providing physical infrastructure, (e.g. transport), social infrastructure, (e.g. education) and market infrastructure, (e.g. planning and site development – town centre or out-of-town developments).

- **Technological issues**: Is retailing technology evolutionary or revolutionary? Will it be costly or labour saving? Will inventory control be facilitated – so saving costs? Technology contributes to overall economic growth. It can increase total output with gains in productivity, reduced costs and new types of product. It influences the way in which markets are identified – database systems make it much easier to analyse the marketplace. Information technology encourages de-layering of organisational hierarchies and better communications.

- **Competitive issues:** It will be necessary to assess the likely responses of both carpet distributors and carpet manufacturers to the proposed incursion by Bowland Carpets. Will the reactions be benign or will they be aggressive?

Test your understanding 16 – (Integration question)

Application of the value chain to university process

Tutorial note

A specialist value chain question that would warrant a brief introduction and possibly a diagram. Don't go mad with the diagrams that do not 'add value' that much. Value chain analysis (VCA) is a method of reviewing all the activities of an organisation and how they interact with each other. Key linkages are identified and areas that create value are focused upon. VCA is not restricted to just the organisation but also the suppliers and customers.

In this question we will have to address the issue of university suppliers of resources:

- students

- staff

- premises

- facilities.

And customers/consumers:

- degree holders

- employers

- society.

The starting point is to identify the objectives for the university in this context. There appear to be three particular issues.

- Students dropping out in the first year.

- Students transferring to another university or just leaving.

- Students swapping courses within the university.

The idea is to look at the primary and support activities to establish why these problems may be arising.

Primary activities

Inbound logistics	Operations	Outbound logistics	Marketing & sales	Service
• Student supply • Staff supply • Facilities supply • Course selections	• Course • Lecturing • Research • Library • IT access • Premises	• Skills base • Employer view • Graduate view	• Marketing mix structure • USP/CA? • Promotions • Research? • Price elasticity	• Support functions • Admin. functions • Social aspects • Post-qualification career assistance

Secondary activities

Procurement	Technology	HRM	Infrastructure
• Food & drink • Accommodation • Building work • Support staff • Books • Students & staff	• Availability • Content • Training • Change	• Staff selection processes • Staff turnover rates • Appraisal processes • Admin. Staff processes	• Culture • Layout • Org. Structure • Faculties • Planning systems • Control systems (FFWD & FBK)

These are some of the things that should be looked at within this context. Processes need to be viewed at first hand and discussed to see how the 'chain' links up. All that needs to happen for the chain to fail is for one link to break.

How will it help?

This model is twenty years' old and designed for application in the private sector but it does have its uses here. The model acts as a **simple starting point** to focus management attention onto the issues. It is not designed to provide an answer, rather to get the 'ball rolling' for management in trying to identify where the problems lie. Managers will have seen it before and be vaguely familiar with it so there will be less resistance. Solutions to these kinds of problems come from reasoned debate from informed people.

VCA will start management thinking where they can add value. They will consider how they differ from the competition and on what basis they will attract staff and students in the future. It will force them to identify the order winners or **'core competences'**.

At the same time, the process will identify the **threshold competences**, or order qualifiers, that are needed. Failure to satisfy threshold competences will lead to consumer dissatisfaction. This would lead to the student problems evident in this case so it looks like VCA would be useful here in spotting those threshold competences that are not being satisfied. Universities are age-old organisations and are not well known for embracing change. It is possible that this university may be suffering from competence slip – that is the situation that arises when a past core competence becomes threshold as a result of increasing consumer sophistication. That means, as the consumer gains more experience of the product, they become more expectant of the service offered. The VCA will force management to consider the issues of **competitive advantage and disadvantage**.

The analysis will see research into student, employer and staff perceptions whilst at the same time may see the application of benchmarking techniques. This would compare a similar institution with ours to see where any issues may exist. So VCA:

- Is the starting point for discussion.
- Gets people from all areas of the business talking – team perspective so a range of opinion and expertise.
- Starts or improves communication, and feedback and forward are encouraged.
- Step-by-step analysis allows the competences to be analysed.

Framework for generating strategic options

Chapter learning objectives

Lead	Component
B1: Analyse the elements of the ecosystem	(a) Markets and competition
C2: Discuss how to generate and develop options	(c) Forecast potential organisational operating ecosystem
	(d) Use various frameworks to generate options
E2: Advise on resource allocation to support strategy implementation	(b) Align resource allocation to support strategic choices

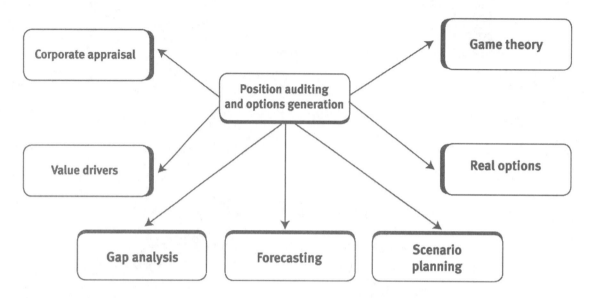

1 Position auditing

In the previous five chapters we have examined the methods that can be used to analyse the current situation of an organisation and its ecosystem – internally, externally and with specific reference to its stakeholders, mission and objectives.

This analysis can be summarised in a formal corporate appraisal, which is typically referred to as a SWOT analysis (strengths, weaknesses, opportunities and threats).

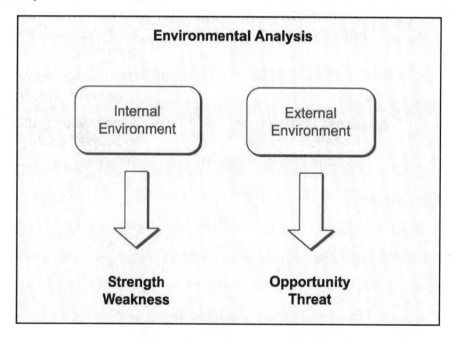

Internal environmental analysis will look for the **strengths and weaknesses** of the organisation and the role it can play in its ecosystem.

External environmental analysis will look for the **opportunities and threats** that the organisation needs to be aware of, both for itself and other components of its ecosystem.

Resource Based (Internal)

S	**W**
• The things we are doing well	• The things we are doing badly (need to correct or improve)
• The things we are doing that the competition are not	• The things we are not doing but should be
• Major successes	• Major failures

O	**T**
• Events or changes in the external environment that can be exploited	• Events or changes in the external environment we need to protect ourselves from or defend ourselves against
• Things likely to go well in the future	• Things likely to go badly in the future

Position Based (External)

The internal and external appraisals of SWOT analysis will be brought together and it is likely that alternative strategies will emerge.

This is an essential part of the strategic management process as it helps the organisation answer the question – **'Where are we now?'**

If an organisation is unsure of its current position then it will be very difficult to plot a successful strategy, one that fully appreciates the organisation's relationship with its wider ecosystem. The ecosystem collectively will be looking to create value; the organisation must question how it is able to contribute to such value creation. Therefore a full analysis of the current position establishes the starting point for the process of strategic choice to help create value successfully.

Key points

- SWOT analysis is a tool to assist the position audit process. It is not the only tool: e.g. the competitor analysis framework works well in this context and can provide a useful framework to analyse a company.

- Position auditing asks the question 'Where are we now?' and is viewed by many as being the starting point for the process of strategic choice.

- The audit will usually be undertaken by a team with a pre-set budget, objectives listing and support functions.

- The management accountant will be involved with delivering and monitoring the information flows into the process.

The position audit would seek to identify:

- **Threats focusing on weakness:** This would usually have top priority and the company should seek to identify and consider possible solutions. This requires a defensive response of some kind and may well necessitate rapid change.

- **Threats focusing on strength:** this requires a review of the supposed strength to ensure that it is still as strong as previously thought. Remember what is good today, may not be so tomorrow.

- **Opportunity focusing on strength:** this gives the organisation the chance to develop strategic advantage in the marketplace. Check the research and assess the strengths again.

- **Opportunity focusing on weakness:** this will require management to make a decision as to whether to change and pursue the opportunity or, alternatively, ignore the prospect and ensure resources are not wasted in this area in future. Usually substantial change will be required if the company is going to pursue the opportunity. Check that the company's internal competencies will allow them to exploit the opportunity.

The review should initially seek to identify what would happen if the organisation chose to do nothing. Remember this is always a strategic option!

The exercise is designed to allow the following:

- identification of the **current issues** relating to the organisation concerned

- analysis and identification of the relevant **problems** facing the organisation

- consideration of the **strategic capability** of the company and its history.

 Test your understanding 1

C Ltd is a large company and is a market leader in a highly competitive industry. It has recently undertaken a corporate appraisal and identified that it has a significant amount of cash available for future investment. It is considering using this to purchase one of its smaller rivals.

Within the corporate analysis, which ONE of the following categories would C's cash surplus be included within?

A   Weakness

B   Strength

C   Opportunity

D   Threat

Test your understanding 2

VVV plc is an organisation that manufactures stationery. It has used various analysis tools in order to identify key issues surrounding the business. It has identified four major issues – one from each of the four major analysis tools that it used.

	VVV's issues		Analysis tool
A	Increased government subsidies for recycled paper	**1**	SWOT
B	Low levels of staff morale within VVV	**2**	Five forces
C	Customers do not see VVV's after sales care as important	**3**	PEST
D	Customers have relatively low levels of influence over VVV's strategy	**4**	Value chain

Identify which analysis tool was used to identify each of VVV's issues by pairing the appropriate letter and number (e.g. A1, B4, etc.).

Test your understanding 3 – (Integration question)

Qualispecs has a reputation for quality, traditional products. It has a group of optician shops, both rented and owned, from which it sells its spectacles. Recently it has suffered intense competition and eroding customer loyalty, but a new chief executive has joined from one of its major rivals, Fastglass.

Fastglass is capturing Qualispecs' market through a partnership with a high-street shopping group. These shops install mini-labs in which prescriptions for spectacles are dispensed within an hour. Some competitors have successfully experimented with designer frames and sunglasses. Others have reduced costs through new computer-aided production methods.

Qualispecs has continued to operate as it always has, letting the product 'speak for itself' and failing to utilise advances in technology. Although production costs remain high, Qualispecs is financially secure and has large cash reserves. Fortunately the country's most popular sports star recently received a prestigious international award wearing a pair of Qualispecs' spectacles.

The new Chief Executive has established as a priority the need for improved financial performance. Following a review she discovers that:

(a) targets are set centrally and shops report monthly. Site profitability varies enormously, and fixed costs are high in shopping malls

> (b)   shops exercise no control over job roles, working conditions, and pay rates
>
> (c)   individual staff pay is increased annually according to a predetermined pay scale. Everyone also receives a small one-off payment based on group financial performance.
>
> Market analysts predict a slowdown in the national economy but feel that consumer spending will continue to increase, particularly among 18- to 30-year-olds.
>
> **Required:**
>
> Produce a corporate appraisal of Qualispecs, taking account of internal and external factors, and discuss the key strategic challenges facing the company.
>
> **(30 minutes)**

2   Value drivers

Part of the process of conducting a corporate appraisal is to consider the value drivers of the organisation.

Value drivers are anything that can be used to create additional value to a consumer in respect of the product or service that the organisation deals in. Such additional value helps to differentiate that product or service compared to those of competitors, and so gives greater appeal to the consumer.

The more value drivers that the organisation can create or use, the greater will be its competitive advantage. Value drivers can be tangible or intangible.

Examples of tangible value drivers:

- State of the art production facilities, including automated processes that increase quality and reduce costs. For example, the car manufacturer Nissan has enjoyed the reputation of being the most efficient car manufacturer in Europe, measured as cars made per employee, due to continued investment at its plant near Sunderland in the North East of England.

- Distribution facilities that are strategically placed to enable rapid and efficient delivery to customers. For example, supermarkets may locate warehouses close to major road systems such as motorways so that delivery of fresh goods into stores can occur more quickly.

- Raw materials that are either better quality or cheaper than those used by rivals.

However, in the modern business environment it is felt that tangible drivers of value can be copied, over time, by rivals, and therefore will not necessarily lead to *sustainable* competitive advantage. Greater strategic importance needs to be placed on the intangible drivers of value; organisations are recognising that, if they want to survive and succeed in the long term they need to strategically manage their intangible assets and create value from them. Sustainable competitive advantage is gained from intangible value drivers.

Examples of intangible value drivers:

- Brands

- Intellectual property and patents

- Relationships with customers

- Relationships with suppliers

- Employees

- Reputation

- Know-how.

Illustration 1 – Tesla

For a period of time, Tesla was valued at more than the Ford Motor Company, despite not having reported a profit and having much lower revenues. The value attributed to the company was derived from its technological know-how, its ability to produce an electric car that had a battery power much greater than any rivals could produce, and therefore which could travel much greater distances before needing to be recharged.

It might also be argued that value was attributed to Tesla's charismatic founder Elon Musk, an entrepreneur with a vision for changing business models, as evidenced through his success with the online payment platform PayPal.

Test your understanding 4

In the English football Premier League, Manchester City have enjoyed great success since being taken over by Sheikh Mansour of Abu Dhabi in 2009.

Which THREE of the following would be classified as intangible drivers of value behind that success?

A   Attracting Pep Guardiola to become manager

B   Having Etihad stadium, with a capacity of just over 55,000 people, as the home ground

C   The network of football clubs owned by the same group, in Melbourne, New York and Yokohama

D   The players that make up the first team squad

The data needed to describe and measure value drivers will be considered in more detail in chapter 9.

3   Gap analysis

Once an organisation has undertaken a detailed corporate appraisal, it may wish to check whether it is on course to meet its longer term strategic objectives.

For example, a large company may have announced that it aims to double its profits within the next five years. The question is, given the current state of the organisation, is this really likely to happen?

To answer that question, many organisations undertake gap analysis. This involves forecasting the organisation's future position (if it continues with its current strategies) and examining whether this future position will meet the organisation's goals.

Gap analysis is the comparison between an entity's ultimate objective and the expected performance from projects, both planned and under way, identifying means by which any identified difference or gap might be filled.

CIMA official terminology

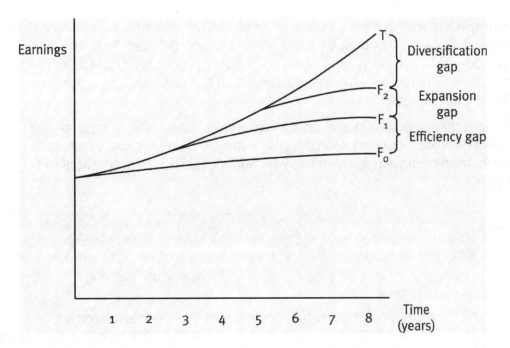

(1) The firm sets its key strategic objective for some time in the future (T), such as achieving a certain level of sales in five years time.

(2) The firm then forecasts its likely performance from current operations (F_0), after efficiency savings have been made (F_1) and after new strategic initiatives (F_2). (Note: These are often separated out as there is a greater degree of uncertainty associated with new initiatives.)

(3) Identify any remaining 'gap'. New strategies will be needed to close this gap. This gap is referred to as the 'diversification' gap.

Closing the gap

There are a number of possible ways of closing the gaps identified by the company:

Closing an efficiency gap – this typically involves undertaking an 'efficiency drive'. The organisation looks to make cost savings and any other actions that will improve the output for a given set of inputs. This is usually the easiest way of closing a gap and is therefore normally undertaken first.

It can also involve looking at market penetration strategies, which involve considering how to sell more of the organisation's current products in their current markets (such as through price cuts, advertising or new packaging, for example).

Closing an expansion gap – this involves looking at ways that the organisation can expand its sales. It could either adopt a market development approach, where it looks to sell its existing products to new markets, or alternatively it could choose a product development strategy where it tries to sell new products to its existing customer base.

Closing a diversification gap – this involves the organisation taking a riskier strategy where it looks to sell new products to new markets (e.g. a pharmaceutical company starting to sell beauty products). Due to the higher risk of failure, this is typically the last strategy that the organisation would adopt in order to close its gap.

Note that the strategies mentioned here (market penetration, market and product development and diversification) are all closely linked to Ansoff's product/market growth framework, which is discussed in more detail in chapter 7.

 Illustration 2 – gap analysis

KOB is a large company which operates a mobile phone network in country C. KOB's strategic goal is to have annual earnings of $85m in ten years' time.

KOB's strategic management accountant has undertaken detailed forecasts of KOB's expected performance over the next ten years and discovered that, if the company continues with its current strategies, it will only have earnings of $78m in ten years' time, giving an overall strategic gap of $7m.

KOB's managers have therefore identified a number of strategies to close this gap.

- **Closing the efficiency gap** – KOB have identified a number of telephone masts that are currently not required. By decommissioning these, as well as outsourcing customer service to overseas call centres, KOB estimates that earnings will rise by $4m after ten years.

- **Closing the expansion gap** – the mobile phone market is highly competitive within country C. However, KOB is considering rolling out its mobile phone services into nearby country G. The market here is less developed and KOB estimates that it will be earning around $1m of earning each year from country G in ten years' time.

The previous strategies should close $5m of the overall strategic gap. As they have not covered the entire gap, KOB may consider undertaking a riskier diversification strategy in order to close the remaining gap.

- **Closing the diversification gap** – KOB is considering selling fixed line internet access to customers in country C. KOB has no experience of this product and believes that it will be mainly selling to consumers who are not its current customers. However, KOB predicts that, due to its well-known brand name, it will be able to earn over $1m each year within ten years.

The various strategies adopted by KOB have therefore closed the strategic gap and KOB should be able to meet (or exceed) its target of $85m in annual earnings within the ten year window.

It is worth noting that a plan is what you want to happen whilst a forecast is what you predict will happen given the current context and assumptions. The whole approach of gap analysis is based upon the feed forward control concept, i.e. the comparison of plan with forecast.

The aim is to identify deviance before the problems of missed targets arise so enabling corrective action to take place in advance. The strategy is too important to leave to reactive control systems. A proactive approach is needed and this will see the need for a significant spend on the forecasting systems. Spending will normally include:

- the team
- IT
- data sourcing and audit
- scenario planning
- time to facilitate the action
- uncertainty evaluation techniques such as 'what if' analysis, high-low forecasting and simulation exercises.

The problems with gap analysis

The whole concept revolves around dealing with uncertainty in the environment. Recent times have seen the business environment becoming increasingly uncertain. This increasing amount of uncertainty makes the predictive capabilities of systems less effective. The predictive process works to an extent if the environmental context can be identified. The uncertainty that exists brings with it new unexpected parameters that can render the whole process a costly waste of time. This has been held as a reason for the abandonment of gap analysis.

The other issue is that in recent years there has been an increasing number of powerful stakeholder groups emerging with the knock-on effect being that there is a greater range of often conflicting objectives. Gap analysis does not entertain the multiplicity of objectives with conflict and compromise running through the whole system.

The benefits of gap analysis

(1) The approach acts as a simple starting point to initiate further debate and consideration.

(2) It is easy to understand and as such acts as an effective communication device.

(3) It highlights the need to keep an eye on the long-term time horizon and draws attention away from the short-term focus.

(4) It provides some basic options that may be considered for closing the gap.

(5) If it is held as a tool to assist and not as the solution provider, the approach still has a place in most planning systems within organisations.

(6)   It allows the questioning of the realism of the objective – if there is a gap, it may be that the objective is unrealistic given the strategic capability of the organisation. This may lead to a reappraisal of the objectives and the generation of more realistic versions.

(7)   Stable environments will still provide a basis for effective gap analysis.

> ### Test your understanding 5
>
> F's strategic management accountants have recently undertaken gap analysis. They have forecasted the likely position of the company after taking account of planned efficiency savings as well as after all planned strategic initiatives. They have identified that there is still a gap between F's forecast position and its ideal position.
>
> This remaining gap is referred to as the _____ gap.
>
> **Required:**
>
> Insert the missing word in the above sentence.

4   Forecasting

A key part of gap analysis is forecasting.

A forecast is a prediction of future events and their quantification for planning purposes.

CIMA official terminology

Clearly gap analysis relies on accurate forecasts of future performance. The strategies developed as a result of gap analysis are only as good as the quality of the forecast that they rely on. So how do we forecast company or market performance – in some cases looking ahead over a number of years?

Statistical models

An organisation could adopt one of several statistical models to try and quantify key forecast figures.

Regression analysis

This looks at how a particular variable correlates (or varies) with another variable.

For example, an airline may wish to investigate the link between passenger numbers and average ticket prices (usually the number of passengers falls as the ticket price rises). Regression will allow the airline to calculate an estimate of the relationship between the two factors, based on past results. This can then be used in its forecasts for coming years. For example, if it intends to raise ticket prices to increase earnings, it can predict what effect this will have on passenger numbers, giving it an accurate forecast of expected earnings.

Time series analysis

Time series analysis involves the identification of short- and long-term trends in previous data and the application of these patterns for projections. In other words, it looks at how a particular factor varies over time.

For example, a jewellery firm may find that its results are strongly affected by the price of gold. Time series analysis will help the firm look at the past gold price movements and use them to predict what the future price of gold will be. This can then be used in forecasting to help the firm estimate its cost of goods sold, or to decide on a pricing strategy (amongst other things).

Trend analysis is a particularly useful tool for companies who have to forecast demand that is influenced by seasonal fluctuations, or where demand is strongly influenced by the business cycle.

Drawbacks of statistical models

While the above models can be useful in helping quantify key forecast figures, they have a number of inherent limitations, including:

- they assume that past results are a good indication of the future. For instance, our jewellery firm may find that the price of gold has risen sharply in past years. This is not conclusive proof that it will continue to do so.

- regression analysis assumes that the two factors are strongly correlated (i.e. linked to each other). The airline firm mentioned above could plot passenger numbers in past years against the average cost of a newspaper on its flights. Regression analysis would calculate the relationship – but there is not likely to be a causal link between the two, giving rise to misleading forecasts.

- regression analysis is only likely to be accurate within the range of the past data collected.

- it can be very difficult to accurately build in seasonal and other fluctuations into time series analysis, meaning that forecast results using this method can be inaccurate.

Other forecasting models

There are a number of other forecasting models that can be used by management to consider what might happen in the future. Each of these methods enables management to identify the resource requirements and availability when considering strategic choices.

System modelling

Many large firms seek to develop sophisticated programmes to model economic systems, market competition and so on.

The difficulty lies in identifying all the variables and defining how they relate to each other.

A number of software products are available to help with this. Most large accounting packages will include forecasting facilities, and Enterprise Resource Management (ERM) software generally includes facilities to model business processes.

Intuitive forecasting methods

What distinguishes intuitive techniques is the relative emphasis they place on judgement, and the value of such techniques lies not in their statistical sophistication but in the method of systematising expert knowledge.

Intuitive forecasting techniques include the use of think tanks, Delphi methods, scenario planning, brainstorming and derived demand analysis.

Intuitive forecasting methods

Think tank

A think tank comprises a group of experts who are encouraged, in a relatively unstructured atmosphere, to speculate about future developments in particular areas and to identify possible courses of action. The essential features of a think tank are:

- the relative independence of its members, enabling unpopular, unacceptable or novel ideas to be broached

- the relative absence of positional authority in the group, which enables free discussion and argument to take place

- the group nature of the activity that not only makes possible the sharing of knowledge and views, but also encourages a consensus view or preferred scenario.

Think tanks are used by large organisations, including government, and may cross the line between forecasting and planning. However, the organisations that directly employ, or fund, them, are careful to emphasise that their think-tank proposals do not necessarily constitute company or government policy.

Think tanks are useful for generating ideas and assessing their feasibility, as well as providing an opportunity to test out reactions to ideas prior to organisational commitment.

The Delphi technique

Delphi seeks to avoid the group pressures to conformity that are inherent in the think tank method. It does this by individually, systematically and sequentially interrogating a panel of experts.

- Members do not meet, and questioning is conducted by formal questionnaires.

- Where the experts are speculating about the future, they are asked for subjective probabilities about their predictions.

- A central authority evaluates the responses and feeds these back to the experts who are then interrogated in a new round of questions.

The system is based on the premise that knowledge and ideas possessed by some but not all of the experts can be identified and shared and this forms the basis for subsequent interrogations.

Brainstorming

This is a method of generating ideas. There are different approaches but a popular one is for a number of people (no fewer than six, no more than fifteen) drawn from all levels of management and expertise to meet and propose answers to an initial single question posed by the session leader.

- Each person proposes something, no matter how absurd.

- No one is allowed to criticise or ridicule another person's idea.

- One idea provokes another, and so on.

- All ideas are listed and none rejected at this initial stage.

- Rationality is not particularly important, but what is essential is that a wide range of ideas emerges and in the ensuing discussion that these ideas are picked up, developed, combined and reshaped.

- Only after the session are ideas evaluated and screened against rational criteria for practicality.

Brainstorming provides a forum for the interchange of ideas without erecting the normal cultural, behavioural and psychological barriers that so often inhibit the expression of ideas.

Derived demand

Derived demand exists for a commodity, component or good because of its contribution to the manufacture of another product.

For example, the demands for the chromium, copper and rubber used in the manufacture of many different products, including cars, are derived demands.

The forecasting technique involves analysing some aspects of economic activity so that the level of other aspects can be deduced and projected. The principle is simple, but the practice is complex and costly.

Take the example of chrome matched with car manufacture. In order to forecast the demand for cars (thus chrome) the forecaster will be faced with the mammoth task of analysing an enormous number of influences and correlated factors.

Due to its cost and complexity the technique has a very restricted use.

5 Foresight

 Foresight goes beyond simple forecasting and tries to identify possible ways that the future of the organisation could develop.

The value of strong brands, loyal customers, etc. has diminished over time as the business environment has become more dynamic. Whereas once a company could rely on these things to bring them future success, they are increasingly unable to do so. Organisations must therefore develop vision and foresight.

For organisations, foresight means not only predicting the future but developing an understanding of all the potential changes, which if managed properly could produce many new opportunities.

By carrying out techniques to develop foresight, management try to shape the future, rather than 'wait' for it to happen and become a victim of changes they are unable to adapt to. The concept is crucial in the global commercial environment, where technological changes for example, or non-traditional competition can erode a company's dominant position overnight.

 Advantages of foresight

In their book 'Research Foresight: Creating the future', John Irvine and Ben Martin give the characteristics of foresight as the 5Cs:

- **Communication** – bringing together groups of people and providing a structure in which they can communicate.

- **Concentration** – on the longer term.

- **Coordination** – enabling different groups to harmonise their future R&D activities.

- **Consensus** – creating a measure of agreement on future directions and research priorities.

- **Commitment** – to the results among those who will be responsible for translating them into research advances, technological developments and innovations for the benefit of society.

Techniques to improve an organisation's foresight include:

- **Scenario planning** – see below.

- **Visioning** – involves management developing a 'mental image' of the organisation in the future. This should be realistic, attractive and better than the company's current state. Management can then devise ways to reach this future ideal.

- **The Delphi method** – see above.

- **Morphological analysis** – the systematic investigation of all the components of large-scale problems. A matrix is used to identify new, reasonable combinations of these components that could result in plausible new outcomes.

- **Relevance trees** – start with a clear goal, which is traced back through the trends and events on which it depends so that the organisation can determine what needs to change or be developed for the desired outcome to be achieved.

- **Issues analysis** – issues arise through the convergence of trends and events. Potentially significant issues should be analysed in terms of probability and impact (i.e. risk).

- **Opportunity mapping** – identifying gaps in the current environment in order to reveal new business opportunities.

- **Cross impact analysis** – involves recording events on a matrix and at each matrix intersection analysing how the event in the row could affect the likelihood of occurrence of the event in the column.

- **Role-playing** – a group of people are given a description of a hypothetical future situation and are told to behave as they believe they would if that situation were true.

Test your understanding 6

Y plc is attempting to forecast future events in its market. It has therefore hired a number of industry experts to identify possible developments over the next ten years. Y plc wishes to avoid any risk of the experts it has hired simply conforming with each other's opinions, so it has decided to interrogate them by questionnaire, meaning that they will never meet in person.

Which ONE of the following approaches to forecasting is Y adopting?

A   Think tank

B   Brainstorming

C   Derived demand

D   Delphi method

6   Scenario planning

Competence slip and organisational failure have been linked to the notion that management have failed to grasp the way that society is moving and have not conceptualised a possible future ecosystem. It has been suggested that managers need a picture or scenario of where the world may be in a few years' time.

For example, how would an accountancy training college meet its objectives under the following circumstances:

(1) a merger between three accountancy bodies

(2) wide demand for computer-based training

(3) changes to immigration laws leading to a reduction in the number of overseas students.

The steps involved in scenario planning

Scenario planning involves the following steps:

(1) Identify high-impact, high-uncertainty factors in the environment.

Relevant factors and driving forces could be identified through a strategic analysis framework such as a PESTEL analysis. Once identified, factors need to be ranked according to importance and uncertainty.

For example, in the oil industry there may be a need to form a view of the business environment up to twenty-five years ahead and issues such as crude oil availability, price and economic conditions are critical.

(2) For each factor, identify different possible futures.

For example, oil companies would consider possible political uncertainty in oil-producing countries and the attitudes of future governments to climate change, pollution and energy policy.

Precision is not possible but developing a view of the future against which to evaluate and evolve strategies is important.

At 3M, for example, the general manager of each business unit is required annually to describe what his or her industry will look like in fifteen years.

(3) Cluster together different factors to identify various consistent future scenarios.

For example, two key factors may have been identified as:

(a) the threat of new entrants

(b) new legislation that may reduce the potential for profit.

Clearly, if new legislation is passed that reduces industry profit potential, then the likelihood of new entrants will fall.

This process usually results in between seven and nine mini-scenarios.

(4) 'Writing the scenario' – for the most important scenarios (usually limited to three), build a detailed analysis to identify and assess future implications.

As part of this, planners typically develop a set of optimistic, pessimistic and most likely assumptions about the impact of key variables on the company's future strategy.

The result of this detailed scenario construction should include:

- financial implications – anticipated net profits, cash flow and net working capital for each of three versions of the future
- strategic implications – possible opportunities and risks
- the probability of occurrence, usually based on past experience.

(5) For each scenario, identify and assess possible courses of action for the firm.

For example, Shell was the only major oil company to have prepared for the shock of the 1970s oil crisis through scenario planning and was able to respond faster than its competitors.

Some strategies make sense whatever the outcome, usually because they capitalise on or develop key strengths of the firm. For example, the firm concerned may have a global brand name and could seek to strengthen it by increasing its advertising spend in the short term.

However, in many cases, new resources and competences may be required for existing strategies to succeed. Alternatively, entirely new strategies may be required.

(6) Monitor reality to see which scenario is unfolding.

(7) Revise ("redeploy") scenarios and strategic options as appropriate.

Construction of scenarios

These need to be well thought out if they are to be effective. Hence the following should be considered:

- use a team for a range of opinions and expertise
- identify time-frame, markets, products and budget
- stakeholder analysis – who will be the most influential in the future?
- trend analysis and uncertainty identification
- building of initial scenarios
- consider organisational learning implications
- identify research needs and develop quantitative models.

As mentioned above, Shell makes use of scenario planning extensively in order to predict future changes in the energy industry so that it can attempt to prepare for them.

How useful is scenario planning?

The downside

- Costly and inaccurate – uses up substantial resources and time
- tendency for cultural distortion and for people to get carried away
- the risk of the self-fulfilling prophecy, i.e. thinking about the scenario may be the cause of it
- many scenarios considered will not actually occur.

The upside

- Focuses management attention on the future and possibilities
- encourages creative thinking
- can be used to justify a decision
- encourages communication via the participation process
- can identify the sources of uncertainty
- encourages companies to consider fundamental changes in the external environment.

Test your understanding 7

Which THREE of the following are disadvantages of scenario planning?

A   Bounded rationality

B   Reduced communication within the organisation

C   High cost

D   Risk of self-fulfilling prophecy

E   Wastes management time

F   Discourages creative thinking

Test your understanding 8 – UHJ – (Case style)

UHJ is a multinational company, based in Europe, which manufactures aircraft components. This is a fast–moving, dynamic market with a large number of innovative competitors attempting to take UHJ's market share.

UHJ recently expanded into the North American market and set up a new division with two factories on the west coast. Since this expansion, however, the North American market has been hit by a significant economic downturn. This downturn has continued for the last year and analysts are uncertain of how far and when it will recover.

This has led to a large reduction in orders for aircraft components and has meant that the North American division of UHJ is now barely breaking even. Its future profitability for the next few years depends on a large order from a North American airline, VTH. VTH will announce a decision on this order next month.

UHJ has recently been approached with an offer by one of its rivals to buy the factories for what UHJ considers to be a fair price. UHJ wishes to avoid closing the factories as it feels that the closure costs and redundancy payouts that would be required would be extremely high.

Your manager has recently attended a seminar on scenario planning, but is concerned that he did not fully understand what is involved.

He has asked you to prepare him some briefing notes, explaining what scenario planning is and how it would benefit UHJ.

Required:

Prepare the briefing notes as requested by your manager.

(10 minutes)

Test your understanding 9 – NSF – (Case style)

The National Sports Foundation (NSF) for Country Z is a public body which operates within the central government department for Sport and Culture. NSF's role is to support and develop a sporting environment across all communities in Country Z and to increase the number of people participating in sport.

NSF is mainly funded by the Government of Country Z. Up until 2010, it employed several hundred staff and also relied upon thousands of volunteers throughout Country Z to run the various sporting clubs and associations, such as amateur football clubs and children's out of school sports activities. Following cuts in Government funding in 2010, NSF's level of staffing was considerably reduced. This resulted in NSF relying more on private sector partnerships and volunteers.

Until three years ago, the economic, social and technological environment in Country Z had been relatively stable, with NSF receiving guaranteed funding from the Government and the numbers of sports participants and volunteers being reasonably predictable. Therefore, the Board of NSF has not considered frequent and regular environmental analysis to be necessary.

NSF's Board has been taken by surprise by the changes that have occurred in the environment in the last three years. In addition to Government funding cuts, local administrative government bodies have been forced to sell off local community sports grounds and facilities to raise finance. Furthermore, the level of financial and operational support provided by private sector organisations has also declined due to similar economic challenges. Increasingly stricter regulations and rules have resulted in fewer volunteers throughout the country. The rapid growth in technology-based entertainment products has been blamed for the reduction in the number of young people participating in sports. In addition, NSF has failed to consider the changing demographics and ageing population of Country Z and the impact that this will have on sports participation in future years.

The Chairman of the Board of NSF has recently attended several conferences where the value of undertaking thorough 'environmental analysis' has been discussed. The Chairman now realises that there is a serious gap in NSF's knowledge about the environment in which it operates. He considers that if NSF is to continue successfully in the future then it must improve its foresight to actively plan for the future.

The Chairman has therefore contacted you and asked you to produce some briefing notes to help him apply this knowledge to NSF. His email is shown below:

To: A. Waterman

From: C. H. Airman

Date: 15/08/XX

Subject: Scenario planning for NSF

Hi A,

Hope you are well. As you know I have recently attended a number of conferences on foresight and scenario planning and I want to try and decide how they could be applied to NSF. I know this is a topic you have studied recently and I would like you to outline a few things to me.

To start, please explain the concept of foresight and TWO techniques (other than scenario planning) which could be used by NSF in the development of foresight.

I also need you to analyse each of the key stages that would be included in a scenario planning process which could be used by NSF.

I'm going into a meeting with the other board members about this in about thirty minutes, so please email back by then.

Kind regards

C.H.

Required:

Draft the email requested by the Chairman.

(30 minutes)

7 Game theoretic approaches to strategic planning

A key aspect of strategic planning is anticipating the actions of competitors and acting accordingly. Game theory has been used to great effect in this matter.

Game theoretic approaches to strategic planning

Game theory

In many markets it is important to anticipate the actions of competitors as there is a high interdependency between firms – i.e. the results of my choice depend to some extent on your choices as well.

Game theory is concerned with the interrelationships between the competitive moves of a set of competitors and, as such, can be a useful tool to analyse and understand different scenarios.

Game theory has two key principles:

(1) Strategists can take a rational, informed view of what competitors are likely to do and formulate a suitable response.

(2) If a strategy exists that allows a competitor to dominate us, then the priority is to eliminate that strategy.

Despite the simplicity of these principles, game theory has become very complex.

Many of the bidders for third-generation mobile phone licences in the early 2000s and the governments auctioning those licences used game theory principles. In the UK this resulted in over a hundred rounds of bidding and revenue raised of £22 billion.

Example

The most famous example of game theory is the "Prisoner's dilemma" game. This can be applied to companies as follows:

Suppose there are two companies, A and B, who between them dominate a market. Both are considering whether to increase their marketing spend from its current low level.

- If just one firm decides to increase their spend, then it will see their returns increase.

- However, if both increase the spend then both end up with lower returns than at present.

These could be shown by the following pay-off table (figures = net profit).

		Competitor A	
		High spend	Low spend
Competitor B	High spend	A = 5 B = 5	A = 3 B = 10
	Low Spend	A = 10 B = 3	A = 7 B = 7

Viewed individually the dominant strategy for both firms is to invest heavily. Taking A's perspective:

- If B does not increase spending, then the best plan of action for A would have been to invest heavily.

- If B does increase spending, then the best plan of action for A would have been to invest heavily.

However, the end result ("equilibrium") is likely to be that both firms increase spending and thus end up worse off than if they had both kept their marketing spend at its current low level. Some degree of collusion to keep the spend low would benefit both parties.

Note: The original version of the prisoners' dilemma.

Suppose two men perpetrate a crime together and are later arrested by the police.

Unfortunately the police have insufficient evidence for a conviction, and, having separated both suspects, visit each of them to offer the chance of betraying their accomplice. Suppose the possible outcomes are as follows:

- If one testifies (defects from the other) for the prosecution against the other and the other remains silent (cooperates with the other), the betrayer goes free and the silent accomplice receives the full 10-year sentence.

- If both remain silent, both prisoners are sentenced to only six months in jail for a minor charge.

- If each betrays the other, each receives a five-year sentence.

Each prisoner must choose to betray the other or to remain silent. Each one is assured that the other would not know about the betrayal before the end of the investigation.

How should the prisoners act?

The unique equilibrium for this game is that rational choice leads the two players to both play defect, even though each player's individual reward would be greater if they both played cooperatively.

Application

A common application of this is to price wars. Price wars between two evenly matched competitors usually results in lower profits for all concerned and no change in market share. No one wins, except the customer.

Test your understanding 10

TRT is a large company that manufactures light bulbs. The light bulb market has been mature for many years, with little innovation and TRT has only three other rivals in the market – all of roughly equal size to TRT. The markets that TRT operate in have strict legislation restricting collusion between competing companies.

A new type of lightbulb has recently been developed by an entrepreneur, Mr B, which provides the same light as a current lightbulb, but which uses a fraction of the electricity of traditional bulbs and which (in theory) will never need to be replaced. Mr B has stated that he is absolutely unwilling to sell this patented new product exclusively to just one supplier. Instead, he wishes to license the technology to any company who is willing to pay a fixed annual fee for a pre-set 15 year period.

TRT's strategic management accountant has calculated that if TRT is the only company that decides to license the new lightbulb, it will earn around $5m each year for the foreseeable future. It will make a loss of around $2m each year if one of its rivals also licenses the product and this loss will widen the more of its rivals decide to enter the market.

Which ONE of the following options is the most appropriate for TRT to take in order to deal with this situation?

A   Attempt to copy the technology behind the new lightbulbs, avoiding having to pay a license fee to Mr B

B   Negotiate with rival companies and agree a mutually beneficial strategy when negotiating with Mr B

C   Attempt to negotiate an exclusive deal with Mr B

D   Invest in the new lightbulbs as quickly as possible in the hope that rival companies will avoid investing

8   Real options

When deciding on a strategic project, there are three possible 'real options' that a manager may wish to take into account.

- **Option to follow on**

    When choosing a project, many managers will make their choice on the basis of Net Present Value (NPV). Projects with a positive NPV will be accepted as they increase shareholder wealth. Negative NPV projects will be rejected.

    However, under options theory this may not always be the case. This is because a project with a negative NPV could provide the business with the opportunity to invest in other, more profitable projects in the future.

    For example, an electronics company may find that designing, manufacturing and selling printers has a negative NPV due to the low prices that can be charged in this market. However, the investment will allow the company to sell a range of ink cartridges that have much higher profit margins and a larger positive NPV.

- **Option to abandon**

    If a project requires a large capital investment and has an uncertain outcome, the option to abandon may be valuable.

    For example, if a civil engineering company enters a fixed price contract to build a stadium, having an option to abandon the project will significantly reduce its risk. Should the costs spiral above the value of the contract, the company will be able to abandon the project and limit its losses.

- **Option to delay**

    The option to delay the beginning of a project can also be valuable to a business.

    A UK house-building company, for example, may have an option to build on a plot of land at any point over the next several years. Unfortunately, due to the current economic downturn, house prices have fallen sharply. The company can therefore delay the building of the homes until the market has recovered and house prices rise to a more acceptable level.

    Generally these options will become more valuable as their duration increases and as the level of uncertainty in the project rises. Remember that you will not be asked for complex calculations in this area of the syllabus.

Test your understanding 11

UPP is an organisation that sells custom-made accountancy software to large or complex organisations. It has recently been approached by the government of country L, which wishes to employ UPP to create an accountancy software solution for country L's national health service, which runs the hospitals and doctors surgeries throughout the country.

UPP is concerned that the government demands a fixed fee contract. It is aware that costs on software development are often hard to accurately estimate and this could lead to UPP making significant losses if the contract becomes more complex than originally anticipated. It is therefore negotiating with the government a clause in the contract that will allow UPP to exit the contract if costs rise above a certain level.

Under real option theory, the clause UPP is negotiating is referred to an option to _____.

Required:

Insert the missing word in the above sentence.

Test your understanding 12

Which ONE of the following changes would BOTH lead to a rise in the value of a real option?

	Option duration	Project uncertainty
A	Increases	Increases
B	Increases	Decreases
C	Decreases	Increases
D	Decreases	Decreases

9 Summary

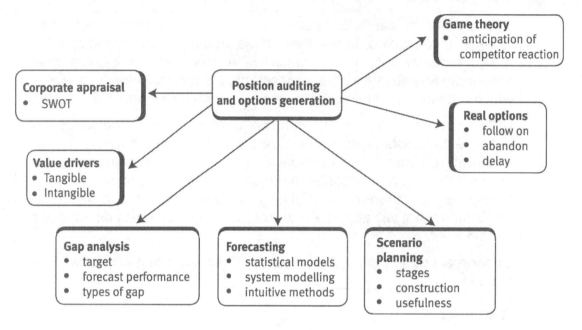

Test your understanding answers

Test your understanding 1

The correct answer is B

Strengths are internal to the organisation. Note that the opportunity to purchase C's rival would likely be classified as an opportunity.

Test your understanding 2

The correct answers are: A3, B1, C4, D2

Increased government subsidies is likely to be identified within a PEST analysis, under the 'economic' heading.

Low levels of staff morale is an internal weakness within VVV and would be identified within a SWOT analysis.

Note that it could be argued that increased subsidies could also be identified by a SWOT analysis as an opportunity/threat. However, as staff morale would only be identified within a SWOT, these subsidies must have been found by VVV's PEST analysis (as we must pair each point to one analysis tool).

After sales care (or service) is part of Porter's value chain, while customer power and its influence over strategy is a key part of the five forces model.

Test your understanding 3 – (Integration question)

Corporate appraisal

A corporate appraisal is an overview of an organisation's current position. It leads on from the internal and external analysis undertaken as part of the business planning process.

As the company works towards achieving its objectives, the corporate appraisal is a summary of the company's:

- strengths within the organisation relative to competitors

- weaknesses within the organisation relative to competitors

- opportunities available from the external environment

- threats from the external environment.

The company must develop a strategy which:

- capitalises on the strengths

- overcomes or mitigates the impact of weaknesses

- takes suitable opportunities

- overcomes or mitigates the threats.

In the case of Qualispecs:

Strengths

- Reputation for quality.

  Quality is a major reason why people buy products, and continuing to build on this reputation will ensure customers continue to buy Qualispecs's products.

- Financially secure/large cash reserves.

  Qualispecs does not need to rush into the implementation of new strategies. It can take its time to ensure strategies chosen are appropriate for the business and implemented effectively. They also have funds to invest in new ventures without having to raise external funds.

- Backing of a famous sports star.

  This helps to improve the image of Qualispecs's products which in turn should result in higher sales, particularly amongst the younger market that might be influenced by the sports star.

- New chief executive.

  The group has a new chief executive who has joined from a rival, Fastglass. Fastglass has been a successful and innovative company and the chief executive may be able to bring new ideas and provide a fresh approach.

- Established group with many stores.

  The group has a good basic infrastructure including many stores and experienced staff. This allows them to implement new strategies quickly and easily.

Weaknesses

- Slower dispensing of spectacles.

  Customer service is worse than competitors in this respect and may be a reason for the reducing customer loyalty.

- Less trendy products than competitors.

  Some competitors have successfully sold designer frames. These are likely to be stylish and trendy compared to Qualispecs' traditional products. Qualispecs may need to update products more often with the latest designs.

- Smaller product range than competitors.

  Some competitors have a wider product range than Qualispecs. This provides more choice, which may attract customers, and also gives competitors the opportunity to on-sell products, i.e. selling prescription sunglasses at the same time as standard spectacles.

- Older production methods causing higher costs.

  This will either cause prices to be higher than competitors or margins to be less. In either case competitors have a distinct advantage.

- Varying performance around the group.

  Little action is being taken to improve performance of poorly performing stores causing varying performance around the group. This indicates a weakness in internal control systems and perhaps also in development and training programmes.

- Little autonomy for shops.

  Without autonomy there is little a shop manager can do to improve local operations. In London, for instance, pay may need to be higher to attract the right staff. With no local control over pay levels, shop managers may find it hard to employ good staff and hence improve their business.

  This lack of autonomy may also be demotivating to managers. Responsibility was one of the major factors outlined by Hertzberg in his motivation theory as a way to motivate staff.

- No incentive to improve for staff.

  The use of group-based bonuses means that people cannot be rewarded for good individual performance. Individuals have little incentive to improve therefore.

Opportunities

Note: Opportunities should be in relation to the market as a whole. They therefore need to be available to all competitors in the market.

- To adopt new technologies to reduce costs (see earlier)
- to stock a wide range of up-to-date products (see earlier)
- consumer spending will continue to increase.

Despite a slowdown in the economy, consumer spending is likely to increase, suggesting an increasing market size in the future. There is therefore further opportunity for all competitors to increase sales.

- Targeting 18- to 30-year-olds.

  The 18- to 30-year-old age group offers a particular opportunity since its spending is likely to increase especially quickly. There is therefore an opportunity to understand this group's needs and to target it specifically.

- Develop a partnership with a high-street shopping group.

  Fastglass has already done this successfully and Qualispecs could follow suit. There are likely to be limited suitable partners so Qualispecs must act quickly before other firms make arrangements with the best partners.

Threats

- Intense competition/eroding customer loyalty.

  Existing competitors are adopting new strategies with great success (e.g. Fastglass developed joint ventures). This has resulted in Qualispecs' customers moving to competitors, thus reducing profits. This is likely to be a continued threat to Qualispecs, who needs to respond.

Test your understanding 4

The correct answer is A, C, D

The manager brings skills in selecting teams and identifying strategies for each game, and is an employee of the organisation. The same can be said of the players that make up the first team squad; their skills are unique and cannot be copied.

The network of clubs within the same group enables Manchester City to exploit marketing opportunities in areas of the world where demand to watch Premier League football is growing, as well as to identify players that it might wish to bring into the club.

The stadium is a tangible asset.

Test your understanding 5

The correct answer is DIVERSIFICATION

By definition.

Test your understanding 6

The correct answer is D

By definition.

Test your understanding 7

The correct answers are: A, C and D

Test your understanding 8 – UHJ – (Case style)

UHJ is faced with a dynamic and rapidly changing environment in the North American market. Scenario planning is the detailed and credible analysis of how the business environment might develop in the future, based on various environmental influences and drivers for change. The target for this analysis should be areas where the organisation considers there to be a high degree of uncertainty or opportunity.

Scenario planning would therefore enable UHJ to calculate and examine various possible strategic outcomes.

For example, UHJ would be able to examine the possible impact of the economic downturn lasting for several years, or alternatively beginning to reverse immediately. It could also compare combinations of events, such as:

- the sale of the division, followed by an economic recovery, but the loss of the VTH order

- the retention of the division, followed by a continuation of the economic downturn, along with the acquisition of the VTH order

and so on.

This approach will have two key benefits:

(1) It will help the directors of UHJ to see 'worst-case' scenarios. Should the North American economy suffer a prolonged downturn and the division lose the VTH order, there could be a significant impact on the division, along with the rest of the company. This may help the directors to decide how much of a risk maintaining the North American division is and whether it would be best to sell immediately.

(2) Scenario planning will also help the directors to anticipate potential problems with, or opportunities from, the North American division. For example, if UHJ wants to sell the division and the VTH order is lost, the price it achieves from the sale may well be much lower than is currently on offer. Alternatively, the market may recover in the near future and the sale of the division now may compromise UHJ's future growth prospects.

Test your understanding 9 – NSF – (Case style)

To: C.H. Airman

From: A. Waterman

Date: 15/08/XX

Subject: Re: Foresight

Dear C.H.

Thank you for your email. I've outlined the issues below as requested.

Foresight has been described as the 'art and science of anticipating the future'. For organisations such as NSF, foresight not only means predicting the future, but also developing an understanding of all potential changes which, if managed properly, could produce many new opportunities. There are a number of techniques which can be used to improve the foresight of an organisation. These include:

Visioning

A possible or desirable future state of the organisation is developed as a mental image by the management of the organisation. This vision may start off vaguely as a dream but should be firmed up into a concrete statement of where the organisation wants to be. The critical point is that the vision articulates a view of a realistic, credible and attractive future for the organisation, which is viewed as being an improvement on the current state of affairs.

Issues analysis

Issues arise through the convergence of trends and events. A trend is a trajectory that an issue takes because of the attention it receives and the socio-political forces that affect it. This convergence usually manifests itself because there are unfavourable events, which are sudden and unanticipated, public interest develops and becomes more important or there is increased political pressure. The issues should be analysed in terms of their impact on the organisation and their probability of occurrence.

Role Playing

This is where a group of people are given a description of a hypothetical future situation and are asked to consider what their role would be.

Delphi Technique

This seeks to avoid the group pressures of conformity that are inherent in other group based forecasting methods. It does this by interrogating a panel of experts individually and sequentially and is based on the premise that knowledge and ideas possessed by some, but not all, of the experts can be identified and shared and this forms the basis of future interrogations.

Others which could be discussed are:

- Opportunity mapping
- Cross impact analysis
- Relevance trees.

Note: Your answer only needs to explain two of the above techniques.

Scenario planning, as a tool, will provide NSF with a better understanding of what could happen in the environment in which it operates and help to minimise surprises.

The stages could be as follows:

(1) **Define the scope of the scenario**

NSF will need to decide what knowledge is most important to it. Consideration of its most important market segments and customers and the time frame it wishes to consider (i.e. how far into the future) should be paramount. It will need to decide whether the scenario is to be focussed on a specific issue e.g. the impact of the technology on the participation of children or a more blue sky approach where it asks a question such as; 'what is the future of community participation in sport in Country Z?'

(2) **Identify and map the major stakeholders**

A consideration of who the main stakeholders are in the sporting environment should be undertaken and how they are likely to drive change over the period under consideration. For NSF this would most probably include the Government of Country Z (as the main funder), its volunteers and its customers. All of these stakeholders would need to be evaluated in terms of their impact and power to influence the future activities of NSF.

(3) **Identify the basic trends and uncertainties affecting the business**

In assessing the trends and factors that would be identified in an environmental analysis and considering how they may change in the future, NSF would most probably want to focus upon the technological advances and the increasing use of the internet by children and young adults and its effect upon sport participation. Since it is very dependent upon the Government for its revenue it would also consider the trends in the economy which would affect its income. Also the changing demographics would be a major consideration for NSF.

(4) Identify the key trends and uncertainties

Of the basic trends that have been identified NSF would need to decide which are the key uncertainties. These trends and uncertainties will be the 'drivers for change' which will require contingency planning activities and will shape the future of the industry. In the case of NSF this would certainly include the declining Government funding and societal and demographic changes. These will be the main drivers forcing change in NSF.

(5) Construct initial scenario themes, or skeleton outlines

Possible future scenarios should then be created by forming the key trends and uncertainties into coherent themes. Usually two alternative scenarios are produced but more can be identified if necessary. NSF might develop one scenario where the economy continues to be depressed and funding continues to decline with sport becoming less important to society. This would be the 'negative' scenario. The alternative 'positive' scenario might feature a booming economy with many members of society both volunteering and actively participating in sport activities.

(6) Check for plausibility and internal consistency

Effective scenarios are both internally consistent and plausible. This means that different directions that the trends have taken in the scenario could logically happen together and the events described could happen within the timescale chosen.

(7) Develop learning scenarios

The next stage would be to 'flesh out' the scenarios so that they become full descriptions of the sector and conditions that are expected to prevail in the future timeframe. This is often done by writing a detailed piece of narrative. The managers of NSF would need to consider the detailed aspects of each scenario in terms of impact upon NSF's staff, possible plans for re-training, more detailed financial analysis and an overall view of the sporting environment in Country Z.

Note: There is no one perfect method of producing scenario plans and the following answer is one of a number of ways in which scenarios can be developed. Candidates will be rewarded for appropriate stages which are applied to the NSF.

I hope this helps you for your meeting – if you need any more information, please let me know.

Kind regards

A.

Test your understanding 10

The correct answer is D

The technology is patented, meaning that it cannot be copied. This means that A cannot be the correct option.

B would involve TRT colluding with its rivals, which would likely breach the strict anti-trust regulation in its markets.

C is unlikely to be a success as Mr B has stated that he will not offer an exclusive contract to any one company.

D may be the best approach. If TRT can gain a license from Mr B first, it may reduce the chances of a rival company attempting to also obtain a license as doing so would incur significant losses.

Test your understanding 11

The correct answer is ABANDON

By definition.

Test your understanding 12

The correct answer is A

The value of a real option will rise as the project becomes more uncertain and as the duration of the option rises.

Strategic options and choice

Chapter learning objectives

Lead	Component
C2: Discuss how to generate and develop options	(a-b) Discuss how to frame key strategic questions and diagnose an organisation's starting position
D1: Evaluate options	(a) Develop criteria for evaluation (b) Evaluate options against criteria (c) Recommend appropriate options
D2: Produce strategy by the integration of choices into coherent strategy	(b) Portfolio analysis
E2: Advise on resource allocation to support strategy implementation	(b) Align resource allocation to support strategic choices

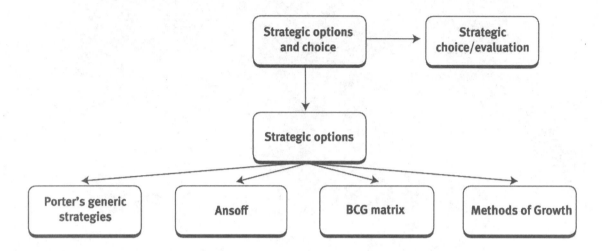

1 Strategic evaluation and choice

Once the position has been identified, the organisation will be aware of the environment within which its ecosystem functions, and the current strategic capability of the organisation within that ecosystem. So the question is "What should we do now to enable us to have the best chance of achieving our objectives?" In other words, which strategy should we follow?

There are many ways to achieve the end result! There is no one strategy that should be deployed in any given circumstance, rather a range of possible strategies that could be used singly or jointly.

2 Key strategic questions

As part of strategic choice there are three key levels of strategy to consider:

(1) **Where to compete?**

Which markets/products/SBUs should be part of our portfolio?

(2) **How to compete?**

For each SBU, what should be the basis of our competitive advantage?

(3) **Which investment vehicle to use?**

Suppose an attractive new market has been identified. Should the organisation enter the market via organic growth, acquisition or some form of joint expansion method, such as franchising?

3 Strategic options – the strategic models

There are several models that you must be familiar with.

- Porter – generic strategies – looks at competitive strategy

- Ansoff – product/market matrix – directions for growth

- Boston Consulting Group (BCG) – growth/share matrix.

Each of these models suggests several possible strategies that the organisation could adopt. The organisation can then pick the one that best fits its circumstances, which it will have identified from the internal and external analysis that it has undertaken.

You need to understand the basics of each model. However, the key to examination success will be to successfully demonstrate your ability to apply them in a scenario.

Benefits

- These models provide a useful starting point for the discursive process as they initiate discussion amongst the management teams.

- They are well-known and as such have credibility. This results in their easy application with minimal resistance.

- They generate options that can be used in the debate and allow comparison.

- They can in some instances be linked to each other to enhance the analysis.

- They can be used simply or be developed into more complicated applications.

Limitations

- They are simplistic – most are two-by-two models.

- Given their prominence in management education, undue emphasis tends to be placed upon them and there is a tendency at times to think that the models will provide a solution.

- They are dated and were produced when environments were very different. They tend to suggest that strategic choice is a straightforward process.

- They serve as a good basis for analysis, but are not perfect and do not apply to every situation.

4 Porter's Generic Strategies

Porter suggests that competitive advantage arises from the selection of a generic strategy which best fits the organisation's environment and then organising value-adding activities to support the chosen strategy.

		Competitive stance	
Strategic scope	Broad scope. Targets whole market.	Cost leadership	Differentiation
	Narrow scope. Targets one segment.	Focus	

Cost leadership – being the lowest-cost producer.

Differentiation – creating a customer perception that the product is superior to that of competitors so that a premium can be charged, i.e. that it is different and that customers are willing to pay more for this difference.

Focus – utilising either of the above in a narrow profile of market segments, sometimes called niching.

Porter argues that organisations need to address two key questions:

- Should the strategy be one of differentiation or cost leadership?

- Should the scope be wide or narrow?

He argues that organisations can run the risk of trying to satisfy all three and end up being 'stuck in the middle'. This seems to suggest that Porter was advocating that organisations need to make a basic competitive decision early on in the strategic determination process.

Cost leadership strategy

This approach is based upon a business organising itself to be the lowest-cost producer.

Note that this does not mean producing an inferior product – cost leadership means that the organisation's product is comparable to those of its rivals, but is made more efficiently.

Potential benefits are:

- business can earn higher profits by charging the same price as competitors or even moving to undercut where demand is elastic

- lets a company build defence against price wars

- allows price penetration entry strategy into new markets

- enhances barriers to entry

- develops new market segments.

Care needs to be taken when deciding on a pricing strategy as a cost leader. Cutting prices to below those of rivals can trigger a damaging price war, as well as potentially suggesting to customers that the product is inferior to those produced by more expensive competitors. Cost leaders may therefore choose to sell their products at a comparable price to those charged by rivals, but earn more profit which can be reinvested (such as in advertising, expansion or research and development) to gain competitive advantage.

Value chain analysis (see chapter 5) is central to identifying where cost savings can be made at various stages in the value chain. Attainment depends upon arranging value chain activities so as to:

- reduce costs by copying rather than originating designs, using cheaper materials and other cheaper resources, producing products with 'no frills', reducing labour costs and increasing labour productivity

- achieving economies of scale by high-volume sales allowing fixed costs to be spread over a wider production base
- use high-volume purchasing to obtain discounts for bulk purchase
- locating in areas where cost advantage exists or government aid is possible
- obtaining learning and experience curve benefits.

Differentiation strategy

This strategy is based upon the idea of persuading customers that a product is superior to that offered by the competition. Differentiation can be based on product features or creating/altering consumer perception (i.e. through superior brand development to rivals). Differentiation can also be based upon **process as well as product**. It is usually used to justify a higher price.

Benefits:

- Products command a premium price so higher margins.
- Demand becomes less price elastic and so avoids costly competitor price wars.
- Life cycle extends as branding becomes possible – hence strengthening the barriers to entry.

Value chain analysis can identify the points at which these can be achieved by:

- creating products which are superior to competitors by virtue of design, technology, performance, etc. Marketing spend becomes important
- offering superior after-sales service by superior distribution, perhaps in prime locations
- creating brand strength
- augmenting the product, i.e. adding to it.
- packaging the product
- ensuring an innovative culture exists within the company.

Focus strategy

This strategy is aimed at a segment of the market rather than the whole market. A particular group of consumers are identified with similar needs, possibly based upon age, sex, lifestyle, income or geography and then the company will either differentiate or cost focus in that area.

Benefits:

- smaller segment and so smaller investment in marketing operations
- allows specialisation
- less competition
- entry is cheaper and easier.

Requires:

- reliable segment identification
- consumer/customer needs to be reliably identified – research becomes even more crucial
- segment to be sufficiently large to enable a return to be earned in the long run
- competition analysis – given the small market, the competition, if any, needs to be fully understood
- direct focus of product to consumer needs.

Niching can be done via specialisation by:

- location
- type of end user
- product or product line
- quality
- price
- size of customer
- product feature.

If done properly it can avoid confrontation and competition yet still be profitable. The attractiveness of the market niche is influenced by the following:

- the niche must be large enough in terms of potential buyers
- the niche must have growth potential and predictability
- the niche must be of negligible interest to major competitors
- the firm must have strategic capability to enable effective service of the niche.

Illustration 1 – Cost leadership

Casio Electronics Co. Ltd – Casio has sold over 1 billion pocket calculators. It follows an industry-wide cost leadership approach. Its calculators are certainly not inferior products, being able to perform over two hundred basic scientific functions. How does it do it? Consider its value chain:

- Operations – mass manufactured in China, which has cheaper labour and economies of scale.

- Operations – 'buttons', display and instructions manuals are multi – lingual – reducing the need to make calculators specific to one target country.

- Procurement – mass purchase/production of components.

- Outbound logistics – packaging is robust, yet allows a considerable number of calculators to be shipped at any time.

Illustration 2 – Differentiation

British Airways (BA) is a multinational passenger airline. It has adopted a differentiation approach by offering passengers a higher-quality experience than many of its rivals. This allows it to charge a premium for its flights compared to many other airlines. Again – examination of its value chain may help to explain how it achieves this:

- Procurement – prime landing slots are obtained at major airports around the world.
- Procurement – high-quality food and drink is sourced from suppliers.
- Operations – well-maintained, clean and comfortable aircraft are sourced.
- Operations – high numbers of attendants on each flight.
- Marketing – advertising based on quality of service provided.
- Human resources – training in customer care and the recruitment of high-quality staff.

Illustration 3 – Focus

Ferrari is an example of a company that focuses on a niche market in the automobile industry. It produces extremely high quality cars which command a high premium price. However, this means that Ferrari only has a very small percentage of the global car market, as the majority of consumers will be unable to afford its high sales prices.

This is a risk of the focus approach. The niche targeted may be small and fail to justify the company's attention. In addition the niche may shrink or disappear altogether over time as consumer tastes and fashions change.

Limitations of Porter's generic strategies

In spite of its popularity, there are a number of problems with Porter's generic strategies model, including:

- Porter argues that any business that attempts to adopt more than one of the generic strategies will become 'stuck in the middle'. He suggested that this is because a business will be unable to successfully implement more than one at the same time, leading to strategic drift. In reality this may be too simplistic.

  A number of companies do not fit into one of the classic generic strategies and adopt a 'hybrid' approach. Successful UK supermarket chain Sainsbury's uses a slogan 'Live well for less', suggesting to its potential customers that its products are both lower price than rivals and good quality – both differentiation and cost leadership.

- Cost leadership in itself may not give competitive advantage.

  Failure to pass on cost savings to customers through lower prices may mean that the business fails to gain an edge over rivals. Passing on the cost savings may trigger a price war with rivals, meaning that the company fails to benefit from the strategy.

- Differentiation may not always lead to a business being able to command a high price for its goods. It may be used to generate increased sales volume – which Porter argued was typically the purpose of a cost leadership approach.

Test your understanding 1

Company W makes motor vehicles. Several years ago, W restructured its value chain to significantly reduce production costs and improve quality. This was in response to similar activities by its W's major rivals.

Because of this, W has been able to maintain its prices at a similar level to those of its competitors, while continuing to produce a wide range of cars that are tailored to a variety of market segments.

W has recently decided to undertake a significant investment in advertising, as it feels that its brand is one of the most recognised in the market. W wishes to further increase the desirability of its brand, which it feels could allow it to raise its prices slightly in the coming year, while still maintaining its overall sales volume.

According to Porter's generic strategies model, W's current approach to its market is an example of which ONE of the following?

A   Cost leadership

B   Focus

C   Stuck in the middle

D   Differentiation

Test your understanding 2

Y is a small business that sells furniture in country H. It is considering its future corporate strategy.

The furniture market is dominated by large manufacturers, who have large factories as well as close relationships with key suppliers of raw materials. Y is currently the twentieth largest manufacturer of furniture in country H.

Y's market analysis has identified that there are a moderate number of self-employed individuals in country H who work from home and who desire standard office furniture that is also fashionable. However, there are several companies who have built up established brand names in this sector of the market.

Y currently makes furniture for small to medium sized businesses (such as desks and office chairs). Products in this segment of the market are fairly generic as businesses typically choose a furniture supplier based on price. There are a large number of other suppliers of this style of furniture in country H – including several of the larger manufacturers.

Y is concerned that it lacks the appropriate skills to make other types of furniture.

Which ONE of the following strategies is the most appropriate for Y to adopt?

A   Focus

B   Differentiation

C   Cost leadership

D   Y is stuck in the middle

Test your understanding 3 – AVA – (Case style)

You work as a strategic management accountant for AVA, an airline company that offers regular passenger flights from several countries in country L to destinations all over the world.

AVA is a long-established company which has historically offered a low-cost service with few passenger comforts or luxuries. Customers have to book seats online, with no chance for interaction with an AVA staff member. Seats (which are renowned by customers for their lack of leg room) cannot be pre-booked and AVA has a poor record for delays and cancellations.

In spite of this, AVA has managed to achieve reasonable profits by being able to offer its flights at extremely low prices. In recent years, however, the company's profits have fallen as the economy of country L has started to recover from a long recession. This has led the company to start looking at ways of improving profitability.

You have been contacted by the Finance Director (FD) of AVA. His email is shown below:

To: H. Pimm

From: FD

Date: 16/09/XX

Subject: AVA Strategic direction

Hi H,

As you know, last year the directors felt that the company was missing out on the lucrative first class service market – currently dominated by several major international airlines which are significantly larger than AVA. While first class travellers require more services and better facilities, we would be able to charge them a relatively high ticket price.

> The company therefore converted the front section of several of its aircraft into 'first class' with fewer seats and more leg room. Passengers book these seats through a separate system which enables them to speak to an adviser if they had any problems. AVA also offers free food and drink on the flight to first class passengers. This service is not be available to standard class customers.
>
> The airplanes AVA upgraded were all based on one of its major routes. Unfortunately, uptake was disappointing and AVA wishes to try and understand why.
>
> The directors would like you to evaluate our first class offering. They feel that examining our existing and first class strategies using Porter's generic strategies would be a good place to start.
>
> Please have the report on my desk in thirty minutes, so I have time to consider it before speaking to the other directors.
>
> Thanks
>
> FD
>
> **Required:**
>
> Draft the report as requested in the FD's email.
>
> **(30 minutes)**

5 Ansoff

The product/market growth framework

A commonly used model for analysing the possible strategic directions that an organisation can follow. Hence useful in areas of strategic choice:

		Products	
		Existing	*New*
Markets	Existing	Market penetration	Product development
	New	Market development	Diversification

Market penetration

The main aim is to increase market share using existing products within existing markets.

Approach

First attempt to stimulate **usage by existing customers:**

- new uses of advertising
- promotions, sponsorships
- quantity discounts.

Then attempt to attract **non-users** and **competitor customers** via:

- pricing
- promotion and advertising
- process redesign, e.g. Internet/e-commerce.

Key notes:

Considered when:

- overall market is growing
- market not saturated
- competitors leaving or weak
- strong brand presence by your company with established reputation
- strong marketing capabilities exist within your company.

Market development

Aims to increase sales by taking the present product to new markets (or new segments). Entering new markets or segments may require the development of new competences which serve the particular needs of customers in those segments, e.g. cultural awareness/linguistic skills.

Movement into overseas markets is often quoted as a good example as the organisation will need to build new competences when entering international markets.

Approach

- Add **geographical** areas – regional and national
- add **demographic** areas – age and sex
- new **distribution** channels.

Key notes

- **Slight** product modifications may be needed

- advertising in different media and in different ways

- research – primary research at this point given significance of the investment

- company is structured to produce one product and high switching costs exist for transfer to other product types

- strong marketing ability is needed, usually coupled with established brand backing, e.g. CocaCola.

Product development

Focuses on the development of new products for existing markets.

Offers the advantage of dealing with known customer/consumer bases.

Approach:

- develop product features of a significant nature

- create different quality versions.

Key notes:

Company needs to be innovative and strong in the area of R&D and have an established, reliable marketing database.

Constant innovation allows for the developing sophistication of consumers and customers and ensures that any product-related competitive advantage is maintained.

Diversification

The risky option?

Approach:

New products to new markets.

Key notes:

Appropriate when existing markets are saturated or when products are reaching the end of their life cycle. It can spread risk by broadening the portfolio and lead to 'synergy-based benefits', allegedly.

This goes through periods of being in and out of favour and the debate is always continuing as to whether this is a good strategic option. Critics argue that it is madness to take resources away from known markets and products only to allocate them to businesses that the company essentially knows nothing about. This risk has to be compensated for by higher rewards, which may or may not exist.

Brand stretching ability is often seen as being the critical success factor for successful diversification – this is a possible discussion point. The new business and its strategy may well have 'teething problems' with its implementation and this may damage brand reputation.

Reasons suggested:

- Objectives can no longer be met in known markets – possibly due to a change in the external environment.

- Company has excess cash and powerful shareholders.

- Possible to 'brand stretch' and benefit from past advertising and promotion in other SBUs.

- Diversification promises greater returns and can spread risk by removing the dependency on one product.

- Greater use of distribution systems and corporate resources such as research and development, market research, finance and HR leading to synergies.

Overall

It is worth noting that, unlike Porter's generic strategies model, Ansoff does not argue that a business should only adopt **one** of the four possible strategies. It is possible for an organisation to adopt multiple strategies simultaneously. For example, UK retailer Marks and Spencer has launched a number of new advertising campaigns designed to boost sales of its products (market penetration), while also offering its existing food ranges in motorway service stations (market development).

Illustration 4 – Ansoff

- Kellogg's have repositioned their products through various advertising campaigns (**market penetration**). For example, the 'have you forgotten how good they taste?' campaign was to remind adults, who buy cereals for their children, of the virtues of their product.

- Kwik Fit, a motor repair company, took the opportunity to cross sell insurance to customers on their database who had visited their outlets to have equipment fitted (**product development – 'piggybacking'**).

- Kaplan now sell their ACCA courses in Eastern Europe and Asia, amongst other countries, rather than just their traditional UK markets (**market development**).

- Virgin, a multinational conglomerate, has expanded into a wide range of different activities, including airlines, trains, cosmetics, wedding wear and so on (**diversification**).

Limitations of Ansoff's matrix

Limitations of Ansoff's matrix include:

- The matrix is seen as being too simplistic as it fails to take account of the external environment, such as competitor strategies. For a complete picture it is essential that the organisation undertakes detailed external analysis with, for example, SWOT, PESTEL and Five Forces.

- The matrix focuses on ways that the organisation can grow. In reality, not all companies want to grow their business. They may wish to simply defend their current position or may be focused on survival.

- Any decision made by management using Ansoff's matrix is subjective – the model does not show the company which strategy is optimal. As such, ineffective strategies can still easily be selected.

Test your understanding 4

Consider the following diagram of Ansoff's matrix:

		Market	
		New	Existing
Product	**New**	A	C
	Existing	B	D

Which ONE of the following strategies is located in quadrant B on the above diagram?

A   Market penetration

B   Product development

C   Diversification

D   Market development

Test your understanding 5

HUF is a business that retails wine, beer and other alcoholic beverages through a large number of stores. It has recently launched a new radio advertising campaign (HUF's normal advertising medium) offering discounts to all customers if they spend more than a certain amount of money in one of HUF's stores.

According to Ansoff, which type of strategy is HUF adopting in the above scenario?

A   Diversification

B   Market development

C   Market penetration

D   Product development

Test your understanding 6 – (Integration question)

Esso is a successful oil company. It has run a 'pricewatch' campaign to ensure its fuels are priced at a similar level to supermarkets and other competitors. It has expanded its range of products available at Esso minimarkets to include groceries and household goods. It has signed agreements with China to sell fuels there and is contemplating acquisitions of engineering and textiles companies.

Required:

Categorise these actions using Ansoff's matrix. Explain your choices.

(5 minutes)

As outlined in Ansoff's model (see previous section), diversification refers to a business entering a new market or industry which it is not currently, while also developing new a new product or products for this new market.

Diversification is usually seen as the riskiest of the growth strategies suggested by Ansoff as the business has no experience of the market or the product that it is planning to sell.

6 Diversification

Diversification can take **two** main forms:

6.1 Related diversification (concentric diversification)

- Growth into similar industries.

- Growth forward into the customer marketplace.

- Growth backward into the existing supply chain:

  - **Vertical backward** – a company seeks to operate in markets in which it currently obtains its resources, e.g. a supermarket producing some of the products it buys – the benefit would arise from greater control over resource supply.

  - **Vertical forward** – a company seeks to move into its customer base, e.g. a brewery establishing its own chain of pubs and off-licences.

  - **Horizontal** – involves a company entering into complementary or competing markets, e.g. Honda motorcycles and cars.

Vertical integration

Taking over a supplier (backwards vertical integration) or customer (forwards vertical integration). Key issues relate to

- Cost.

  Is it cheaper to make a product in-house and avoid paying towards a supplier's profit margin or might the supplier have sufficient economies of scale for them to sell it cheaper than you can make it?

- Quality.

  Making a component in-house means you can tailor it to your own needs and use proprietary expertise... if you have the necessary resources and competences.

- Risk/flexibility.

  Outsourcing gives a firm the flexibility to switch suppliers and so exercise buyer power to drive down prices.

Vertical integration

Backward integration refers to developments into activities which are concerned with inputs to the company's present business, for example a company becoming a supplier of its own raw materials. Sometimes this form of integration is called "upstream" integration.

Forward integration refers to development into activities which are concerned with the company's outputs. For example, a company could set up its own distribution channels rather than relying on outside retailers. Sometimes this form of integration is called "downstream" integration.

Vertical integration can have important benefits and costs which need to be considered in any decision.

Benefits of integration

- Economies of combined operations, e.g. proximity, reduced handling.

- Economies of internal control and coordination, e.g. scheduling and coordinating operations should be better. Information about the market can be fed back to the production companies.

- Economies of avoiding the market, e.g. negotiation, packing, advertising costs are avoided.

- Tap into technology. Close knowledge of the upstream or downstream operations can give a company valuable strategic advantages. For example, computer manufacturers have instituted backwards integration into semi-conductor design and manufacturing to gain a better understanding of the technology and its potential.

- Safeguarding proprietary knowledge. If a firm makes components itself, it does not have to supply specifications to its suppliers; this information therefore stays confidential.

- Assured supply and demand. The firm will have first call on supplies in scarce periods and the greatest chance of having an outlet in periods of low demand. Fluctuations in supply and demand are not eliminated but can, perhaps, be better planned.

- Reduction in bargaining power of suppliers and customers. Two of Porter's forces on a firm are customer and supplier bargaining power. So if your suppliers are giving you a rough time, take them over or set up your own supply company. Similarly with distribution channels.

- Enhanced ability to differentiate. More of the product comes under your control so you have a greater ability to differentiate it. For example, a specialist chain of shops could be established with a distinctive brand image.

- Defend against "lock out". It may be necessary to defend against being cut off from access to suppliers or distributors. For example, if a competitor were buying up your suppliers you would have to acquire your own supplier to ensure continued supply of components.

Costs of integration

- Increased operating gearing. Vertical integration increases the proportion of the firm's costs which are fixed. For example, if the firm were to purchase from an outside source, all those costs would be variable. If the input is produced internally the firm has to bear all the fixed costs of production. Vertical integration increases business risk from this source.

- Reduced flexibility to change partners. If the in-house supplier or customer does not do well, then it is not easy to switch to outsiders. You will probably have to get rid of the in-house company first.

- Capital investment needs. Vertical integration will consume capital resources and must yield a return greater than, or equal to, the firm's opportunity cost of capital, adjusting for strategic considerations, for integration to be a good choice.

- Cut off from suppliers and customers. By integrating a firm may cut itself off from the flow of technology from its suppliers or market research information from its customers. For example, a firm will have to take responsibility for developing its own technology. Other potential suppliers may be reluctant to share their technology as they would be supplying it not only to a customer, but a customer who is also a competitor.

- Dulled incentives. The captive relationship between buyer and seller can quickly lead to inefficiencies. These can quickly spread through the group as too high cost products are passed through.

- Differing managerial requirements. Different businesses need different management skills. Because a company is a successful manufacturer, this does not mean that it can turn its hand to retailing with a reasonable chance of success. Many companies have found that they do best doing what they do best.

Horizontal diversification

Horizontal diversification refers to development into activities that are competitive with, or directly complementary to, a company's present activities. There are three cases.

(a) Competitive products. Taking over a competitor can have obvious benefits, leading eventually towards achieving a monopoly. Apart from active competition, a competitor may offer advantages such as completing geographical coverage.

(b) Complementary products. For example, a manufacturer of household vacuum cleaners could make commercial cleaners. A full product range can be presented to the market and there may well be benefits to be reaped from having many of the components common between the different ranges.

(c) By-products. For example, a butter manufacturer discovering increased demand for skimmed milk. Generally, income from by-products is a windfall: any you get is counted, at least initially, as a bonus.

6.2 Unrelated diversification (conglomerate diversification)

This type of diversification occurs when a business expands into completely new markets or industries with which the business currently shares no common ground.

Advantages

Conglomerate diversification tends to occur when there are limited opportunities for expansion in the organisation's current markets. The only way for such a business to grow may be through unrelated diversification. It provides an opportunity for return if there is nothing else to do with the resources. The company may need to be seen as an 'aggressive' organisation and may embark on this course of action in order to appease powerful stakeholder groups.

The fact that the organisation is operating in a range of different markets reduces the organisation's overall risk. It is unlikely that all of the markets that the organisation operates within will enter decline at the same time, reducing variability of returns.

Even unrelated markets may have some synergies with each other, which could reduce the overall costs of the organisation.

Disadvantages

There is significantly more risk for the organisation if they adopt this strategy as they are launching a new, unproven product into a market that they have little experience or knowledge of. This significantly increases the chances of failure. This can be eliminated to a degree by acquiring an existing business in the new target market (thereby acquiring the industry knowledge required).

For many larger organisations, there will be little gain to shareholders. Shareholders are already likely to hold a diverse portfolio of investments, meaning that they have already diversified away much of their risk.

Diversification by one of the companies that they own shares in will therefore do little to help them.

Attempting to operate in new industries may mean that management lose focus on the core markets that the company currently operates within. This could lead to reduced returns for the organisation as a whole.

Test your understanding 7

Which THREE of the following would be likely reasons for an organisation to adopt an unrelated diversification strategy?

A   Reduced risk for diversified institutional shareholders

B   Increased synergies

C   Reduced variability in returns for the organisation

D   Possibility of 'brand stretch'

E   Increased management focus on core activities

F   Existing markets are saturated

G   Improved employee morale

Test your understanding 8 – C – (Case style)

C operates several hundred coffee shops across country U. Its stores offer a wide variety of coffee and tea-based drinks that customers can either drink on the premises or take away. In addition to drinks, C also offers a range of sandwiches and cakes.

C has a large number of rivals in the intensely competitive coffee shop market in country U, all of which offer a similar range of products to C and at a slightly lower price.

C has built a reputation for high quality service and is currently the market leader, allowing it to achieve high margins on its products – even in the current economic downturn in country U.

This has allowed C to build a significant cash surplus and it is considering how to further grow its business. At the most recent meeting of the Board of Directors, three directors made suggestions for how to expand the business.

The Finance Director (FD) suggested that C should consider offering a range of other products in its shops. These would include wine and soft drinks as well as hot food. The cash surplus could be used to re-fit the kitchens of C's shops and launch a large advertising campaign across the country. The FD suggested that the margins on these items were even higher than those currently achieved on coffee, leading to higher profits for C in the future.

The Marketing Director (MD) disagreed as she felt that C's coffee shops were currently successful and should not be changed. She recommended investing the cash into opening up branches in neighbouring countries. She stated that C's current branding and product range would be suitable for neighbouring countries with few, if any changes. Many of C's competitors have already entered the countries surrounding country U.

The Operations Director (OD), however, stated that he felt that the coffee and food market in the region was simply too saturated to make further investment worthwhile. Instead, he feels that C should look to invest in a totally new area.

A successful online music store has recently posted significant growth in profits in country U. The OD has identified this as a high-growth market and feels the cash surplus should be used to purchase this business.

Required:

(i)   Explain and justify where each of the director's proposals would be placed on Ansoff's matrix.

(**Note:** A diagram is NOT required)

(ii)   Identify the strategy suggested by Ansoff that the directors have failed to consider and suggest how this could be applied to C.

(iii)   Discuss the advantages and disadvantages of the CEO's proposal to purchase the online music store.

(45 minutes)

7   Product Portfolio Theory – Boston Consulting Group (BCG)

Boston Consulting Group Growth / Share Matrix

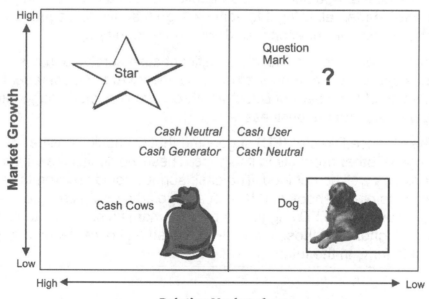

Relative Market share

Developed originally to assist managers in identifying cash flow requirements of different businesses or products within their organisation's portfolio and to help to decide whether change in the mix of businesses is required. A broad portfolio indicates that a business has a presence in a wide range of products and market sectors – this may or may not be a good thing!

Using the BCG matrix typically requires four main steps:

(1) divide the company into SBUs

(2) allocate into the matrix

(3) assess the prospects of each SBU and compare against others in the matrix

(4) develop strategic objectives for each SBU.

Relative market share – the ratio of SBU market share to that of largest rival in the market sector. BCG suggests that market share gives a company cost advantages from economies of scale and learning effects. The dividing line is set at 1 – i.e. a high market share suggests that the product is a market leader. A figure of 4 suggests that SBU share is four times greater than the nearest rival. A figure of 0.1 suggests that the SBU is 10% of the sector leader.

Market growth rate – represents the growth rate of the market sector concerned. High-growth industries offer a more favourable competitive environment and better long-term prospects than slow-growth industries. The dividing line is set at 10%.

SBUs are entered onto the matrix as dots with circles around the dots denoting the revenue relative to total corporate turnover. The bigger the circle, the more significant the unit.

Using the matrix

The model suggests that appropriate strategies would be:

- **hold** – adopt strategies to keep the product in its current quadrant – i.e. invest heavily in advertising or promotion for a star product in order to maintain its current high market share.

- **build** – increase investment in the product in an attempt to boost its market share.

- **harvest** – reduce investment in the product in order to maximise the net cash return from the product to the business.

- **divest** – disposal/closure of the product in order to release any cash currently tied up within it.

Cash cows – hold or harvest

These products or SBUs have a high market share in a low-growth market. They have usually reached the 'maturity' stage of their life cycle (see chapter 4 for more information on the product/industry life cycle).

Cash cows, as the name suggests, are usually strongly profit and cash generating. This is because they are market leaders with relatively high sales and this has often allowed them to create significant economies of scale.

The fact that the market is low growth indicates that it is no longer attractive for new entrants, or for heavy investment by any participating company. This means that capital requirements are low for the cash cow and that the cost of defensive strategies (such as advertising) are also likely to be fairly low.

A company will often adopt a harvesting strategy towards its cash cows, maximising cash flows by keeping investment to a minimum where possible, while trying to maintain the product and prevent it from entering decline for as long as possible.

Note that profits from cash cows can be used to support other products in their development stage. Therefore for a company to have a balanced portfolio, it needs some of these cash cow products.

Stars – hold or build

Stars have high market share in an attractive, high-growth market. They are most likely in the 'growth' stage of their life cycle.

As they are likely to be the market leader, they offer attractive long-term prospects and, if maintained could one day become a cash cow when the rate of market growth finally slows.

Stars rarely generate significant amount of cash or profits for the company. While they generate high levels of sales, they operate in an attractive, high-growth market meaning that they are likely to be facing significant levels of competition. This requires the company to spend large amounts of money to beat off competitor attack strategies, through marketing and research and development (amongst other things), as well as having to aggressively try and win new customers in the expanding market.

In addition, in order to sustain the level of growth in the market, stars require high levels of capital investment.

The company therefore usually adopts a 'build' strategy, involving heavy investment to keep attracting new customers (as well as defending those it already has).

Question marks (also known as problem children) – build or divest

Questions marks have low market share in an attractive, rapidly growing market. They may be at the 'growth' or 'introduction' stage of their life cycle.

Given the rapid growth in the market, there is opportunity for significant development of question marks. However, given the currently low market share, there is high risk of failure – the product may fail to grow its market share and will not therefore become a star.

As such, management typically adopts a 'double or quits' approach to question marks. If they feel that the product stands a good chance of success, they will adopt a build strategy and try to grow market share through heavy investment in expansion, marketing and promotion. If they are not confident in the future success of the product, they may choose to divest, exiting the market.

Ultimately, question marks are risky – they will usually absorb substantial management time and cash and may not be successfully developed.

Dogs – harvest or divest

Dogs have a low market share of a slow growing (or even contracting) market. It may be a product which has entered the 'decline' stage of its life cycle, or could even be a question mark that never successfully grew. It is likely to be making small profits or losses and will be fairly cash neutral.

There is usually seen as being little point for the business to try and grow market share. The market is no longer attractive and it is dominated by other, rival products. To invest in the dog would require significant cost and risk, with relatively little chance of a reasonable return. This most commonly leads to the BCG matrix suggesting that the product is divested.

However, it is important not to divest the product without further analysis. Some dog products support other, more valuable products sold by the business. For example, a computer printer manufacturer may accept a 'dog' printer model as it allows them to sell more valuable ink cartridges, which enjoy very high profit margins. Alternatively a 'dog' product may be used as a retailer as a loss leader to attract customers.

The dog may also still be profitable. There is little point divesting a product which is still making acceptable returns and may still be helping to earn shareholders money.

Be aware that sometimes dogs cannot be divested – particularly in the public sector where failing schools for example will need to be reinvested in and possibly restructured but certainly not divested.

Whatever the reason for keeping the dog, a harvest strategy would be adopted, keeping costs low and maximising what little profit or cash flow can be made from the product.

BCG recommendations

Once the company has completed its portfolio analysis, it can identify a number of overall portfolio issues:

- Is the portfolio in balance? While the business does not necessarily need any dog products, it would expect to have products in the other three quadrants of the grid. It needs cash cows to support stars and develop question marks, but if it only has cash cows it may find that they all enter decline at the same time – stars and question marks may be the successful products of the future.

- Some less attractive parts of the portfolio may be divested – in particular dog products (if not profitable or support for other products) and question marks that the management lacks confidence in.

Limitations of the BCG

Limitations

- Simplistic – only considers two variables

- connection between market share and cost savings is not strong – low-market share companies use low-share technology and can have lower production costs

- cash cows do not always generate cash – cash cows may still require substantial cash investment just to remain competitive and defend their market share.

- fail to consider value creation – the management of a diverse portfolio can create value by sharing competencies across SBUs, sharing resources to reap economies of scale or by achieving superior governance. BCG would divert investment away from the cash cows and dogs and fails to consider the benefit of offering the full range and the concept of 'loss leaders'.

- over-emphasis on being the market leader – many companies have products that are not market leaders, but which are highly profitable.

Test your understanding 9

You have been given the following data regarding four products currently sold by company YX:

Product	Revenue – total market ($m)	Revenue – YX ($m)	Market share of largest competitor	Market growth rate
Whizz	400	40	45%	1%
Bang	60	20	10%	4%
Wallop	100	5	1%	15%
Pop	96	4.8	30%	–5%

Show where each product would be categorised using the BCG matrix below. You can place more than one product in each category.

Stars	Question marks
Cash cows	**Dogs**

Test your understanding 10

O sells four products.

Product H1 is a type of protective shoe. It has recently lost its market leader position as the market for protective clothing continues to shrink. Financially, H1 is breaking even.

Product E2 is a vented umbrella. It has only recently been launched and has yet to see strong sales growth in the market. O feels that the umbrella market is likely to grow strongly over the next few years due to global warming.

Product Y4 is a waterproof coat. It is the top selling coat in O's market and, as with product E2, O expects ongoing growth due to the changing climate.

Finally, product B3 is a waterproof boot. B3 is far superior to the market leaders, but is struggling to gain acceptance in the popular, rapidly growing footwear market.

According to the BCG matrix model, which ONE of the above four products would O be most likely to adopt a holding strategy for?

A   H1

B   E2

C   Y4

D   B3

Test your understanding 11 – GC – (Case style)

GC is a conglomerate that comprises five strategic business units (SBUs), all operating as subsidiary companies. Your manager has sent you an email attachment which gives information relating to each SBU (and the market leader or nearest competitor):

Current market share

	GC %	Market leader %	Nearest competitor %	Market growth expected by GC
Building brick manufacturer (Declining profitability)	3	25		Small
Parcel carriage service (Long established, faces strong competition. Turnover and profitability over last three years have been stable but are expected to decline as competition strengthens)	1	6		Nil
Food manufacturer producing exclusively for household consumption (Long established with little new investment. High levels of turnover and profitability, which are being sustained)	25		5	Slowly declining
Painting and decorating contracting company (Established three years ago. Continuous capital injections from group over that period. Currently not making any profit)	0.025	0.5		Historically high but now forecast to slow down

Software development and supply company (Acquired two years ago. Market share expected to increase over next two years. Sustained investment from the group but profitability so far low)	10		8	Rapid

Your manager has left a note on your desk asking you to prepare briefing notes for him covering the following issues:

(a) Comment on GC's overall competitive position by applying the Boston Consulting Group growth/share matrix analysis to its portfolio of SBUs.

(b) Discuss how GC should pursue the strategic development of its SBUs in order to add value to the overall conglomerate group.

Required:

Prepare the briefing notes as requested by your manager.

(45 minutes)

8 Methods of growth

Businesses may choose to grow in one of several main ways, including acquisitions, mergers or organic growth.

8.1 Acquisition

Acquisition refers to a corporate action in which a company buys most, if not all, of the target company's ownership stakes in order to assume control of the target firm.

Illustration 5 – Facebook

Facebook has grown its presence in the social media industry through the acquisitions of Whatsapp in February 2014 for an estimated $22 billion and Instagram (2012 – $1 billion). It also reportedly tried to acquire Snapchat in 2013 for $3 billion, but the Snapchat CEO Evan Spiegel refused to agree to a sale.

8.2 Merger

 Mergers are business combinations that result from the creation of a new reporting entity formed from the combining parties.

Illustration 6 – Sainsburys and Asda

In April 2018, UK supermarket giants Sainsburys and Asda announced that they were to merge. This was in response, in part, to the growing threat from discount food retailers Aldi and Lidl. However, there is considerable doubt as to whether the deal will be allowed to proceed due to concerns on the part of the Competition Authority over whether the deal is in the public interest (the merged entity would have too great a market share and therefore restrict choice for the consumer).

Note that, for our purposes in the E3 examination, there is little or no strategic difference between an acquisition and a merger.

8.3 Organic growth

 Organic growth is growth through internally generated projects, such as increased output, customer base expansion, or new product development.

Illustration 7 – Sainsburys and organic growth

As well as looking to grow by acquisition or merger, Sainsburys has also adopted strategies of organic growth in the UK. It increased the number of edge of town supermarkets it operated by identifying suitable locations, applying for planning permission, building premises and then opening for trade.

It increased the range of products in-store, adding items such as books, dvds, clothes etc. to the more traditional foodstuffs.

It also branched out into convenience stores, opening a chain of Sainsburys Local stores in high street locations.

The above growth strategies were largely by organic means.

Acquisition may be more expensive than organic growth because the owners of the acquired company will need to be paid for the risks they have already taken. On the other hand, if the company goes for organic growth it must take the risks itself so there is a trade-off between cost and risk.

A company can gain synergy by bringing together complementary resources in their own business and that being acquired. Synergy is defined as **'the advantage to a firm gained by having existing resources which are compatible with new products or markets that the company is developing'.**

For example, sales synergy may be obtained through the use of common marketing facilities such as distribution channels. Investment synergy may result from the joint use of plant and machinery or raw materials.

An acquisition must add value in a way the shareholder cannot replicate in order to avoid the risks associated with diversified companies (see Ansoff).

Acquisition v organic growth

Advantages of acquisitions over organic growth

Acquisition has some significant advantages over internal growth.

- High-speed access to resources – this is particularly true of brands; an acquisition can provide a powerful brand name that could take years to establish through internal growth.

- Avoids barriers to entry – acquisition may be the only way to enter a market where the competitive structure would not admit a new member or the barriers to entry were too high.

- Less reaction from competitors – there is less likelihood of retaliation because an acquisition does not alter the capacity of the competitive arena.

- It can block a competitor – if Kingfisher's bid for Asda had been successful it would have denied Walmart its easy access to the UK.

- It can help restructure the operating environment – some mergers of car companies were used to reduce overcapacity.

- Relative price/earnings ratio – if the P/E ratio is significantly higher in the new industry than the present one, acquisition may not be possible because it would cause a dilution in earnings per share to the existing shareholders. But if the present company has a high P/E ratio it can boost earnings per share by issuing its own equity in settlement of the purchase price.

- Asset valuation – if the acquiring company believes the potential acquisition's assets are undervalued, it might undertake an asset-stripping operation.

Disadvantages of acquisitions growth

There are some disadvantages associated with this method of growth

- Acquisition may be more costly than internal growth because the owners of the acquired company will have to be paid for the risk already taken. On the other hand, if the company decides on internal growth, it will have to bear the costs of the risk itself.

- There is bound to be a cultural mismatch between the organisations – a lack of 'fit' can be significant in knowledge-based companies, where the value of the business resides in individuals.

- Differences in managers' salaries – another example of cultural mismatch that illustrates how managers are valued in different countries.

- Disposal of assets – companies may be forced to dispose of assets they had before the acquisition. The alliance between British Airways and American Airlines was called off because the pair would have had to free up around 224 take-off and landing slots to other operators.

- Risk – of not knowing all there is to know about the business it seeks to buy.

- Reduction in return on capital employed – quite often an acquisition adds to sales and profit volume without adding to value creation.

9 Joint methods of expansion

Mention has already been made of the importance of networks within an organisational ecosystem. In some situations it might lead to greater value being created if an organisation adopts a collaborative approach to strategy i.e. it works in partnership in some way with another organisation or organisations. For example, sales synergy may be obtained through the use of common marketing facilities such as distribution channels. Investment synergy may result from the joint use of plant and machinery or raw materials.

There are a number of joint development methods that you should be aware of.

Joint development methods

These include:

- Joint venture
- strategic alliances
- franchising
- licenses
- outsourcing.

In any joint arrangement key considerations are

- sharing of costs
- sharing of benefits
- sharing of risks
- ownership of resources
- control/decision making.

Joint development methods

Joint venture

A separate business entity whose shares are owned by two or more business entities. Assets are formally integrated and jointly owned.

A very useful approach for:

- sharing cost
- sharing risk
- sharing expertise.

In the UK, an example of a joint venture is Virgin Trains – a company whose share capital is 51% owned by the Virgin Group and 49% owned by Stagecoach. The joint venture allowed the two companies to work together to take advantage of the privatisation of the nationalised British Rail.

A further example is that of Sainsburys Bank, which was originally a joint venture between Sainsburys and Bank of Scotland. The joint venture started in 1997, with Sainsburys then taking full control in 2014.

Strategic alliance

A strategic alliance can be defined as a cooperative business activity, formed by two or more separate organisations for strategic purposes, that allocates ownership, operational responsibilities, financial risks, and rewards to each member, while preserving their separate identity/ autonomy.

Alliances can allow participants to achieve critical mass, benefit from other participants' skills and can allow skill transfer between participants.

The technical difference between a strategic alliance and a joint venture is whether or not a new, independent business entity is formed.

A strategic alliance is often a preliminary step to a joint venture or an acquisition. A strategic alliance can take many forms, from a loose informal agreement to a formal joint venture.

Alliances include partnerships, joint ventures and contracting out services to outside suppliers.

Seven characteristics of a well-structured alliance have been identified.

- **Strategic synergy** – more strength when combined than they have independently.

- **Positioning opportunity** – at least one of the companies should be able to gain a leadership position (i.e. to sell a new product or service; to secure access to raw materials or technology).

- **Limited resource availability** – a potentially good partner will have strengths that complement weaknesses of the other partner. One of the partners could not do this alone.

- **Less risk** – forming the alliance reduces the risk of the venture.

- **Co-operative spirit** – both companies must want to do this and be willing to co-operate fully.

- **Clarity of purpose** – results, milestones, methods and resource commitments must be clearly understood.

- **Win-win** – the structure, risks, operations and rewards must be fairly apportioned among members.

Some organisations are trying to retain some of the innovation and flexibility that is characteristic of small companies by forming strategic alliances (closer working relationships) with other organisations. They also play an important role in global strategies, where the organisation lacks a key success factor for some markets.

An example of a strategic alliance is that announced by Uber and Volvo in August 2016 with a view to developing self-driving (or autonomous) vehicles. Volvo agreed to develop and share base vehicle technology and Uber would develop and add its own self-driving technology. Both companies committed a combined US$300m to the alliance, and this was then taken further when Uber agreed to buy 24,000 vehicles from Volvo in late 2017, Volvo's biggest corporate sale to date.

Franchising

The purchase of the right to exploit a business brand in return for a capital sum and a share of profits or turnover.

- The franchisee pays the franchisor an initial capital sum and thereafter the franchisee pays the franchisor a share of profits or royalties.

- The franchisor provides marketing, research and development, advice and support.

- The franchisor normally provides the goods for resale.

- The franchisor imposes strict rules and control to protect its brand and reputation.

- The franchisee buys into a successful formula, so risk is much lower.

- The franchisor gains capital as the number of franchisees grows.

- The franchisor's head office can stay small as there is considerable delegation/decentralisation to the franchisees.

A classic example of franchising is McDonalds. Within the UK, for example, around half of all McDonalds restaurants are franchises.

Licensing

The right to exploit an invention or resource in return for a share of proceeds. Licensing differs from a franchise because there will be little central support.

In the UK, many beers such as Heineken and Fosters were 'brewed under licence' in the UK for many years, with the original companies that developed the beers simply taking a share of the proceeds from the local brewers.

Outsourcing

Outsourcing means contracting out aspects of the work of the organisation, previously done in-house, to specialist providers. Almost any activity can be outsourced – examples include information technology or payroll.

Mobile telecommunications company O2 has recently announced plans to outsource its customer contact centres in the UK.

The public sector may also undertake outsourcing. For example, in 2013 Barnet Council in London announced plans to outsource much of its corporate procurement, IT and HR services to Capita – a private sector company.

Test your understanding 12

H Ltd wishes to rapidly expand its popular chain of retail stores, but does not have the capital needed to do so. It has decided to consider joint development methods in order to aid its growth, but H Ltd's owner T is uncertain about which method to use.

T is unwilling to allow any other individual or organisation to have significant influence over H's strategic operations as he is used to having the final say over all major decisions within the company.

T wishes to avoid any damage to H's brand name. As such, he wants staff to continue to be trained centrally, as well as all fixtures, fittings and inventory to be purchased from authorised suppliers only.

Which ONE of the following methods of joint development would be most appropriate for H Ltd?

A   Licensing

B   Franchising

C   Joint venture

D   Strategic alliance

Test your understanding 13 – (integration question)

Which of licensing, joint venture, strategic alliance and franchising might be the most suitable for the following circumstances?

(1) A company has invented a uniquely good ice cream and wants to set up an international chain of strongly branded outlets.

(2) Oil companies are under political pressure to develop alternative, renewable energy sources.

(3) A beer manufacturer wants to move from their existing domestic market into international sales.

10 Divestment

May occur because:

- The SBU no longer fits with the existing group. The company may wish to focus on core competences.

- The SBU may be too small and not warrant the management attention given to it.

- Selling the SBU as a going concern may be a cheaper alternative to putting it into liquidation if redundancy and wind-up costs are considered.

- The parent company may need to improve its liquidity position.

- There may be a belief that the individual parts of the business are worth more than the whole when shares are selling at less than their potential value, e.g. ICI's demerger of its bio-sciences business, later called Zeneca.

- An MBO (management buy out) is one way a divestment can occur.

11 International growth

When deciding whether to expand abroad, a business has several possible strategies that it can adopt:

- **Exporting strategy** – the firm sells products made in its home country to buyers abroad. This often starts with the receipt of a chance order or perhaps poor sales at home force the business to export or collapse.

- **Overseas manufacture** – the firm may either manufacture its products in a foreign country and then either import them back to its home country or sell them abroad. Either way, the firm is involved in direct foreign investment because it is purchasing capital assets in another country. For example, Nissan Motors is a Japanese company, but operates plants to build its motor vehicles across the world, including North-East England.

- **Multinational** – these firms co-ordinate their value-adding activities across national boundaries. For example, a multinational car manufacturer will have engine plants in one country, car body plants in another and electrics in a third. Production capacity is often duplicated around the world.

- **Transnational** – these are 'nation-less' firms that have no 'home' country. Employees and facilities are treated identically, regardless of where they are in the world. The company may be listed on several national stock exchanges. This is often considered to be (currently) largely theoretical.

When deciding between which approach to take if expanding abroad, consideration should be given to the following points:

- **Exposure to risk** – both foreign exchange risk and political risk.

- **Need for capital investment** – this will be lower if an exporting strategy is used.

- **Customer relationships** – given the distance between the manufacturer and its foreign consumers, this can be hard to maintain in an exporting strategy.

- **Transportation costs** – manufacturing at a distance from your target market will increase the cost of getting the units to them.

- **Ethical issues** – if operating in countries with less developed labour laws, should the company take advantage of this to keep costs low?

- **Cultural issues** – managing operations in foreign countries can be difficult due to differences in language and customs. This can also make advertising and operational control difficult.

Test your understanding 14

YH operates a large number of food production facilities, based in country N. In particular, YH's operations focus on the growing and harvesting of soft fruit. YH then sorts and grades the fruit, before shipping it to retailers, such as large supermarkets.

YH has struggled to find the amount of farmland it needs in order to expand its production in its home country. In recent years, therefore, YH has been buying farmland and facilities in several new countries around the world. This has allowed it to expand its sales into a number of new geographical markets and grow its business.

This business model has been so successful that a significant majority of YH's fruit is now grown abroad, with some of it even being brought back into country N to meet demand from YH's customers.

> Which ONE of the following options is the best match to the international growth strategy being adopted by YH?
>
> A   Transnational
>
> B   Exporting
>
> C   Multinational
>
> D   Overseas manufacture

12   Evaluating strategies – making a strategic choice

So far in this chapter we have looked at a number of models which provide the company with different options for strategies. Management can then select the strategy that they believe is most appropriate for the organisation – for example if following Porter's generic strategies, managers may decide that a cost leadership approach would be the best strategy to adopt.

This raises a very important question – **how do managers know whether a particular strategy should be adopted by the organisation?**

Strategies need to have 'strategic fit' with their environment if they are to be effective. This 'fit' will be with both their internal and external environments and so the ability to assess viability relies very much on the reliability of the position audit.

Strategic options will be generated by various stakeholder groups (and by use of the various models discussed earlier in this chapter) and debate/discussion will need to follow to assess the viability of each option and make a final selection.

The final selection will be a function of the following:

(1)   Relative stakeholder power and their personal characteristics

(2)   information available and perceived reliability

(3)   historical experience

(4)   presentation of options – manner

(5)   other corporate experiences

(6)   expectations for the future

(7)   objectives ordering and perceived ordering – there will be a significant political involvement at this stage.

Viability – a basic approach

According to Johnson and Scholes, potential strategies can be evaluated against the following three criteria:

- **Suitability** is concerned with whether the strategy addresses the circumstances in which an organisation is operating – its strategic position.

- **Feasibility** is concerned with whether the strategy could be made to work in practice and as such looks at more detailed practicalities of strategic capability.

- **Acceptability** is concerned with the expected performance outcomes (such as return or risk) of a strategy and the extent to which these would be in line with the expectations of stakeholders.

 For a strategy to be accepted, it must meet all three of these criteria.

Suitability

Is the proposed strategy a suitable response to environmental events and trends? Do we have **strategic fit**? You should consider whether the proposed course of action fits with the existing position. Will it cause any problems elsewhere in the company?

(1) Will it take advantage of **opportunities?**

(2) Will it build on our **strengths?**

(3) Will it help us meet our **mission and objectives?**

(4) How will new products fit with existing ones? Is the new **portfolio balanced?**

Use within Ansoff's matrix

A market development strategy would 'fit' where:

- Channels of distribution are available

- a business has a strong marketing presence

- products are superior to competitors

- an unsaturated markets exist

- spare production capacity exists

- economies of scale are possible.

A product development strategy would 'fit' where:

- brand reputation is high

- the brand is transportable

- strong research capabilities exist.

A market penetration strategy would 'fit' where:

- current markets are not saturated
- present customers will rebuy
- competitors are weak
- spare production capacity exists.

A consolidation strategy would 'fit' where:

- there is a lack of funding
- owners do not want to grow
- human resources not available
- any kind of restraining factor exists.

A diversification strategy would 'fit' where:

- there is a strong brand presence
- significant resources are available to enable the development of new competencies
- market research base is reliable and competent.

Example

Gucci sought growth in sales and so expanded into lower-priced goods and stretched its brand. It also pushed its products in department stores and duty-free channels. It let its name appear on many licensed products such as watches and perfumes.

Sales soared – the company was very happy!

But it soon found that sales in its traditional high-priced, high-margin segment were plummeting as its traditional buyers became disillusioned by the fact that Gucci was now worn by many people thus removing the exclusivity of the product.

Gucci's strategy was not suitable.

Feasibility

Can the necessary resources and competencies be obtained and the required changes be implemented? Any new strategy will require change of some kind and this is likely to meet resistance from some quarters. We will need to question whether the company concerned has the strategic capability to pursue the course of action concerned.

So the key questions revolve around:

(1)   Resources – basic and unique.

(2)   Competences – threshold and core.

(3)   Implementation issues with regard to dealing with strategic change.

Considerations should cover:

- Cultural change required and realism of change
- timescales
- potential resistance
- raw materials availability
- human resources availability
- distribution channel access
- marketing requirements
- IT requirements and skills
- finance:
    - How much is needed?
    - Where will it come from?
    - What options exist?
    - What will the impact be on our financial position and performance?

Don't forget the basic analysis relating to identifying the threshold and core competencies. Are there any sources of competitive advantage or disadvantage?

Acceptability

Any proposed strategy will need to be acceptable to the stakeholders of the organisation, both in terms of "returns" and risk.

All stakeholders will need to be considered relative to their power – the more powerful the stakeholder group, the greater the influence they will have and the more the strategist will have to consider their views.

Some areas for consideration:

- A new strategy usually involves some internal changes and due consideration will need to be given to the **staff** who may have to confront different work practices. Resistance is likely.

- **Financiers** often have required rates of return and liquidity positions.

- **Owners** may well have non-financial requirements of their investment.

    They may prefer to have less risk and accept a lower reward as the inevitable cost. They could require that all actions conform to their cultural expectations, e.g. Anita Roddick at the Body Shop.

- **Customers, consumers and suppliers** may also have required standards that must be met by the company.

- Local and national **governments** may have some concerns about any strategic proposals with regard to legality and political implications.

- Don't forget the **public** and their ability to form into 'pressure groups'. Ethical considerations may need to be included in the evaluation.

Evaluating "acceptability" will often involve quantitative analysis such as NPV calculations. However, it must be noted that conventional NPV analysis tends to undervalue projects with significant future flexibility. Real option theory, covered in more detail in the F3 paper, is an attempt to incorporate such flexibility into a "strategic NPV".

Tests of a winning strategy

The SAF (suitability, acceptability, feasibility) approach is very useful but other considerations have been added which are worthy of note.

The first is referred to as the **competitive advantage** test and raises the questions:

- What is it?

- How long can it last?

The second question highlights that competitive advantage may not be sustainable, in other words does the **performance measurement** system show predicted improvement?

Thompson poses this strategic management principle:

'The more a strategy fits the enterprise's external and internal situation, builds sustainable competitive advantage and improves company performance, the more it qualifies as a winner.'

Strategy evaluation – the role of the management accountant

Making strategic decisions

Strategic options can be evaluated using the suitability, feasibility, acceptability framework.

The strategic management accountant will contribute to the acceptability and feasibility aspects in particular:

Aspect	Key concerns	Typical financial analysis
Acceptability	Returns to stakeholders	• Cash flow forecasts to ensure dividend growth requirements can be met dividend growth requirements can be met • NPV analysis • ROCE • Valuation of real options • Shareholder value analysis • Economic value added • Cost/benefit analysis • Ratio analysis (e.g. dividend yield, growth)
	Risk	• Sensitivity • Break-even • Ratio analysis (e.g. gearing, dividend cover) • Expected values
Feasibility	Resources	• Cash flow forecast to identify funding needs • Budgeting resource requirements • Ability to raise finance needed • Working capital implications • Foreign exchange implications

Test your understanding 15

LL is a company that makes and sells clothing made out of wool. It has been having problems manufacturing sufficient garments for its customers for several years as demand has increased significantly. LL's current wool spinning process has been identified as a bottleneck process.

It is considering the purchase of an automated spinning machine that it believes will significantly improve the speed of its manufacturing process. In addition it will allow LL to lay off around fifty members of staff (who are heavily unionised).

The machine will cost around $5m. LL does not have this cash available, but believes that it will be able to raise these funds from its investors.

LL will only purchase the machine if it is:

(i)   suitable

(ii)   acceptable; AND

(iii)   feasible

From the information given above, which ONE of these three criteria does the acquisition of the machine meet?

A   Suitable and acceptable only

B   Suitable only

C   Acceptable and feasible only

D   Suitable and feasible only

Test your understanding 16

When evaluating the acceptability of a new strategy, which ONE of the following analysis tools would be the most useful?

A   BCG matrix

B   Porter's five forces

C   Mendelow's matrix

D   Porter's value chain

Test your understanding 17 – (Integration question)

You work for Blueberry – a quoted resort hotel chain based in Europe.

The industry

The hotel industry is a truly global business characterised by the following:

- Increasing competition.

- An increasing emphasis on customer service with higher standards being demanded.

- In particular the range of facilities, especially spas, is becoming more important as a differentiating factor.

Performance

- Blueberry offers services at the luxury end of the market only, based on a strong brand and prestigious hotels – although its reputation has become tarnished over the last five years due to variable customer satisfaction levels.

- Despite a reputation for having the most prestigious coastal resort hotels along the Mediterranean in 20X0, Blueberry was loss-making in the financial years 20X4/5 and 20X5/6.

- To some extent this situation has been turned around in 20X6/7 with an operating profit of €11 million. However, shareholders are putting the board under pressure to increase profits and dividends further.

- Management have responded to this by setting out an ambitious plan to upgrade hotel facilities throughout the company and move more upmarket. The bulk of the finance is planned to come from retained profits as Blueberry has historically kept its financial gearing low.

Acquisition opportunity

Your manager has arrived in the office and has said the following:

'I've just been told that the Board of Blueberry have been approached by the owner of 'The Villa d'Oeste', a luxury hotel on the shores of Lake Como in Italy, who is considering selling it. The hotel has an international reputation with world-class spa facilities and generates revenue throughout most of the year due to Lake Como's mild micro-climate. The asking price will be approximately €50m. Please spend the next 15 minutes writing some brief notes of issues we should take into account when evaluating the purchase.'

Required:

Draft the notes for your manager.

(15 minutes)

Test your understanding 18 – GGG – (Case style)

You are L. Carter, a strategic management account working for HF&H – a large accountancy practise. One of HF&H's clients is GGG. A partner in HF&H has left the following note on your desk:

Note

Hi L,

I'm going to be meeting several key managers from GGG shortly and I need you to prepare some briefing notes for me. I've left you a briefing document giving you some background information about the company.

Once you've familiarised yourself with the briefing document, please prepare some notes, which need to include the following:

- Analyse the opportunities available to GGG, using Ansoff's strategic directional growth vector matrix.

- Evaluate the opportunities available to GGG in each of the four areas of the Ansoff strategic directional growth vector matrix using Johnson, Scholes and Whittington's Suitability, Acceptability and Feasibility framework.

- Recommend, with your justifications, which strategic directions, as set out in Ansoff's strategic directional growth vector matrix, would be most appropriate for GGG to follow.

I'm meeting the clients in 45 minutes, so please have the notes ready by then.

Thanks

P.

Briefing document – GGG

GGG is a privately owned unlisted company which runs 20 residential care homes for the elderly. A residential care home for the elderly is a building where a number of older people live and receive care (that is, their physical needs are provided for), normally on a full-time basis. The elderly residents may pay the care home fees themselves or they may be paid by their relatives or by the local government authority.

The elderly residents of GGG's care homes are all capable of making decisions for themselves. All of GGG's care homes are located in and around two cities both located in the south of country X. GGG employs around 400 staff in the care homes, some of whom work part-time, and a small team of highly experienced administrators. GGG's care homes all have modern facilities and their staff are highly trained and dedicated. GGG has always been a profitable business, even though its care homes normally have a small amount of spare capacity. GGG has approximately 25% market share in the south of country X. The remainder of the market is shared by a small number of local government funded and operated care homes and some other small private businesses.

Due to the rising costs of operating care homes as a result of increased regulation and the general economic environment, a number of small privately owned care homes in the region have recently closed. The owners of some other privately owned care homes are considering closing or selling them. GGG is also aware that this trend is occurring nationally across country X.

A national shift in the demographics of the population in the last 30 years has resulted in a significant rise in the proportion of elderly members of society. Added to this, the increased social movement of families has resulted in an increasing demand for care home places for the elderly. GGG undertakes limited advertising, relying more on word-of-mouth recommendations and referrals from local hospitals and doctors to obtain its customers.

The prices charged to care home residents by the local government authority run care homes are lower than those charged by GGG, due to central government subsidies. However, the Managing Director of GGG is confident that the services and facilities provided by GGG are superior to those offered by the local government funded care homes.

Although GGG currently offers only full-time care for its elderly residents, there is a growing need for the market to offer 'relief care' packages. This is where elderly people, who do not normally live in residential care homes, could use any of the 20 care homes' facilities for short periods of time (normally 1 week), in order to enable their normal carers (usually family members) to take holidays or rest periods.

A number of GGG's elderly residents are often referred to local hospitals by their doctors for treatments and therapies. Many of GGG's staff are fully qualified nurses and these treatments and therapies could be undertaken by the staff of GGG in each of its care homes. These hospital visits for treatments and therapies can be disruptive and upsetting for residents who often prefer to remain in GGG's care homes and be cared for by staff with whom they are familiar. However, if GGG were to offer these additional facilities within its care homes it will need investment in training and new facilities.

Required:

Prepare the notes as requested in the note from P.

13   Summary

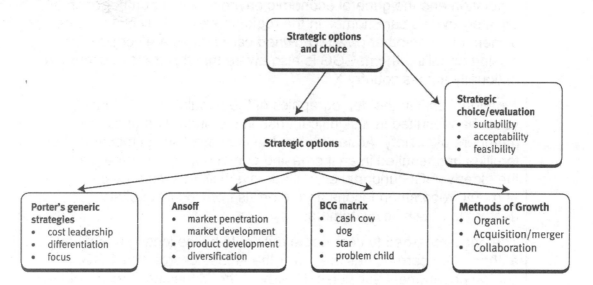

Test your understanding answers

Test your understanding 1

The correct answer is D

W is currently trying to gain competitive advantage by using its brand name to differentiate it from its rivals.

Test your understanding 2

The correct answer is D

Y appears to be stuck in the middle.

Its size prevents it from achieving the economies of scale of its larger rivals, meaning that cost-leadership appears unlikely.

The product that Y currently produces seems to be fairly generic and Y seems to lack the skills to do anything different. Note that Y's current customers seem to mainly be interested in price, so a differentiation strategy would be difficult to undertake here.

Finally, there seems to only be one niche market that Y has identified – that of home workers. However this is a relatively small part of the market and it appears to be well served by the several existing companies.

Overall, this is a very difficult market for Y as it will find it difficult to find a way to out-compete its rivals.

Test your understanding 3 – AVA – (Case style)

Report

To: FD

From: H. Pimm

Date: 16/09/XX

Title: Evaluation of AVA first class offering

Introduction

Porter argued that organisations could adopt one of three main strategies in order to gain competitive advantage – focus, differentiation and cost leadership. This report will use Porter's model to analyse the first class strategy at AVA.

Current strategy in AVA

AVA has adopted a classic cost leadership approach. It has removed a number of 'extras' from the service it provides to customers – such as excess leg room, direct customer service and seat reservations.

AVA has done this in order to keep its costs low. These savings can then be passed onto the customer in the form of low ticket prices, driving demand and enabling AVA to outcompete its rivals.

Cost leadership requires the price elasticity of the market to be high – in other words if AVA offers a low price for its product it needs to be able to generate a high volume of sales. This will allow it to cover its high fixed costs in spite of the relatively low contribution made by each ticket sale.

As the economy in country L has returned to growth, it is likely that customers will have more disposable income and therefore be willing to spend more money on flights with additional features – such as increased leg room. AVA has started to see the effect of this as its passenger numbers start to fall.

First class strategy in AVA

AVA's new approach is to offer a section of 'first class' seats to customers at the front of each airplane which provide more leg room and free food and drink, as well as better customer service.

This seems to be an attempt to move into a differentiation approach, where AVA will be starting to charge a premium for some of its flights due to additional features that wealthier clients may value.

For this to work, AVA must be able to offer a real alternative to the existing first class airline services – either through the actual services offered to its customers or through its brand name and image.

Evaluation of the proposal

Expansion into the first class market could provide a limited amount of diversification for AVA. Its low cost approach would seem to be struggling as customers are able to afford better quality flights and this problem is likely to continue as the economy grows.

In addition, the move into first class flights would help to improve AVA's profitability as first class tickets command higher margins than AVA's standard tickets.

However, there are a number of practical problems with the proposals.

Firstly, AVA may be struggling to attract more affluent customers as the new first class model is inconsistent with its brand image. AVA has a poor reputation in the market for comfort and reliability – things that are likely to strongly appeal to first class customers.

In addition, the first class market is already dominated by several major airlines that have experience of catering to the needs of this market segment. Unless AVA is able to find some way of truly differentiating its product from these rivals, it is unlikely that it will ever outperform them in the market.

It is worth noting that attempting to operate both differentiated and cost leadership approaches is likely to cause the organisation considerable cultural problems – staff may find it difficult to offer an excellent service to some customers but not others.

Conclusion

Overall by proceeding with its first class strategy, AVA risks becoming 'stuck in the middle' and failing to compete effectively within the market. It may therefore wish to consider an alternative plan which is more in keeping with its current strategy.

Test your understanding 4

The correct answer is D

By definition.

Test your understanding 5

The correct answer is C

HUF is trying to sell more of its existing product lines (and is therefore not adopting a product development strategy) to its existing customers. Note that HUF is continuing to use radio advertising, indicating that it is not trying to attract new market segments (and is therefore not adopting a market development strategy).

If HUF was diversifying, it would be offering new products to new markets, which is clearly not happening in the scenario.

Test your understanding 6 – (Integration question)

- **Pricewatch** – market penetration – building sales from existing customer base via lower prices (cost leadership).

- **Esso minimarkets** – product development – addressing customer bases who already use Esso outlets. Could also be categorised as market development if minimarkets are effectively acting as local ('corner') shops.

- **Distribution to China** – market development – taking existing products/technologies and selling them to a new market.

- **Acquisitions** – diversification – this involves Esso moving into completely new markets/industries.

Test your understanding 7

The correct answers are C, D and F

Operating in several unrelated markets diversifies the risk of the organisation, reducing the variability in its returns. Note that this is unlikely to be of benefit to institutional investors, who will likely already hold a diversified portfolio of shares.

If the company believes that its existing brand name will also be recognised in its new venture (or it can 'stretch' its brand), this may increase the likelihood of a diversification strategy being adopted.

Finally, a diversification strategy is useful if the organisation's existing markets are saturated. Diversification may be the only way for the organisation to continue to grow.

Test your understanding 8 – C – (Case style)

(i) **Ansoff's matrix**

Ansoff identified four main growth strategies in his matrix, depending on whether new or existing products were being offered to new or existing markets.

New products in C's coffee shops

While the products that the FD is suggesting, such as wine and ice-cream, are food and drink – like C's current products – they represent a significant departure from C's current image of a 'coffee-shop'. They should therefore be classed as new products.

The FD seems to feel that C will manage to grow its profits due to the higher margins achieved on these new items, rather than due to any significant increase in volume. This would seem to indicate that C will be relying on its existing customers.

C would therefore be attempting to sell new products to our existing customers. In Ansoff's matrix, this would be called product development.

Expansion into new countries

Expansion abroad will clearly help C to break into new markets and attract a whole new set off customers. Given the success of the current product range, the MD is suggesting that no changes are made when opening up foreign stores.

Overall, C would be attempting to sell its existing products to a new market – an approach that Ansoff called market development.

Online music

This is a completely new business area for C. It would involve selling music – a completely different range of products to its current offering.

In addition, it is likely to appeal to a totally new range of customers – especially as it will involve trading online, which does not appear to be something that C currently does.

C will therefore be selling new products to new markets – which Ansoff termed diversification. In this case, it would appear to be unrelated or conglomerate diversification.

(ii) **Alternative strategy**

The only strategy suggested by Ansoff that has not been suggested by the directors would involve C attempting to sell more of its existing products to its current market.

This is referred to by Ansoff as market penetration.

Application to C

C will need to look for ways to increase its market share. This may be difficult given the competitive nature of the market it operates in and the fact that its rivals offer similar products to it at a similar price.

C does achieve high margins on its products. This could give it scope to consider lowering its prices – especially as it is currently more expensive than its competitors. This may be attractive to customers in the current economic downturn and could encourage customers to 'defect' from rival coffee chains.

It should be noted that if C does lower its prices, this could have a detrimental effect on the perceived quality of its products and services by customers.

Alternatively, C could attempt to make use of its unique selling point – good quality service. This has made it a market leader in country U and stressing this in its advertising could also grow its market share further.

(iii) **Proposed acquisition of online music store**

As mentioned earlier, this is an example of unrelated or conglomerate diversification. This could have several advantages and disadvantages for C.

Advantages:

Saturated current market – the coffee market appears to be saturated in country U. In addition, many of U's competitors have already expanded into the countries around country U, indicating they may also be highly competitive already. C may find it difficult to achieve future growth if it stays within its current market.

Spreading of risk – by operating in two unrelated markets, C will be spreading its risk. Online music sales have performed well over the last year in country U – in spite of the poor economic climate which has seen a fall in the amount spent on coffee. By operating in both markets, C may be able to enjoy more stable returns.

Surplus cash – the acquisition of the music store would allow C to get a return on the surplus cash it currently holds. This may be seen favourably by investors.

Disadvantages:

Increased risk

C is planning to enter a new market that is has no experience of. It currently does not appear to have an online presence, meaning that it may well not know how to best run the online music store once it has been purchased.

No economies of scale

By expanding into the online music industry, C is unlikely to enjoy significant synergies.

In fact, the opposite may well be true. C's managers may find that operating such an unfamiliar business takes up a significant proportion of their time. This may have a negative effect on C's core coffee shop business.

Brand Damage

An unsuccessful venture into the online music industry could affect the brand of "C" which in should a highly competitive industry could have severe consequences.

Lack of a clear generic strategy

Using Porters understanding of strategic thinking C is clearly a differentiator – Entering into new industries such as online music could negatively affect this clear generic strategy.

Shareholder reaction

Shareholders often dislike unrelated diversification as it often has few benefits to them. If C's shareholders had wished to spread their risk, they could simply invest some of their money in the shares of a company in a different industry to C.

Test your understanding 9

Stars	Question marks
Wallop	
Cash cows	**Dogs**
Bang	Whizz
	Pop

Test your understanding 10

The correct answer is C

H1 appears to be a dog, suggesting a divestment strategy would be appropriate.

E2 and B3 are question marks. These need to be divested or built on. Given the attractive nature of the market for these products, O may wish to consider investing heavily to try and increase its market share.

Y4 is a star. It is a market leader in a growing market. O needs to adopt a holding strategy, defending its market share and maintaining its position as a star until the market slows and Y4 becomes a cash cow.

Test your understanding 11 – GC – (Case style)

Part (a)

- **Brick manufacturer** – dog
- **Parcel service** – dog
- **Food manufacturer** – cash cow, maybe dropping from star. Largely depends upon the current growth rate
- **Painting and decorating** – problem child. High growth at present but forecast to decline. Opportunity to turn this into a star
- **Software development company** – star

(May consider a diagram with SBUs located on the matrix.)

Representations in all sectors of the matrix with two dogs present. May need to question what to do with the problem child and the dogs. Dogs may need to be divested or harvested. Problem child needs management attention to stop it becoming a dog.

Food manufacturer (cash cow) will generate cash flows that can be used to fund the development of the star software company. Little need for strategic investment will see the cash surpluses rising.

Star will need investing in and penetration strategies will be appropriate. Branding strategies may be initiated with a view to future defence when star becomes the cash cow. Current cash cow will need defending.

SBUs will each need different business strategies as positions vary. Levels of competition and demand sophistication will vary across the SBU marketplaces and the research and information systems will become ever more important.

Part (b)

Considerations

Divest dogs – gets rid of the poor products quickly. But may not be poor performers! May be better to Harvest instead – slow decline leads to less damage elsewhere within the group in terms of bad publicity.

Niche dogs – a deliberate strategy to take the SBU into a specialist marketplace by aiming at a specific market segment and seek to earn high return from this focused approach.

Market development for dogs and problem children – aiming to expand market share and improve value via improved profitability.

Product development for the cash cow as a form of defensive strategy to extend the life cycle and the subsequent cash flows – but will the cash cow really be cash generative? Will it not need to reinvest to maintain threshold competence in the market place?

Market penetration for the star – the market is expanding with many new users and strategies should be aimed at building market share.

Aim to develop **synergy*** within the group:

- Possible **brand stretching** – taking the good reputation and respect from one brand name and attach it to other products in the form of either aggressive or defensive strategy, e.g. use a link from the food manufacturing to painting and decorating and/or software development.

- Possible sharing of **distribution channels** – there seems to be little scope for this given the diverse nature of the product portfolio.

- Possible use of **central resources** – scope here for central marketing function if a common linkage could be found (such as a brand). HR and IT functions offer scope for value added via cost savings on the functions.

McKinsey approach

- Manage investor relations
- turnaround strategies at SBU level
- outsourcing
- benchmarking
- cost reduction programmes
- manage structure of portfolio via acquisition, divestment and demerger
- consider and deploy value adding "group" activities such as brand stretching.

* The idea that combining certain operations/functions will produce a benefit in numerical terms that will be greater than the sum of the individual parts. The creation of 'excess value' from combination – what some refer to as '2 + 2 = 5'

Test your understanding 12

The correct answer is B

T has two major requirements – consistency with the existing H stores and the need to retain control of H and its operations.

Licensing another organisation to trade as H would not allow T to maintain control over the day to day operations of the new stores.

Strategic alliances and joint ventures, by their nature, would require T to form partnerships with third party organisations who would work together (or set up a jointly owned company) to operate the new H stores. Again, this would lead to H losing control and being forced to compromise with the other organisation(s) he had entered an alliance with.

Franchising would allow H to control many of the day to day operations of the new stores and would also enable him to still make the key strategic decisions for the organisation. The franchisee would have to work within the pre-set guidelines in the franchise agreement, which may include central training of staff and supplier selection.

Test your understanding 13 – (integration question)

(1)   A franchise arrangement would work well here. There is more than just manufacturing involved – there is the whole retail offering, and entering into franchise agreements would be a quick, effective way of expanding.

(2)   Unless the oil companies felt that, because of their size, there was no need for joint research, development, marketing and lobbying, a strategic alliance of some sort could be useful. Research costs and findings could be shared. Together they could bring powerful pressure to bear on governments to, for example, allow more generous time scales for implementation of the new technology. Alternatively, the new energy technology could be developed within a joint venture organisation.

(3)   Almost certainly, this company would expand by licensing local brewing companies to make and distribute its product.

Test your understanding 14

The correct answer is D

YH is currently manufacturing (or growing) the bulk of its products overseas to meet demand, with some of this produce even finding its way back to country N. This would suggest an overseas manufacture strategy.

YH does grow some of its fruit in its home country, but given that this is a minority of its goods, it cannot be convincingly matched to an exporting strategy.

As YH does not obviously co-ordinate value adding activities between its overseas facilities (they are all similar growing and processing facilities in each country) it is not a multinational. The fact that it still has a home country in which it is based would indicate that it is not a transnational.

Test your understanding 15

The correct answer is D

The purchase appears to be suitable as it will help the company deal with the problems it is facing with supplying its customers by removing a major bottleneck.

It will also be feasible as the company has the ability to raise the cash needed to complete the purchase.

However, it is unlikely to be acceptable to employees due to the reduction in staff numbers it will cause. This is likely to be a problem for LL as employees are heavily unionised and could act collectively to resist the layoffs.

Test your understanding 16

The correct answer is C

Acceptability looks at the reaction of key stakeholders to the proposed strategy. Mendelow's matrix would be the most appropriate way of identifying these stakeholders as well as their relative interest and power.

Test your understanding 17 – (Integration question)

Suitability

- The hotel market is becoming increasingly more competitive, so it might make more sense for Blueberry to try to diversify its activities more.

- Furthermore, the acquisition does not address Blueberry's underlying problems of inconsistent customer service levels.

- On the other hand, the Villa d'Oeste already has a world class spa facility and would fit well into Blueberry's current strategy of moving more 'upscale'.

- Also the goodwill attached to the Villa's reputation could enhance Blueberry's image, depending on branding decisions.

Feasibility

- Financing the acquisition could prove problematic:

- Debt finance: Historically the Board have chosen to keep Blueberry's financial gearing level relatively low. Blueberry's existing clientele of shareholders may thus resist any major increase in gearing.

- Equity finance: Given losses in two out of the last three years, Blueberry may struggle to raise the purchase price via a rights issue.

Acceptability

- Growth by acquisition is generally quicker than organic growth, thus satisfying institutional shareholders' desire to see growth in revenues and dividends.

- Further work is needed to assess whether the €50m asking price is acceptable.

- Buying another hotel should enable Blueberry to gain additional economies of scale with respect to insurance, staff costs such as pensions and purchasing economies on drinks. This should boost margins and profitability further.

- The new hotel would fit well into Blueberry's existing portfolio of hotels, for example, by having significant cash inflows throughout the year in contrast to Blueberry's highly seasonal business, thus reducing the overall level of risk.

Preliminary recommendations

- The opportunity to acquire the Villa d'Oeste should be rejected on the grounds that financing the acquisition would be problematic at present.

- Blueberry should instead focus on improving facilities and quality in existing hotels before looking to expand through acquisition.

Test your understanding 18 – GGG – (Case style)

Briefing notes

Ansoff

GGG could utilise the Ansoff growth vector matrix to analyse the possible future strategic directions it could follow.

Market penetration

GGG could attempt to increase its market share with its existing services to its current market or region. The market is a growing one; with the change in demographics, therefore, market penetration is a real option for GGG. As it currently has 25% of its region's market with the rest fragmented between local government run and privately owned care homes, there is potential for GGG to undertake promotional activities in order to obtain business from these competitors. In particular, the sale and closure of a number of the privately run care homes could be an opportunity to obtain a greater share of the market through targeting these care homes customers. GGG may have to consider its pricing strategies however, as its prices may well be higher than its competitors. It may need to consider a reduction of prices or some form of discounted offer to attract customers who are currently paying less than they would be charged in GGG's care homes.

Product Development

GGG could attempt to offer new services to its existing market or region.

Within the scenario, there is mention of a new 'relief package' facility that is becoming popular with customers. GGG could consider offering its facilities for customers within its region for this new service. This would have to be investigated further to ensure that GGG has the capacity and facilities to offer such a service. If there is clearly a growing need for this type of package, then GGG could try to gain early market entry in order to gain early mover advantage. The issue for GGG is likely to be capacity constraints and the need to weigh up the benefits and costs of the option against those of offering continued longer term care to its residents.

In addition, the additional services that could be offered by the qualified staff and nurses of GGG to its patients as an alternative to referral to hospitals could be a form of product development. However, this is likely to involve investment in re-training and facilities.

Market Development

GGG could attempt to increase its revenues by offering its current services to new customers or at a different geographical location. One option would be to consider moving into another geographical region in its own country to offer its services to the elderly. This is a possibility as the national geographic trend suggests increasing demand nationally for elderly care. However, this is a riskier strategy as GGG currently has no experience of its competitive environment outside its own region and the competitive market may be very different. In addition, GGG would require heavy investment in facilities outside of the region. However, the market conditions are likely to be the same as in its own region and, therefore, it could consider buying or merging with another private care home outside of its current region. However, GGG must consider the rising costs of running care homes and the consequent need for it to price its services accordingly.

Diversification

GGG could consider offering new services to new customers. For example, the trained staff and nurses could be used to offer other nursing and rehabilitation services to individual customers, other care homes or to GP surgeries. These could be offered within the facilities of GGG or could be offered on site in customers' homes.

GGG's administrators are also highly experienced and GGG could consider utilising their experience to offer consultancy and management services to other care homes which might consider outsourcing their management and administration function to GGG.

Evaluation of opportunities

According to the Johnson, Scholes and Whittington approach, an organisation's potential strategies can be evaluated against the following criteria:

- Suitability: whether a strategy fits with the organisation's operations and its strategic position.

- Acceptability: whether a strategy fits with the expectations of the stakeholders.

- Feasibility: whether the strategy can be implemented, taking into consideration practical considerations such as time, cost and capabilities.

GGG must consider if the proposed strategy is suitable to respond to environmental events and opportunities and whether it fits with the current strategic position. It would need to consider whether it had the right level of resources and competences. It would also have to consider its key stakeholders in terms of both risk and return. It is important to note that GGG must also consider 'who' their customers are, as customers will include not only the actual residents of the care home but also their families or their current carers. Reviewing each of the strategies identified in the Ansoff matrix, GGG should consider:

Market penetration

Suitability: This strategy would appear suitable as GGG has spare capacity and also this option builds upon GGG's current expertise so there is clear strategic fit.

Acceptability: The key stakeholders such as staff and management are unlikely to be opposed to this strategy as it is a mere development of the current activities of GGG. Existing customers should find it acceptable as long as current standards of operation are not affected if the care homes now take on more customers.

Feasibility: GGG has the resources in terms of capacity and competences to undertake this strategy. However, further growth could mean the need to invest in more facilities if spare capacity limits are exceeded. GGG would also need to consider the costs of advertising.

Product Development

Suitability: This strategy continues to fit with GGG's strategic position and would certainly exploit an obvious market opportunity. It will complement the existing long term care facilities and should help to balance GGG's portfolio. Therefore it is suitable.

Acceptability: Staff may find this strategy unacceptable if it requires additional training or detracts them from the care of GGG's existing long term care customers. Existing customers should be neutral in the decision as long as it does not affect the standard of their care and potential customers are likely to be positive towards the proposal.

Feasibility: Investment in facilities and training may make this option unfeasible but GGG would have to weigh up the long term benefits of building market share through subsequent conversion from short-term care residents into long-term residents and by improving quality of care by providing services in-house rather than necessitating referral to hospital.

Market Development

Suitability: There is certainly a potential for opportunities outside of its current geographical region. The national trend suggests increasing demand nationally for elderly residential care. However, GGG has no experience of its competitive environment outside its own region and the competitive market may be very different. GGG does not know whether its own service would be superior from that offered by competitors.

Acceptability: Staff and managers may not find this strategy acceptable as it might affect their own workloads, location and roles. However, current customers are likely to be neutral to the proposal.

Feasibility: Can GGG find the right facilities or a suitable partner to merge with or acquire? Costs of relocation of some staff or recruitment and training would need to be carefully considered. There might be some resistance from staff and competitors. Also, GGG needs to consider timescales and possible local Government resistance. Therefore, market development may not be feasible.

Diversification

Suitability: GGG has the necessary skills to undertake diversification although additional training may be required. In the present climate it would appear that the opportunities for this development may be limited. It would fit with the current activities of GGG and therefore has strategic fit.

Acceptability: The staff may find this acceptable as it would develop their skills and enhance their job roles. Existing customers are also likely to find this acceptable as it would not mean disruption to them assuming the new services do not detract from their own care. However, GPs and hospitals may not find this acceptable as they may not agree that the same level of care can be offered by GGG's staff.

Feasibility: GGG will have to invest heavily in training and facilities which may make this unfeasible. There may also be resistance to this from local GPs and hospitals. Therefore, GGG may find this strategy unfeasible.

Recommendation

In the current market and competitive environment, where GGG is managing to remain profitable despite other similarly businesses failing, the recommended options for GGG would be to follow a market penetration strategy with product development.

The current geographical market clearly has potential for GGG so there is no need for a market development strategy. A market penetration strategy would allow GGG to exploit the current trends and build upon its own strength and reputation. It is also the least risky option in a time when costs are clearly rising. Product development with the care relief packages should also be considered as it has clear potential for GGG to exploit its current spare capacity and to use its expertise to develop a clearly growing market need.

Developing strategic performance management systems

Chapter learning objectives

Lead	Component
C2: Discuss how to generate and develop options	(d) Use various frameworks to generate options
E1: Develop strategic performance management system	(a) Develop detailed action plans
	(b) Communicate action plans
	(c) Monitor implementation
	(d) Align incentives to performance

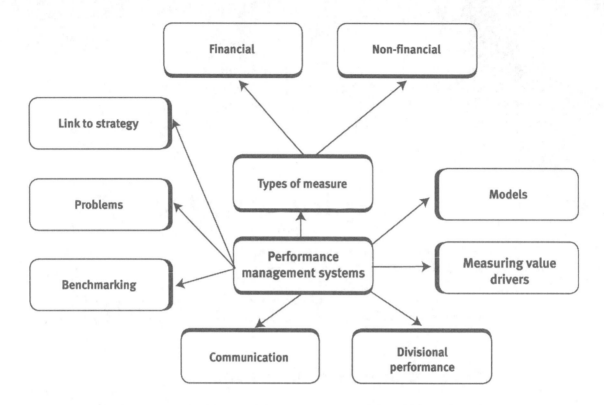

1   Performance management

So far we have looked at how an organisation decides on an appropriate strategy to undertake. The next step is to introduce a process by which the strategy can be properly controlled so that it delivers the benefits to its organisational ecosystem that had been anticipated. Such a control process involves the careful selection and introduction of appropriate **performance measures**.

 Performance measurement is the process of assessing the proficiency with which a reporting entity succeeds, by the economic acquisition of resources and their efficient and effective deployment, in achieving its objectives. Performance measures may be based on non-financial as well as on financial information.

CIMA official terminology

Selecting appropriate performance measures is important for two reasons:

- management must be able to identify whether the strategy is having the desired effect on the organisation's output

- setting performance measures is a way of communicating targets to staff and other key stakeholders, indicating the organisation's priorities. Rewards can be linked to the achievement of these measures.

For example, an organisation may have decided to implement a new strategy to improve the quality of its output. It will want to create a range of performance measures that support this – such as monitoring the number of defective products produced, or the number of customer complaints. This will allow the organisation to see whether its strategy is having the desired effect and is actually improving quality. Management will also be able to set targets for staff in each of these areas, focusing the attention of workers on the need to improve quality.

Setting performance measures is often more difficult than would first be imagined.

For example, is the measure of 'waiting times for patients' a good measure of a hospital's performance? There is much discussion in the media about resources made available to the NHS in the UK and its impact on healthcare services. A shortage of hospital beds might lead to patients waiting a long period of time for a necessary procedure, such as a hip replacement operation. And so much focus is placed on hospital waiting times.

Surely the answer then is to shorten the length of time to perform a procedure (so that more procedures can be carried out each day), and then send the patient home immediately to recuperate in their own bed (so that fewer hospital beds are taken up). This would seem appropriate in one sense, in that one measure of performance is now improved.

However, this would surely have potential negative effects on another means by which the NHS is assessed, the quality of healthcare provided. Procedures being performed more quickly might result in patients not being properly cured. Recovering at home, perhaps without the necessary supervision from healthcare experts, might lead to patients having to move about before they are ready and so injuring themselves again.

Action taken to improve one objective (improve waiting times) has had a negative effect on another, equally important objective (quality of healthcare provided).

The challenge is therefore to be able to design a performance measurement system that can be used in the control process and not prove to be a burden and/or misleading.

How do performance measures control what people do?

In Measuring Business Performance: Why, What, How (1998), Neely suggested that there were four ways in which performance measures could act to control the behaviour of people within the organisation. He referred to these reasons as the 'four CPs'.

Imagine that the managers of a manufacturing business have just informed staff that they will be assessed on the quality of the goods that they produce.

- **Confirm priorities** – the fact that management have chosen to measure and report on quality indicates to workers that this is an area that is important and that needs to be prioritised.

- **Compel progress** – workers will want to ensure that they meet quality targets as failure to do so may adversely affect their pay or career prospects. Remember that measures can be the basis for bonus payments (giving rise to an additional CP not identified by Neely – cash prizes!)

- **Check position** – the management of the business (as well as individual staff members) will be able to monitor progress relating to quality and see whether they are on course to meet their targets or not. If not, action can be taken to improve performance.

- **Communicate position** – measures of production quality can be used by management (and other interested parties, such as quality control organisations, trade associations or even investors) to assess and understand how the organisation is performing.

2   Critical success factors and their link to performance measurement

It is clear that the organisation needs to ensure that its performance measurement system ties into its overall strategy. How can this be accomplished? If our overall strategy is to, for example, become a cost leader in our market in order to outperform our rivals, what do we measure to help us ensure that we are doing this successfully?

One useful way of generating a performance measurement system for the organisation is to identify the critical success factors (CSFs) that are determined by our strategy. CSFs were discussed in detail in chapter 5.

Critical success factors are the limited number of areas in which results, if they are satisfactory, will ensure successful competitive performance for the organisation.

CSFs tie in to the organisation's overall strategy. For example, if our strategy is cost leadership, our CSFs could include:

- lower labour costs than rivals

- efficient production.

These CSFs would then be translated into key performance indicators (KPIs) – which are specific, measured targets that can be used to assess whether the CSF has been achieved.

For example, KPIs for 'efficient production' could include:

- maximum kg of materials wasted

- average time taken to produce one unit of the product, etc.

A strong performance measurement system is likely to reflect the CSFs and KPIs identified by the organisation, as these are areas that the organisation needs to do well at in order to outperform its rivals – a key issue for most businesses.

Remember that whatever the organisation chooses as its performance measurement system will need to be monitored going forward. Management will need to ensure that information systems are put in place to collect data to allow performance in these areas to be measured on an ongoing basis.

If our cost leader (above) wishes to target its staff performance based on the average time they take to produce units, it will need to create systems to keep track of how long each employee works for and how many units they individually produce.

Note that, as with the organisation's KPIs, the performance measurement system is likely to cover a wide range of criteria – both financial and non-financial.

Changes to the performance measurement system

The changing environment presents new risks and opportunities and these must be monitored and identified as early as possible. It is therefore likely that new measures will be added to the system over time. However, consideration must also be given to keeping the system as uncomplicated as possible and as such old unnecessary measures should be dropped.

When changing the performance measurement system, management need to be aware of the following points:

- too many changes may lead to 'indicator overload', confusing employees about what the company wants them to do.

- if something is included as part of the performance measurement system, the importance of this item is being highlighted to staff. If you change the system, what are you telling people?

- if a measure is dropped from the measurement system, you are telling your staff that this item is no longer important. Is this what you want to achieve?

3 Financial and non-financial measures

Financial performance measures

These indicators concentrate on the revenue, profits, cash and capital position of the business.

Typical indicators may include (but are not limited to):

Sales margin (gross profit margin):

$$\frac{\text{Revenue} - \text{cost of sales}}{\text{Revenue}} \times 100\%$$

- this indicator focuses on the profitability of the business' trading account.

Net profit margin:

$$\frac{\text{Profit (before interest and tax)}}{\text{Revenue}} \times 100\%$$

- this indicator focuses on the profitability of the business in both its trading and its net operating expenses.

Return on capital employed:

$$\frac{\text{Profit (before interest and tax)}}{\text{Capital employed}} \times 100\%$$

- ROCE measures the profitability of a business or division against the assets utilised in that business. (Capital employed is normally measured as shareholders' funds + long–term debt).

Remember the principle of **controllability** when using these measures to assess divisional performance. The costs used in both cases should only be those that the division can directly control. Expenses such as head office costs would normally be excluded as it would be unfair to assess divisional managers on spending that they cannot alter.

Advantages of financial measures of performance

- Culturally expected
- focus on financial objectives
- comparable across companies
- cheap
- established framework for preparation in many cases
- tend to focus onto resource generation and so survival in the long term.

Disadvantages of financial measures of performance

- Inflation distortion
- leads to suboptimal and short-termist behaviour
- lack of comparability
- understood by the 'select few' – i.e. trained accountants and managers
- subjectivity can exist in calculation, e.g. depreciation.

Non-financial performance measures

Non-financial performance indicators are measures of performance based on non-financial information that may originate in and be used by operating departments to monitor and control their activities without any accounting input.

CIMA official terminology

Put simply, businesses also need to focus on factors that actually cause profits to be earned – the non-financial measures.

For instance in an accountancy training business, sales and market share (financial issues) are caused by student pass rates, student satisfaction, class sizes, tutor quality, etc. (non-financial issues). These non-financial issues will also need to be measured. If performance in these areas begins to fall, it will not be long before the financial measures deteriorate as well.

Advantages of non-financial measures

- Wider view
- easier to calculate
- easy to understand (sometimes)
- not distorted by inflation
- can emphasise broad spectrum of management
- positive motivational implications.

Disadvantages of non-financial measures

- Some can be difficult to calculate
- subjectivity exists in design, interpretation and calculation
- can lead to indicator overload
- costly
- culture clash implications
- constant change requires constant monitoring.

Test your understanding 1

Which THREE of the following are advantages to an organisation of using non-financial performance measures, rather than traditional financial measures?

A   Culturally expected

B   Gives a wider view of business performance

C   Less subjective measurement

D   Allows earlier problem identification

E   Not distorted by inflation

F   Cheaper to measure

Test your understanding 2

Y plc has noticed that its return on capital employed (ROCE) has fallen significantly over the last twelve months. One of the junior management accountants has made the following statements regarding this:

(i)   Y's gearing must have risen in the year.

(ii)   Y may find it hard to raise additional finance in the coming year.

(iii)   The ROCE may have fallen due to reductions in Y's gross profit margins.

(iv)   The ROCE may have fallen due to large dividends paid out during the last year.

Which of the above statements is/are correct?

A   (i) and (ii) only

B   (i) and (iii) only

C   (ii) and (iii) only

D   (ii) and (v) only

4   The balanced scorecard

Presented by **Kaplan & Norton** in 1992 – 'Kaplan's cockpit'

'An approach to the provision of information to management to assist strategic policy formulation and achievement. It emphasises the need to provide the user with a set of information which addresses all relevant issues of performance in an objective and unbiased fashion. The information provided may include both financial and non-financial elements and cover areas such as profitability, customer satisfaction, internal efficiency and innovation'.

Its aim is to provide a broad range of both financial and non-financial measures designed to reflect the complexity and diversity of business circumstance. Such breadth is key to successful **implementation** of strategy.

It was a response to traditional performance measurement which had tended to focus on a narrow range of performance measures and caused management to adopt a short-term focus.

Kaplan likened running a business to flying a plane – airspeed, altitude, direction and fuel level are just a few of the pieces of information needed. Yet, in many businesses, managers have to rely on a narrow set of financial indicators to support their decision making – and this in an environment with many more complexities than a plane.

The balanced scorecard approach brings together a wide range of measures to give managers a broader perspective of their business performance.

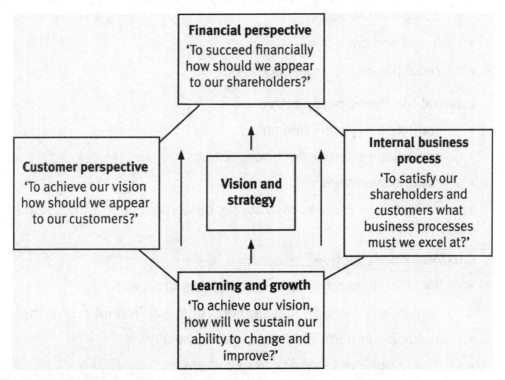

This is a powerful tool that assists in the running of an organisation. Gains in one area need to be considered with the losses that may arise in other areas and vice versa. Thus the manager's view is broadened and the tendency to concentrate on one measure is reduced, hopefully removed.

Possible measures for the balanced scorecard

The measures used within the balanced scorecard will vary between organisations, but some typical examples are shown below for each of the four perspectives:

Financial perspective

- increased revenue
- improvements to key ratios, such as gross margin, net margin or ROCE
- rising market share
- increased cash flow
- reduction or increase in gearing.

Internal business perspective

- reduction in production time
- reduction in number of errors/defects
- reduced wastage
- reduction in time taken to supply customers/deal with customer queries.

Customer perspective

- increase in number of new customers attracted
- increase in number of customers returning (repeat business)
- reduction in number of customer complaints
- rise in positive feedback from customers
- reduction in returns from customers
- number of orders delivered on time to customers.

Innovation and learning (learning and growth)

- number of days of staff training
- number of new products or services launched
- increase in number of sales made through new channels – such as online
- increase in proportion of sales of new products
- reduction in staff turnover (increased staff satisfaction)
- number of new business ideas generated by staff.

Remember that this list is not exhaustive. In your exam you will need to select the performance measures that best fit the organisation in question.

Illustration 1 – The balanced scorecard

For a train company, a balanced scorecard could include indicators such as:

Customer perspective

- Percentage of trains running on time/cancelled

- percentage of trains running per hour between destinations

- cleanliness levels

- seat availability.

Internal business process

- Staff attendance rates

- average time taken to process ticket enquiries

- percentage of trains in full working order.

Learning and growth

- Investment in new rolling inventory

- number of training days per annum per staff member

- investment in new passenger facilities (e.g. internet access on–board).

Financial perspective

- Profit levels

- revenue growth

- revenue by activity

- cost control versus budget.

Strategy mapping

Strategy mapping – implementing the balanced scorecard more effectively

Strategy mapping was developed by Kaplan and Norton as an extension to the balanced scorecard and to make implementations of the scorecard more successful.

The steps involved are:

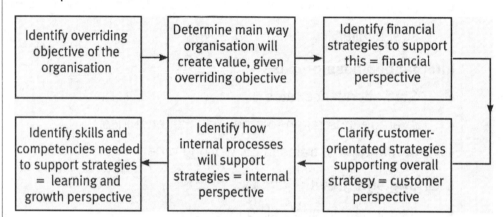

- At the head of the strategy map is the overriding objective of the organisation which describes how it creates value. This is then connected to the organisation's other objectives, categorised in terms of the four perspectives of the balanced scorecard, showing the cause-and-effect relationships between them.

- The strategy map helps organisations to clarify, describe and communicate the strategy and objectives, both within the organisation and to external stakeholders, by presenting the key relationships between the overall objective and the supporting strategy and objectives in one diagram.

Problems:

- Organisations have often found it difficult to translate the corporate vision into behaviour and actions which achieve the key corporate objectives.

- In practice many employees do not understand the organisation's strategy, and systems such as performance management and budgeting are not linked to the strategy.

Test your understanding 3

A bus company uses Kaplan and Norton's balanced scorecard as a way of developing its performance measurement mix.

One of the measures it has chosen to use is the number of days of driver training each year. The company feels that this will reduce the number of accidents and casualties due to more skilled and motivated drivers.

Which ONE of the balanced scorecard perspectives would this measure relate to?

A   Learning and growth

B   Internal business processes

C   Customer perspective

D   Financial perspective

Test your understanding 4 – (Integration question)

Suggest some critical success factors (CSFs) and key performance indicators (KPIs) for each perspective of the balanced scorecard for an electronics manufacturer.

Benefits and drawbacks of the balanced scorecard

The main benefits are:

- It avoids management reliance on short-termist or incomplete financial measures.

- By identifying the non-financial measures, managers may be able to identify problems earlier. For example, managers may be measuring customer satisfaction directly as part of the balanced scorecard. If this changes, steps can be taken to improve it again before customers leave and it starts to impact on the company's finances.

- It can ensure that divisions develop success measures for their division that are related to the overall corporate goals of the organisation.

- It can assist stakeholders in evaluating the firm if measures are communicated externally.

The drawbacks are:

- It does not provide a single overall view of performance. Measures like ROCE are popular because they conveniently summarise 'how things are going' into one convenient measure.

- There is no clear relation between the balanced scorecard and shareholder analysis.

- Measures may give conflicting signals and confuse management. For instance, if customer satisfaction is falling along with one of the financial indicators, which should management sacrifice?

- It often involves a substantial shift in corporate culture in order to implement it.

Test your understanding 5 – CCC – (Case style)

T is the Chief Executive Officer of a motor car insurance company, CCC. T, together with the Board of Directors, developed a mission statement in 20X3 following a detailed analysis of the company's operations and market place. The mission statement states that 'CCC wants to continually grow through its commitment to quality and delivering value to its customers'. CCC has developed a complementary vision statement which aspires to:

- Provide superior returns to our shareholders

- Continually improve our business processes

- Delight our customers

- Learn from our mistakes and work smarter in the future.

CCC's overriding objective, also developed in 20X3, is to double the size of its revenue by the end of 20X7.

T has identified the following areas of concern:

- Poor customer service has led to CCC losing 15% of its customers in 20X3/20X4. The customer sales manager had sponsored an initiative to reward customers with a discount if they renewed their motor insurance. However, most of the sales executives were not familiar with the details of this scheme and did not mention it to customers considering renewing their insurance. The discount scheme had not affected the rate of loss of customers.

- The average age of CCC's personal computers (PCs) was five years. There have been many complaints from CCC's staff that their PC's are not adequate for the demands of 2014. The last time an initiative had been undertaken to bring PCs up to date was in 20X1.

- CCC's internal auditors had conducted performance reviews in three departments during 20X3. They found a common pattern in all three departments: many of the staff had only minimal educational qualifications which were inadequate for the jobs they were doing. This resulted in an unacceptable level of errors being made. No initiatives had been undertaken to address this problem.

- Investors have been critical of the low dividend yield on their CCC shares.

T is worried because, despite the time and effort put into the development of the mission and vision statements and the overriding objective, CCC is not making sufficient progress towards achieving its revenue target. Its revenue growth rate in 20X3 was 10%.

CCC's shortfall against its revenue target was discussed at a recent Board meeting. The Corporate Affairs Director stated that "the Board is 100% behind our strategy and vision but it's just not happening. I have experience in my previous company of working with an integrated model, the Balanced Scorecard. Could the Balanced Scorecard help CCC?"

T has asked you, a strategic management accountant working in CCC, for a report covering the following areas:

(i)   Advice on how a Balanced Scorecard could assist in delivering CCC's vision and strategy.

(ii)   Assume that CCC has adopted a Balanced Scorecard approach to help it achieve its vision. Recommend FOUR perspectives and for each perspective show:

  –   An objective

  –   A measure

  –   A target

  –   An initiative.

(iii)   Discuss briefly TWO drawbacks of the Balanced Scorecard.

Required:

Draft the report as requested by T.

(45 minutes)

5   The performance pyramid

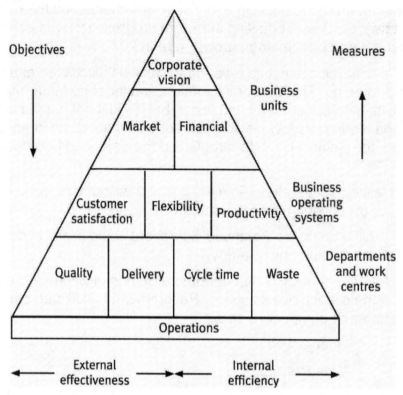

The performance pyramid framework

The performance pyramid was developed by Lynch and Cross as a model to understand and define the links between objectives and performance measures **at different levels** in the organisation.

The performance pyramid is designed to ensure that the activities of every department, system and business unit support the overall vision of the organisation.

At the top of the pyramid is the vision through which the organisation describes how it will achieve long-term success and competitive advantage.

The second level, **the business unit**, includes the critical success factors (CFSs) in terms of market-related measures and financial measures that need to be achieved to meet the organisation's overall vision.

The third level, the **business operating systems**, includes measures which relate to the internal systems and processes which are needed to meet the needs of customers. For example, measures of flexibility which relate to how responsive the system is to customer demands. They will link to the market and financial measures identified at level two.

The lowest level of the pyramid, **departments and work centres**, contains the day-to-day operational measures that can be used to monitor the status of the level three measures.

The left-hand side of the pyramid contains measures which have an external focus and which are predominantly non-financial. Those on the right are focused on the internal efficiency of the organisation and are predominantly financial.

Objectives cascade down through the organisation, while measures and information flow from the bottom up.

The performance pyramid does tend to concentrate on two groups of stakeholders – shareholders and customers. It is necessary to ensure that measures are included which relate to other stakeholders as well.

Value drivers

In chapters 6 & 7 we introduced the concept of value drivers within an organisational ecosystem, and how such drivers might be either tangible or intangible. We identified that, over time, tangible drivers of value do not necessarily lead to sustainable competitive advantage as they can be copied by competitors. Intangible drivers of value, such as the organisation's brand, its reputation, or its know-how, are much more difficult for another business to replicate.

The performance pyramid framework is a useful means to assess the drivers of value in an organisation and to adopt suitable measures of performance within the management system. This is because many elements of the pyramid can be classified as tangible or intangible.

For example, the measure of 'quality' could be said to have a tangible nature, perhaps measured by the % of units sold that are returned because they are defective.

Alternatively, the measure of quality might be seen as an intangible driver of value; the product may function as intended, but does it really meet the expectations of the customer/user? Is it, in their eyes, fit for purpose and meeting their needs?

Similarly, 'waste' might be seen in a tangible context (such as a restaurant measuring the amount of food that gets thrown away), or an intangible context (perhaps taking too long to prepare meals and irritating the customer, a waste of the time in the kitchen due to inefficient cooking methods).

Note that the Lynch and Cross model is not the only framework that could be used to assess value drivers; the same thought processes could equally be applied to other models such as the Balanced Scorecard.

Test your understanding 6

Which ONE of the following would be classified as an internal efficiency measure within the performance pyramid?

A   Customer satisfaction

B   Cycle time

C   Delivery

D   Quality

Test your understanding 7

G plc has set its staff targets relating to improvements in the number of customer complaints received.

Which level of the performance pyramid is G measuring?

A   Corporate vision

B   Departments and work centres

C   Business units

D   Business operating systems

Test your understanding 8 – Ochil – (Case style)

Ochil is an engineering manufacturing company specialising in the production of mobile machinery for the construction industry. The company has identified and defined a market in which it wishes to operate. This will provide a new focus for an existing product range. Ochil has identified a number of key competitors and intends to focus on close co-operation with its customers in providing products to meet their specific design and quality requirements. Efforts will be made to improve the effectiveness of all aspects of the cycle, from product design to after-sales service to customers. This will require inputs from a number of departments in the achievement of the specific goals of the new proposal. Efforts will be made to improve productivity in conjunction with increased flexibility of methods.

An analysis of forecast financial and non-financial data relating to the new proposal is shown in Schedule 1 below.

Schedule 1

	20X4	20X5	20X6
Total market size ($m)	120	125	130
Ochil sales ($m)	15	18	20
Ochil total costs ($m)	14.1	12.72	12.55
Ochil sundry statistics			
Production achieving design quality standards	95%	97%	98%
Returns from customers (% of deliveries)	3.0%	1.5%	0.5%
Cost of after-sales service ($m)	1.5	1.25	1.0
Sales meeting planned delivery dates	90%	95%	99%
Average cycle time (customer enquiry to delivery) (weeks)	6	5.5	5
Components scrapped in production (%)	7.5%	50%	2.5%
Idle machine capacity (%)	10%	6%	2%

The company is considering the implementation of a new performance measurement system in an attempt to make a clear link between performance and strategy and to be flexible and adapt to an ever changing business environment. The directors are therefore considering implementing the performance pyramid.

The managing director of Ochil has asked you to prepare an analysis of the new proposal for the period 20X4 to 20X6. The analysis should use the information provided in the question, together with the data in Schedule 1.

The analysis should contain the following:

(i) Discussion of the external effectiveness of the proposal in the context of ways in which (1) Quality and (2) Delivery are expected to affect customer satisfaction and hence the marketing of the product.

(ii) Discussion of the internal efficiency of the proposal in the context of ways in which the management of (1) Cycle time and (2) Waste are expected to affect productivity and hence the financial aspects of the proposal.

(iii) Discussion of the potential benefits to Ochil of implementing the performance pyramid.

Required:

Prepare an analysis as requested by the managing director.

(30 minutes)

Fitzgerald and Moon

The building block model

```
                    Dimensions
                      Profit
                  Competitiveness
                     Quality

                  Resource Utilisation

                    Flexibility
                    Innovation


        Standards              Rewards
        Ownership              Clarity
       Achievability          Motivation
         Equity             Controllabilitiy
```

Fitzgerald and Moon adopted a framework for the design and analysis of performance management systems. The model was first devised as a solution to performance measurement problems in service industries. But it can be applied successfully to other manufacturing and retail businesses to evaluate business performance.

Fitzgerald and Moon based their analysis on three building blocks:

- **Dimensions**

  Dimensions are the goals for the business and suitable measures must be developed to measure each performance dimension. Below are six dimensions in the building block model, along with examples of measures that could be used under each.

  - **Profit**

    Measures: successful financial performance and growth, increased sales or margins.

  - **Competitiveness**

    Measure: number of new customers, repeat business, market share.

  - **Resource utilisation**

    Measure: optimum use of scarce resources, wastage, idle time.

- **Quality issues**

  Measure: minimising defects and errors, reliability of service/ delivery to the customer, response times.

- **Innovation**

  Measure: product/service development – including time taken to develop new products and services, as well as the number of new products or services launched.

- **Flexibility**

  Measure: the ability to respond to changing needs, customer waiting times, overtime worked by staff.

- **Standards**

  These are the measures used. To ensure success it is vital that employees view standards as achievable and fair and take ownership of them.

- **Rewards**

  To ensure that employees are motivated to meet standards, targets need to be clear and linked to controllable factors.

Financial performance and competitiveness were seen as the "results" and the others as "determinants" of success.

Fiztgerald and Moon suggested that these six dimensions could be used to generate the key performance measures that the business would need to monitor.

Again, applying this framework whilst thinking about the value drivers of the organisational ecosystem (both tangible and intangible) will be of benefit.

Test your understanding 9

JKJ is a small company that sells office stationery, such as paper and pens. It has set targets in the following areas as performance measures for its employees:

- number of new product lines offered to customers
- increased revenue and margins
- number of defective products returned by customers.

Which of the following dimensions from the Fitzgerald and Moon building block model have **not** been considered by JKJ as part of the above measures? Select all that apply.

A   Resource utilisation

B   Innovation

C   Flexibility

D   Profit

E   Quality issues

6   Benchmarking schemes

Benchmarking is 'the establishment, through data gathering, of targets and comparators, through whose use relative levels of performance (and particularly areas of underperformance) can be identified. By the adoption of identified best practices it is hoped that performance will improve.'

CIMA Official Terminology

Most organisations have systems in place to help management monitor key factors such as profits and sales. However, if the financial results or market share of the firm start to deteriorate, management needs to know the reasons why.

The purpose of benchmarking is to help management understand how well the firm is carrying out its key activities and how its performance compares with other, successful, organisations who carry out similar operations (often those considered **best in class**).

A famous example of this is the Rank Xerox company. In the 1970s, such was the dominance of the firm that the word 'Xerox' meant 'photocopier'. A decade later and they had serious competition, most notably from Canon. Something had gone wrong...but what?

Rank Xerox found that clients were switching to other providers because Rank Xerox machines were perceived to always be out of order. It used benchmarking to restore its fortunes.

Types of benchmarking

Seber identifies **three** basic types:

Internal

- This is where another branch or department of the organisation is used as the benchmark
- used where conformity of service is the critical issue – either threshold or core competence
- easily arranged, cheaper and culturally relevant
- but, culturally distorted and unlikely to provide innovative solutions.

Competitor

- Uses a direct competitor with the same or similar process
- essentially aims to render the competition core competence as threshold
- relevant for the industry and market
- but, will the competitor really be keen to hand over their basis for success?

Process or activity

- Focus upon a similar process in another company which is not a direct competitor, e.g. an airline and a health service

- looks for new, innovative ways to create advantage as well as solving threshold problems

- takes time and is expensive

- but, resistance likely to be less and can provide the new basis for advantage.

Implementing a benchmarking scheme

This will involve:

(1) identifying what is wrong within the current organisation

(2) identifying best practice elsewhere

(3) contacting, preparing for a site visit

(4) gathering, evaluating and communicating the results.

It will need:

- key executive commitment from the outset

- establishment of teams for those ranges of opinions and expertise

- a team to manage the project

- a team for the site visit

- budget allocations and training to be given

- a formalised process.

Problems

- Best practice companies unwilling to share data

- what is 'best practice'?

- costly in terms of time and money – opportunity cost

- provides a retrospective view in a turbulent environment – what is best today may not be so tomorrow. As one writer put it: 'Benchmarking is the refuge of the manager who's afraid of the future.'

- successful benchmarking firms can find themselves inundated with requests for information from much less able firms from whom they can learn little

- managers may become demotivated if they are compared against a better-resourced rival.

Test your understanding 10

J plc is a medium-sized training organisation based in country V. It operates fifteen centres in major towns and cities across V. Each centre offers IT training accredited by the ITTO (International Technology Training Organisation). Staff are required to follow centrally produced teaching plans which have been approved by J's head office and the ITTO when delivering these courses. J believes that ITTO accreditation is a vital part of its operations.

J has one major competitor, IHG Ltd, within country V. IHG Ltd also offers IT training, but their courses are not ITTO accredited and course content and style varies significantly between IHG centres.

J is aware that a number of universities offer ITTO accredited courses within country V. However J does not see these as competitors as they typically attract school-leavers, rather than the corporations that are J's main customers. The average university pass rate for ITTO courses is currently higher than J's.

J wishes to undertake a benchmarking exercise. Which ONE of the following types of benchmarking would be most appropriate to J?

A   Competitor

B   Process

C   Internal

D   Strategic

Test your understanding 11 – K and L – (Case style)

A company which manufactures and distributes industrial oils employs a team of salespeople who work directly from home and travel around different regions in the country. Each member of the sales team has his or her own geographical area to cover and they visit clients on a regular basis.

The sales team staff are each paid a basic monthly salary. Each member of the team is set an identical target for sales to be achieved in the month. A bonus payment, in addition to the basic salary, is made to any member of the team who exceeds his or her monthly sales target.

Generally, experience has been that the members of the sales team succeed in improving on their sales targets each month sufficiently to earn a small bonus. However, the managers are unclear whether all the team members are achieving their maximum potential level of sales.

Consequently they are considering introducing a system of benchmarking to measure the performance of the sales team as a whole and its individual members.

The Human Resources Director (HRD) is uncertain how best to accomplish this and has sent you the following text:

> *Hi K, could you please send me a quick email setting out how a system of benchmarking could be introduced in the company to measure the performance of the sales team, both as a team and as individuals who will be compared with each other. I'm going into a meeting about this in fifteen minutes, so please make this a priority. Thanks. L.*
>
> **Required:**
>
> Prepare the email as requested by the HRD.
>
> **(15 minutes)**

7 Divisional performance

While the Balanced Scorecard and performance pyramid both identify the need for a wide range of performance measures, financial performance is still extremely important – especially when monitoring the performance of divisions or other strategic business units (SBUs) within the organisation.

There are a wide number of measures that can be used to examine divisional performance, including:

- Economic value added (EVA)
- Shareholder value analysis (SVA)
- Triple bottom line.

8 EVA and SVA

EVA™ (Economic Value Added)

EVA (developed by Stern Stewart & Co) is an estimate of true economic profit after making corrective adjustments to GAAP accounting.

EVA refers to the profit less a charge for capital employed in the period. Accounting profit may be adjusted, for example, for the treatment of goodwill and research and development expenditure, before economic value is calculated.

CIMA official terminology

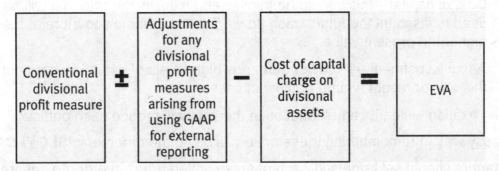

- Adjustments are made to avoid the immediate write-off of value-building expenditure such as research and development expenditure, advertising expenditure or the purchase of goodwill.

- Adjustments are intended to produce a figure for capital employed which is a more accurate reflection of the base upon which shareholders expect their returns to accrue, and to provide a profit after tax figure which is a more realistic measure of the actual cash yield generated for shareholders from recurring business activities.

SVA (Shareholder Value Analysis)

A variation along the same theme as EVA. The main aim of the organisation is to add value to shareholder wealth. This can be defined in a variety of ways and usually results in a form of balanced scorecard being used.

Shareholder value is the total return to the shareholders in terms of both dividends and share price growth, calculated as the present value of the future free cash flows of the business discounted at the weighted average cost of the capital of the business less the market value of its debt.

CIMA official terminology

Essentially this means that management need to ensure that their strategies maximise the wealth of the shareholders of the company, by ensuring that they increase the present value of the returns that they will receive from their shares.

Rappaport has a model that is frequently mentioned. He suggested that future cash flows should be discounted at a suitable cost of capital and that shareholder value would be increased if this measure were to increase.

In order to maximise future cash flows and reduce the cost of capital, he identified seven value drivers:

- **S**ales growth rate – assuming sales are profitable, this should increase cash flow.

- **L**ife of the project – if the firm can forecast growth over a longer period, there will be more cash flows to discount.

- **O**perating profit margin – if this is increased, the amount of cash generated from each sale should rise.

- **W**orking capital – this should be minimised to reduce the amount of cash tied up in inventory and receivables.

- **C**ost of capital – this should be minimised as this is the rate that will be used to discount the future cash flows. The lower the discount rate, the higher the present value.

- **A**sset investment – if growth demands high levels of capital investment, this will represent a large outflow of cash.

- **T**axation – clearly, any reduction in this rate will reduce cash outflow.

An easy way of remembering these drivers is using the mnemonic **SLOW CAT**.

Managers should set targets in each of these seven areas in order to ensure they are maximising shareholder wealth.

It is important to remember that value is not just a financial concept. Shareholders can attach non-financial value, e.g. social responsibility of the company – not testing on animals, positive human rights record or even football club membership.

Later work has developed to include other stakeholders and also non-financial perspectives such as social responsibility. Remember, look after the environment in which you operate and you will get a longer life – the implications for increasing future cash flows as a result are substantial.

Advantages of EVA/SVA approaches

- Adjustments made to profit effectively mean we are looking at cash-flow based measures

- consistent with NPV so should ensure better goal congruence between divisional performance and maximising shareholder value. (Note: You can show that the present value of future EVA figures equates to the increase in shareholder value measured by discounted cashflows)

- cost of financing emphasised.

Drawbacks of the EVA/SVA Systems

- Uses accounting data which has been prepared for other purposes and involves subjective provisions and estimates

- it ignores items that don't appear on balance sheets such as brands, staff and inherent goodwill

- confuses management as they are seldom trained fully in its operation and it varies from one company to another

- costly to maintain and resistance is usually high when first deployed

- assumes value can be measured in money terms

- judgement involved by users in evaluation and selection of cost of capital rate to be used.

Test your understanding 12

YU Ltd is a multinational company that makes and sells one major product, the TRT. The company is aware that the TRT is starting to show signs of decline. YU wishes to undertake one or more of the following strategies to deal with this:

(i)   Rebranding TRT. YU believes that this will extend the life of the TRT by five years.

(ii)   Replacing the current computerised inventory management system which is coming to the end of its useful life.

(iii) Altering YU's internal transfer pricing to reduce its overall tax liability.

(iv)   Adjusting YU's reported profit figures to remove the effect of GAAP for external reporting.

> Which of the above strategies will be consistent with a shareholder value analysis (SVA) approach?
>
> A   (ii) and (iv)
>
> B   (i) and (iii)
>
> C   (ii) and (iii)
>
> D   (i) and (iv)

9   Triple Bottom Line

As outlined in chapter 3, many organisations are concerned about their impact on the environment and wish to monitor whether they are sustainable.

Triple Bottom Line (TBL) expands traditional accountancy reporting systems, looking at social and environmental performance, rather than simply financial performance. This can be used to help encourage each division and manager within the organisation to act in a socially responsible manner.

The model suggests measuring three areas:

- **profit** (or economic prosperity) – the economic value created by the company, or the economic benefit to the surrounding community and society

- **people** (social justice) – the fair and favourable business practices regarding labour and the wider community in which the company conducts its business

- **planet** (environmental quality) – the use of sustainable environmental practices and the reduction of the environmental impact of the organisation.

TBL has a number of advantages, most of which relate to its improvement of the organisation's corporate social responsibility position:

- attracting ethically aware customers

- attracting better quality staff

- cost reductions (i.e. savings in energy, reduced pollution clean-up costs)

- reduced chance of government legislation.

However, there are a number of drawbacks, including:

- **Difficult to quantify**

  It is often difficult to quantify appropriate social and environmental measures. When a business makes a commitment to protecting the environment by recycling, for example, its impact is not always easily discernible.

- **Management conflict**

  The organisation's management usually aims to maximise shareholder return. TBL reporting might create conflict as the benefits of any social and environmental actions that a business engages in are likely to emerge over the long term. However, they could have a short-term negative impact on profits, leading to conflict with shareholders.

Test your understanding 13

Which ONE of the following benefits is consistent with the use of triple bottom line (TBL) reporting?

A   Cost savings through reduced wastage

B   Measures are all based on objective cash-flows, rather than subjective accounting profits

C   Decisions made ensure shareholder wealth is maximised

D   Cheap and easy measurement of targets

10 Communication

Whatever an organisation's chosen performance measurement system, it is essential that the targets set for employees and divisions are appropriately communicated by senior management.

This will involve:

- communicating the targets being set and how they will be measured

- identification of why the targets have been selected – why they are important and how they feed into the organisation's overall strategy

- explaining to employees how they will personally be affected by achieving (or failing to achieve) the targets set

- getting feedback from employees about the appropriateness of the targets being set.

Why is effective communication of the performance measures important?

Benefits include:

- if employees understand the reason for the performance targets that they are being set, they are more likely to 'buy in' to the performance measurement system and see it as important

- an explanation of how the employee's performance is going to be measured will increase the likelihood that they will understand how to meet the targets they are being set

- explaining the impact of hitting or missing their targets (i.e. impact on pay rises or bonuses) will ensure that the employee is aware of the advantages to them personally of conforming to the performance measurement system, improving their motivation to meet the targets set

- getting feedback from employees can ensure that targets set are achievable. If employees feel that targets are unattainable, they will not be motivated to work to achieve them.

Stretch target

Communication with employees is particularly important if an organisation sets stretch targets.

Stretch targets are where the organisation sets goals for its employees that are possible, but very difficult for them to meet. The employee is 'stretched' in that they have to perform extremely well in order to achieve the target.

For example, many accountancy firms pay for their junior employees to sit professional accountancy exams. Instead of simply requiring these students to pass their exams, a firm may require a mark of, say, 75% or higher.

In theory, this requirement will stretch the student, making them work hard to achieve the target.

While stretch goals can work well to motivate staff to work hard, care has to be taken when setting them:

- if employees see the stretch target as unachievable it will be demotivating.
- a stretch target may encourage unethical or risk-taking behaviour – a student may be more likely to cheat on their exam in order to achieve the required grade!

As such, setting the right goal is crucial to avoiding behavioural problems.

It is also worth noting that if the employee has performed exceptionally well and met their stretch targets, the organisation will need to offer them sufficient rewards to maintain their motivation. These could include:

- pay rises
- bonuses
- promotions
- more responsibility.

Excellent performance by an employee should be communicated throughout the organisation as this can motivate other employees to work harder, as well as proving that the stretch targets are achievable.

The high-achieving employee could also be asked to share their approach to meeting their targets, so that others are able to imitate their example throughout the organisation.

11 Problems with performance measurement

Problems in performance measurement and control in complex business structures

A main feature in modern business management is the practice of splitting an enterprise into semi-autonomous units with devolved authority and responsibility.

Such units could be described as 'divisions', subsidiaries or SBUs, but the principles are the same.

This raises the following potential problems.

- How to co-ordinate different business units to achieve overall corporate objectives.

- Goal congruence – managers will be motivated to improve the performance of their local business unit, possibly at the expense of the larger organisation.

- The performance of one unit may depend to some extent on others, making it difficult to implement responsibility accounting effectively.

- Whether/how head office costs should be reapportioned.

- How transfer prices should be set as these effectively move profit from one division to another.

Controllability

Managers should be made accountable for those factors that they can control. This would see a focus onto divisional contribution. This issue of controllability and design poses a few problems:

- What exactly is controllable? Consider shared assets.

- Does controllability change when the long run is considered?

- Transfer pricing issues – should the sales and purchases be included?

- Managerial performance and divisional economic performance are not necessarily the same thing – uncontrollable factors would need to be included when considering economic performance.

- Where does the data originate from? The financial accounting system may not be suitable for performance evaluation of SBUs and may need to be adapted by the management accountant. Reporting or accuracy –which is most important? The faster you go the less reliable the information may become.

- The cultural situation and factors that are likely to motivate the divisional management team.

Test your understanding 14

H runs a small manufacturing company. She is concerned that production levels and production quality have been declining in the last several months. H is therefore planning to set stretch targets for her staff relating to the number of units they produce. Typical production levels require staff to make 25 units per hour. After careful analysis and discussion with staff, H feels that this can be increased to 28 per hour, though this will be difficult for staff to achieve. Any employees who manage to hit the new target will be given a significant bonus at the end of the month.

Which ONE of the following problems is H most likely to face with the stretch targets she has set?

A   Staff will see the target as unachievable and are demotivated

B   The stretch target may lead to staff producing poor quality work

C   Staff will feel no motivation to work towards the stretch target

D   The stretch target will be ignored by staff due to lack of communication

Cost centres, profit centres and investment centres

Key considerations

When assessing divisional performance it is vital that the measures used match the degree of decentralisation in the division:

Type of division	Description	Typical measures
Cost centre	• Division incurs costs but has no revenue stream	Total cost • Cost variances • Cost per unit and other cost ratios • NFPIs (nonfinancial performance indicators) related to quality, productivity, efficiency, etc.
Profit centre	• Division has both costs and revenue • Manager does not have the authority to alter the level of investment in the division	All of the above PLUS • Sales • Profit • Sales variances • Margins • Market share • Working capital ratios (depending on the division concerned) • NFPIs related to customer satisfaction.

| Investment centre | • Division has both costs and revenue

 • Manager does have the authority to invest in new assets or dispose of existing ones | All of the above PLUS

 • Return on Investment (ROI)

 • Residual Income (RI)

 • SVA/EVA

 These are discussed in more detail above. ROI and RI should be familiar to you from your earlier studies. |

In most exam questions you will meet SBUs that are investment centres.

Sub-optimisation

Sub-optimisation refers to actions taken to improve the divisional situation at the expense of the company as a whole. This can arise for a number of reasons:

- **Short-termism**

  Short-termism refers to actions taken to improve the short-run performance at the expense of the long run. For example, cutting discretionary costs such as advertising and training budgets to hit a profit target.

- **Problems intrinsic to the targets used**

  Most measures are linked to profit, which does not have a high correlation with shareholder value.

- **Wrong signals**

  Excessive pressure to hit targets may result in a culture where it is felt to be acceptable to use 'creative accounting' to achieve results.

Wrong signals and inappropriate action

There are many ways in which poorly designed performance management systems can send managers the wrong signals, resulting in dysfunctional behaviour. Berry, Broadbent and Otley identified the following problem areas:

- Misrepresentation – 'creative' reporting to suggest that a result is acceptable.

- Gaming – deliberate distortion of a measure to secure some strategic advantage.

- Misinterpretation – failure to recognise the complexity of the environment in which the organisation operates.

- Short-termism – leading to the neglect of longer-term objectives.

- Measure fixation – measures and behaviour in order to achieve specific performance indicators which may not be effective.

- Tunnel vision – undue focus on stated performance measures to the detriment of other areas.

- Sub-optimisation – focus on some objectives so that others are not achieved.

- Ossification – an unwillingness to change the performance measure scheme once it has been set up.

Test your understanding 15 – (Integration question)

HIH is a large, multinational chain of high-quality hotels. Recently they have expanded rapidly, with growth of over a hundred hotels in the last two years.

Each new hotel is fitted to a high standard by HIH. The head office of HIH is responsible for all advertising and special offers, the setting of prices and any branding changes.

The local hotel managers are responsible for operational decisions, such as which staff to hire and employee training.

HIH sets targets for local managers based on total sales and customer satisfaction feedback. The customer feedback is collected by hotel staff from customer questionnaires.

Required:

Comment on the suitability of the targets set for local hotel managers.

(15 minutes)

> ## The role of the management accountant in performance
>
> The Chartered Management Accountant has a crucial role to play within the organisation when considering the performance measurement mix.
>
> They will help management to decide on the performance measurement mix itself. Management accountants can help managers analyse the organisation's strategy and suggest what measures will ensure this strategy is achieved.
>
> Management accountants will also help managers to decide what targets to set staff in each area of the performance measurement mix. This could include work studies to identify what employee roles involve, followed by calculation of what they can reasonably be expected to achieve.
>
> Management accountants will also help the organisation to design systems to capture relevant information relating to the measurement mix. They will then communicate this to management, enabling them to identify whether the organisation's strategy is being successfully implemented.

12 Integrated Reporting

12.1 Introduction

In the modern business environment, stakeholders will have multiple expectations, not just profitability. How a business actually behaves is just as important, and this has led to the emergence of Integrated Reporting (IR). IR is seen as a **key strategic communication tool,** both internally and externally, and helps management adopt suitable incentives for good performance.

With IR, instead of having environmental and social issues reported in a separate section of the annual report, or a standalone 'sustainability' report, the idea is that one report should capture the strategic and operational actions of management in its holistic approach to business and stakeholder 'wellbeing'.

12.2 The management accountant's role in providing key performance information for IR

The management accountant must now be able to collaborate with top management in the integration of financial wellbeing with community and stakeholder wellbeing. This is a more strategic view considering factors that drive long-term performance.

IR will bring statutory reporting closer to the management accountant and will make management accountants even more important in bridging the gap between stakeholders and the company's reports.

The management accountant will be expected to produce information that:

- is a balance between quantitative and qualitative information. The information system must be able to capture both financial and non-financial measures

- links past, present and future performance. The forward looking nature will require more forecasted information

- considers the regulatory impacts on performance

- provides an analysis of opportunities and risks that could impact in the future

- considers how resources should be best allocated

- is tailored to the specific business situation but remains concise.

There is clearly a need for the profession to accept the challenge for being the mechanism for a new type of transparency and accountability; one that incorporates social and environmental impacts as well as economic ones.

The role of the management accountant in sustainability is as yet not well established. However, it is anticipated that over time, IR will become the corporate reporting norm. This will offer a productive and rewarding future, not only for the management accountant but for society as a whole.

12.3 The International Integrated Reporting Council (IIRC)

The IIRC was formed in August 2010 and aims to create a globally accepted framework for a process that results in communication by an organisation about value creation over time.

The IIRC seeks to secure the adoption of an Integrated Reporting Framework (an alternative to the recommendations by the Global Reporting Initiative) by report preparers. The Framework sets out several **guiding principles** and **content elements** that have to be considered when preparing an integrated report.

Illustration 2 – Guiding principles

There are **seven** guiding principles, as follows:

Strategic focus and future orientation – the report should provide and insight into the organisation's strategy and how it relates to the organisation's ability to create value in the short, medium and long term.

Connectivity of information – the report should show a holistic picture of the combination, inter-relatedness and dependencies between the factors that affect the organisation's ability to create value over time.

Stakeholder relationships – the report should provide an insight into the nature and quality of the organisation's relationships with its stakeholders.

Materiality – the report should disclose information about matters that substantively affect the organisation's ability to create value.

Conciseness – the report should be concise and include relevant information only.

Reliability and completeness – the report should include all material matters, both positive and negative, in a balanced way and without material error.

Consistency and comparability – the report should be consistent and comparable over time.

Illustration 3 – Content elements

There are **eight** content elements.

Organisational overview and external environment – what does the organisation do and what are the circumstances under which it operates? The organisation's mission and objectives, stakeholder analysis and PESTEL analysis would be relevant in this section.

Risks and opportunities – what are the risks and opportunities, both internal and external, that affect the organisation's ability to create value over the short, medium and long term and how is the organisation dealing with them?

Strategy and resource allocation – where does the organisation want to go and how does it intend to get there? This section may make use of Porter's 5 Forces, the BCG matrix and the value chain.

Business model – what is the organisation's business model, i.e. what activities will it carry out to create value? The Value Chain is likely to be highly relevant here.

Future outlook – what challenges and uncertainties is the organisation likely to encounter in pursuing its strategy and what are the implications for future performance? PESTEL and Porter's 5 Forces are likely to be particularly relevant here.

Performance – to what extent has the organisation achieved its strategic objectives for the period? The most appropriate performance indicators should be chosen here.

Governance – how does the organisation's governance structure support its ability to create value in the short, medium and long term?

Basis of preparation and presentation – how does the organisation determine what matters to include in the integrated report and are such matters quantified or evaluated?

12.4 IR and capital

The IR Framework recognises the importance of looking at financial and sustainability performance in an integrated way – one that emphasises the relationships between what it identifies as the "six capitals":

- Financial capital

  This is what we traditionally think of as 'capital' – e.g. shares, bonds or banknotes. It enables the other types of Capital described below to be owned and traded.

- Manufactured capital

  This form of capital can be described as comprising of material goods, or fixed assets which contribute to the production process rather than being the output itself – e.g. tools, machines and buildings.

- Intellectual capital

  This form of capital can be described as the value of a company or organisation's employee knowledge, business training and any proprietary information that may provide the company with a competitive advantage.

- Human capital

  This can be described as consisting of people's health, knowledge, skills and motivation. All these things are needed for productive work.

- Social and relationship capital

  This can be described as being concerned with the institutions that help maintain and develop human capital in partnership with others; e.g. Families, communities, businesses, trade unions, schools, and voluntary organisations.

- Natural capital

  This can be described as any stock or flow of energy and material within the environment that produces goods and services. It includes resources of a renewable and non-renewable materials e.g. land, water, energy and those factors that absorb, neutralise or recycle wastes and processes – e.g. climate regulation, climate change, CO_2 emissions.

The fundamental assumption of the IR Framework is that each of these types of capital – whether internal or external to the business, tangible or intangible – represents a potential source of value that must be managed for the long run in order to deliver sustainable value creation.

As well as external reporting to a range of stakeholders, the principles of IR can be extended to performance management systems. This is sometimes referred to as 'internal IR'.

An emphasis on these types of capital could result in more focussed performance management in the following ways:

- KPIs can be set up for each of the six capitals, ensuring that each of the drivers of sustainable value creation are monitored, controlled and developed.

- These can be developed further to show how the KPIs connect with different capitals, interact with, and impact each other.

- The interaction and inter-connectedness of these indicators should then be reflected in greater integration and cooperation between different functions and operations within the firm.

- This should result in greater transparency of internal communications allowing departments to appreciate better the wider implications of their activities.

- Together this should result in better decision making and value creation over the longer term.

Test your understanding 16

For each of the six capitals outlined in the Integrated Reporting Framework, suggest appropriate KPIs.

12.5 The Global Reporting Initiative (GRI)

The most accepted framework for reporting sustainability is the GRI's Sustainability Reporting Guidelines, the latest of which 'G4' – the fourth of the guidelines – was issued in May 2013. The G4 Guidelines consist of principles and disclosure items.

- The principles help to define report content, quality of the report and give guidance on how to set the report boundary.

- The disclosure items include disclosures on management of issues as well as performance indicators themselves.

Reporting principles and disclosures

Reporting principles

Reporting principles are essentially the required characteristics of the Report Content and the Report Quality. The Principles for Defining Report Content are given as:

- Stakeholder Inclusiveness

- Sustainability Context

- Materiality

- Completeness.

The Principles for Defining Report Quality are given as:

- Balance

- Comparability

- Accuracy

- Timeliness

- Clarity

- Reliability.

Standard disclosures

Two types of disclosure are required: General standard disclosures:

- Strategy and Analysis

- Organisational Profile

- Identified Material Aspects and Boundaries

- Stakeholder Engagement

- Report profile

- Governance

- Ethics and Integrity.

Specific Standard Disclosures

- Disclosures on Management's Approach

- Indicators.

The G4 guidelines encourage disclosure of various 'aspects' in the three categories: Economic, Environmental and Social.

Illustration 4 – Categories and aspects in the G4 guidelines

Examples of the aspects grouped by category are:

Economic

- Economic Performance

- Market Presence.

Environmental

- Materials, energy and water

- Biodiversity

- Emissions

- Effluents and Waste.

Social – this category is split into four sub-categories, each with several aspects associated with it as follows:

Labour Practices and Decent Work

- Labour/Management Relations
- Occupational Health and Safety
- Training and Education
- Diversity and Equal Opportunity.

Human rights

- Non-discrimination
- Child Labour
- Human Rights Grievance Mechanisms.

Society

- Local Communities
- Anti-corruption.

Product responsibility

- Customer Health and Safety
- Product and Service Labelling.

13 Summary

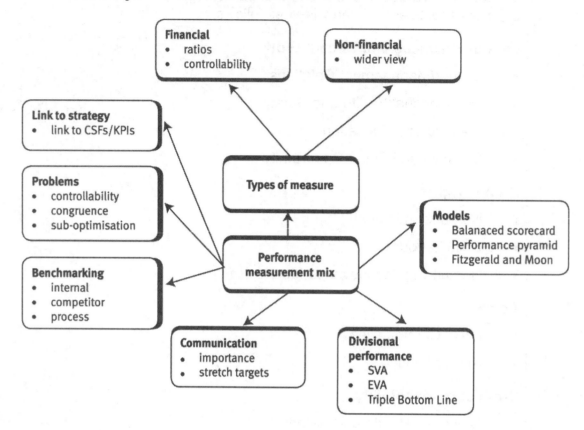

Test your understanding answers

Test your understanding 1

The correct answers are B, D and E

A, C and F are advantages of using financial measures.

Test your understanding 2

The correct answer is C

The return on capital employed (ROCE) is calculated by taking the profit before interest and tax and dividing this by capital employed (shareholders' funds plus long-term debt).

Note that the proportions of debt to equity do not matter in this calculation, meaning that a shift in gearing will not necessarily affect the ROCE.

In addition, large dividends would tend to reduce the shareholders' funds, which could actually cause an increase in the ROCE, rather than a reduction.

Test your understanding 3

The correct answer is A

Learning and growth relates to both innovation and training for staff though this could also have a positive effect on both customers and service quality.

Test your understanding 4 – (Integration question)

Perspective	Goals/CSFs	Measures/KPIs
Customer	New products	% of sales from new products
	Responsive service	% ontime delivery
	Preferred supplier	Customer ranking
	Partnership ventures	Number of cooperative operations
Internal business	Manufacturing excellence	Production cycle time, unit cost
	Design productivity	Material efficiency
	New product development	Introduction times, actual versus plan
Learning and growth	Time to market	Introduction times v competition
	Product focus	% of products giving 80% of sales
	Manufacturing	Process time to maturity
	Learning technology	Time to develop next generation products
Financial	Survival	Cash flow
	Success	Quarterly sales growth
	Prosperity	Increase in market share and return on equity (ROE)

Test your understanding 5 – CCC – (Case style)

Report

To: T

From: A. N. Accountant

Date: 15/01/XX

Subject: Balanced scorecard analysis for CCC

Introduction

The Balanced Scorecard (BS) helps an organisation, like CCC, to identify key issues that it needs to consider in order to maximise the efficiency of its performance measurement mix.

How the Balanced Scorecard could assist CCC

In a widely published model, Johnson and Scholes characterise the strategic management process as consisting of three inter-related elements:

- strategic analysis
- strategic choice
- strategic implementation.

CCC has developed both mission and vision statements and an overriding objective so they have dealt with the first two elements. However, the comments of the Corporate Affairs Director that 'our strategy and vision ..(are)..not happening' indicate that CCC has been unsuccessful in strategic implementation. This is not an unusual situation as firms often experience a disjunction between the three elements. This is one of the reasons that the Balanced Scorecard (BS) was developed by Kaplan and Norton 'to assist strategic policy formation and achievement'.

The BS (See example below) comprises four perspectives surrounding the organisation's vision and strategy. Each of these perspectives can be associated with an aspect of CCC's vision statement.

Vision and Strategy

Our vision aspires to:

- provide superior returns to our shareholders
- continually improve our trading methods
- delight our customers
- learn from our mistakes, work smarter in the future.

Our strategy is to double the size of our revenue by 20X7. Customer perspective.

To achieve our vision how should we appear to our customers?

Delight our customers.

Financial perspective

To succeed financially how should we appear to our shareholders?

Provide superior returns to our shareholders.

Learning and growth

To achieve our vision, how will we sustain our ability to change and improve?

Learn from our mistakes and work smarter in future.

Internal business process

To satisfy our shareholders and customers, what business processes must we excel at?

Continually improve our business processes.

Example application of the Balanced Scorecard to CCC

The Balanced Scorecard can be made operational by using:

- Objectives: what CCC wants to achieve
- Measures: these will express the progress made towards an objective
- Targets: these give specific values and timescales for the achievement of the measures
- Initiatives: these are the actions taken to achieve a target.

Examples of these four aspects are given below:

Financial perspective

- Objective: Provide increasing dividend returns
- Measure: Dividend yield
- Target: 6% dividend yield by end 20X4
- Initiative: Cost cutting exercise to increase profits.

Customer perspective

- Objective: Increase customer satisfaction
- Measure: Customer complaints
- Target: Reduce customer complaints to 1% of transactions by mid 20X5
- Initiative: Increased training for sales executives.

Learning and Growth

- Objective: Raise the educational level of staff
- Measure: Number of graduates
- Target: 50% of staff to be graduates by 20X6
- Initiative: Sponsor staff on degree courses.

Internal processes

- Objective: Be at the forefront of the use of Information technology
- Measure: Replacement rate for PCs
- Target: All PCs to be no older than 2 yrs by the end of 20X4
- Initiative: Seek new PC suppliers.

Tutorial note: the examples given above are not exhaustive: candidates were given credit for other appropriate examples.

Potential drawbacks of the Balanced Scorecard

It is possible that the pursuit of one perspective may adversely affect another one. For example, if customer satisfaction was to be increased by increased investment in inventory, the financial perspective could be damaged. In this case, CCC would have to prioritise one of the perspectives even though both of them were helping to deliver the vision and strategy.

As CCC has not used the BS before there may have to be a cultural change for it to work successfully: cultural change can be hard to achieve.

The BS may require substantial investment in dedicated software and training costs.

The BS does not provide a single overall view of performance. Managers and analysts often favour measures which capture overall performance.

Conclusion

The BS could be used to great effect within CCC. However, before the organisation decides to adopt this approach, it needs to ensure that they have fully understood the drawbacks and prepared strategies to handle these.

Tutorial note: any other appropriate drawbacks identified by candidates would be given credit.

Test your understanding 6

The correct answer is B

The others are all measures of external effectiveness.

Test your understanding 7

The correct answer is D

By definition.

Test your understanding 8 – Ochil – (Case style)

(i)   The marketing success of the proposal is linked to the achievement of customer satisfaction. The success will require an efficient business operating system for all aspects of the cycle from product design to after-sales service to customers. Improved quality and delivery should lead to improved customer satisfaction. Schedule 1 shows a number of quantitative measures of the expected measurement of these factors:

Quality is expected to improve. The percentage of production achieving design quality standards is expected to rise from 95% to 98% between 20X4 and 20X6. In the same period, returns from customers for replacement or rectification should fall from 3% to 0.5% and the cost of after-sales service should fall from $1.5m to $1.0m.

Delivery efficiency improvement that is expected may be measured in terms of the increase in the percentage of goods achieving the planned delivery date. This percentage rises from 90% in 20X4 to 99% in 20X6.

(ii) The financial success of the proposal is linked to the achievement of high productivity. This should be helped through reduced cycle time and decreased levels of waste. Once again Schedule 1 shows a number of quantitative measures of these factors:

The average total cycle time from customer enquiry to delivery should fall from 6 weeks in 20X4 to 5 weeks in 20X6. This indicates both internal efficiency and external effectiveness.

Waste in the form of idle machine capacity is expected to fall from 10% to 2% between 20X4 and 20X6. Also, component production scrap is expected to fall from 7.5% in 20X4 to 2.5% in 20X6. These are both examples of ways in which improved productivity may be measured.

(iii) Performance pyramid

The performance pyramid should ensure that Ochil's performance measurement system remains dynamic and relevant in a changing business environment. The pyramid measures performance across nine dimensions from corporate vision to individual objectives. The pyramid links the business strategy with the day to day operations ensuring that the different levels support each other.

The measures go far beyond traditional financial measures such as profitability and cash flow. The measures relate to business operating systems and address the driving forces that guide the strategic objectives of Ochil.

Customer satisfaction, flexibility and productivity are the driving forces upon which company objectives are based. The status of these can be monitored using the lower level indicators of waste, delivery, quality and cycle time.

The pyramid views a range of objectives for both external effectiveness and internal efficiency. It makes clear the difference between measures that are of interest to external parties, e.g. customer satisfaction and quality, and measures that are of interest to the business, e.g. productivity and cycle time.

The measures are seen to interact both horizontally at each level and vertically across the levels.

Test your understanding 9

The correct answers are: A and C

The number of new product lines relates to the innovation dimension. Increased revenue and margins is linked to the profit dimension, while the number of defective products is most closely linked to quality issues. The remaining dimensions have not been well covered by the measures set up by JKJ.

Test your understanding 10

The correct answer is B

Competitor benchmarking is not appropriate here as J's rival is not ITTO accredited and is highly inconsistent with its approach to tuition. Neither of these things is likely to make it a suitable candidate for benchmarking.

While J does operate a number of centres, their operations are strictly controlled by central teaching programmes and ITTO requirements. This means it is unlikely that internal benchmarking will identify any major improvements that can be made.

The only group likely to be useful for a benchmarking exercise is universities. These are not rivals to J, so it is likely that this would be a process, or activity, benchmarking exercise. Universities are currently achieving a higher pass rate than J, so benchmarking could be useful for J.

Test your understanding 11 – K and L – (Case style)

Email

To: L From: K

Date: 19/09/XX

Subject: Re: Benchmarking

Hi L,

As per your text, I've outlined the impact of benchmarking on the department and individuals below.

The areas of the sales department as a whole which will be affected by the introduction of a system of benchmarking are:

Planning: It is important that the company's current practises are reviewed and assessed. If comparisons are made with similar organisations, it is essential that the present processes are understood to allow an objective view to be taken of the firm's current sales management function. An effort will need to be made to identify a firm which is prepared to share information that may be regarded as confidential by many firms.

Research: It will be necessary to identify the activities which can be compared. In a sales department this could include, for example, the number of calls per week, the distances covered by each salesperson, etc. These might be useful starting points for the benchmarking process.

Analysis: The method used and the specification of the variables should be established before comparisons are made with another organisation. It is likely that operating costs, past sales levels and new business generated could all be performance indicators that can be analysed to provide the basis on which benchmarking can be undertaken.

Implementation: The information obtained in the benchmarking exercise will be invaluable in the future in order to monitor the selling activities of the company. In addition it will assist in making better decisions regarding sales in the future.

The impact of benchmarking on individual salespeople would be in the following areas:

Planning: As the activities of each salesperson need to be monitored, it is essential to get their co–operation if the benchmarking process is to be successful. Staff may need to be reassured that it will not affect them adversely.

Research: It is necessary to establish performance measures in a flexible manner as it may be difficult to make direct comparisons. For example, travelling times and the size of purchases by customers are likely to be major performance measures. These targets are currently the same for each sales area, but this may need to be flexed in order to be fair to each salesperson.

Analysis: It will become possible to compare performance within the firm and with other firms operating in the same areas. This could make comparisons more realistic and more effective for determining bonuses.

Implementation: Benchmarking will provide a better appreciation of the factors involved in setting sales targets. By helping to improve the performance of individual salespeople, the performance of the company as a whole can be improved.

I hope that helps – if you need any more information, please let me know.

Kind regards

K

Test your understanding 12

The correct answer is B

(i)   will increase the life of the project, while (iii) will reduce the tax liability. Both will specifically improve YU's SVA.

(ii)   will not necessarily add to SVA as it will require additional asset investment and there is no evidence that it will reduce YU's overall working capital levels. (iv) relates to EVA, not SVA.

Test your understanding 13

The correct answer is A

Triple bottom line requires measuring the 3Ps – profits, people and planet. This can encourage staff to save money by reducing wastage as they are targeted on their environmental impact. Reducing wastage will help them achieve this and save the company money.

However, measuring the 3Ps can be time consuming and complex. Note that options B and C are benefits of EVA/SVA.

Test your understanding 14

The correct answer is B

H is worried about production levels AND quality. The targets she is proposing are likely to encourage staff to work quickly – not with more care. This could see H suffering from further declines in quality.

The stretch targets set have been created after discussion with staff - this suggests that they are achievable and that have been fully communicated by H. This means that A and D are incorrect.

The sizeable bonus would indicate that staff will feel motivated to work towards the stretch target, meaning that C is also incorrect.

Test your understanding 15 – (Integration question)

Suitability of targets

Remember that targets set for managers need to be based around areas that they can directly control.

Managers do make the operational decisions in the hotel, meaning that they should have a large degree of control over the customer experience and therefore customer satisfaction.

However, as pricing and special offers are set by head office, they do not have total control over the sales made by the hotel. Should head office set an inappropriate price per room, sales will suffer. It would be unfair to blame the manager for this.

Test your understanding 16

Obviously (!) KPIs need to be matched to CSFs, which will depend on the precise circumstances of an organisation and the environment within which it operates. However, some generic KPIs could include the following:

Financial capital

- Conventional performance measures may be relevant here including revenue growth, margins, ROCE, interest cover, key costs as a % of revenue, etc.

- EVA™.

Manufactured capital

- Inventory days, inventory turnover, size of forward order book compared to annual production, etc.

- Investment in different classes of NCAs. These could also include intangible assets, such as measuring annual investment in R+D as a % of revenue.

Intellectual capital

- Staff turnover of skilled staff

- Utilisation of skilled staff

- Percentage of patented products

- A measurement of brand strength such as elasticity of demand (i.e. the change in demand as a result of a change in price)

- R+D expenditure.

Human capital

- Number of staff, staff turnover

- Productivity/efficiency measures such as sales per employee for a sales team

- Sickness rates.

Social and relationship capital

- Staff satisfaction surveys, looking in particular at staff confidence in leadership, opinions about growth and wellbeing.

Natural capital

- Any environmental KPIs could be used here such as energy consumption and efficiency, output of greenhouse gasses and carbon footprint, water usage, % of waste recycled verses landfill, % of products produced that can be recycled, etc.

Understanding the impact and context of change

Chapter learning objectives

Lead	Component
E3: Recommend change management techniques and methodologies	(a) Assess impact of strategy on organisation (b) Recommend change management strategies

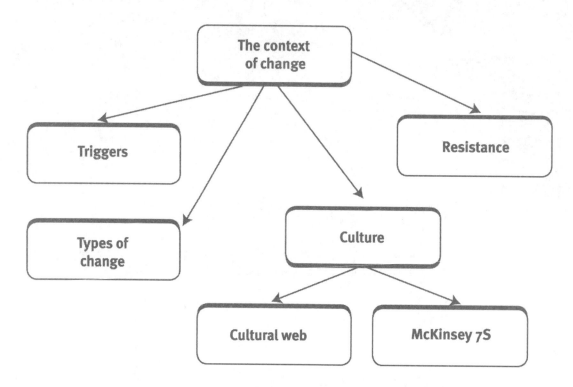

1 Introduction

Internal and external pressures make change inevitable. 'Adapt or die' is the motto of almost every organisation. Some strive to meet the challenge by leading those in the marketplace whilst others hide in niches, snapping at the heels of the major players.

The key questions for all companies are not whether to change or not but rather:

- **What to change?**

- **What to change to?**

- **How to change successfully?**

2 Triggers for change

External triggers

Environmental pressure for change can be divided into two groups.

- General (indirect action) environmental factors – these can be identified using the familiar PESTEL framework and

- Task (direct action) factors – these can be assessed using Porter's five forces model.

Examples of external triggers

Indirect triggers (PESTEL)

Political	Changes in government
	New environmental protection policies
	Private/public partnerships
Economic	Growth or recession
	Changes in currency and interest rates
	Local labour costs
	Regional prosperity/opportunities
	Disposable income
Social	Attitudes to work and leisure
	Environmentalism
	Attitudes to health/education
	Fashion trends
	Changing national/regional culture
Technological	Growth in Internet
	Public use of IT
	Global sourcing/call centres
	Innovations
Environmental	Visible impact (e.g. plastic in oceans)
	Demands from customers
Legal	New labour laws
	European directives

Direct triggers (Porter's five forces)

Competitive rivalry	Powerful rivals may force the firm to have to adapt to survive, either through innovation, if a differentiator, or cost cutting if a cost-leader.
Power of customers	Powerful customers could trigger a firm to consider forwards vertical integration.
Power of suppliers	Supplier power could encourage a firm to redesign products in order to reduce the reliance on specialist components and thus facilitate multi-sourcing.
Threat of new entrants	New entrants may force incumbent firms to improve quality to maintain market share.
Threat of substitutes	New technologies may result in substitutes that render existing products obsolete. This could lead to factory closure and reorganisation.

Internal triggers

The reasons for change within the organisation could span any functional area of operation or level of control from strategic to operational.

Philosophy	New ownership
	New CEO
	New initiative/management style
Reorganisation	Takeover/merger
	Divisional restructuring
	Rationalisation/cost reduction
Personnel	Promotions/transfers
	Rules/procedures
	Training/development
Conditions	Location change
	Outsourcing
	Rosters/flexible working
Technology	New procedures/systems
	Changing information demands
	Integration of roles

Problem identification as a precursor to change

The above triggers can be reasons **why** change is considered or even necessary. However, further strategic analysis is needed to determine **what** needs changing.

Illustration 1 – Problem identification as a precursor to change

For example, TGH Textiles is a UK-based clothing manufacturer that has seen falling profits, declining margins and a loss of market share over the last two years. The main reason for this decline is increasing competition from manufacturers in China and India.

The external trigger for change is increased competitive rivalry, but what needs changing?

The first step would involve analysing the firm's cost base and determining customer perceptions regarding relative quality. This should help TGH to see how its competitive advantage is being eroded. Suppose poor quality is identified as the underlying problem.

Even then, it is not obvious what needs changing. "Poor quality" could be an underlying problem of customer perception related to brand or design flaws, the quality of raw materials, production problems or an underlying culture where quality is not valued highly enough. Determining the main cause(s) could involve discussions with customers, competitor analysis, Porter's value chain analysis, SWOT and/or benchmarking.

Only then will the directors have a clear idea of what needs changing.

3 Classifying change

Types of organisational change

Change can be classified by the extent (or scope) of the change required, and the speed with which the change is to be achieved:

Types of change

Speed of change	Extent of change: Transformation	Extent of change: Realignment
Incremental	**Evolution:** Transformational change implemented gradually through inter-related initiatives; likely to be proactive change undertaken in participation of the need for future change	**Adaptation:** Change undertaken to realign the way in which the organisation operates; implemented in a series of steps
Big Bang	**Revolution:** Transformational change that occurs via simultaneous initiatives on many fronts: • more likely to be forced and reactive because of the changing competitive conditions that the organisation is facing	**Reconstruction:** Change undertaken to realign the way in which the organisation operates with many initiatives implemented simultaneously: • often forced and reactive because of a changing competitive context

(Exploring strategic change – Balogun, Hope Hailey)

Note that incremental change is also known as "continuous" change while "discontinuous change" refers to the big bang above.

- Transformation entails changing an organisation's culture. It is a fundamental change that cannot be handled within the existing organisational paradigm. This is likely to be a top down process and is normally driven by major external events.
- Realignment does not involve a fundamental reappraisal of the central assumptions and beliefs.
- Evolution can take a long period of time, but results in a fundamentally different organisation once completed. It is normally taken in anticipation of a need for change.
- Revolution is likely to be a forced, reactive transformation using simultaneous initiatives on many fronts, and often in a relatively short space of time. It is rapid and likely to affect most, if not all, aspects of what the business does and how it operates – in other words it represents a fundamental change to the organisation's paradigm. It is therefore critical that this type of change is managed effectively.

Illustration 2 – Strategic change

Strategic change is by definition far-reaching. We speak of strategic change when fundamental alterations are made to the business system or the organisational system. Adding a lemon-flavoured Coke to the product portfolio is interesting, maybe important, but not a strategic change, while branching out into bottled water was a major departure from Coca-Cola's traditional business system.

Evolution or revolution?

Another way that evolution can be explained is by conceiving of the organisation as a learning system. However, within incremental change there may be a danger of strategic drift, because change is based on the existing paradigm and routines of the organisation, even when environmental or competitive pressure might suggest the need for more fundamental change.

In selecting an approach to strategic change, most managers struggle with the question of how bold they should be. On the one hand, they usually realise that to fundamentally transform the organisation, a break with the past is needed. To achieve strategic renewal it is essential to turn away from the firm's heritage and to start with a clean slate. On the other hand, they also recognise the value of continuity, building on past experiences, investments and loyalties. To achieve lasting strategic renewal, people in the organisation will need time to learn, adapt and grow into a new organisational reality.

The 'window of opportunity' for achieving a revolutionary strategic change can be small for a number of reasons. Some of the most common triggers are:

- competitive pressure – when a firm is under intense competitive pressure and its market position starts to erode quickly, a rapid and dramatic response might be the only approach possible. Especially when the organisation threatens to slip into a downward spiral towards insolvency, a bold turnaround can be the only option left to the firm.

- regulatory pressure – firms can also be put under pressure by the government or regulatory agencies to push through major changes within a short period of time. Such externally imposed revolutions can be witnessed among public sector organisations (e.g. hospitals and schools) and highly regulated industries (e.g. utilities and telecommunications), but in other sectors of the economy as well (e.g. public health regulations). Some larger organisations will, however, seek to influence and control regulation.

- first mover advantage – a more proactive reason for instigating revolutionary change, is to be the first firm to introduce a new product, service or technology and to build up barriers to entry for late movers.

Test your understanding 1

Strategic change can be classified as evolution, adaptation, reconstruction or revolution. The classification depends on both the scope and speed of the change.

Which ONE of the following combinations of extent and speed of change would be classified as an evolutionary change?

	Extent	Speed
A	Transformation	Big bang
B	Realignment	Big bang
C	Transformation	Incremental
D	Realignment	Incremental

Test your understanding 2

H makes and sells a patented chemical, known as LKL, widely used in cosmetics. LKL has recently been found to increase the risk of cancer of users. This has led to a ban on all cosmetics containing LKL.

H has therefore started urgently looking for alternative uses for LKL. It has identified that LKL can be an effective pesticide and, due to its lack of contact with humans the increased risk of cancer will not be an issue. H has therefore started looking for pesticide manufacturers to sell to.

Which ONE of the following types of organisational change is occurring at H?

A   Reconstruction

B   Evolution

C   Revolution

D   Adaptation

Test your understanding 3 – (Integration question)

Historically the directors of Zed Bank have resisted change, seeking to offer a traditional approach to its customers. However, recent problems within the banking industry and an increasingly competitive market has forced the Board to consider a number of important initiatives, including:

- enhancing its current services to customers by providing them with on-line internet and telephone banking services; and

- reducing costs by closing many of its rural and smaller branches (outlets).

In an attempt to pacify the employee representatives (the Banking Trade Union) and to reduce expected protests by the communities affected by branch closure, a senior bank spokesperson has announced that the changes will be 'incremental' in nature. In particular, she has stressed that:

- the change will be implemented over a lengthy time period

- there will be no compulsory redundancies

- banking staff ready to take on new roles and opportunities in the online operations will be retrained and offered generous relocation expenses.

H For customers, the bank has promised that automatic cash dispensing machines will be available in all the localities where branches (outlets) close. Customers will also be provided with the software needed for Internet banking and other assistance necessary to give them quick and easy access to banking services.

The leader of the Banking Trade Union is 'appalled' at the initiatives announced. He has argued that the so-called 'incremental' change is in fact the start of a 'transformational' change that will have serious repercussions, not only for the Union's members but also for many of the bank's customers.

Required:

Distinguish incremental change from transformational change. Explain why the bank spokesperson and the trade union leader disagree over their description of the change.

(15 minutes)

4   Organisational culture

Definition

 Culture is the set of values, guiding beliefs, understandings and ways of thinking that are shared by the members of an organisation and is taught to new members as correct. It represents the unwritten, feeling part of the organisation.

Culture is 'the way we do things around here' (Charles Handy).

Culture is a set of 'taken-for-granted' assumptions, views of the environment, behaviours and routines (Schein).

Cultural processes of change

The inherent culture of the organisation is important for two reasons:

Firstly the existing culture can become "embedded" and hence resistant to change. Overcoming this resistance can be a major challenge.

Secondly the existing culture can limit the types of strategy development and change that are considered.

- Faced with forces for change, managers will seek to minimise the extent to which they are faced with ambiguity and uncertainty by defining the situation in terms of that which is familiar.

- This can explain why some firms adopt incremental strategies and, worse, why some fail to address the impact of environmental triggers, resulting in strategic drift (that is, having no sense of strategy).

 Illustration 3 – Cultural process of change

Faced with a change trigger such as declining performance, management are likely to react as follows:

(1) First managers will try to improve the effectiveness and efficiency of the existing strategy

    e.g. through tighter controls.

(2) If this is not effective, then a change in strategy may occur but in line with existing strategies

    e.g. through market development, selling existing products into markets that are similar to existing ones and managing the process in the same way as they are used to.

(3) Even when managers know intellectually that more radical change is needed, they find themselves constrained by existing routines, assumptions and political processes.

The cultural web

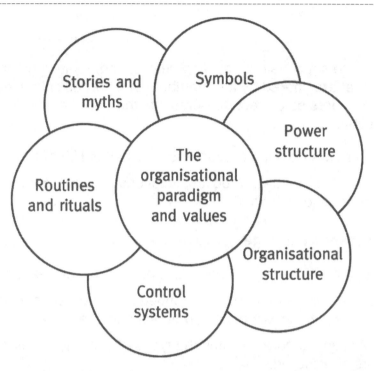

The cultural web was devised by Gerry Johnson as part of his work to attempt to explain why firms often failed to adjust to environmental change as quickly as they needed to. He concluded that firms developed a way of understanding their organisation – called a paradigm – and found it difficult to think and act outside this paradigm if it was particularly strong.

Using the cultural web to map change

The concept of the cultural web is a useful device for mapping out change but its real worth is in the fact that we can identify which elements of culture need to change.

Key questions to ask include:

Stories	
	• What stories do people relate within the organisation and what do they say about the organisation's values?
	• How pervasive are these beliefs (through the levels of the organisation)?
	• What do current staff tell new staff when they join?
	• Do stories relate to: strengths or weaknesses, successes or failures, conformity or mavericks? Who are the heroes and villains?
	• What norms do the mavericks deviate from?

Routines and rituals	• What behaviour do routines encourage? Which would look odd if changed?
	• What are the key rituals that staff undertake regularly? What core beliefs do they reflect?
	• What do training programmes emphasise?
	• How easy are the rituals/routines to change?
	• What do employees expect when they come to work?
Organisational structures	• Is there a very formal organisational structure? Are there any informal reporting mechanisms?
	• How flat/hierarchical are the structures? How formal/informal are they?
	• Do structures encourage collaboration or competition?
	• What type of power structure does the overall organisational structure support?
Control systems	• What is most closely monitored/controlled in my organisation?
	• Is emphasis on reward or punishment? Are there many/few controls?
	• Are all employees aware of the control mechanisms in place?
	• Is the organisation well controlled?
Power structures	• What are the core beliefs of the leadership in my organisation?
	• Who has the power to make decisions?
	• Is power used effectively and appropriately?
	• How is power distributed in the organisation?
	• What are the main blockages to change?

Symbols	• What language and jargon are used in the organisation?
	• How internal or accessible are they?
	• What aspects of strategy are highlighted in publicity?
	• What status symbols are there?
	• Are there particular symbols that denote the organisation to the outside world/customers?
Overall	• What are the key underlying assumptions that are the paradigm?
	• What is the dominant culture?
	• How easy is this to change?

Illustration 4 – The cultural web

Suppose you are acting as a consultant to the technical services department of a local government authority. You have found that departments are not very responsive to the needs of users and that service is inconsistent from one branch to another.

A strategic change workshop with managers resulted in the following cultural web:

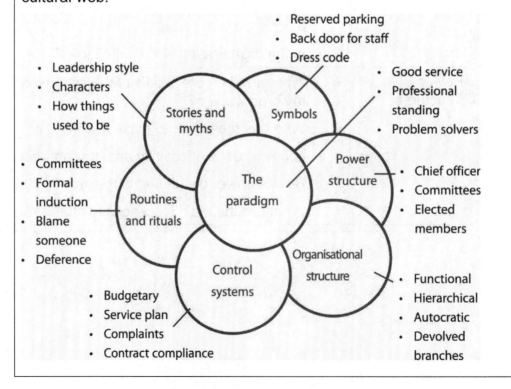

What is notable about the paradigm is that staff believe they are providing a "good service", that they have a high professional standing and see themselves as problem solvers. Unfortunately their problem solving and professional standards do not appear to be customer focused. The fact that stories and myths focus on how things "used to be" indicate staff are out of touch with user needs.

Furthermore, given the degree of local autonomy, an emphasis on status symbols such as parking spaces and a blame culture, it is hardly surprising that co-operation and standardisation across branches is poor.

These are the cultural challenges that must be met if effective change is to be implemented.

Test your understanding 4

D has recently been hired by B Brothers Ltd, a large department store which is owned and run by the Bond family. The family has owned and run the store for 75 years and little has changed in the management approach.

D has been hired in order to make suggestions relating to strategic changes needed within B Brothers, which has seen falling profitability for the last five years.

His first suggestion was to eliminate the private dining room that was set aside for senior managers. D suggested that this room was too expensive to run and damaged management's ability to interact with more junior members of staff.

D's suggestion was met with significant opposition, with senior management suggesting that he had 'failed to understand the culture of B Brothers'.

Which ONE aspect of B Brothers' corporate culture would D's suggestion have directly impacted upon?

A   Power structure

B   Control systems

C   Symbols

D   Stories and myths

Test your understanding 5

G Ltd is a training organisation based in country S. G's mission statement, which is regularly promoted by management is 'to enable students to achieve their long-term goals in the workplace'.

Employees, however, believe that the company's main aim is to simply make a profit and this has caused problems with customer service and student satisfaction at G Ltd.

According to the cultural web model, there appears to be confusion between managers and students over the organisation's _____.

Which ONE of the following words correctly fills the gap in the sentence above?

A   Mission

B   Paradigm

C   Objectives

D   Vision

Test your understanding 6 – HBY – (Case style)

HBY is a manufacturer of children's toys based in country U. It makes scale models of motor vehicles and trains using traditional methods. This means there is a heavy reliance on manual labour with a focus on quality. HBY's sales have declined since their peak around twenty years ago, although they have been static for many years. The company is owned by the founding family (who also occupy most of the senior positions on HBY's Board of Directors) and has always returned acceptable profits, with the family regularly consulting their workers regarding the strategic decisions made by the board – in spite of the organisation's rigid, bureaucratic structure. The many levels of management create a defined career path for staff, and the directors place a strong emphasis on individual growth and development.

Recently, the family have decided to sell the company to a large, multinational toy-maker, WDG, who wishes to add HBY's well-known brand name to its portfolio. WDG is a listed company and is under pressure from its shareholders to increase dividends and profits.

HBY's employees have been informed of many of WDG's plans for the company, including a move to cheaper, more automated production processes. WDG has not spoken with any staff representatives of HBY to date and redundancies have not been confirmed, though staff expect them to be significant.

WDG has announced that it will be replacing several levels of HBY's managers with a single tier of their own senior staff, who will have oversight over all of HBY's employees and remaining managers. Whereas staff at HBY have historically been left to get on with their work, unless there were specific problems, WDG's Board have stated that they will be more hands-on, helping train staff on the 'new, improved manufacturing processes being introduced by WDG'.

WDG has also suggested that the company's pay structure will be altered. Previously, staff were awarded a bonus based on a range of indicators, including sales and customer complaints. WDG wishes to pay staff on a piecework basis and is planning to cut back on the regular social gatherings that HBY has historically provided for its workers.

Finally, WDG has indicated that it no longer wishes to pursue the quality accreditation that HBY has attained for the last ten years, as the 'costs outweigh the benefits'.

The staff of HBY have expressed their concern to the current owners. Staff are unionised and they have stated their intention to strike over the proposals. A number of HBY's senior managers have stated that WDG 'clearly fails to understand the culture of HBY and should not be allowed to destroy the organisation that HBY's staff have worked so hard to build.'

Required:

Draft a report to the management of WDG, which identifies the various aspects of the existing culture of HBY, using an appropriate model to structure your report.

You should also use your report to explain the reasons for HBY's staff resisting the proposed takeover by WDG.

(25 minutes)

5   McKinsey 7S Model

Like the cultural web, McKinsey's 7S model looks at corporate culture and the various components that it is made up of. McKinsey saw culture as seven interconnected elements, each beginning with the letter S.

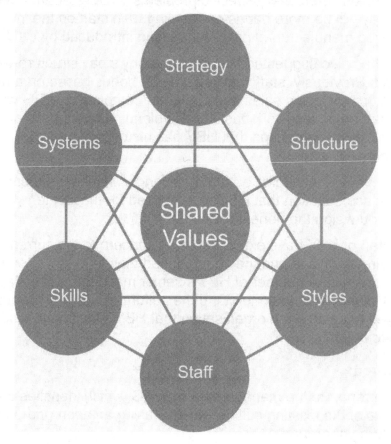

Three of these factors are referred to as 'hard' (tangible and easy to quantify):

- **Structure** – this looks at the way the organisation is structured and who reports to whom.

- **Strategy** – relates to the ways in which the organisation plans to gain a competitive advantage or achieve other objectives.

- **Systems** – these are the daily activities and procedures followed by staff.

The remaining four factors are 'soft' (less easily quantified and more subjective):

- **Skills** – the skills, abilities and competences of the organisation's employees.

- **Style** – the style of leadership adopted within the organisation.

- **Staff** – the people that make up the organisation.

- **Shared values** – the core values of the organisation (i.e. the paradigm).

The model suggests that all seven elements have to be aligned with each in order for the organisation to operate effectively.

In the context of change, McKinsey's 7S model can be used to look at the factors that could be affected by the change process, as well helping improve the organisation's understanding of the wider effect of change. If one of the S factors changes, it will have a knock-on effect on other S factors.

For instance, if the organisation introduces a new automated assembly process, this would be a change to the company's systems. However, this would also likely impact elsewhere in the organisation. Staff may find they lack appropriate **skills**, leading to uncertainty and resistance. It may lead to a reduction in the number of workers, affecting the **staff** and **structure** of the organisation. If staff require fewer skills to undertake their roles, the **style** of management within the business may be affected. Even a small change can therefore have wide-ranging impacts on the organisation.

Test your understanding 7

Which THREE of the following are elements within McKinsey's 7S model of corporate culture?

A   Symbols

B   Stories and myths

C   Structure

D   Support

E   Skills

F   Styles

Test your understanding 8

Which ONE of the following factors of the McKinsey 7S model is classified as a 'soft' element?

A   Structure

B   Strategy

C   Staff

D   Systems

6   Resistance to change

Resistance to change is the action taken by individuals and groups when they perceive that a change that is occurring is a threat to them.

 Resistance is 'any attitude or behaviour that reflects a person's unwillingness to make or support a desired change'

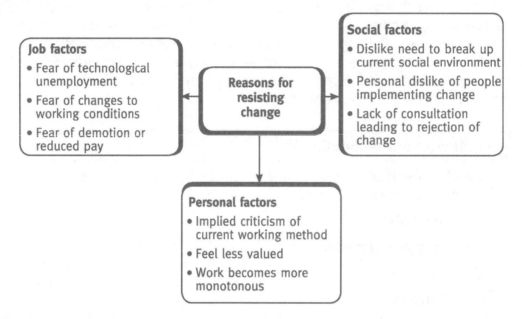

Resistance may take many forms, including active or passive, overt or covert, individual or organised, aggressive or timid. For each source of resistance, management need to provide an appropriate response, e.g.:

Source of resistance	Possible response
• The need for security and the familiar • Having the opinion that no change is needed • Trying to protect vested interests	• Provide information and encouragement, invite involvement • Clarify the purpose of the change and how it will be made • Demonstrate the problem or the opportunity that makes changes desirable

Reasons for resisting change (Kotter and Schlesinger)

According to Kotter and Schlesinger (1979) there are four reasons that explain why certain people resist change.

- Parochial self-interest (some people are concerned with the implication of the change for themselves and how it may affect their own interests, rather than considering the effects for the success of the business).

- Misunderstanding (communication problems; inadequate information).

- Low tolerance to change (certain people are very keen on security and stability in their work).

- Different assessments of the situation (some employees may disagree on the reasons for the change and on the advantages and disadvantages of the change process).

Understanding the causes of resistance to change is vital if management are to deal with such resistance in the appropriate way. This is looked at in detail in the next chapter.

Test your understanding 9

Which THREE of the following would usually be classed as social factors leading to resistance to change?

A   Fear of unemployment

B   Dislike of person leading change

C   Lack of consultation regarding the change

D   Changes to current social environment

E   Implied criticism of current methods

F   Fear of demotion or reduced pay

G   Work becoming less interesting

Test your understanding 10

J runs a small business manufacturing personalised stationery (such as envelopes and paper). She has recently decided to automate parts of this process, meaning that all four of her current staff members will see their overtime pay reduced (though there will be no effect on their basic pay). The main activities of each staff member will not change significantly as a result of the introduction of automation.

J feels that the current overtime payments are unsupportable and that the business will be unable to grow unless the new system is introduced. Local competitors are already currently using this automated process.

Although J has communicated the situation to the staff and they are all fully aware of the problems faced by the business, they have complained bitterly to J about the proposal and have suggested that they will refuse to use the new automated system.

According to Kotter and Schlesinger, which ONE of the following is the primary reason for resistance among J's employees?

A   Differing assessments of the situation

B   Parochial self-interest

C   Misunderstanding

D   Low tolerance to change

7 Summary

```
                    ┌─────────────────┐
                    │   The context   │
                    │    of charge    │
                    └─────────────────┘
```

Resistance
- job factors
- social factors
- personal factors

Triggers
- internal
- external

Culture
- 'the way we do things round here' – Handy

Types of change
- evolution
- adaption
- revolution
- reconstruction

Cultural web
- stories and myths
- symbols
- power structure
- organisational culture
- control systems
- routines and rituals
- paradigm

McKinsey 7S
- strategy
- structure
- systems
- shared values
- skills
- styles
- staff

Test your understanding answers

Test your understanding 1

The correct answer is C

By definition.

Test your understanding 2

The correct answer is A

Change is classified with reference to two factors – extent and speed of the change.

The change in H is clearly rapid, as all the traditional products used for its chemical have been banned. It is urgently looking for alternatives to prevent a total collapse of the company.

The scope of change seems small (a realignment). H will still be producing LKL – it will simply be selling it to a different type of organisation. While this may require some changes (such as marketing and customer management), H is still fundamentally producing and selling LKL.

Test your understanding 3 – (Integration question)

Incremental change means step-by-step changes over time, in small steps. When incremental change occurs within an organisation, it is possible for the organisation to adapt to the change without having to alter its culture or structures significantly. Employees are able to adapt to the gradual changes, and are not unsettled by them.

In contrast, transformational change is a sweeping change that has immediate and widespread effects. The effect of transformational change is usually to alter the structure and culture of the organisation, often with major staff redundancies and the recruitment of new staff with new skills.

The spokesperson for the bank has argued that the change will be incremental. Since the change will take place over a long period of time, staff will have time to adapt to the new structure. There will be no compulsory redundancies and staff will be re-trained in new skills. Although some branches will close, others will remain open, and customers will be offered additional facilities through on-line banking.

The trade union leader believes that the change will be much more dramatic. He might believe that many employees will leave the bank because they are unable to adapt to the new service, or because they are unwilling to re-locate from the branches that are closed down. The bank might push through the branch closure programme more quickly than it has currently proposed, and staff redundancies could be made compulsory if there are not enough individuals willing to take voluntary redundancy.

Essentially, the two individuals take differing viewpoints because they are looking at change differently. The spokesperson for the bank wants to persuade employees to accept the change, and even welcome it. The trade union representative wants to warn employees about the potential consequences, and has therefore stressed the risks.

Test your understanding 4

The correct answer is C

The private dining room is a symbol of the authority and position of the senior managers. Trying to remove this is likely to cause resistance as senior managers will see D's suggestion as a way of reducing their status within the organisation.

The proposed change does not directly affect the senior manger's authority or position within the business, suggesting that it will not affect the power structure of B Brothers.

The removal of the private dining room is also unlikely to impact the way that the organisation controls its staff (there is no change to the way that staff are rewarded or punished) and there is no evidence that it will alter the stories and myths – i.e. what staff members believe and say about the organisation.

Test your understanding 5

The correct answer is B

The paradigm is the overall aim and purpose of the organisation. This is clearly confused at G Ltd, leading to problems with customer management.

There is no confusion over the mission itself. This has been published, meaning that staff are aware of the current mission statement. They simply do not agree that it represents the actual purpose of the organisation.

Test your understanding 6 – HBY – (Case style)

Report

To: The Board of Directors, WDG

From: A. Consultant

Date: 18/08/XX

Subject: Cultural issues and resistance at HBY

Introduction

This report will examine the impact of WDG's proposals relating to the takeover of HBY. Specifically, it will look at how these proposals will affect the culture of HBY post-acquisition.

According to Handy, culture is defined as 'the way we do things round here'.

When analysing an organisation's corporate culture, the most logical model to use is the Cultural Web. This suggests that the culture of an organisation can be broken down into six different aspects. Any attempt to significantly change the culture of the organisation, as WDG is attempting to do with HBY, is likely to lead to significant resistance.

Symbols

This looks at the symbols or symbolic actions that typify the organisation.

Within HBY, the symbols include the regular social gatherings supplied by the company. This indicates that staff wellbeing and happiness is valued by the company. Cutbacks to this area are likely to cause resistance as staff will feel that WDG is indicating that they are no longer as valued as they once were.

Power structure

This examines who is in charge (or who has the power) within the organisation.

HBY currently appears to have several levels of management, with the original founding family having ultimate control over the organisation. WDG intends to replace many of these managers with a single layer of their own management.

This is likely to upset many of HBY's employees as it will not only lead to redundancies, but it will also change the reporting system that they are currently used to.

Organisational structure

The current management structure of HBY appears to be bureaucratic, with a number of levels of management. WDG is planning to replace this with a single level of its own management, flattening the structure.

This may lead to resistance as it may reduce the chances for internal promotion for HBY's existing staff. There will be fewer management positions, many of which will be filled by WDG's staff for the foreseeable future.

Control systems

Controls appear to be few and far between under the traditional approach taken by HBY. Staff were largely expected to get on with their own jobs, with management only getting involved if there was a problem.

The new management systems proposed by WDG involve a much more hands-on approach, with employees being trained in the new systems by WDG managers. This is likely to cause resistance as staff will feel that they are no longer trusted by their management to get on with their work in an effective manner.

The shift from a bonus based on a range of indicators, which focused on quality, to pay which is piecework, and therefore only based on the level of productivity, also indicates a shift in what the business expects from its employees. This is likely to cause confusion amongst workers who are used to a quality focus.

Routines and rituals

Linked to control systems, WDG are suggesting that the existing methods used by HBY's workers for many years are inferior to the 'new, improved' WDG methods.

Employees may therefore feel that there is an implied criticism of their existing working methods by WDG, increasing resistance.

The fact that WDG has no interest in pursuing the quality accreditation that HBY have historically obtained also indicates that it places little value on the work currently being done by HBY and this, in turn, will increase resistance.

Stories and myths

The staff of HBY feels that, due to the participative style of the existing management, they have 'helped to build' the company and that they are a major reason for its historic success.

Whether this is the case or not, WDG's desire to implement the changes without any staff consultation is a departure from the management style that staff of HBY are used to and is likely to upset them.

Paradigm

Overall, HBY's approach has been a participative one, with defined roles and a strong focus on quality. WDG seems to want to shift this towards a focus on output and profitability. This fundamental move in culture is, understandably, a difficult one for the staff of HBY to accept.

Test your understanding 7

The correct answers are: C, E and F

Note that A and B are factors from the cultural web model.

Test your understanding 8

The correct answer is C

Soft factors are those that are less easy to analyse and evaluate.

Test your understanding 9

The correct answers are B, C and D

A and F are job factors, E and G are personal factors.

Test your understanding 10

The correct answer is B

J's employees are motivated by their own self-interest, rather than the ongoing success of the business.

J's staff are fully aware of the situation that the business is in – including the fact that J's rivals have adopted similar automated systems. There is no evidence that they have failed to understand how much of a threat this may be to J's operations. This suggests that options A and C are incorrect.

It is unclear whether J's staff have faced changes in their working practices in the past, so there is no evidence to support a low tolerance of change. It is therefore unlikely to be the primary reason for resistance.

Change management – the role of the leader in managing change

Chapter learning objectives

Lead	Component
E3: Recommend change management techniques and methodologies	(c) Discuss the role of the leader in managing change

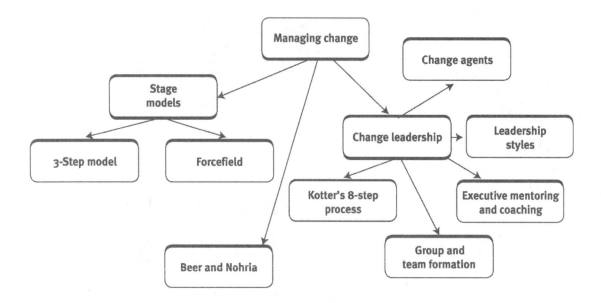

1 Introduction

As can be seen from the previous chapter, understanding the factors that impact on change management can be complex. However, even when a manager has a good understanding of the context of change within their organisation, they still need to be able to successfully implement the change itself.

Given the conflicting views of different stakeholders – such as shareholders, employees and customers – achieving change within an organisation is often difficult and prone to failure. Due to this, a number of different theorists have examined the issue and identified possible approaches to managing the change process within the organisation.

2 The role of the leadership

In order to successfully implement change, most organisations will require someone to take overall control of the change process. This person is referred to as the **change leader**.

Who is the change leader?

The change leader is a key figure within the organisation who takes overall responsibility and control for the proposed change within the organisation.

For a major, organisation-wide change this role may well be best filled by the CEO, but it can be taken on by anyone with the appropriate power and leadership skills within the organisation.

What does the change leader do?

The change leader is responsible for articulating what change is needed and why, acting as a figurehead for the change process, as well as helping to deal with any problems or conflicts that arise during the change process.

Kotter (Leading Change, 1996) suggested that leading change is an 8-step process.

8-step process of change leadership

- **Establish a sense of urgency** – the change leader needs to help others see the need for change and convince them that it must be implemented promptly.

  Failure to create a sense of urgency leads to a lack of motivation from staff – the people who will ultimately be implementing the change you wish to create. Without motivation, they will not see the need to get involved, leading to failure. This sense of urgency is therefore vital and means that change leaders may take drastic action to create it. One company manager commissioned his organisation's first ever customer satisfaction surveys, knowing the results would be adverse and then made them public. This created a strong driving force for change within the organisation.

- **Creating the guiding coalition** – the change leader is unlikely to be able to control the entire change process by themselves. They must therefore assemble a group with enough power to lead the change process and ensure that they are able to act as a team.

  The coalition may not simply be formed from senior management, as it can include anyone with skills or knowledge which could be useful in the change process. However, they will need sufficient power – whether through job titles or reputation, to accomplish the change and (where necessary) force it through against opposition.

- **Developing a change vision** – the change leader needs to create an overall vision of the future, illustrating what the change is designed to accomplish as well as its benefits. Strategies will be developed to achieve the proposed changes.

  Failure to develop a clear, concise vision that can be communicated to stakeholders means that the project can lack focus and goal congruence. The change management process may simply collapse into a series of conflicting projects that do not move the organisation in the desired direction.

- **Communicating the vision** – the leader needs to communicate the vision and strategies identified in the previous stage to as many stakeholders as possible. This will maximise buy-in.

  Implementing major change in an organisation requires the involvement of (potentially) a large number of people at all levels. Without plenty of communication, these people will never see the importance of change and will be unwilling to make any effort towards accomplishing it.

- **Empowering broad-based action** – the change leader needs to remove obstacles to change (restraining forces) and encourage staff to get involved in generating ideas.

  Using Lewin's forcefield analysis (as discussed later in this chapter) can be a useful exercise here. It helps management identify what will cause resistance, so that plans can be created to deal with these issues.

- **Generating short-term wins** – plan for interim achievements that can easily be made visible, then publicise and reward staff members involved.

  Change processes can take a long time to implement – in some cases years. Most people will become demotivated if they do not see any changes within the short to mid-term. Without some short term wins, they will therefore become demotivated and cynical about the success of the change management process.

- **Never letting up** – maintain the change process, hiring, promoting and developing employees who support and implement the required changes. The use of specific change agents may be of use here (the role of change agents are explored later in this chapter).

  It is easy for an organisation to believe that its change process is complete when it has completed all relevant major projects. Unfortunately, as Lewin's three-stage model indicates later in the chapter, it is easy for staff to slip back into old habits and ways of working. Management will need to monitor the change process for a significant amount of time after 'completion' to ensure that the change has indeed become permanent.

- **Incorporating changes into the culture** – continually reinforce the change and communicate and reward achievement. This stage looks at ways of ensuring that the new change a standard part of everyday work and to prevent staff slipping back into their old habits.

  Management need to ensure that they show staff how the changes have improved performance and how they have benefitted. It is also important to ensure that existing and future managers are supportive of the new processes. Choosing new managers who disagree with the changes that have been made could lead to staff slipping back into old habits and practises.

> ### Test your understanding 1
>
> X plc has been performing well for many years, with staff enjoying significant bonuses. However, recent strategic analysis by the Board of X plc has identified that there are a number of rival organisations starting to gain a share in X's traditional markets. They feel that, unless X significantly updates its working practises, it will lose its market position within three years. B was recently hired as CEO of X plc. She was selected as the company felt that she was the best candidate to lead X plc through a period of major change.
>
> After a thorough review of X's operations, B created a powerful group of managers and directors across the organisation to help her implement her proposed, wide-ranging changes. She spent a significant amount of time explaining the process of change that was to be implemented, with a series of staff meetings under the slogan 'changing X for the new markets'. At these meeting she involved staff and tried to build their ideas into the final change strategy. The Board refused to allow B to explain the new entrants to the market, as they felt that the company would see a drop in its share price if this information was leaked to the markets.

> B backed up her proposed changes with a series of interim goals. When the organisation reached these targets, she planned to widely publicise them within the organisation in order to improve motivation amongst the staff.
>
> Unfortunately B struggled to motivate the staff and, in spite of her staff meetings, little change occurred. After six months, B had failed to reach any of her interim goals. She decided to step aside and left the company.
>
> Kotter suggested that there were eight steps required to successfully lead change. B's failure to achieve which ONE of these eight steps led to the ultimate failure of the change process at X plc?
>
> A   Creation of a guiding coalition
>
> B   Communicating the vision
>
> C   Establishing a sense of urgency
>
> D   Generating short-term wins

Group and team formation

One key aspect of change leadership is the ability to form a group of individuals within the organisation who can help to control and implement any proposed changes (Kotter's 'guiding coalition' mentioned above). This group, as well as the other groups and teams that they form within the organisation, will actually implement change throughout the organisation. The change leader therefore **must** be able to manage them effectively.

A 'group' is simply a collection of individuals. The group the change leader selects may well come from various parts of the organisation, such as finance, human resources and sales – any part of the organisation that may be affected by the proposed change or have useful input into it.

There is no guarantee that this group of individuals will work well together. It is therefore very important that the change leader turns this group into a team.

 A team is more than a group. It is a set of individuals who must work together in order to accomplish shared objectives.

Teams usually:

- share a common goal

- enjoy working together

- are committed to achieving certain goals.

A team will have its own culture, leader and should be geared towards achieving a certain goal – in this case, implementing the desired changes within the organisation.

A change leader needs to ensure that his change team works well together to ensure that they will effectively assist in the implementation of the change process.

Team building

Teams are not always able to achieve their goals without some outside intervention. As such, change leaders may need to create 'team-building' exercises. These are tasks that are designed to develop team members and their ability to work together.

Team building exercises tend to be based around developing the team in several areas, including:

- **improved communication**, such as through the use of problem solving exercises which force team members to discuss problems the team is facing.

- **building trust** between team members, which will help them work together effectively.

- **social interaction** between the individuals within the team can help to reduce conflict and increase their ability to work effectively.

Benefits and drawbacks of teams

The change leader needs to be aware of the potential advantages and drawbacks of using a team to help implement change within the organisation.

Benefits include:

- a mixture of skills and abilities within the team. Each member may be from a different part of the organisation and may therefore have unique skills and knowledge that can be used to help the change process

- better control, with opportunities for individual performance to be reviewed and controlled by other team members

- improved communication – this can also lead to increased buy-in by the rest of the organisation. For example, employees within the HR department are more likely to accept change if an HR staff member is part of the change team.

However, there are problems with the use of a team, including:

- slower decision-making, as discussion is needed to come to any agreement – also potentially leading to increased conflict

- decisions may be compromises, rather than decisions that are beneficial to the business and change process as a whole

- group pressure to conform can lead to team members agreeing to decisions that they know are wrong because other team members support it

- teams may have a lack of individual responsibility, as responsibility is shared between all members. They may therefore be more willing to take riskier courses of action than individuals.

Leadership styles – Kotter and Schlesinger

Kotter and Schlesinger set out the following change approaches to deal with resistance:

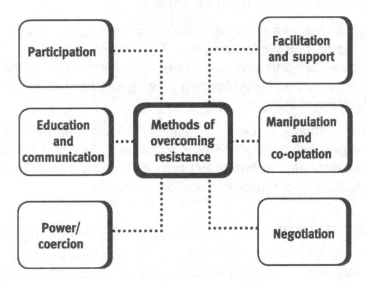

Key considerations when deciding upon a leadership style

- The speed at which change must be introduced
- The strength of the pressure for change
- The level of resistance expected
- The amount of power you hold
- How much information you need before you can implement the change and how long it will take to get that information.

Explanation of the Kotter and Schlesinger styles

- Participation – aims to involve employees, usually by allowing some input into decision making. This could easily result in employees enjoying raised levels of autonomy, by allowing them to design their own jobs, pay structures, etc.

- Education and communication – used as a background factor to reinforce another approach. This strategy relies upon the hopeful belief that communication about the benefits of change to employees will result in their acceptance of the need to exercise the changes necessary.

- Power/coercion – involves the compulsory approach by management to implement change. This method finds its roots from the formal authority that management possesses, together with legislative support. This approach is often required where the speed of change needs to be rapid and where possible crises occur.

- Facilitation and support – employees may need to be counselled to help them overcome their fears and anxieties about change. Management may find it necessary to develop individual awareness of the need for change.

- Manipulation and co-optation – involves covert attempts to sidestep potential resistance. The information that is disseminated is selective and distorted to only emphasise the benefits of the change. Co-optation involves giving key people access to the decision-making process.

- Negotiation – is often practised in unionised companies. Simply, the process of negotiation is exercised, enabling several parties with opposing interests to bargain. This bargaining leads to a situation of compromise and agreement.

Illustration 1 – Kotter and Schlesinger in practice

P is an organisation which wants to undertake a significant restructuring and is concerned about staff resistance. Kotter and Schlesinger's six styles could be a useful way for the business to deal with this resistance.

Education and communication

The management of P could look at ways of helping staff see the need for (and logic of) the proposed reorganisation. This could involve, amongst other things:

- meetings with employees

- presentations

- emails.

This is useful if P's managers believe that the resistance from staff will be based on inaccurate information. For example, employees may believe that the restructuring will lead to job losses. If this is not the case, then an education programme will help put staff fears to rest. Explaining the reasoning behind the restructuring (i.e. the need to deal with new, efficient competitors) can also help improve staff support.

However, the process of communicating with all employees can be time consuming, especially in larger organisations – meaning that if P's proposed changes are urgent, this may not be the best approach. In addition, employees may simply not believe the information that P's managers are providing, meaning that the communication process will fail to be effective.

It is also worth noting that if employees do not have inaccurate information, this approach is unlikely to work. If P's plans will involve significant redundancies, then communicating this to employees will clearly not reduce resistance.

Participation and involvement

This approach requires P's managers to involve employees in the development and implementation of the reorganisation of the business. This means listening to the employees affected by the proposed changes and making use of their advice.

This approach will work well if P's employees are highly skilled and/or experienced, as they may have valuable ideas that will benefit the proposed restructuring. In addition, involving staff members in the restructuring decision-making process will significantly reduce resistance, as it increases employee buy-in.

However, if employees are less skilled or experienced, they may fail to come up with valuable input into the change process. If employees are cautious, they may fail to make the major changes that are required. For instance, if P needs to make significant job cuts in order to compete in its market, it is unlikely that staff members will make that suggestion!

Involving a large number of employees in the design and implementation of a new strategy is likely to be time consuming (as per education and communication) and is likely to therefore be inappropriate if rapid change is needed.

Facilitation and support

This involves management looking at ways of being supportive of employees who may be worried about the changes being proposed. For P this could include:

- training staff in the use of any new systems which are being introduced

- giving employees time off after the reorganisation has taken effect

- giving time off/support for any employees who are being made redundant to find another job

- listening and providing emotional support.

This is a particularly effective approach to managing a situation where resistance is caused by fear and anxiety of the proposals, such as the fear of unemployment, or the fear of not being able to do a new role adequately.

The main drawback of facilitation and support is that it, again, takes time and money – and can still ultimately be unsuccessful.

Negotiation and agreement

This would involve P negotiating with employees to find a restructuring approach which is satisfactory to both P and its staff. This could involve:

- reducing the extent of the restructuring to keep staff happy

- offering alternative benefits to employees if they support the restructuring, such as increased pay or better working conditions. Employees who are made redundant could be offered more attractive redundancy packages.

Negotiation is particularly useful when one party is clearly going to lose out under the proposed change, but still has the power to significantly resist the change process. Within P, this situation could occur if employees are heavily unionised. P may have to offer some compromises to avoid damaging strike action.

Ultimately, however, negotiation can be time consuming for the company. In addition the agreement demanded by powerful other parties may be expensive.

Manipulation and co-optation

This would occur if P's managers try to use covert attempts to influence the staff. It typically involves selective use of information.

P could consider releasing information which makes it look as if the company is in financial difficulties (even if it is not) as a way of convincing staff that the restructuring is necessary for the survival of the business. Staff may simply be scared into thinking there is a crisis coming that only the proposed restructuring can avoid.

Co-optation involves selectively promoting key staff members (or offering them incentives) if they decide to support the proposed change. This is not participation, as P's managers are not interested in these staff member's opinions – they simply want their endorsement, which may reduce resistance elsewhere in the business.

Both of these approaches have possible drawbacks. Manipulation is likely to lead to P's employees feeling that they have been lied to (if the truth ever comes out) and can therefore destroy future working relations between employees and management. Producing misleading information is also a breach of an accountant's professional code of ethics (in particular integrity and professional behaviour) and should therefore not be recommended by P's strategic management accountant.

Co-optation may lead to employees feeling that their managers are trying to 'buy their silence' and this can lead to more bad feeling and increased resistance.

However, both manipulation and co-optation are relatively cheap to undertake and can be implemented quickly. This may therefore be a consideration for P if the proposed restructuring is required urgently.

Explicit and implicit coercion

This involves P's management attempt to force the restructuring through by threatening staff (for example with the loss of their jobs, demotions, or pay cuts) or by actually dismissing them or transferring them.

Like manipulation, this is likely to cause significant bad feeling from employees and this may lead to a breakdown of future working relations.

However, it is fast, cheap and may be the most effective route to take if change is required urgently – especially if it will be unpopular, regardless of how it is introduced.

If P intends to fire a large proportion of its workforce as part of the restructuring process, none of the other methods discussed above are likely to lead to reduced resistance. As such, coercion may be the only possibility for the company.

Test your understanding 2

H has recently announced a series of compulsory redundancies amongst staff. It plans to offer counselling to staff members affected by this process and has offered them time off (at full pay) to allow them to look for alternative jobs.

Which ONE of Kotter and Schlesinger's leadership styles has H adopted?

A   Education and communication

B   Facilitation and support

C   Coercion

D   Participation

Test your understanding 3

U is an organisation which is currently experiencing a crisis. Due to the loss of a major customer, U feels that it has to cut a minimum of 30% of its workforce within the next month or it faces bankruptcy. U's 10,000 employees are not heavily unionised, but U expects significant resistance from staff when it announces the job losses.

Which ONE of Kotter and Schlesinger's leadership styles would be most appropriate for U to adopt when dealing with its employees in this situation?

A   Education and communication

B   Negotiation

C   Manipulation and co-optation

D   Coercion

Test your understanding 4 – Grey – (Case style)

Grey Limited is a conglomerate organisation with two major divisions: A and B. The two divisions are run as autonomous business units as they operate in completely different markets. Both are entering a period of organisational change and the directors of Grey are considering what style of management would be the most effective for each division.

The CEO of Grey has asked you to produce a set of notes for her, suggesting which leadership style(s) would be most appropriate in each division and why. She has sent you the following background information document.

Briefing document – Divisions A and B

Division A is currently highly profitable. However, it is looking at ways of increasing its efficiency. The managers of A have decided to centralise the accounting function within the business, which will reduce overheads and allow for a reduction in the number of employees. Division A has always had an excellent relationship with its relatively small number of highly skilled staff and is concerned about how these plans may affect that.

Division B is currently loss-making. It is also planning on reducing the number of staff it employs, but wishes to do so across all departments. B has a large number of workers and initial estimates are that 18% of all staff members will be made redundant. B has undertaken similar exercises in previous years, leading to significant conflict between the relatively unskilled staff and managers. The directors of Grey have informed the managers of B that if the division does not move back into profit in the near future, the division will be closed.

Required:

Produce the notes as requested by the CEO.

(20 minutes)

Test your understanding 5 – (Integration question)

You are a manager who is in charge of a team that has been given the task of introducing a new management reporting system into regional offices. There is considerable resistance to the changes from the office managers, and comments that you have heard include the following.

- I have more important work priorities to take up my time.

- I'm used to the old system.

- The new system is too complicated.

- The new system will create more paperwork.

- The new system will make me more accountable.

- My job in the new system is not clear.

How would you try to deal with this resistance to change?

(5 minutes)

---

3 Stage models of the change process

Lewin's three-stage ("ice cube") model

The three-stage model of change was proposed by Kurt Lewin in the 1950's. He argued that, in order for change to occur successfully, organisations need to progress through three stages.

This process, shown in the following diagram, includes unfreezing habits or standard operating procedures, changing to new patterns and refreezing to ensure lasting effects.

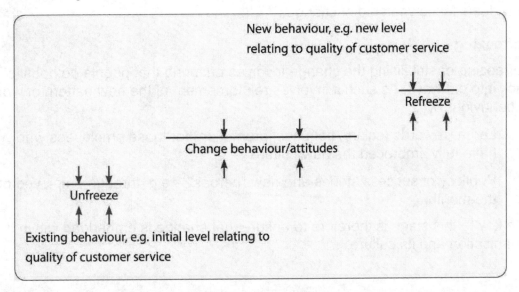

The process of change comprises three stages.

Unfreezing

In this stage, managers need to make the need for change so obvious that most people can easily understand and accept it. Unfreezing also involves creating the initial motivation to change by convincing staff of the undesirability of the present situation. Ways of destabilising the present stability could include:

- Identifying and exploiting existing areas of stress or dissatisfaction.

- Creating or introducing additional forces for change, such as tighter budgets and targets or new personnel in favour of the change.

- Increasing employee knowledge about markets, competitors and the need for change.

Essentially, effective communication and explaining the need for change is vital within the unfreeze stage.

Change

The change process itself is mainly concerned with identifying what the new behaviour or norm should be. This stage will often involve:

- Establishing new patterns of behaviour

- Setting up new reporting relationships

- Creating new reward/incentive schemes

- Introducing a new style of management.

It is vital that new information is communicated concerning the new attitudes, culture and concepts that the organisation wants to be adopted, so that these are internalised by employees.

In the 'change' stage participation and involvement is often necessary so that individuals feel ownership of change.

Refreezing

Refreezing or stabilising the change involves ensuring that people do not slip back into old ways. As such it involves reinforcement of the new pattern of work or behaviour by:

- Larger rewards (salary, bonuses, promotion) for those employees who have fully embraced the new culture

- Publicity of success stories and new "heroes" – e.g. through employee of the month.

The key to this stage is therefore to ensure that change is embedded within the organisation and its culture.

Bank automation

During the economic crisis of 2008, many companies were faced with the need to restructure their organisations in order to cut costs and improve efficiency – with many banks being particularly hard-hit.

A number of banks increased the amount of automation in their branches. This involved the purchase of cash machines that are able to process deposits of cash and cheques as well as performing other basic account management functions. Many other traditional branch functions now require customers to telephone central call centres rather than going into a branch. These changes allowed the bank to reduce the number of staff in their branches, saving money.

However, such an approach was likely to create significant resistance from staff – especially employees who work within the branches themselves. The bank may have wished to use Lewin's three-stage model as a way of managing the change process.

Unfreezing

This involves convincing employees of the initial need for the increased automation in the branches. While this may be difficult to do, especially if employees are heavily unionised, it is a crucial step in the change management process.

The bank may choose to explain to employees about its current position in the market and the effect that the economic downturn has had on profits. If reducing costs will help to secure the long-term survival of the entire bank, many employees may be convinced of the need to proceed with the change.

The directors of the bank may also stress any potential benefits of the proposals for the remaining branch employees. For example, a reduction in the number of basic account queries from customers may free up time for more interesting work, such as helping customers review their finances.

Change

This is the stage where the proposed change actually occurs. It will involve the reduction in the number of branch employees and the installation of new machinery into the branches.

This will require training for employees. They will need to be able to deal with customer queries and complaints about the new branch procedures as well as how to maintain the new cash machines.

Communication is vital at this stage. Employees must know what is expected of them during and after the change management process.

Refreezing

This stage tries to ensure that bank staff do not return to the old systems. In this case managers need to prevent staff from processing basic customer transactions themselves rather than convincing customers to use the new automated systems.

This may involve the creation of new reward schemes to encourage staff to adopt the new procedures. For instance, branch staff could receive an increased bonus if a high proportion of their customers start maintaining their accounts using the automated system. They may be penalised if they continue using the old systems.

Managers can also reinforce the new approach by publicising success stories of branches that have embraced the change and by promoting key members of staff who supported the automation process.

Criticisms of Lewin's three-stage model

Kanter et al suggest that Lewin's ice cube model is too simplistic.

They argue that the model is based on the assumptions that organisations are stable and static so change results only from concentrated effort and only in one direction.

Kanter et al argue that change is 'multi-directional and ubiquitous', that it happens in all directions simultaneously and is often a continuous process.

Test your understanding 6

According to Lewin's three-stage model, which ONE of the following activities would be part of the 'unfreezing' stage?

A Explaining the need for change

B Creation of new reward schemes

C Publicity of success stories

D Training of staff in new ways of working

Test your understanding 7 – WW – (Case style)

WW is a company specialising in industrial paint manufacturing. It has recently experienced significant growth in turnover and has opened two new factories to help it cope with the additional demand.

The managers of WW have become concerned that their current accounting software is no longer adequate for their needs. The current system is a basic one, which is mainly designed to record transactions and produce financial statements at the end of each period. Given the growth in the business, the managers of WW now need additional information, such as the production of monthly management reports and the ability to accurately cost each unit of their products.

The current accounting system does not support these functions, meaning the accounting department is required to produce the information manually, which is both complex and time-consuming. WW's managers are concerned that this delay in obtaining management information may be putting the firm at a disadvantage in the marketplace.

The managers are therefore currently considering the purchase of a new, more complex, accounting package that will easily allow the production of the management accounting information that they need.

WW has a small accounting department with six members of staff. All of these staff members have been employees of the company for many years. The current accounting package has been in use within WW for the last seven years.

Required:

Using Lewin's three-stage model, explain how WW could manage the changeover to the new accounting package.

(15 minutes)

Force field analysis

Lewin also emphasised the importance of force field analysis. He argued that managers should consider any change situation in terms of:

- the factors encouraging and facilitating the change (the driving forces)
- the factors that hinder change (the restraining forces).

Change will only be successful if the driving forces are larger than the restraining forces.

If we want to bring about change we must change the equilibrium by:

- strengthening the driving forces
- weakening the restraining forces
- or both.

The model encourages us to identify the various forces impinging on the target of change, to consider the relative strengths of these forces and to explore alternative strategies for modifying the force field.

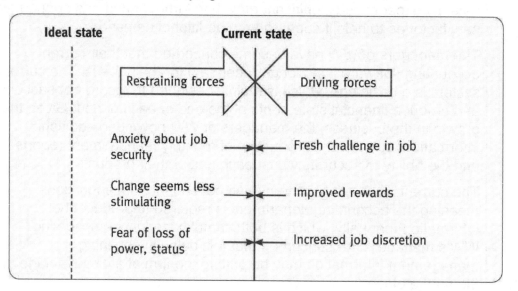

Test your understanding 8

N is the manager of a small division of NNB Ltd, which makes solar cells. N wishes to introduce a new shift system for his staff. A large number of N's staff have stated that they will not accept the new shift pattern.

N was initially uncertain of the reason for this resistance. After investigating, it was discovered that several staff members have misunderstood the proposals and spread the rumour within the division that the new shift pattern would lead to redundancies.

N plans to communicate this error to his employees and explain to them that, while the new shift pattern will improve efficiency, it will not lead to redundancies.

According to Lewin's forcefield model, N's plan to communicate with staff an example of _____ .

Which ONE of the following phrases best fits the gap in the above sentence?

A   Reducing the restraining forces

B   Increasing the restraining forces

C   Reducing the driving forces

D   Increasing the driving forces

Test your understanding 9 – GVF – (Case style)

Great Value Foods (GVF) is one of Bigland's leading supermarket chains, having traded for over fifty years. Though fierce competitive activity had reduced the major players in the industry to six large chains in the last twenty years, the competitive pressures and large-scale capital investment required had not prevented all new entrants to the market. A high proportion of all workers in the supermarket industry are unionised.

A few foreign competitors seeking new markets had managed to secure a market share by offering unbranded goods at extremely low prices. This development increased the pressure on GVF as these new entrants were attracting consumers that had been part of GVF's traditional customer base.

In the midst of these difficulties, GVF was presented with a major opportunity. One of its competitors was experiencing difficulties and offered GVF the chance to purchase 60 of their stores in the south of the country. GVF borrowed $800m and made the purchase, doubling its number of outlets.

As GVF took over management of the new stores, however, it realised that considerable time and funds would be required to convert them to its own distinctive format and to the modern standards now expected by customers. This not only delayed the expected revenue stream, but also required additional borrowing, raising GVF's gearing to uncomfortably high levels. The government of Bigland subsequently raised interest rates, increasing the financial pressure on GVF.

During all this, GVF had been seeking to catch up with its competitors in a number of ways. This had included increasing the number of own-brand products it offered, along with the development of a new central distribution system that experts agreed was one of the best in the country. However, there were delays in distribution of supplies to some stores during the run up to the country's most important festive period. This resulted in a considerable loss for the company and three of the directors considered responsible for the problems were sacked.

These problems, together with an accompanying decline in profits, resulted in a fall in GVF's share price. Investors were concerned that GVF had paid too much for its 60 southern stores and that a rights issue would be needed to reduce the company's debt burden.

GVF has recently appointed a new CEO and she has spent her first few weeks reviewing the company and its problems, She has found that the company has too many layers of management, narrow functional attitudes and a controlling, bureaucratic head office culture. She feels that the business is no longer effective or responding to customer needs.

> You are currently working as a strategic management accountant for the new CEO of GVF. She has told you that she wishes to involve you in the strategic decision-making process within the company and you have just opened up the following email from her:
>
> **To: Anne Sma**
>
> **From: Rebecca Smith (CEO)**
>
> **Date: 12/4/20XX**
>
> **Subject: Strategic change issues within GVF**
>
> Hi Anne,
>
> As you know, I've been trying to analyse the problems within GVF and come to some sensible conclusions about our way forward as a company and I would like your help.
>
> I know that when I was employed by GVF, several key shareholder representatives told me that they were looking forward to seeing how well I could 'turn the business around'. I have some of my own ideas about how this could be accomplished, but could you please give me a summary of the measures you think are required to turn GVF around.
>
> I am also concerned that any proposals I make will be met with resistance by key stakeholders. Could you describe the most likely sources of resistance to change for me, please? I know several managers have mentioned a model by Lewin called 'forcefield analysis', but this isn't a model I have heard of before. I need you to explain the basics of the model to me and explain how it might be used to implement change in GVF.
>
> I've got a meeting in an hour with the board and I need this information in time to have a look at it. If you could get it to me in 35 minutes that would be great.
>
> Thanks
>
> Rebecca
>
> **Required:**
>
> Reply to the email.
>
> **(35 minutes)**

Beer and Nohria – Theory E & Theory O

Beer and Nohria (2000) identified that a large proportion of all business change initiatives fail. They believed that this was caused by managers becoming overwhelmed by the detail of the change management process and failing to focus on the overall goals of the change itself.

Beer and Nohria identified that every organisational change conforms to a variant of either:

- **Theory E strategies** – these are based on measures where shareholder value is the main concern. Change usually involves incentives, layoffs, downsizing and restructuring.

- **Theory O strategies** – these are 'softer' approaches to change, often involving cultural adjustment or enhancing employee capabilities through individual and organisational learning. This involves changing, obtaining feedback, reflecting and then making further changes. This requires involving employees in the change process.

Both approaches have drawbacks. A Theory E approach will tend to ignore the feelings and attitudes of their employees, which will often lead to a loss of motivation and commitment from staff members. This can damage the competitive advantage of the organisation.

Theory O organisations, on the other hand, will often fail to take the 'tough' decisions that may be needed.

To solve these problems, Beer and Nohria recommended that organisations should implement both Theory E and Theory O approaches simultaneously and try to balance the associated tensions.

Illustration 2 – Beer and Nohria

Due to the recent economic slowdown, many high-street retailers have seen a significant reduction in their profits, forcing them to consider a number of strategies to improve their results.

A **Theory E** approach means that the retailer is only concerned with the effect that falling profits has on shareholders – such as reduced dividends and share prices. The managers of the company will usually try to improve this quickly by laying off staff, reducing employee pay or closing stores that are seen as underperforming.

While this can have a positive impact on profits in the short-term, it fails to consider the needs of other stakeholders, such as employees. This can cause problems with employee motivation and commitment as staff members will not feel that the company is acting in their best interests. As such, the company may suffer from poor performance in the long-term.

A **Theory O** approach would see the retailer attempt to improve their profits by developing the organisation's capabilities and culture. For instance, a high-street retailer may train its staff to provide better customer service for shoppers. This will improve the customer experience and therefore, in the longer-term, should improve the profitability of the business. The retailer may well choose to involve staff in the decision-making process, asking for suggestions as to how customer service could be improved.

All of this is likely to make the employees feel more valued and should improve the commitment and motivation of the workforce. However, it may be insufficient in the short–term to deal with the fall in profitability and shareholders may expect more drastic, Theory E action in order to quickly improve their returns.

Beer and Nohria suggested that companies needed to be prepared to take both approaches simultaneously. This could, for example, involve some restructuring as well as a development of remaining employees. This would still need careful management as it would be easy to get the 'worst of all worlds' where staff are demotivated by the job losses while investors feel the cost cuts have not gone far enough.

Balance is needed!

Test your understanding 10

F is a clothes retailer which is struggling in the current economic downturn and is looking for ways to improve performance.

According to Beer and Nohria, which ONE of the following strategies would be consistent with a Theory O approach to change management?

A   Reduction in staff numbers

B   Store closure

C   Improved staff training

D   Reduction in product quality

Test your understanding 11 – (Integration question)

In what circumstances would Theory E be a successful approach?

4   Change agents

Many organisations seek to identify and reward change agents to encourage and facilitate change. They can play a major role in helping deal with resistance to change. Usually change agents are figures who are familiar and non-threatening to other people.

The quality of the relationship between the change agent and key decision makers is very important, so the choice of change agent is critical.

Whether internal or external, the change agent is central to the process, and is useful in helping the organisation to:

- **Define the problem and its cause** – the change agent should be able to identify restraining forces or potential resistance and help management to understand the root causes behind them.

- **Diagnose solutions and select appropriate courses of action** – the change agent will be responsible for proposing ways in which these problems can be overcome and then helping management to select the most appropriate course of action.

- **Implement change** – once management have made their decision about which course of action to take, it will need to be implemented. Given that the change agent will be well informed about the proposed change and the reasons behind it, they are likely to be the best person to take the lead in implementing the change.

- **Transmit the learning process to others and the organisation overall** – the change agent should document the learning process and discussions which the company has undergone during the change process. They can then take the lead in spreading this information throughout the company.

Skills and attributes of change agents

The skills and attributes of the change agent would include:

Goals	• Clarity in defining the achievable • Sensitive to the impact of change on all stakeholders • Flexibility to adapt to internal and external triggers
Roles	• Team-building skills to establish work groups • Networking skills inside and outside the company • Tolerance of ambiguity and uncertainty
Communication	• Skills with colleagues and subordinates • Personal enthusiasm, stimulating commitment • Meeting management
Negotiation	• Creating vision and selling plans • Resolving conflict • Contract negotiation
Managing up	• Political awareness and influencing skills • Balancing goals and perceptions • Helicopter perspective

"Power skills" of change agents (Kanter)

Kanter identified seven 'power skills' that change agents require to enable them to overcome apathy or resistance to change, and enable them to introduce new ideas:

- ability to work independently, without the power and sanction of the senior management hierarchy behind them, providing visible support

- ability to collaborate effectively

- ability to develop relationships based on trust, with high ethical standards

- self-confidence, tempered with humility

- being respectful of the process of change, as well as the substance of the change

- ability to work across different business functions and units

- a willingness to stake personal rewards on results, and gain satisfaction from success.

Using external consultants as change agents

Advantages of using external consultants as change agents are as follows:

- They can bring a fresh perspective to the problem.

- May have state-of-the-art knowledge of the required change – e.g. introducing TQM.

- Being a dedicated resource they may be able to give it more time and energy.

- They may have more experience and hence be better able to avoid traps and pitfalls.

- Greater objectivity as they have no personal stake in the outcomes of the change.

Test your understanding 12

M Ltd is currently considering who to choose to act as a change agent during the implementation of a new JIT system, which M currently has no experience of. M has a strong corporate culture, with excellent working relationships between managers and other employees throughout the organisation.

Which THREE of the following are advantages to M Ltd of using external consultants as change agents, rather than internal managers?

A   They can bring a new perspective to the change process

B   Improved objectivity in decision-making

C   Improved relationship and trust with employees

D   Improved ability to collaborate effectively across different functions

E   Reduced cost of the change management process

F   May have specialist knowledge of the change to be implemented

Test your understanding 13 – (Integration question)

MMM is a small company based in country A. It is currently considering the acquisition of a rival company, POR, which is based in country D. Unfortunately, the employees in country D speak a different language to staff members in country A. The directors of MMM are concerned about the effect that this could have on the viability of the acquisition.

They have decided to appoint a change agent to help control the process.

Required:

Explain how a change agent could aid in the acquisition of POR.

(10 minutes)

5   Executive mentoring and coaching

Part of managing change is helping employees to perform well after the change process is complete. For example, a manufacturing organisation that introduces a new set of targets based around production quality needs to ensure that its staff are comfortable with how best to achieve these goals.

While formal training is useful here, management may also consider initiating a process of mentoring and coaching to support staff.

Mentoring

This refers to a process where a manager (or any other member of staff) offers help, guidance, advice and support to facilitate the learning and development of another.

A mentor is typically a skilled, senior member of staff who:

- offers practical advice and support

- can give technical and general guidance

- can help with the development of key work skills

- can act as a role model.

A manager could act as an ongoing mentor, giving guidance to staff about how to deal with the changes in the organisation and helping them develop the skills and abilities they need on an ongoing basis in order to be successful.

Key features of mentoring include:

- it has no specific period – mentoring is indefinite and may be ongoing until it is no longer considered necessary

- it does not have to be a formal process – mentoring does not have to have a rigid structure and can be flexible to adapt to the needs of both parties (the mentor and the mentee). The agenda is open and will change as necessary over time.

- it seeks to build wisdom – it is supposed to help the mentee apply key skills and experience to new situations.

Coaching

The CIPD defines coaching as 'developing a person's skills and knowledge so that their job performance improves, hopefully leading to the achievement of organisational objectives. It targets high performance and improvement at work. It usually lasts for a short period and focuses on specific skills and goals.'

For example, a coach may help staff improve their IT skills over a one month period, so that they are able to deal with a new computer system being installed.

Most coaching is carried out by a senior person or manager, but the most important requirement is that the coach has sufficient expertise and experience.

Key features of coaching include:

- it tends to take place on a one-to-one basis

- it has a very specific purpose and therefore tends to have a planned 'programme' that is followed over a set time period to help the individual being coached meet pre-set objectives.

Similarities between coaching and mentoring

While the approach may be different, there are similarities between coaching and mentoring.

- **Neither is about teaching, instruction or telling someone what to do.** Mentors and coaches both attempt to help members of staff to find their own solutions to problems or issues, rather than simply telling them what the best approach is.

- **Both are flexible and evolutionary approaches.** While coaching may have more pre-set objectives, these may still change over time as the needs of the member of staff being coached change.

- **They require similar skills from the individual acting as the coach or mentor.** In both cases, the coach or mentor is likely to act as a 'critical friend' who helps the staff member in their care to improve their skills and abilities.

Generally

Note that in either case, the coach or mentor must be someone that supports the change process within the organisation. If an individual is selected that disapproves of the changes being made, their negative attitude may transfer to the employees they are trying to help, leading to increased resistance.

Mentoring and coaching are also important for **all** levels within the business. As well as workers affected by change, it will also often be useful for senior managers. They may need help to ensure they have the relevant leadership and management skills required to lead the change within the organisation.

Ultimately, coaching and mentoring is a key part of the change management process – it can help keep the change management process moving forward and help reduce the amount of resistance that the organisation faces.

Illustration 3 – Mentoring and coaching in action

Mentoring

J works within the human resources department of a large multinational organisation. He has expressed an interest to his line manager about learning more about the organisation's advertising function, with a possible long-term goal of moving departments. J's line manager arranges a secondment to the advertising department and approaches M, an advertising department manager, to act as a mentor for J during his secondment.

M's main roles as part of this mentoring process would include:

- agreeing the objectives for J's secondment – discussing what he wishes to get from the experience

- helping J understand the skills that he will need in the advertising department

- arranging relevant work experience for J during his secondment, such as attending marketing meetings and presentations

- providing relevant information to J about how the marketing department is structured and the various roles within the department

- being available to discuss questions or problems that J has during his secondment.

Coaching

P works in a bank as a cashier. He needs to improve his customer management skills, as this is an area that he currently feels uncomfortable with. P's manager arranges for him to be coached by F, an experienced colleague.

F's role as coach would include:

- discuss with P what the coaching needs to achieve – what does P need/expect to get from the process? What standard of customer service should he be able to reach by the end of the coaching process?

- decide with P on the length of the coaching period and what it will entail – P may, for example, get to shadow F at work and see how she interacts with customers.

- be available for P so that he can discuss any queries or issues as they arise and help him to work towards practical solutions that he can use in his own role.

- regularly review P's progress and evaluate the overall success of the coaching process.

Test your understanding 14

Which ONE of the following statements is consistent with the concept of coaching?

A   It is typically only useful for senior management

B   It is undertaken on an on-going, long-term basis

C   It can only be carried out by senior managers

D   It is designed to help the person being coached achieve specific objectives

6   Managing decline

In reality, businesses are not always successful at expanding their business. Many managers may therefore find themselves having to manage decline rather than growth. The changes required during a period of decline pose particular dilemmas for managers as decisions often affect the organisation's workforce – its pay, conditions and job security.

When attempting to help a business recover from a period of decline, a manager's strategic priorities are likely to be:

- reducing costs to improve efficiency, and

- improving competitiveness in order to increase revenue.

Initially, when facing a downturn, the typical management response is to cut costs. While these can be cut from anywhere in the supply chain, the most obvious starting point is to reduce labour costs. At first, this may simply involve altering working patterns, such as the elimination of paid overtime or the replacement of full-time with part-time jobs. If this does not produce a sufficient cost reduction, management may move on to a program of voluntary or compulsory redundancies.

There is, however, a danger that if staff cuts are too severe then there will be reductions in the quality of the product and services provided to customers. There is also likely to be a serious impact on staff morale, potentially leading to a loss of commitment, a loss of skilled staff and an increase in conflict within the organisation.

Illustration 4 – UK public sector

It is not just businesses that have been affected by the global economic slow-down in recent years. Many governments have had to reduce their level of spending – leading to many public departments having to lay off staff.

In the UK, local and central government departments have shed hundreds of thousands of posts in an effort to cope with the tight budget restrictions that have been imposed upon them, while attempting to continue to maintain their level of service provision.

This has led to angry reactions from the heavily unionised public sector employees, with a number of strikes and protests across the country. The long-term effects of this are unknown, but the government may find it harder to attract good quality staff members in the future as public sector jobs may no longer be seen as secure.

It should be noted that many of the changes that a business may wish to make during a period of decline, such as compulsory redundancies or improving factory layout, may require some initial expenditure. The business may be unable to afford this if it is experiencing falling revenues.

In this case, managers may have to consider a fundamental change to the business strategy. This may involve:

- **Retrenchment** – this involves doing the same as before, but drastically cutting costs.

- **Turnaround** – the organisation repositions itself within the market for competitive advantage.

- **Divestment** – this involves the external sale of part of the organisation, or the internal closure of units as part of a rationalisation programme.

- **Liquidation** – the organisation is sold to one or more buyers. This is an admission of failure by the senior managers and is normally a last resort.

All four of these strategies require managers to make difficult decisions, which may have adverse effects on the organisation's stakeholders – especially employees. Whichever approach is taken, it is important that the business acts ethically towards its stakeholders when making tough decisions.

Test your understanding 15

O Ltd is experiencing a period of declining demand for its products. It has decided to look at ways of sourcing cheaper materials and reduce the number of skilled employees to enable it to maintain its profits as sales volume falls.

What ONE approach to decline is O adopting?

A   Retrenchment

B   Turnaround

C   Liquidation

D   Divestment

Test your understanding 16 – (Integration question)

A business has found itself entering a period of decline. What measures could it consider as alternatives to reducing its labour costs?

Test your understanding 17 – (Integration question)

AV Ltd is a high-quality board game manufacturer. It is part of a larger group of companies that manufacture toys and computer games. While these other businesses have prospered over the last few years, this has been at the expense of the traditional board games that AV manufactures and AV's sales have declined each year for the last several years. In addition, AV has seen increased competition from cheaper board game manufacturers, further reducing demand.

The directors of AV's parent company have met to discuss their approach to AV's problems. They have all agreed that a fundamental change is needed to their strategy with regards to the company, but they are not sure what that change should be.

Required:

Discuss four possible strategies that the directors may consider, given AV's continuing decline.

(20 minutes)

7 Ethics and change management

Most ethical issues focus on how one stakeholder group is benefited at the expense of another, so within any change process there will be a number of potential ethical dilemmas that need managing:

- Whether the change is justified – for example, boosting shareholder profits at the expense of widespread job cuts. If the change involves re-engineering and/or downsizing, then there will usually be redundancies. Ethical issues include:

    - Deciding on who to make redundant (e.g. preference to keep younger employees).

    - Fair treatment of all employees (e.g. discrimination by race, sex or age).

    - What severance package and assistance to offer.

    - Skills obsolescence.

    - Do remember that making employees redundant is not always unjustified. If it is necessary to safeguard the business in the long-term, it cannot be classed as being unethical.

- Management approach used – e.g. manipulation v participation.

- Some managers may seek to exploit change to ensure they benefit personally from new power structures and reward schemes.

- Similarly some may resist change to protect their own interests.

- The extent to which plans are made available or if a "need to know" culture is adopted.

- Whether "misinformation" is used to drive certain phases of the change process – e.g. to unfreeze the existing culture.

- Accountants may be asked to manipulate figures to exaggerate the case for change.

This list is not exhaustive. The CIMA E3 syllabus requires you to apply the Code of Ethics in the context of business change. This means that whenever you read through a scenario, you need to consider whether there are any business ethical issues or challenges occurring in the change process which will impact upon the ethical position of the organisation.

Illustration 5 – Chrysler

Even when tough decisions need to be made, the actions of a business do not have to be uncaring or disrespectful to the individual employees affected. As part of a US government plan to save the struggling Chrysler motor company, Chrysler's CEO was faced with having to close a number of plants.

The CEO decided to soften the blow through a series of associated plans designed to get the employees into self-employment or into other forms of work. Some employees reskilled and moved to jobs in other parts of the Chrysler group, but the majority found employment elsewhere locally.

8 The importance of adaptation and continuous change

Many authors have argued that firms need to look beyond change as an event and develop a culture where change is embraced as an ongoing process. These include:

- change-adept organisations (Kanter)
- excellent firms that seek to create a climate of change (thrive on chaos) (Peters).

Change-adept organisations – Kanter

Kanter's model focuses on two main issues. Firstly, it identifies the **three attributes of companies that manage change successfully**.

- The imagination to innovate.
- The professionalism to perform.
- The openness to collaborate.

The model goes on to examine the **seven key skills for leaders in these change-adept** organisations.

Change adept organisations

Rosabeth Moss Kanter looked at the characteristics of organisations that managed change successfully ('change-adept organisations'), and the qualities of their leaders and managers.

Attributes of change-adept organisations

She suggested that change-adept organisations share three key attributes:

- The imagination to innovate.

  Effective leaders help to develop new concepts, which are a requirement for successful change.

- The professionalism to perform.

  Leaders provide both personal competence and competence in the organisation as a whole, which is supported by workforce training and development. This enables the organisation to perform strongly and deliver value to ever-more-demanding customers.

- The openness to collaborate.

  Leaders in change-adept organisations make connections with 'partners' outside the organisation, who can extend the organisation's reach, enhance its products and services, and 'energise its practices'. 'Partners' will include suppliers working in close collaboration, joint venture partners, and so on.

Kanter argued that change should be accepted naturally by organisations, as a natural part of their existence. Change that is compelled by a crisis is usually seen as a threat, rather than as an opportunity for successful development. Mastering change means being the first with the best service or products, anticipating and then meeting customer requirements (which continually change) and applying new technology. This requires organisations to be 'fast, agile, intuitive and innovative'.

Skills for leaders in change-adept organisations

- Tuning in to the environment.

  A leader can actively gather information that might suggest new approaches, by tuning in to what is happening in the environment. Leaders can create a network of 'listening posts', such as satellite offices and joint ventures.

- Challenging the prevailing organisational wisdom.

  Leaders should be able to look at matters from a different perspective, and should not necessarily accept the current view of what is right or appropriate.

- Communicating a compelling aspiration.

  Leaders should have a clear vision of what they want to achieve, and should communicate it with conviction to the people they deal with. A manager cannot 'sell' change to other people without genuine conviction, because there is usually too much resistance to overcome. Without the conviction, a manager will not have the strength of leadership to persuade others.

- Building coalitions.

  Change leaders need the support and involvement of other individuals who have the resources, knowledge or 'political clout' to make things happen. There are usually individuals within the organisation who have the ability to influence others – 'opinion shapers', 'values leaders' and experts in the field. Getting the support of these individuals calls for an understanding of the politics of change in organisations.

- Transferring ownership to the work team.

  Leaders cannot introduce change on their own. At some stage, the responsibility for introducing change will be handed to others. Kanter suggested that a successful leader, having created a coalition in favour of the change, should enlist a team of other people to introduce the change.

- Learning to persevere.

  Something will probably go wrong, and there will be setbacks. Change leaders should not give up too quickly, but should persevere with the change.

- Making everyone a hero.

  A successful leader recognises, rewards and celebrates the accomplishments of others who have helped to introduce a change successfully. Making others feel appreciated for their contribution helps to sustain their motivation, and their willingness to attempt further changes in the future.

 ## Thriving on Chaos (Tom Peters)

Tom Peters has written extensively on management theory. One of his ideas relates to 'excellent' companies that have succeeded by seeking to create a climate of continual and radical change. Peters called this 'thriving on chaos'. He suggested that:

- Incremental change is the enemy of true innovation, because it makes an organisation less willing to be truly innovative.

- Excellent firms don't believe in excellence, only in constant improvement and constant change.

- A constantly changing environment does not necessarily mean chaos: instead, it may mean that companies can handle the introduction of change successfully.

Peters suggested that the advantages of having a climate of change are as follows:

- Innovation and the introduction of new products and new methods are actively sought and welcomed.

- People who are used to change tend to accept it without resistance.

- Employees develop an external viewpoint, and are less insular and defensive in their outlook.

However, there are possible disadvantages:

- With a climate of change morale might be damaged

- Staff might become involved in office politics because of their concerns about the possible changes that might occur in the organisation.

Test your understanding 18

According to Kanter, which of the following is a required skill for leaders within change-adept organisations?

A   Tuning in to the environment

B   The imagination to innovate

C   The professionalism to perform

D   The openness to collaborate

9   Conclusion

The management of change is never an easy process and it is rare that the final outcome exactly matches the original plans. Remember that there is no recipe for success – it simply does not exist.

However, change is more likely to succeed if there is/are:

- clearly understandable goals,

- realistic time frames, rather than merely looking for a 'quick fix'

- clear guidance as to how each individual's behaviour needs to change

- clear, unified leadership with no conflict between managers

- management support for training and other necessary investment.

Test your understanding 19 – C Co – (Case style)

C is a large multinational confectionary manufacturer which was purchased in a hostile takeover bid one year ago. The new owners, R Co, have been surprised at the number of key staff who have left over the last year. A total of 120 out of 170 managers and executives have resigned since R Co took control of the two-hundred-year-old company. The acquisition of C completed R Co's ten year geographical expansion strategy.

In particular, there have been departures among creative, design and marketing specialists. While some resignations are normal after such a bitterly fought takeover battle, industry specialists are shocked at the extent of the staff losses.

A group of remaining managers have been questioned by the board of R Co on why they think so many employees have left. The managers explained that the rate of change in C was historically slow, with a great deal of pride taken in making confectionary the old-fashioned way. C's products are considered part of the national identity of its home country and the company even has a royal license to make chocolate for the queen.

Since R Co took over, the company has changed suppliers for many of the key ingredients used in C's products, and despite pre-takeover promises to the contrary, begun devising strategies to move production overseas. Many of the managers who have left made it clear they were resisting these changes before their resignation.

R Co is a cost leader in the global confectionary market and wishes to bring C in line with the rest of the group. The board of R Co have also announced plans to remove the C name altogether and bring the newly acquired company into its own functional structure, rather than allowing it to operate as a stand-alone division.

The managers stated that in their view, the rate of change has been a problem for many employees together with what they perceive to be a 'selling out' of the C name and values.

Required:

Prepare a report for the Board of R Co, which covers the following key issues:

(a) Explain what is meant by the phrase 'resistance to change' and discuss the resistance to change at C which led to so many managers leaving.

(15 minutes)

(b) Evaluate the change management process which has been undertaken at C over the last year.

(15 minutes)

(c) Advise the board of R Co on an alternative strategy for C, which may avoid further loss of staff.

(10 minutes)

10   Summary

By the end of this chapter you should be able to discuss the following:

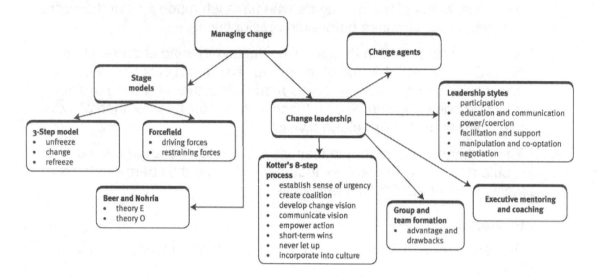

Test your understanding answers

Test your understanding 1

The correct answer is C

B assembled a large group of powerful stakeholders. This suggests that a guiding coalition was indeed formed. Her regular meetings with the staff suggested that she had no problems communicating her change vision – and her request for involvement by staff suggests that she had indeed empowered broad-based action.

However, due to the refusal of the Board to allow her to discuss the new entrants to the market, she was unable to establish a sense of urgency. This is likely compounded by the fact that staff have historically enjoyed high bonuses and that the company is seen to be doing well.

Note that B was unable to generate short term wins, but this was largely due to a lack of staff motivation. Failure was therefore caused by a lack of urgency.

Test your understanding 2

The correct answer is B

This is a classic example of facilitation and support.

Education and communication involve convincing staff of the benefits of the change process being undertaken. Coercion relies on the use of threats, while participation involves employees having input into the change management decision-making process. None of these other options fits this scenario.

Test your understanding 3

The correct answer is D

A is likely to take too long, given the need for rapid change and the large number of employees. B is also likely to be inappropriate due to the lack of a central union to negotiate with and the fact that it needs to lay off many of its staff in order to survive, giving little room for negotiation.

C relates to distortion of the true facts in order to convince staff of the need for change. Not only is this unethical, but it is unnecessary given the dire state of U's actual position. Untruths are not needed.

Coercion involves the use of managerial power to force change. While this is unlikely to be popular with employees, it is rapid and may be U's best option at managing the change process.

Test your understanding 4 – Grey – (Case style)

Division A

Division A appears to be making a relatively small change to its business. It is currently highly profitable – indicating that it is not currently experiencing a crisis.

As such, education and communication may be the best approach. This involves explaining the reasons behind the proposed centralisation of the accounting function and attempts to persuade the employees that this is a beneficial idea. While this is often time-consuming, A has a relatively small number of staff, which makes this approach more realistic. In addition, as the company currently has a good relationship with its workers (and likely needs to maintain this given that its staff are highly skilled and therefore very important to the company), this approach is most likely to keep the majority of staff happy.

It is possible that staff may not be convinced by the need to cut costs given that the division is highly profitable. In this case, A could choose facilitation and support – perhaps helping the staff who will be made redundant to find new jobs, such as by giving them time off for job interviews.

Finally, A could consider participation and involvement. This would see A getting its employees involved in the change process. Perhaps job losses can be avoided if employees are able to think of alternative ways of improving efficiency. This may be very time consuming, although there is no evidence of time-pressure in the scenario.

Division B

Division B is clearly in a crisis, with poor industrial relations and the potential threat of closure.

Given the serious nature of its situation, B could also adopt an education and communication style. If the alternative to job losses is a total closure of the division, this may be enough to convince employees of the need for the change. However, given the poor relations between staff and managers, as well as the tight time-constraints that B is under, this may not be realistic.

As an alternative, B could choose a manipulation and co-optation style. This involves undermining resistance in a more covert manner, perhaps by stressing the potential for the division to be closed, or down-playing the number of job losses that would be involved. It is a faster way of dealing with resistance than education and communication, but if employees feel that they are being manipulated, it may damage industrial relations further.

Test your understanding 5 – (Integration question)

Change introduced through the use of power or manipulation is likely to add to anxiety. Education and communication will rarely succeed on their own when introducing major change. However, they are useful as a support for a negotiation or participation approach. The negotiation approach requires the existence of organised representatives and a formal procedure that is suitable for some items such as change in employment terms but would be inadvisable for other items of changing procedures, organisational changes, decentralisation, etc. In these cases, participation offers the best opportunity of allaying staff anxieties by involving them early in the change process and continuing that involvement through to completion.

Test your understanding 6

The correct answer is A

A is part of unfreezing, B and C are part of refreezing, while D is an element of change itself.

Test your understanding 7 – WW – (Case style)

Lewin's model suggests that, in order to be successful, WW will need to follow three stages in the change-over to a new accounting package.

Unfreeze

Staff need to be convinced of the need for the new accounting package. This could be difficult within WW for several reasons.

WW's six employees have used the current accounting system for many years. This may mean that they are 'stuck in their ways' and unwilling to learn the new skills required for the new system.

In addition, currently management accounting information can only be produced after a time-consuming and complex process. If a new system improves the efficiency of this process, employees may fear that they will become redundant.

To help with this, WW need to convince them of the superiority of the new system. For instance, it appears that it will make the production of management reports much faster, easing the workload for the employees.

WW also needs to communicate well with its employees. Resistance is often caused by a fear of the unknown. Managers could discuss with staff about the level of training that they will be given on the new system and attempt to allay any fears they may have about potential redundancies.

Finally, WW's managers could also stress to staff members that it will benefit the business as a whole. The current system may cause WW to be less competitive in the marketplace, which could threaten the business as a whole.

Change

This involves actually moving staff onto the new accounting system.

This stage will involve training all members of the accounting department on how to use the new system. Enough time must be allowed for employees to be reasonably comfortable with the new system before the change-over is made.

Communication is also vital here – employees must know when the new system will be installed and what will be expected from them. For example, what new reports will the managers expect from the system and when they will need to be prepared.

Refreeze

Finally, WW's managers must ensure that employees do not slip back into old habits and start using the old systems again.

Clearly, if the old accounting system is entirely replaced by the new one, it should be easy to ensure that staff members do not continue to use the original accounting system. However, employees may still continue preparing the management reports manually.

To avoid this, managers could refuse to accept reports in the old, manual format – instead requiring that they be produced from the new system. Staff could be rewarded for using the new system and penalised if the old methods are still used.

Test your understanding 8

The correct answer is A

The current misunderstanding is an example of a restraining force, which is holding the division back from implementing change. N's planned communication will rectify this misunderstanding, reducing the force.

Test your understanding 9 – GVF – (Case style)

To: Rebecca Smith

From: Anne Sma

Date: 12/4/20XX

Subject: Re: Strategic change issues within GVF

Dear Rebecca,

Thank you for your email. I have outlined the points that you requested below.

(a) **Summary of measures needed to turn around GVF**

The inefficiency of GVF management seems to be related to the structure of the company. According to the CEO, there is a need to reduce the number of layers of management, to reduce head office controls and to change attitudes from a narrow concern with departmental objectives to a broader concern for the needs of GVF as a whole.

The reduction in the layers of management will help to reduce costs and to improve communications within the business. Store managers and others may well welcome reduced interference from head office and the increased autonomy may help to motivate them.

The CEO's comment that the company was 'no longer effective or responding to customer needs' is clear from the scenario. Given its loss of customers to new entrants to the market, GVF needs to determine precisely what the needs of its customers are. This may need further investigation – although by increasing the number of own–brand products, it appears to be at least part way through this process already.

(b) (i) **Likely sources of resistance**

Resistance to change in organisations can be considered according to whether the resistance comes from individuals, groups or the organisations themselves.

Individual level

At the individual level, resistance is often caused by fear of the unknown, long-held existing habits and possible threats to position or livelihood.

In GVF, all of the above are likely to be factors. Given the present circumstances of GVF, employees are likely to fear for their job security and whether or not they will be able to continue in their current role or will have to learn a new one.

Managers will be particularly fearful, given the CEO's statement regarding the need to reduce the number of layers of management within GVF. Given that many of these managers may have much to lose and little to gain from such a restructuring, GVF could expect to see significant resistance from them.

Group level

At a group level, there will be collections of individuals who see their positions as threatened and who will join forces to resist and make mutual threats. This will particularly be the case in GVF as many of its employees are unionised, increasing the amount of co-ordinated resistance they are capable of.

Even where trade unions do not exist, it is possible for groups of employees, including managers, to collude informally to resist changes. This may be achieved by withholding information or refusing to co-operate with those seeking to implement change.

For GVF, managers and employees are unlikely to co-operate unless they can see some long-term benefits for themselves.

(ii) **Models of organisational change**

The new CEO of GVF might use the force-field theory of change proposed by Lewin. Lewin's theory suggests that there are two forces present in a change management scenario. One set he refers to as driving forces because they are forces attempting to bring about change; the other set are referred to as restraining forces as they act in the opposite direction and seek to maintain the status quo.

For GVF, the driving forces are likely to include the need for the business to be competitive. Unless GVF can improve its efficiency, its competitors will continue to take its market share. Unless GVF becomes flatter, leaner and more responsive to the market, it may ultimately collapse – especially given its high level of financial gearing.

Organisational level

At the level of the organisation, a number of factors will combine to make the change process difficult. These include the existing culture and structure of the organisation, as well as any past agreements with stakeholders.

Given that the company has traded for over fifty years, the company may be 'set in its ways', with staff unwilling to see significant changes made to longstanding arrangements or ways of working.

The proposed de-layering in GVF will threaten the jobs and status of some layers of management. This will again increase resistance.

The restraining forces will include the reasons for employee resistance mentioned above, such as loss of job security and management levels within GVF.

To be successful, the CEO will need to increase the driving forces – perhaps by improved communication with all employees, laying out the benefits of her proposed changes and the potentially dire consequences to the whole of GVF if they are not implemented.

Alternatively, the CEO may look at reducing the restraining forces. This could involve looking at ways of avoiding voluntary redundancies among managers or by supporting employees who are to be made redundant as they try to find alternative employment.

I hope this helps. If you need any more information, please don't hesitate to get in touch.

Kind regards

Anne Sma

Test your understanding 10

The correct answer is C

Theory O looks at improving the organisation's culture and skill-set for instance through training staff.

Theory E looks at predominantly economic changes that can be made to the organisation.

Test your understanding 11 – (Integration question)

Theory E is often the approach taken in a crisis. If a business needed to make drastic or rapid cuts to its business, or undertake a major restructuring, management may have to make tough decisions in order to secure the long–term survival of the business.

In these circumstances, there may be insufficient time to involve staff in the decision–making process and doing so would likely make it harder to make the difficult choices, such as the number of job losses in the organisation.

Test your understanding 12

The correct answers are A, B and F

The fact that M already has a strong corporate culture with employees that work well together would suggest that C and D are all likely to be advantages of using internal change agents. There is no guarantee that the use of external consultants will be cheaper than using internal managers – in fact, the reverse may well be true.

Test your understanding 13 – (Integration question)

A change agent is a person, or group of people, who help an organisation to achieve its strategic change. If MMM appoints a change agent, he or she would carry out a number of useful functions, including:

Identify any problems and their causes

This is likely to be relatively straightforward for MMM. The biggest problem with their proposed purchase of POR is the language barrier between their staff. MMM and POR will find it almost impossible to work together as they do not understand each other's language.

This could cause the acquisition to fail.

Diagnose solutions and select appropriate courses of action

The change agent is responsible for proposing ways in which the problems that they have identified could be overcome.

For MMM, it could consider:

- sending key members of staff in both companies on external language courses, or

- hiring some additional staff members in both companies who are bilingual.

In many cases there will be a number of possible solutions. The change agent will be responsible for presenting these to management and helping them to decide which option is most appropriate for MMM.

Implement change

Once the management have selected an appropriate strategy, they will need someone to implement it. As the change agent has been part of the decision-making process, they will be the most logical choice to actually carry out the plan. In MMM, the change agent may, for example, investigate and book language courses for appropriate members of staff.

Transmit the learning process to others and the organisation overall

There may be some resistance to the proposed changes. A change agent can champion the proposals, explaining to employees why it is necessary and what the advantages will be.

The change agent will also document the decision-making process and communicate to all members of staff in both MMM and POR. This is a vital step, as employees in both businesses will need to be kept informed about the developments in the company.

Test your understanding 14

The correct answer is D

A is incorrect as coaching can be useful for all levels within the organisation. B relates to mentoring. C is inconsistent with mentoring or coaching as either can be done by any individual with the relevant skills/experience.

Test your understanding 15

The correct answer is A

By definition.

Test your understanding 16 – (Integration question)

The business could attempt to:

- generate additional revenue through more effective marketing

- improve purchasing policies and procedures

- redesign the product or service offered in order to reduce production costs

- contract out services that are not considered essential to the core business (although this may result in job losses)

- consider changes to reduce duplication and improve financial control systems.

Test your understanding 17 – (Integration question)

There are four major approaches that the directors could consider with regards to AV:

Retrenchment

This would involve AV continuing to make board games, but looking at ways to significantly cut costs. This would help increase profits and offset the decline in results that the business is experiencing.

Given that the company currently produces high-quality board games, there may be scope for the business to save money by reducing the quality of materials. This may also allow it to cut its prices and compete with the new, lower-cost market entrants.

Turnaround

For AV this would probably involve much the same approach as retrenchment. AV could attempt to reposition itself within the board games market as a low-cost manufacturer.

Liquidation

The directors could choose to sell AV to one or more investors. Given the current level of decline, they may not realise a high price for the business. This would normally be a last resort for the directors.

Divestment

As an alternative to selling the business, the directors could decide to close the business unit down. The assets could then be sold or transferred to other parts of the organisation.

Test your understanding 18

The correct answer is A

The other three are attributes of change-adept organisations themselves.

Test your understanding 19 – C Co – (Case style)

Report

To: The Board of R Co

From: A. Strategy

Date: 18/09/XX

Subject: Change management at C

Introduction

This report will examine a number of issues surrounding the change management process and the resistance that has been seen at C, a business recently acquired by R Co.

(a) **Resistance to change**

Resistance to change is the action taken by individuals and groups when they perceive that a change that is occurring is a threat to them.

Resistance is any attitude or behaviour that reflects an individual's unwillingness to make or support a desired change.

Reasons for resisting change can stem from three factors.

These are discussed below with reference to the situation at C:

Job factors

Employees may resist change because they fear changes to their working conditions, demotion or reduced pay. The managers in question at C took pride in the traditional ways of making confectionary and obviously saw these methods were under threat from R Co. In particular, the creative managers may have foreseen cuts to design and marketing budgets, since these costs are often viewed as discretionary by cost leader organisations like R.

Reduced pay, demotion and certainly inferior working conditions would all be suggested by R's aggressive strategy over the first few months of ownership.

Personal factors

Managers may have resisted changes as they saw them as a perceived criticism of their performance in C. Changing suppliers of raw materials as well as beginning to move production overseas suggests that R Co sees C as inefficient and its cost base as too high. Altering the supply chain and sourcing overseas partners are typical strategies to reduce variable costs. It is likely that the managers felt less valued under the new management than the old.

The development of C into a cost leader would also signal more monotonous roles for many of its staff, with the emphasis on reducing costs rather than being creative with products.

Social factors

C was a well established part of the national culture in its home nation. The staff's social environment at work would have reflected this, with a great deal of pride being taken in working methods pre-takeover. For new owners to come in and disregard this heritage would lead to personal dislike of R's staff on the part of the C employees. The lack of consultation carried out by R's executives is also likely to have led to rejection of change.

(b) **Evaluation of change management process carried out at C**

There are some positives to the way change management has been carried out at C. Employees are in no doubt as to the intentions of R Co, and although acceptance of that may be difficult in some cases, it could be argued that, the sooner processes of change are begun, the sooner staff can get used to new methods of working.

R Co clearly has a track record of cost leadership, and to maintain a subsidiary which has a different strategy would detract from their corporate image and possibly confuse investors and customers. The sooner this mismatch is dealt with the better.

There is also a clear reason for R Co's rapid changes, in that it is possible for them to save money through moving production abroad and changing suppliers. Such rapid change will in fact increase profit margins and, arguably, benefit stakeholders in C.

C has given a clear message that it is in charge of C and again, this strategic clarity is equivalent to a 'short, sharp shock'. Once the message is communicated, there can be no doubt or confusion as to the company's intentions.

However, the results of such rapid change show that there are significant disadvantages to altering strategy upon acquisition in such a fashion. Firstly, C is a highly valued national institution, with a royal endorsement. R's actions may be seen as disrespectful and result in a consumer backlash.

Rapid transformational change only works if employees believe it is necessary to benefit the company and safeguard their jobs. In the case of C, the opposite is true, with managers feeling so strongly that the change is a mistake and that they would rather resign than see it through. The loss of so many staff, particularly in creative areas, means that new strategies will be harder to implement.

R Co is taking significant risks by adopting a cost leadership strategy for C. If in fact, it is impossible to complete the transfer of C from a differentiator to a cost leader, there will be no return to the previous strategy. C's brand names are, at best, likely to be devalued once it becomes part of the functional structure of R and at worst, completely lost.

In conclusion, the unpopularity of R's actions means they will find it harder to push continued change through and high staff turnover together with resistance to change will both remain as key obstacles to their aims.

(c) **Alternative strategy for C**

Since R Co has purchased C as part of a geographical expansion programme, the simplest alternative is to allow C to continue to operate as a division of R but to use its distribution channels to introduce some of R's products into its markets.

This parallel strategy could work well for some time and R could slowly introduce cost-cutting measures, trying to keep any promises, such as not moving production overseas for the foreseeable future.

It is likely with a slower approach that many managers could be brought on-side. The board of R Co are clearly not averse to consulting with C's staff, since they have asked for their views on the staff turnover issue. If these consultations could be extended to strategic aims and intent, the 'old' C workforce would be much happier to work under R's board, particularly if they saw the attributes of C protected rather than dismantled.

Of course, if R Co is determined to make C part of their empire and remove its identity completely, any kind of change management is likely to meet fierce resistance.

Digital strategy – digital technologies

Chapter learning objectives

Lead	Component
F2: Analyse digital transformation	(a) Analyse digital technologies
	(b) Analyse digital enterprise

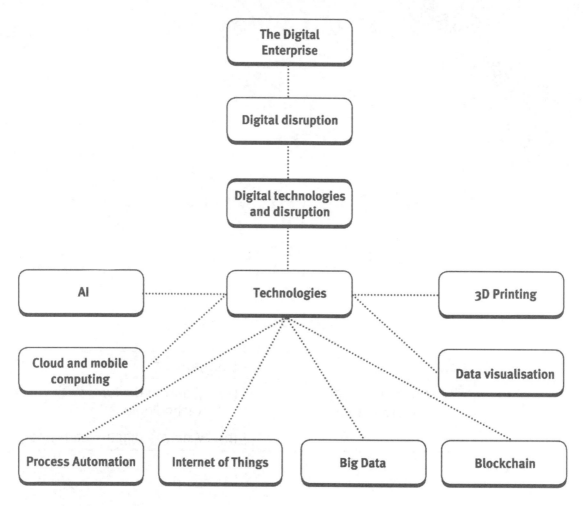

1 Introduction

Throughout the preceding chapters, reference has been made to 'the digital economy' and to a number of digital technologies. The syllabus now contains a section entitled 'Digital Strategy', and it makes up 15% of the overall paper.

It therefore stands to reason that students need to be aware of modern digital technologies and how they can represent both an opportunity and a threat to the organisational ecosystem.

In this chapter we will look at the concept of digital disruption and how management need to perhaps rethink their traditional business models. We will also examine what is meant by a number of technological developments, namely:

- Artificial intelligence
- Cloud and mobile computing
- Internet of Things
- Big Data
- Blockchain
- Data visualisation
- 3D Printing
- Process Automation.

In chapter 13 we will examine the governance of digital transformation and the elements of digital strategies.

2 The Digital Enterprise

In the 21st century there has been unprecedented growth in the use and availability of technologies upon which to base a business model.

Organisations have always relied on technology to innovate and improve productivity; the Industrial Revolution was just such an example, and that begin in around 1760! However, the rate at which this is happening has accelerated enormously in recent years. Consumers are increasing willing to buy goods and services through digital channels, as the examples of the music industry (e.g. Spotify), TV (Netflix, Apple TV+, Britbox, Amazon Prime etc.), and travel can demonstrate (it is reckoned that the majority of flights are now booked online).

This acceleration in the use of technology presents opportunities and threats for all organisations, perhaps at differing speeds. The business that is 'born digital' has an inevitable advantage in some respects, as its proposition is challenging the status quo. For example, compare Uber with an established taxi operator – they have fundamentally different business models. Uber shows that technology can be put at the forefront of operations to reduce costs and offer a very different proposition that customers will find appealing. So identifying that new proposition based on technology is an opportunity – all the entrepreneur has to do is bring it successfully to market!

Businesses that have been established for a long time may see technology as a threat, as newly-formed organisations 'disrupt' their industry. However, technology should also be seen as a potential opportunity, a chance to introduce new revenue streams, augment existing offerings or reduce costs.

Illustration 1 – Kaplan UK

Kaplan Financial Ltd. was founded in 1958, and was originally known as The Financial Training Company. Since it was first created, the company has provided courses to student accountants looking to pass professional qualifications. For many years this was done either by classroom-based tuition or distance learning products, both of which made use of printed study materials. However, this has been supplemented enormously in recent times with the introduction of Live OnLine and OnDemand products, both of which offer students much more choice in terms of how they study through the use of web-based technologies.

So established businesses can adapt through successfully identifying how technology can add to competitive advantage; it is not just newly-created organisations that should be thinking about being digital. Indeed, a failure on the part of management to view their organisation as becoming a digital enterprise may be disastrous – adopting the mind-set of 'what has worked in the past will always work in the future' is blinkered, at best. Admittedly, new start-ups tend to move at a much faster speed and are able to innovate what is proposed to the customer very quickly, whereas established organisations have a history, culture, systems etc. that mean that moving at such speed simply isn't possible. But in the modern business environment, ALL organisations need to consider the need to become, to some degree at least, a digital enterprise.

3 Digital disruption

As mentioned above, in today's business environment many industries are experiencing change at an increasingly rapid rate, and one of the fundamental drivers of such change is digital transformation. Traditional business models are being re-examined as use of technological advances enables organisations to challenge the status quo and create value in new ways.

Illustration 2 – The changing nature of business

A recent article on *TechCrunch,* a digital economy news site, made the following observation:

"Uber, the world's largest taxi company, owns no vehicles. Facebook, the world's most popular media owner, creates no content. Alibaba, the most valuable retailer, has no inventory. And Airbnb, the world's largest accommodation provider, owns no real estate... Something interesting is happening."

Two features are common across all the above-mentioned companies – they have become incredibly valuable in terms of market capitalisation in an astonishingly short space of time; and they have had a profound impact on the businesses that were already present in their industries.

What is it about these businesses which has allowed them to change enormously how their industries work and the ways in which they deliver value? How might organisations in other industries learn lessons from the disruptors mentioned above and other similarly successful companies? And how might that impact on those in senior finance roles?

Much of the answers to these questions lie in the use of disruptive technology.

Disruptive technology

Disruptive technology relates to instances where technology is used to fundamentally change and 'disrupt' the existing business model in an industry.

An example of a disruptor

An example of a disruptor is the passenger service Uber which created a business model using technology which avoided the need for licensed drivers, a vehicle fleet, local booking services etc. Instead, customers use their internet connected device to hail a ride and all payments are handled by a smartphone app.

Uber has disrupted the existing business model for traditional passenger services. Uber was set up in San Francisco in the United States and its initial key competitor was the Yellow Cab Co-operative, but whilst Uber has grown to a business worth over $60bn, the Yellow Cab Co-operative has since filed for bankruptcy.

The key reason for the growth of new disruptive businesses is from technology. Not only from the technology that they employ in order to cut costs and improve efficiency, but also in the access that consumers now have to technology in the modern on-demand economy. For example, many disruptive businesses rely on smartphone applications or have internet-only based transactions.

The two largest growth sectors for disruptive technology are in health services and financial services. Financial technology (commonly known as Fintech) is, for example, completely disrupting the traditional banking sector – long seen as a highly technical, highly regulated industry dominated by giant banks.

Fintech businesses exist which can provide investment advice, offer banking services, transfer money internationally, provide mortgages and loans, exchange currency etc. These are typically big earners for traditional financial institutions. Goldman Sachs estimates that upstarts could steal up to $4.7 trillion in annual revenue, and $470 billion in profit, from established financial services companies.

Fintech examples

Zopa is a peer-to-peer (or person-to-person) loan company. What this means is that Zopa has technology which allows a person who wants to borrow money to be matched with a person who wants to lend money. This completely removes the role of traditional banks from the transaction. Lenders receive higher returns than they would from depositing in a bank but it is still cheaper for borrowers to borrow directly from lenders rather than pay bank margins. Zopa has a low margin fee for setting up the transaction. Zopa has no physical branches and therefore avoids many of the overheads and operating costs of traditional lenders.

The loans are unsecured but credit scores are available to lenders so that they can match lending rates to different credit scores. Lenders can also sell their loan if they want to cash in early (for a 1% fee).

Some borrowers and lenders who use peer-to-peer markets suggest that they do this for ethical reasons. They argue that traditional banks often have unethical practices and a peer-to-peer system avoids giving big banks more profits.

New entrants into the market such as Funding Circle are now offering a similar service for business customers with larger loans and longer periods.

Another example of a Fintech is a company called Betterment. Betterment aims to become a financial portfolio management platform – taking business away from the typically person-to-person financial advisers. Users can use a smartphone app to get investment advice and manage their investment portfolio.

Here is an extract from Betterment's mobile app description:

Why we're here

Betterment is an online financial advisor with one purpose: to help you make the most of your money. We're taking investment strategies that have worked for decades and using technology to make them more efficient. Our goal: to increase your long-term returns.

What we do for you

We make tailored recommendations, from how much to invest to how much risk to take on in your portfolio. Then, we invest your money in a globally diversified portfolio of low-cost Exchange Traded Funds (ETFs) and help lower taxes in ways many traditional investment services can't match.

Seek higher returns:

- Automated portfolio management

- Globally diversified portfolio of ETFs

- Tax efficient investing features, like tax loss harvesting and asset location.

Get a better investing experience:

- Sync your external investments

- Customer support 7 days per week

- Access to Certified Financial Planner (CFP®) professionals and licensed financial experts.

Invest and save with transparency:

- Low-cost, straightforward pricing plans

- Low fund fees

- No trading or rebalancing fees.

The advantages that Fintechs have are:

- better use of data – providing better understanding of their customer and giving customers a wider choice

- a frictionless customer experience using elements such as smartphone apps to provide a broad and efficient range of services

- more personalisation of products/services to individual customers

- the lack of a physical presence (with associated overheads and operating costs)

- access to cheap capital to fund growth – much like when internet based businesses first came to prominence in the 1990's, investors want to get in on the growth potential that Fintechs offer. This gives Fintechs a wide scope for raising cheap finance in order to fund their future expansion.

Of course, Fintech is just one example of how an industry has been disrupted in recent times; there are many others, as was demonstrated at the start of this chapter (AirBnB – the hospitality industry). There are also many examples of industries that are about to be disrupted or are in the early stages of disruption.

For example, autonomous vehicles are forecast to change the way in which people use cars, and detailed testing has been underway in some countries for a while. How soon before they become the 'norm'? And what sort of impact might it have on who is successful in the industry? Will traditional names such as Ford, Mercedes, Renault etc. come up against significant competition from organisations such as Apple, Dyson, and Alphabet (the parent company of Google)? All of these latter names have been investing major sums in vehicle research and development.

Surviving digital disruption

So how might management ensure that their organisations survive digital disruption and rethink their business models so that they can thrive in a digital age?

The consultancy group Accenture wrote a report in 2015 called Accenture Technology Vision, which highlighted five emerging trends that were shaping the digital landscape for organisations and which business leaders should focus on in developing digital strategies:

1 **The Internet of Me** – users are being placed at the centre of digital experiences through apps and services being personalised.

2 **Outcome economy** – organisations have an increased ability to measure the outcomes of the services that they deliver; customers are more attracted to outcomes than just simply to products, and this is what organisations should focus on.

3 **The Platform (r)evolution** – global platforms are becoming easier to establish and cheaper to run. Developments such as cloud computing and mobile technology offer huge potential for innovation and quicker delivery of next-generation services. The rate of evolution is only going to increase.

4   **The intelligent enterprise** – using data in a smart way enables organisations to become more innovative and achieve higher degrees of operating efficiency.

5   **Workforce reimagined** – whilst greater use is made of smart machines, the role of human beings is not being removed altogether; they are simply being used in a different way. Ways need to be identified in which man and machines can work effectively together to create better outcomes.

There are also a number of myths about digital transformation that are common. This is perhaps understandable given the rate of change that has been seen in many industries over the last few years, but such impressions need to be shown as misleading if management are to see digital transformation as an opportunity as opposed to a threat.

Myth 1 – those organisations that are not digital already have missed their chance

It is true that a number of recently-formed businesses have achieved huge valuations in a very short space of time, and successfully attacked traditional markets (Uber, AirBnB, Amazon etc.). This is because they have successfully exploited new technologies and understood the changing tastes of consumers.

However, existing businesses that have been around for a long time have substantial assets – know-how, customer relationships, brands, distribution channels, data – and should look to leverage these to their advantage. The business model simply needs to adapt.

Myth 2 – becoming a digital business is an administrative exercise that focusses on achieving operational efficiencies

The reality is that successful organisations today are not just looking to cut costs through using technology; they are looking to increase the revenue sources available to them. Using technology is an important way to achieve this.

Myth 3 – digital transformation can be successfully achieved just by creating a digital business unit headed up by a Chief Digital Officer

Whilst such business units and roles may be created, the process of digitisation will impact on all employees in the business. Digital transformation needs to be driven at the very top of the organisation, with the CEO taking responsibility for it and achieving buy-in from everybody else.

The lesson from the above myths is that organisations need to recognise how technological development requires them to question their business model, to enquire how adopting such technologies can bring benefits, and to understand how employees and their roles are also evolving and how to get the best out of them.

Test your understanding 1

JKP company manufactures handmade chocolates which it markets and sells in the local area. It was established many decades ago and until recently its board was still dominated by the founding family. However recent changes have brought in some new board members who wish to encourage a fresh approach.

The newly constructed board is now meeting to discuss the future. One area for discussion is the need for the company to develop a digital strategy and become a digital business – something heavily resisted by many of the original board members.

Which of the following statements made by members of JKP's board during the discussion on digitisation are correct?

Select ALL that apply.

A   Digitisation of the company will mean replacing all current equipment with internet enabled versions.

B   The main aim of digitisation is the achievement of operational efficiencies.

C   If JKP digitises all its data will be stored in the cloud.

D   JKP can successfully implement a digitisation programme by setting up a digital business unit headed up by a specially appointed Chief Digital Officer.

E   Digitisation can be adapted to suit any business model.

The rest of this chapter will examine what technologies should be considered.

4 Artificial Intelligence (AI)

Definition

Artificial Intelligence is an area of computer science that emphasises the creation of intelligent machines that work and react like human beings. Some of the activities that computers with artificial intelligence are designed for include:

- Voice recognition

- Planning

- Learning

- Problem solving.

Companies such as Apple and Amazon have developed and marketed voice recognition systems, either to be built into an existing product (such as Apple with its Siri system) or developed new products whose main function is voice recognition (such as Amazon and Alexa).

A further simple example is that of Facebook, and its process of recommending new friends for users to connect with.

There are many, more complex examples of Artificial Intelligence, but a common factor to both the simple and the more involved is **machine learning**.

Machine learning

Most recent advances in AI have been achieved by applying machine learning to very large data sets. Machine learning algorithms detect patterns and learn how to make predictions and recommendations by processing data and experiences, rather than by explicit programming instruction. The algorithms themselves then adapt to new data and experiences to improve their function over time.

There are three major types of machine learning:

- Supervised learning

- Unsupervised learning

- Reinforcement learning.

Supervised learning

In this instance an algorithm uses training data and feedback from humans to learn the relationships of given inputs to given outputs. For example, if the objective is to predict future house prices, the inputs might be "time of year" and "interest rates".

This sort of approach can be used when the user knows how to classify the input data and the type of behaviour that they want to predict, but the algorithm is needed to calculate it on new data.

There are three steps to how supervised learning works:

1   A human labels every element of the input data (e.g. "time of year", "interest rates" etc.) and defines the output variable (e.g. "house prices").

2   The algorithm is trained on the data to find the connection between the input variables and the output.

3   Once training is complete – typically when the algorithm is sufficiently accurate in providing output data from input – then the algorithm is applied to new data.

Unsupervised learning

With unsupervised learning, an algorithm interrogates input data without being given any explicit output variable. For example, the input data might be "customer demographic data" and the algorithm is then used to explore and identify patterns.

This can be used when there is no known classification of the data, and the user wants the algorithm to find patterns and classify the data for them.

The three steps for using unsupervised learning are:

1   The algorithm receives unlabelled data; for example, a set of data describing customer journeys on a website.

2   The algorithm then infers some sort of structure on the data.

3   The algorithm identifies groups of data that exhibit similar behaviour; for example, clusters of customers of similar age that exhibit similar buying patterns, such as choice of destination, length of trip, amounts spent etc.

Reinforcement learning

This is when an algorithm learns to perform a task by trying to maximise the rewards it receives for the actions it takes. For example, in managing an investment fund, the rewards would be gains in value of the fund based on which investments it has decided to put capital into.

Reinforcement learning can be used when there isn't a lot of training data available, the ideal end state cannot be clearly defined, or the only way to learn about the environment is to interact with it.

The three steps for reinforcement learning are:

1   The algorithm takes an action on the environment; for example, it makes a trade in a financial portfolio.

2   It receives a reward if the action taken brings the machine a step closer to its objective. For example, it makes a return on the investment chosen.

3   The algorithm optimises for the best series of actions by correcting itself over time. For example, if it makes losses, or could have made better returns through investing elsewhere, it will do better at the next time of investing.

Rewards for reinforcement learning will depend on the application to which the AI is put.

For example, a courier company that decides to adopt AI in this way might see reductions in fuel consumption, or an increase in the number of deliveries made to customers on time, as a gain.

Reinforcement learning has famously been used in training computers how to play games.

Illustration 4 – AlphaGo

In May 2017, reinforcement learning helped the AI system AlphaGo to defeat the world champion Ke Jie in the ancient Chinese board game of Go.

A particular advantage of reinforcement learning compared to supervised and unsupervised learning is that it is not based on the limitations that can result from human labelling. Even experienced operators can introduce natural and social bias into labels, which will limit the learning process for the machine.

In a recent development, the AI system AlphaGo Zero defeated its predecessor AlphaGo at the board game Go, even though it had not been "trained" to play by human beings; instead, it learnt to play Go from scratch, rather than training on Go games played by and with human beings.

Illustration 5 – 'Intelligent' vehicles

Jaguar LandRover has introduced self-learning vehicles into its range of vehicles. The system within the vehicle integrates with different passengers'' mobile phones, and learns to recognise their individual behaviours and preferences. It can then apply such understanding to adapt issues such as comfort controls within the vehicle, and the entertainment choices that are offered.

For example, the car can link up with the fitness and activity tracker worn by the driver to detect a visit to the gym, and start the air conditioning to create a cooler interior as the driver returns to the vehicle once the gym session is over.

Test your understanding 2

RTY company sells a wide range of products via its website. Management believe that in order to maximise sales the company needs to understand the way customers navigate around its website and the interaction between customer purchasing patterns and a range of other factors such as competitor behaviour, economic indicators, and local weather conditions.

RTY plans to use an Artificial Intelligence Application to interrogate the data. First staff will label the relevant input data and then an algorithm will be used to find the relevant connections.

Which ONE of the following forms of machine learning is RTY planning to adopt?

A   Supervised learning

B   Unsupervised learning

C   Reinforcement learning

D   Feature learning

Artificial Intelligence and finance

Although artificial intelligence techniques such as machine learning are not new, and the pace of change is fast, widespread adoption in business and accounting is still in relatively early stages.

Increasingly, we are seeing systems that are producing outputs that far exceed the accuracy and consistency of those produced by humans. In the short to medium term, AI brings many opportunities for finance professionals to improve their efficiency, provide more insight and deliver more value to businesses. In the longer term, AI brings opportunities for much more radical change, as systems increasingly carry out decision-making tasks currently done by humans.

AI, no doubt, will contribute to substantial improvements across all areas of accounting, equipping those in finance with powerful new capabilities, as well as leading to the automation of many tasks and decisions.

Examples include:

- using machine learning to code accounting entries and improve on the accuracy of rules-based approaches, enabling greater automation of processes

- improving fraud detection through more sophisticated, machine learning models of 'normal' activities and better prediction of fraudulent activities

- using machine learning-based predictive models to forecast revenues

- improving access to, and analysis of, unstructured data, such as contracts and emails.

Despite the opportunities that AI brings, it must remembered that it does not replicate human intelligence. The strengths and limits of this different form of intelligence must be recognised, and we need to build an understanding of the best ways for humans and computers to work together.

5 Cloud and mobile computing

Cloud and mobile computing is computing based on the internet. It avoids the needs for software, applications, servers and services stored on physical computers. Instead it stores these with cloud service providers who store these things on the internet and grant access to authorised users.

Benefits of cloud and mobile computing

- **Store and share data** – cloud services can often store more data than traditional, local physical drives, and the data can be shared more easily (regardless of physical location).

- **On-demand self-service** – customers and users can gain access to technology on demand. For example, every time you download an app from iTunes or the Play store you are downloading it from a cloud service where it is stored.

- **Flexibility** – work can be done more flexibly as employees no longer need to be 'plugged into' work networks or facilities to access the data they need.

- **Collaboration** – the cloud facilitates better workforce collaboration – documents, plans etc. can be worked on by many different users simultaneously.

- **More competitive** – smaller firms can get access to technology and services that, without significant financial investment, may otherwise only be available to the largest organisations. This can allow small organisations to compete better with larger rivals.

- **Easier scaling** – cloud services provide high levels of flexibility in terms of size, number of authorised users etc. This means that the service can grow as the business grows, and allows businesses to scale up much more easily.

- **Reduced maintenance** – there is no longer need on the part of the organization for regular maintenance and (security or software) updates of IT services; the cloud provider will take care of this.

- **Back-ups** – it can be used to back up data. This adds an extra layer of security and removes the need for physical devices to store backed-up data.

- **Disaster recovery** – this means that it can also aid disaster recovery. Using cloud technology makes this faster and cheaper.

- **Better security** – the cloud can increase security of data. For example, if in the past an employee were to lose a laptop with sensitive data on it, this would be a high risk security event for the organisation. Keeping data stored in the cloud should reduce such risks associated with hardware.

Risks of cloud and mobile computing

- **Reliance on the service provider** – as with any outsourcing decision, relying on the cloud service provider means that any failings at the service provider could be more problematic without back-up plans for bringing services back in-house. There is not only issues with the trust and security required with the service provider: it also needs to be considered whether the providers services are suitable for the tasks required; whether the technology is advanced enough to give adequate competitiveness; whether the service provider will continue as a going concern; whether the service provider can ensure continuity in the light of external events such as system failure; whether initial prices will be maintained, etc.

- **Regulatory risks** – data security is often highly regulated in terms of what can be stored, who can access it, how long it can be stored for, how it can be used etc. Organisations will be reliant on cloud service providers for this compliance. This may become a problem if the service provider is based in a different jurisdiction with different regulations and rules.

- **Unauthorised access of business and customer data** – this can come in two forms. Firstly, the cloud service provider is more likely to be a target of hacking than the individual small businesses that use it. If the service provider is targeted all users suffer, even if they were not individual targets themselves. Secondly, providing business and customer data to an outsourced service provider means that the data can be accessed by that service provider's staff. It will also be important that the service provider does not share this data with unauthorised users such as other users of that service provider's services.

Test your understanding 3

TRY company provides financial advice to business clients in P-Land. The P-Land financial regulator requires financial advisors to keep all client data confidential. TRY has a large workforce operating in offices across the country. At present all its systems are held within the company offices and connected via a company network. Advisors visit clients at their business premises to discuss options and existing financial plans but currently no changes may be made to client accounts until the advisors return to the TRY offices.

The board of TRY company is now considering updating its digital strategy by adopting cloud computing and allowing advisors access to mobile computing.

Which of the following statements about the use of mobile and cloud computing by TRY company are correct? Select ALL that apply.

A TRY cannot hold client's financial data using cloud storage as this would breach their obligation to keep it confidential.

B Using cloud computing would reduce the risk of losing sensitive data in the event that a mobile device was mislaid or stolen.

C Providing advisors with mobile computing would provide them with additional flexibility to work remotely.

D Using cloud computing will reduce the risk that hackers will attempt to access the company's data.

E The use of mobile computing will expand TRY's network and therefore increase the importance of endpoint security.

Application to finance

A simple example of how cloud and mobile computing might be of use to finance professionals can be seen in the budgeting process. Any organisation which has a number of different locations (such as a multinational company) has historically experienced difficulties and time delays in constructing budgets which require input from people in different places. Cloud computing means that budget templates can be worked on simultaneously by many people without them having to be in the same location.

6   Internet of Things (IoT)

The Internet of Things can be described as the inter connection via the internet of computing devices embedded in everyday objects, enabling them to send and receive data.

This data can then be used for practical applications to the potential benefit of both individuals and businesses.

> **Illustration 6 – Intelligent refrigerators**
>
> The concept of "smart" devices has been around for many years. The much-quoted example is of the refrigerator in the home which can tell the owner about the contents at any point in time and then turn such knowledge to some use. For example, an alert as to the sell-by date of particular goods might make the owner plan to use those ingredients in the next meal, so as to reduce food waste. Or perhaps the fridge can identify when the house is about to run out of milk, and thereby prompting the householder to buy some more on the way home from work. The truly smart fridge might even be able to add milk to the next online order from a supermarket automatically.

It is reckoned that, at the start of 2017, there were 8 billion devices globally that were connected to the internet – laptops, smartphones, wearables etc. That figure is forecast to grow to 1 trillion by 2030 (source: Digital Transformation Initiative), and this therefore represents potential opportunity for businesses.

This is already a reality in everyday lives.

> **Illustration 7 – Motor insurance**
>
> Many young drivers now have "black boxes" installed in their cars as a requirement of their motor insurance policy. These black boxes record data about how the car is driven – speed, acceleration, braking distance, how corners are taken etc. – and the agreement to provide such data to the insurance company should result in less chances of an accident and therefore lower insurance premiums.

The cost saving to the motorist, and the reduced chances of a claim to the insurance company, are not the only benefits. The fact that the motorist knows that their driving habits are being recorded should lead to more careful driving, and therefore result in fewer injuries and fatalities among a group statistically more at risk of suffering such incidents.

 Illustration 8 – Smart meters

In the UK the government has an initiative to encourage energy companies to persuade homeowners to have smart meters installed (at no cost to the homeowner) which will enable that owner to control what happens in the home remotely.

For example, you could turn on the heating just as you are about to leave the office so that the home is warm as you arrive. Or set the meter to turn down the temperature if it's a sunny day, or even turn the heating off altogether if there is nobody home and the house is likely to be empty for a while. It would even be possible to turn your heating on whilst you are abroad on holiday, for example if there is unexpectedly cold weather and you are concerned about pipes bursting in your absence.

The truly smart meter might simply be able to tell that the smartphone – and therefore the owner – has left the building and therefore the heating should be turned down or off.

The government is keen for homeowners to adopt a smart meter so that overall energy consumption can be reduced, thereby helping the UK to hit environmental targets.

Commercial applications

It stands to reason that, in a business context, there must be a commercial logic to exploiting technology and the IoT. Just because use *can* be made of technology does not mean that it will be.

For example, a factory owner may well be able to understand the temperature of different parts of their factory via smart technology but, unless this can then be used to improve productivity and therefore profit, it is unlikely that such technology will be taken up.

There needs to be some strategic justification for exploiting the potential of the IoT.

Illustration 9 – Dairy farming

A dairy farm in Essex was used to trial smart collars attached to a herd of cows. A sensor was inserted into each collar which then fed back information to the farmer's computer about the cow's behaviour.

Two principle issues affect the profitability of each cow. The first is illness (such as mastitis and going lame); this is reckoned to cost the UK dairy industry around £100 million per year. The second is a cow's ability to conceive.

The cows' behaviour was monitored, and then classified as either "normal" or "abnormal". Abnormal behaviour could then in turn lead to action being taken by the farmer.

For example, if a cow starts showing initial signs of sore feet, treatment could be applied immediately which prevents the bigger problem of it going lame, thereby improving productivity of milk from the cow and saving vets' bills.

The typical cost per cow going lame was estimated at £300; the farm therefore has to decide if implementing such technology is justified on a cost/benefit basis.

Illustration 10 – UPS

The courier company UPS fitted its fleet of vehicles in the US with smart devices that tracked fuel consumption. It identified that making left turns at traffic lights lead to increased amounts of idle time and therefore longer journey durations and fuel consumption.

It therefore re-routed deliveries so as to avoid unnecessary left turns. This resulted in 9 million gallons of fuel (and $31 million of costs) being saved.

Illustration 11 – Vitality

The insurance company introduced a scheme whereby policyholders who took out health insurance with the company were given an Apple watch. A condition of the deal was that the member had to download the Vitality Members app on their iPhone.

The watch was "free" provided that the wearer met the target with regards to exercise taken in a specified time. For example, if the wearer walked 12,500 steps per day for 5 days in a week, the amount payable in respect of buying the watch was £NIL.

If, however, the target was not achieved, a contribution would be paid via direct debit to the insurance company; the greater the amount by which the target was missed, the more was paid.

This had a number of benefits. It gave Vitality a marketing edge in the insurance market and increased the number of members.

It also made policyholders think about taking exercise, thereby staying healthier and reducing the amount of health insurance claims.

Test your understanding 4

BGH company is a supplier of vintage wines and uses many types of technology in its business.

The temperature and humidity in its chain of atmosphere-controlled warehouses is recorded by sensors and automatically transmitted to head office so that any problems can be identified and dealt with as soon as they arise. Wine barrels are fitted with barcodes which are scanned by despatch staff as the barrels pass through the warehouse to record the movement of inventory. The data from the barcodes is recorded on BGH's system, updated overnight and can then be accessed by staff via the company network.

BGH's sales teams visit potential customers at their homes or places of business and use their work laptops to make sales and record transaction details remotely. Many of the sales staff also wear wrist mounted health monitors which relay real time information about their heart rate, physical activity etc. to the company. Those willing to wear the devices are provided with an upgraded health care insurance package. The company has also ensured that the sales team's cars are fitted with satellite navigation systems. Staff complain that the systems cannot provide real time traffic information but they are updated for new road networks every time the cars are serviced.

The board of BGH has been warned by the company's IT director that the Internet of Things has extended their network and will require a fresh assessment of their security risks.

Based on the information provided, which of the following devices used by BGH would be categorised as being included in the Internet of Things?

Select ALL that apply.

A   Warehouse atmosphere sensors.

B   Barcode readers in the warehouse.

C   Sales team's laptops.

D   Wrist mounted health monitors.

E   In-car satellite navigation systems.

7 Big Data

 Big Data is a term for a collection of data which is so large that it becomes difficult to store and process using traditional databases and data processing applications.

Big Data often also includes more than simply financial information and can involve other organisational data (both internal and external) which is often unstructured.

Examples of data that inputs into Big Data systems can include:

- social network traffic
- web server logs
- traffic flow information
- satellite imagery
- streamed audio content
- banking transactions
- web page histories and content
- government documentation
- GPS tracking
- telemetry from vehicles
- financial market data.

The shift to Big Data

Traditionally, businesses gathered structured information on relevant issues from a variety of sources and placed them into a database, or data warehouse.

As the world has increasingly moved towards digitisation (and especially through the growth of the internet), almost all information relating to the organisation and its environment can be stored electronically. The amount of unstructured data generated by electronic interactions increased significantly – through emails, online shopping, text messages, social media sites as well as various electronic devices (such as smartphones) which gather and transmit data. In fact, it is estimated that around 90% of the information in the world today has been created in the last few years.

The amount of data which businesses have to store and interrogate has therefore increased at an exponential rate, requiring new tools and techniques to make the most of them.

Illustration 12 – Big Data

Ford's modern Hybrid Fusion model of car (which has a hybrid petrol/electric engine) generates up to 25 GB of data per hour and the company is experimenting with vehicles that produce ten times that amount. This data can be used for many purposes, including:

- A computer model has been developed that projects CO_2 emissions generated by the fleet of vehicles on roads worldwide for the next 50 years. This helps Ford to balance fuel economy requirements and environmental considerations.

- Mathematical models have analysed millions of possible vehicle combinations to assist in the construction of a technology roadmap which has resulted in the development of new features such as Ford Auto Start-Stop.

- Ford researchers have developed specific tools such as the Ford Fleet Purchase Planner, which analyses fleet customers' needs and identifies their optimal vehicle choice.

The features of Big Data

According to Gartner, Big Data can be described using the '3Vs':

- **Volume** – this refers to the significant amount of data that the organisation needs to store and process. Match.com (an online dating company) estimates that it has 70 terabytes of data about its customers.

- **Variety** – Big Data can come from numerous sources. For example, Match.com (with user permission) also gathers data on users' browser and search histories, viewing habits and purchase histories to build an accurate view of the sort of person the customer might like to date.

- **Velocity** – data is likely to change on a regular basis and needs to be continually updated. For Match.com, new customers will join the service, or existing customers will find their needs and wants from a partner may change. Match.com needs to continually gather data to ensure that they are able to deal with this.

Another V which is sometimes added by organisations to the above list is:

- **Veracity (truthfulness)** – it is vital that the organisation gathers data that is accurate. Failure to do so will make analysis meaningless. Match.com has found that when gathering customer data, customers may lie to present themselves in the most positive light possible to prospective partners. This will lead to inaccurate matches. Using non-biased sources of information (such as purchasing or web browser histories) rather than relying on customer feedback is therefore important.

Test your understanding 5

U has recently started looking at ways of gathering Big Data for her business. She is concerned that some of the sources of data she has chosen are unreliable and may therefore lead her to inaccurate conclusions.

Which of Gartner's features may be missing from U's Big Data?

A   Variety

B   Velocity

C   Veracity

D   Volume

Illustration 13 – Big Data

Netflix has over 120 million users worldwide who watch billions of hours of programmes a month. The company uses information gathered from the analysis of viewing habits to inform decisions on which shows to invest in. Analysing past viewing figures and understanding viewer populations and the shows they are likely to watch allows the analysts to predict likely viewing figures before a show has even aired. This can help determine if the show is viable.

Illustration 14 – Big Data

Big Data analysis is being used by some organisations to help increase crop yields by providing information to farmers about when to plant, manage and harvest their crops.

The Climate Corporation, a company acquired by agricultural conglomerate Monsanto in 2013, operates an information system that keeps track of weather measurements from 2.5 million locations every day, along with 150 billion soil observations. It processes this data to generate 10 trillion weather simulation data points.

With this information, the company claims it can provide US farmers with temperature, rain and wind forecasts for areas of 200 acres and above for the next 7 day period.

This allows the farmers to decide optimal times to sow, spray and harvest crops to maximise their yields and reduce wastage.

Benefits of Big Data

Big Data has several stated benefits to the organisation, including:

- **Driving innovation** by reducing the time taken to answer key business questions and therefore make decisions.

- **Gaining competitive advantage** by identifying trends or information that has not been identified by rivals.

- **Improving productivity** by identifying waste and inefficiency, or identifying improvements to working procedures.

A recent study by Bain & Co suggested that, of 400 large companies, those that had adopted Big Data analytics have gained a significant market advantage.

Illustration 15 – Big Data benefits

Delivery company UPS equips its delivery vehicles with sensors which monitor data on speed, direction, braking performance and other mechanical aspects of the vehicle.

Using this data to optimise performance and routes has led to significant improvements, including:

- Over 15 million minutes of idling time were eliminated in one year, saving 103,000 gallons of fuel.

- 1.7 million miles of driving were also eliminated in the same year, saving a further 183,000 gallons of fuel.

Big Data problems

As mentioned before, one of the difficulties with Big Data is the ability to convert it to useful information. To help with this, a number of new open-source platforms have emerged to help organisations make sense of Big Data, such as Hadoop and Cassandra, though these may be difficult to integrate with existing data warehouses.

New roles are also emerging in business – such as 'data scientists' whose role is to help the organisation get meaning from the data it stores. However, due to the rapidly changing nature of Big Data analysis, there is a shortage of skills and support for these systems.

It is important to realise that just because something CAN be measured, this does not mean it should be. There is a risk that valuable time and money will be spent measuring relationships and information that has no value for the organisation.

The organisation needs to consider how to keep its data secure from viruses and hackers.

Does the organisation actually own the data it has collected on individuals? There may be legal (Data Protection) and privacy issues if it holds large amounts of data on potential customers.

Illustration 16 – Risks of Big Data

It is widely reported that Walmart tracks data on over 60% of adults in the US, including online and in-store purchasing patterns, Twitter interactions and trends, weather reports and major events. The company argues that this gives them the ability to provide a highly personalised customer experience.

Walmart detractors criticise the company's data collection as a breach of human rights and believe the company uses the data to make judgements on personal information such as political view, sexual orientation and even intelligence levels.

Test your understanding 6

S Ltd is a large business that produces online tax returns for businesses and individuals. It has a large cash surplus and has invested significantly in its IT infrastructure in the last several years. It currently has a large database which stores a wide variety of information about its customers.

The CEO of S believes that S has failed to fully understand its market. He has proposed that S adopt a Big Data approach. This would involve expanding the current database to enable the storage of information recorded on customer tax returns.

S is confident that it could use this to tailor its products and services to customer needs, as well as identify possible additional services that could be offered to customers. It does not believe that its rivals have adopted this approach to date.

Which of the following concerns should S have about the use of Big Data in this way?

A   High setup costs

B   Lack of IT knowledge

C   Privacy issues

D   Lack of competitive advantage

Test your understanding 7

BDT company is an on-line retailer and gathers data on a range of business factors such as its sales patterns, the economy, its customers and competitors, and the market for its products.

BDT has convened a board meeting to discuss how the company should manage the data. The marketing director believes that insufficient use is currently being made of the information contained within the data and wishes to exploit the opportunities it presents. The marketing department is not clear how best to classify the data but wishes to understand the patterns within it. The IT director is concerned that the data changes almost daily and will need continual updating.

Which of the following comments made by directors at the board meeting are correct?

Select all that apply

A   BDT will need to use supervised machine learning to interrogate the data.

B   Moving to cloud computing would help BDT to store the vast volumes of data it is currently gathering.

C   The speed of data change being faced by BDT is often described as its Veracity.

D   Big Data refers specifically to the amount of financial data being gathered by a company on its customers' purchasing patterns.

E   It will be vital for BDT to analyse all the data it collects and so maximise the available information.

Test your understanding 8 – (Integration question)

PL is a global firm of accountants and business advisors offering a large range of services to a wide range of clients. The company originally offered just two services (accounting and audit), but has branched out in the last ten years to provide tax, forensic accountancy (in partnership with a large law firm), consulting, insolvency and certain niche advisory services such as environmental reporting.

Evaluate the advantages to PL of adopting a Big Data approach.

(15 minutes)

8   Blockchain

What is blockchain technology?

A blockchain has been described as a decentralised, distributed and public digital ledger that is used to record transactions across many computers so that the record cannot be altered retroactively without the alteration of all subsequent blocks and the consensus of the network.

Alternatively, it has been defined by the Bank of England as a technology that allows people who do not know each other to trust a shared record of events.

Benefit of a blockchain

The main benefit of blockchain is security. In the digital era, cyber security is a key risk associated with the use of IT systems and the internet. This is because traditional systems have been 'closed', and so modifications to data have been carried out by just one party. If the system is hacked, there is little control over such modification to prevent it from happening.

> ### Illustration 17 – Credit cards
>
> A simple illustration is the relationship that individuals have with their banks or credit card companies. If a transaction is carried out with either (for example, you use your credit card to pay for goods or services) there is only one party that records the transaction, your credit card company. How is that company to know that the transaction is valid? If the details appear reasonable, the transaction will be authorised. This allows those who carry out credit card fraud to make their (illegal) gains.

Key features of a blockchain

- In a blockchain system, transactions are recorded by a number of participants using a network which operates via the internet. The same records are maintained by a number of different parties; as a transaction is entered, it is recorded by not just two parties, but instead by all of the parties that make up the overall chain. This can happen because all of the records in the blockchain are publically available and distributed across everyone that is part of that network.

- When a transaction takes place (for example, between a buyer and a seller) the details of that deal are recorded by everyone – the value, the time, the date and the details of those parties involved. All of the ledgers that make up the blockchain are updated in the same way, and it takes the agreement of all participants in the chain to update their ledgers for the transaction to be accepted.

- The process of verifying the transaction is carried out by computers; it is effectively the computers which make up the network that audit the transaction. If all of the computers review the transaction and verify that the details are correct, the systems of all participants in the blockchain have updated records. The computers work together to ensure that each transaction is valid before it is added to the blockchain. This decentralised network of computers ensures that a single system cannot add new blocks to the chain.

- When a new block is added to a blockchain, it is linked to the previous block using a cryptographic hash generated from the contents of the previous block. This ensures that the chain is never broken and that each block is permanently recorded. It is intentionally difficult to alter past transactions in the blockchain because all of the subsequent blocks must be altered first.

It is this control aspect of blockchain technology which addresses the main concern of cyber security. If anyone should attempt to interfere with a transaction, it will be rejected by those network parties making up the blockchain whose role it is to verify the transaction. If just one party disagrees, the transaction will not be recorded.

Illustration 18 – Cryptocurrency

Bitcoin is a digital currency that was introduced in 2009. Other cryptocurrencies exist, such as Ethereum and Litecoin.

There is no physical version of Bitcoin; all Bitcoin transactions take place over the internet. Unlike traditional currencies, Bitcoin is decentralised, meaning it is not controlled by a single bank or government. Instead, Bitcoin uses a peer-to-peer (P2P) payment network made up of users with Bitcoin accounts.

Bitcoins can be acquired in 2 different ways: 1) exchanging other currencies for bitcoins; and 2) bitcoin mining.

The first method is by far the most common, and can be done using a Bitcoin exchange such as Mt.Gox or CampBX. These exchanges allow users to exchange sterling, dollars etc. for bitcoins.

Bitcoin mining involves setting up a computer system to solve maths problems generated by the Bitcoin network. As a bitcoin miner solves these complex problems, bitcoins are credited to the miner. The network is designed to generate increasingly more complex maths problems which ensures that new bitcoins are generated at a consistent rate.

When a user obtains bitcoins, the balance is stored in a secure 'wallet' that is encrypted using password protection. When a bitcoin transaction takes place, the ownership of the bitcoins is updated in the network on all ledgers, and the balance in the relevant wallets updated accordingly.

> There is no need for a central bank to authorise transactions, since they are verified by those computers that make up the system. This therefore has the advantages of speed, reduced cost (transaction fees are small, typically $0.01 per transaction), and increased security.
>
> Additionally, there are no pre-requisites for creating a Bitcoin account, and no transaction limits. Bitcoins can be used around the world, but the currency is only good for purchasing items from vendors that accept Bitcoin.

Test your understanding 9

TRS company is a component manufacturing company. It is one of a number of companies working together as part of a just-in-time supply chain for the production of medical sterilisation units.

A meeting has been convened by the heads of the companies involved to discuss a secure way for the companies to transact with each other and provide absolute certainty over the current location and ownership of goods.

Which ONE of the following digital technologies would be MOST likely to achieve this objective?

A   Machine learning

B   Blockchain technology

C   Process automation

D   Cloud computing

The relevance of Blockchain technology to finance professionals

Much of the accountancy profession is concerned with ascertaining or measuring rights and obligations over property, or planning how best to allocate financial resources. For accountants, using blockchain provides clarity over ownership of assets and existence of obligations and can dramatically improve efficiency.

Examples of how blockchain can enhance the accounting profession include:

- Reducing the costs of maintaining and reconciling ledgers

- Providing absolute certainty over the ownership and history of assets

- Helping accountants gain clarity over available resources

- Freeing up resources to concentrate on planning and valuation, rather than record-keeping.

9 Data visualisation

 Data visualisation is a general term that describes any attempt to take data and help people to understand it better by presenting it in a visual context. Patterns, trends, correlations and other relationships that might otherwise not be noticed in a narrative-type presentation can become clearer and more obvious when presented using some sort of data visualisation software.

Presentation of information

Presenting information in a diagrammatic form has been around for many years. Standard charts and graphs from using spreadsheet software have helped users appreciate content at a glance. However, as data analytics has become more sophisticated and the use of Big Data more commonplace, the way in which data is presented has had to evolve. In the digital era, the use of data visualisation tools and technologies are seen as essential to be able to analyse meaningfully massive amounts of information and to be able to make data-driven decisions.

There are many common general types of data visualisation, including:

- Charts
- Tables
- Graphs
- Maps
- Infographics
- Dashboards.

More specific examples of methods to visualise data include:

- Bubble clouds
- Cartograms
- Heat maps
- Histograms
- Radial trees.

This is not an exhaustive list, merely some examples in the ways in which data can be presented.

Illustration 19 – Motor insurance

An article on the World Economic Forum website ("How businesses can benefit from visual analytics") cites the example of how data visualisation can be of use to companies that sell motor insurance.

Historically, the insurance industry has offered vehicle insurance cover based on age, sex, previous claims, location, etc. It is now able to offer usage-based vehicle insurance, alternatively called pay-as-you-drive (PAYD) insurance to its customers.

The insurance value under such schemes is determined based on type of vehicle used, distance covered, vehicle braking pattern, etc. Volumes of such data are collated and stored through as telematics tracking device. However, insurance companies find it challenging to exploit the data in analysing and rolling out suitable premiums across all sections of their customers. As a result, this means that they might operate at a sub-optimal level.

This can be overcome by means of data visualisation. For example, for a selected geographic category, provision can be made to show a map with bubbles for each customer segment.

The map can then be zoomed in to multiple sub-layers to study the relationship between two parameters and seek correlations in real time. For example, the insurance company can determine the appropriate premium by comparing parameters such as age of the insured, gender, profession, type of road driven, average miles driven per year, probability of accident, etc.

This helps the insurance companies to price their products and charge different sections of their customers accordingly.

Illustration 20 – Pharmaceutical companies

Visual analytics can be used in the pharmaceutical industry to compare gene sequence from multiple patients in real time. This enables the pharmaceutical companies to analyse new trends and take better-informed decisions on drugs trials. Additionally, it helps them to modify their research methodologies as per the results of trials so far and therefore enables them to bring their drugs to market more quickly.

In essence, data visualisation techniques help organisations to understand their home-grown data in more detail and therefore to exploit it better to achieve growth and flexibility. This will then lead to competitive advantage as the organisation moves ahead of its rivals through being proactive in its markets rather than having to follow a trend.

Test your understanding 10

The board of BUL company is meeting to discuss the staffing levels needed in its large retail store. The store's visitor numbers fluctuate throughout the day, with differing patterns on different week days. The board wants to understand how the density of customer numbers changes over each day in order to identify peak periods and quieter times.

The sales director is considering how best to illustrate the fluctuations in customer numbers.

Which ONE of the following types of data visualisation would be most suitable for the sales director to use?

A   Heat map

B   Radial tree

C   Cartogram

D   Pie chart

10   3D Printing

3D Printing, also known as Additive Layer Manufacturing (ALM) is a process whereby three-dimensional solid objects are created from digital files. Each item produced is created by laying down successive layers of material, each of which is a thinly-sliced horizontal cross section of the final object. The end product is gradually built up by repeatedly adding these cross sections.

Applications for 3D Printing

Until the mid-2000s, the only viable application for 3D printing was with soft plastic, and this was limited. However, the technology has advanced significantly, and the range of materials that can be used in 3D printing applications has expanded enormously. It is now seen in sectors of industry as diverse as aerospace, car manufacturing, electronics, healthcare and education.

Illustration 21 – Airbus

Airbus Group uses 3D printers for tooling, prototyping and making parts for test flights and aircraft in commercial service. The Airbus A350 is a long-range, twin-engine airliner, and is the first Airbus aircraft with both fuselage and wing structures made primarily of carbon fibre reinforced polymer.

More than 1,000 of the plane's components are now 3D-printed. The Group sees this as an important step in reducing manufacturing waste and making its aircraft lighter, resulting in greater fuel efficiency and less harmful to the environment.

Benefits of 3D Printing

3D Printing has several stated benefits, including:

- **Reduced waste** – it is estimated that 3D printing generates 5–10% waste material (which can then be recycled or reused) instead of the much higher rate of waste that results from traditional manufacturing techniques that create a part by cutting away a solid block of material, rather than building it up layer by layer.

- **Eliminate transport costs** – as production can occur at the point where the product is required, the organisation will not have to incur shipping costs to have it brought in from a 3rd party supplier.

- **Less environmental impact** – the reduction in 'travel miles' in getting the product to its required location will mean lower overall carbon emissions.

- **Shorter lead times** – components can be produced as they are required, meaning lower lead times between identifying a need and taking possession of the product. This should result in less requirement for holding inventory and therefore reduced investment in working capital.

- **Greater customisation** – the component may be tailored better to specific requirements if made in-house.

- **Increased profitability** – if a component can be made in-house rather than sourced from a supplier, the organisation will not have to pay an element of overall profit to that supplier to give them a return. This should result in increased margins for that organisation.

- **Social benefits** – in certain sectors of industry, 3D Printing can help solve social issues that traditional manufacturing processes cannot.

Illustration 22 – 3D Printing in the construction industry

Apis Cor is a construction company based in San Francisco. Founded in 2014, it claims to have created a 3D Printer that is capable of building an entire house in just 24 hours – and that will last for 175 years.

Not only does this mean that construction can be hugely accelerated to meet global housing shortages (traditional houses naturally take much longer to build), but Apis Cor built its first house in Stupino in Russia at a time when construction would not normally take place because of the cold (usually cement cannot be used when temperatures drop below 5 degrees centigrade). Apis Cor placed its 3D Printer inside a large tent when temperatures outside went as low as –35 degrees.

The video showing the house being built can be seen here:

www.youtube.com/watch?v=xktwDfasPGQ

Dubai has announced that 25% of the emirate's new buildings will be made by 3D printers by 2025. The Dubai Future Foundation claims that this strategy will reduce labour by 70% and cut costs across different sectors by as much as 90%.

Illustration 23 – 3D Printing in the healthcare industry

There are many applications for 3D printing in the healthcare industry, including hearing aids, personal prosthetics, dental crowns, surgical implants and facial reconstruction. This is because 3D printing allows for much greater personalisation, meaning that a bespoke product can be created for a particular person's needs and style/shape of body. This also has benefits to the healthcare providers – if units are made bespoke to each consumer, there is no need to buy items in bulk.

3D printing also has uses in creating pills and tablets. For example, if a patient suffers from multiple ailments, a bespoke pill can be made aimed at solving different illnesses simultaneously. The 3D printed pill can contain multiple drugs at once, each with different release times. This can make life much simpler for patients.

Problems of 3D Printing

There are however a number of problems of 3D printing, including:

- **Cost** – the cost of creating a 3D printer can be high, meaning that small businesses may find it a technological area that is beyond their financial means.

- **Quality concerns** – the fact that products made using a 3D printing process can be bespoke means that there is no universally accepted standard. This then leads to concerns over quality, strength and reliability, meaning that organisations forego the potential benefits of 3D printing for the perceived lower risk in traditional manufacturing processes.

- **Lack of skills** – as with any new technology, 3D printing requires specific expertise. Until it is firmly established, organisations may struggle to recruit/train staff to have skills needed to exploit it properly.

- **Legal concerns** – 3D printing may make it possible for manufacturers to "steal" the intellectual property of companies by copying products that, under traditional manufacturing laws, they would not be allowed to make. It is possible that new legislation will need to be drafted to cover such areas, but this takes time.

- **Environmental impact** – a study at Loughborough University in 2009 found that a 3D printed product would have taken as much as 50-100 times the amount of energy to produce compared to traditional moulded manufacturing techniques. Furthermore, plastic is commonly used in 3D printing, and the environmental concerns over use of such product are growing.

- **Ethical concerns** – for example, in the healthcare industry, pharmaceutical companies have to go through rigorous trials before a product can be licenced for sale by the regulatory bodies. Creating a bespoke medication for a particular patient may mean that such approval processes are not possible.

Test your understanding 11

BQP hospital uses surgical implants in many operations – for example in the treatment of hip, knee and other joints. Once an operation has been scheduled, the implants are ordered from external suppliers, and then transported to the hospital via road and rail. Implants are often an inexact fit so high volumes of inventory are held to provide surgeons with the greatest possible choice.

After reviewing the increasing costs associated with the use of surgical implants the hospital's Technical Director has suggested BQP should acquire a 3-D printer to make the components within the hospital.

Which THREE of the following potential outcomes are MOST likely should BQP decide to acquire the 3-D printer?

A   Improved implant quality

B   Reduced expenditure on shipping

C   Greater customisation

D   Higher inventory levels

E   Shorter lead times

11   Process Automation

Process automation (also known as Robotic, Digital or Business Process Automation) refers to the use of digital technology to perform a process or processes to accomplish a workflow or function. Or, to put it another way, processes that used to be done manually become automated.

A simple illustration is the example of Apis Cor in the previous section, which has devised a means of building a house using a 3D printer instead of traditional labourers.

As part of digital transformation, processes can be automated in almost any industry.

Illustration 24 – Airports

Much of the process for checking in and dropping bags off at airports has now been automated, meaning that passengers no longer have to wait in (sometimes long) queues in order to receive their boarding passes and check their luggage in.

The boarding pass can be printed at home or simply shown via a smart phone, having been emailed in advance by the airline.

Machines with scales enable passengers to weigh and print the relevant baggage tags on arriving at the airport. The bag is then simply dropped off at one of the conveyor belts, leaving the passenger to go straight to security checks and passport control.

Automation results in a speedier and more satisfying experience for the passenger, and cost reductions for the airline as it no longer has to employ as many check-in staff.

Benefits of Process Automation

There are a number of benefits associated with Process Automation:

- **Productivity** – employees can be released from mundane activities and redeployed to more value-adding tasks.

- **Accuracy** – as processes are automated, this eliminates the risk of human error. This should mean that the right result, decision or calculation is achieved at the first attempt.

- **Consistency** – identical process and tasks should be achieved in standardised activities, resulting in no variations.

- **Audit trail** – automation of activities should result in a complete log being recorded of all tasks carried out and the outcomes. This can be essential for compliance purposes.

- **Flexibility** – if processes are subject to spikes or troughs in demand (for example, a seasonal business) automating the process will allow the organisation to deal better with such variations without compromising quality or service.

- **Staff retention** – if repetitive or mundane activities can be carried out in the workplace automatically, employees can be redeployed on more stimulating jobs of work, resulting in greater job satisfaction. This is particularly important in roles requiring skilled or semi-skilled staff.

- **Availability** – automated processes can be carried out 24/7, 365 days a year.

- **Cost savings** – significant cost savings can be produced through automation, as certain roles can become redundant in the organisation.

Illustration 25 – Finance departments

Many organisations have typically busy month-end procedures, whereby results for the month just passed are collated into templates, variances calculated and commentary provided in order to give management a detailed basis on which to make future decisions about the business. This can be a stressful time for finance staff, as a lot of work has to be completed in a short space of time.

Relevant software can be introduced which enables data to be drawn automatically from integrated sources to complete the necessary templates. Furthermore, if the software is sophisticated enough to be able to interrogate the source data, variance commentary can be provided with little or no human intervention. This can result in a much speedier reporting process with less stress for finance staff.

Challenges of Process Automation

- **Lack of integration in IT systems** – in large businesses with many different components to IT, there may be a lack of integration that makes process automation impossible without first investing significant time and money in making the systems more aligned. For example, in a group comprising a parent company and many subsidiaries, it might be possible to automate processes in just 1 company but not across the group as a whole because the IT systems are incompatible.

- **Lack of standardisation** – automation works when processes are high volume, based on set rules, repetitive and needing no element of human judgement. Organisations where this is not found will struggle to benefit from process automation.

- **Reluctance to reduce headcount** – the automation of work processes has a natural consequence in many people's eyes that it leads to job losses. This may not necessarily be the case; it can be argued that people are still a necessary resource, but will be deployed to more value-adding activities rather than routine and repetitive work. However, there may be resistance from employees if they feel that their positions are threatened.

- **Cost** – acquiring or developing the necessary software may be beyond the budget of the organisation, even though it might produce long-term cost savings.

- **Lack of skills** – this may be within the business itself. For example, new skills will be needed in implementing, monitoring and servicing the automated systems, and may require new roles to be created and filled.

  Alternatively, it could be in terms of software providers. Process Automation is still a young industry, and it may be that there are not enough suppliers with the necessary skills to create the solution needed for a particular organisation or industry.

> **Test your understanding 12**
>
> BHJ is a tax advisory organisation operating in H-Land. It has a large number of offices, many acquired in the last two years, and most of its IT systems have not yet been integrated. Clients come to BHJ requiring a range of services from the completion of their routine tax returns to the provision of detailed tax advice about the implications of a group restructuring. The tax authorities in H-Land have strict compliance requirements for tax returns which must be fully supported with the relevant corroborating documentation. BHJ is growing fast; its highly skilled workforce is currently struggling to cope with the workload and a back log of work is building up.

The board of BHJ is meeting to discuss how best to manage the organisation's growth. The IT director has suggested that BHJ should introduce business process automation into its service provision business model. Not all of the directors are currently in support of the idea.

Based on the information provided, which of the following comments about process automation made by BHJ's directors are correct?

Select ALL that apply.

A   BHJ's lack of IT systems integration would be no obstacle to the use of process automation.

B   The use of process automation could help to reduce the back log currently faced by BHJ.

C   Process automation could simplify the provision of the compliance documentation required by the tax authorities.

D   Process automation would allow BHJ to make better use of its highly skilled workforce.

E   Process automation would not be suitable for BHJ because some clients require highly technical advice.

Test your understanding 13

During a business conference about the issues involved in process automation, its potential drawbacks are being discussed. Managers from several companies are comparing the features of the businesses they work for and considering the reasons why process automation may therefore not be suitable.

Which THREE of the following business features would be an obstacle to process automation?

A   The accuracy of processes is of vital importance to product safety.

B   A highly unionised workforce will make it difficult for the company to reduce its headcount in routine work roles.

C   The relevant processes are subject to significant fluctuations in demand.

D   The company currently has no IT department and a severely limited budget.

E   The company's processes are run on a large number of unintegrated systems.

12   Summary

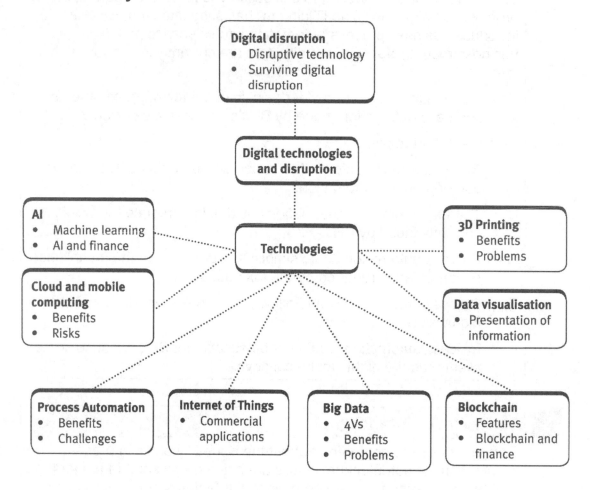

Test your understanding answers

Test your understanding 1

The correct answer is E

Digitisation is the process of converting information into a digital format. All businesses can adopt this approach. It may help the company to achieve operational efficiencies but it also offers opportunities for innovation, expansion and competitive advantage. It does not mean that a company must use cloud computing nor that all devices must be able to access the internet. However the process of introducing a successful programme should not be underestimated and simply setting up a business unit to manage the process will not be sufficient. Top level responsibility and full organisational buy in will be needed.

Test your understanding 2

The correct answer is A

RTY is using supervised learning where the machine is given data classifications and then applies them to the data. Unsupervised learning is used where no clear classifications can be identified in advance and the algorithms are used to explore the data and find the intrinsic patterns. Reinforcement learning is where the algorithm has a result to achieve (like maximising returns) and then interacts with the environment to learn the best way to achieve it. Feature learning is a technique used in machine learning which allows the system to discover what is needed to identify features or classifications from raw data.

Test your understanding 3

The correct answers are B, C and E

One of the main advantages of mobile computing is that it allows workers greater flexibility to work remotely. However all the additional devices (such as tablets and laptops) which are then joined to the company's network increase the risk of unauthorised access and so endpoint security will need to be strengthened. The need to keep client data confidential does not preclude the use of cloud computing and indeed many companies do keep such data 'in the cloud' but hackers may be more likely to target cloud service providers than individual businesses and so care must be taken to select a reliable provider. Additionally with cloud computing no actual data is stored on the remote device, so losing it would not carry the same risks of losing sensitive data.

Test your understanding 4

The correct answers are A and D

The key component of items included in the Internet of Things is that they communicate without human intervention using the internet. This would therefore exclude devices such as laptops and barcode readers which require human involvement and the in-car satellite navigation systems which do not currently access the internet. The warehouse sensors and wrist mounted health monitors are examples of items included in the Internet of Things.

Test your understanding 5

The correct answer is C

By definition.

Test your understanding 6

The correct answer is C

S already has a significant amount of IT infrastructure and seems to have the relevant skills to maintain, suggesting that this would not be a problem of adopting Big Data. The fact that the organisation would be the first in its industry to adopt this approach (which it seems confident will improve its service provision) would also seem to suggest that it will gain competitive advantage from such a move.

However, storing such a large amount of personal information opens up the organisation to issues surrounding privacy and data protection. Customers may be unwilling to allow the company to use their personal data in this way and there may be legal implications as well.

Test your understanding 7

The correct answer is B

Big Data includes all types of internal and external data. It describes the position where the collection of data is so large that it becomes difficult to store and process using traditional databases and data processing applications.

Machine learning is where algorithms are used to make predictions and recommendations by processing data and experiences. Unsupervised learning means that the algorithm interrogates input data without being given any explicit output variable and is needed where the data can't be classified as is the situation here. Supervised learning requires human input to first classify the data which BDT cannot do.

The speed by which data changes is known as its 'Velocity'. Big Data analytics can help the companies to control and manage this flow of data. However firms should be wary of spending resources on analysing data that cannot provide it with valuable information, and care should be taken to interrogate only that data that will be genuinely useful.

Using cloud computing would mean that an external service provider would store BDT's data on the internet rather than companies storing it on its in-premises systems which would provide them with greater capacity.

Test your understanding 8 – (Integration question)

Capturing Big Data and having the capability to manage and analyse such data has many business benefits, but also comes with risks.

Companies like PL will gather huge amounts of data about their clients in a wide range of different formats. This data will cover fairly straightforward transactional data, such as the clients' sales history, but will also include less structured data regarding products, services, competitive environment and key personnel.

Traditionally accountancy and advisory firms would have used the data collected to make a very specific conclusion (for example a calculation of tax liability), but wouldn't have harnessed the data gathered to better understand the client and business opportunities for PL. If Big Data management principles were applied, PL could perform analysis on all of this additional information to make decisions regarding cross-selling opportunities, more targeted marketing activity and identify further niche advisory options.

Despite having access to such a wide variety of data, PL needs to take greater care than some companies when using this data. As a professional services firm, they will need to ensure that they are complying with all relevant ethical codes, which may restrict the amount of data shared between departments. PL will also need to observe any relevant data protection legislation as large amounts of data gathered will be sensitive business information about their clients.

Another area that PL can use Big Data management is during the recruitment process. Firms in this industry receive thousands of applications for graduate schemes each year and have traditionally relied on academic qualifications to shortlist candidates.

A wider range of data through networks such as Facebook and LinkedIn can lead to a more meaningful and effective selection process.

Test your understanding 9

The correct answer is B

Blockchain technology allows for the synchronisation of all data and transactions across a network and each member must verify the transaction before it can be approved. It is increasingly being used to link supply chains as it provides certainty over the current location and ownership of goods.

Process automation is the conversion of processes that used to be done manually so that they become automated. Machine learning is where algorithms are used to make predictions and recommendations by processing data and experiences. Cloud computing involves service providers storing software, applications, servers etc. on the internet rather than companies storing them on in-premises systems.

Test your understanding 10

The correct answer is A

The main use of heat maps is to help visualise the volume of locations or events within a collection of data by using variations of colouring. This would be ideally suited to showing the density of visitor numbers throughout the day with stronger shading being used to represent greater densities.

A radial tree is used to lay out hierarchical relationships which radiate out from a central point. A mind map is an example of a radial tree.

A cartogram is a map in which a chosen mapping variable – such as population size, or income per head – is substituted for land area or distance and the land sizes are distorted accordingly.

A pie chart is used to show proportions or percentages between categories by dividing a circle into appropriately sized chunks.

Test your understanding 11

The correct answers are B, C and E

If the hospital owns a 3-D printer it will be able to produce more components as needed without the need to wait for external deliveries (so lower shipping costs and shorter lead times) and will be able to customise the implants to exactly match the needs of each patient. This should lead to lower inventory levels. However the quality control mechanisms within the medical supplies market may well be tighter than those over a hospital operated printer and so implant quality may be less certain.

Test your understanding 12

The correct answers are B, C and D

Process automation involves using digital technology to perform repeatable work flows or functions. Completion of routine tax returns would therefore appear to be a suitable process for automation. It would not matter that some clients require complex advice as process automation can be applied to individual processes and need not be rolled out across all the organisation's activities. It could simplify the provision of the audit trail required by the tax authorities in H-Land and since it can run 24/7 it could also help to reduce BHJ's back log. However process automation does require integrated IT systems to run effectively and this could be an obstacle to its successful introduction.

Test your understanding 13

The correct answers are B, D and E

Two of the strengths of business process automation are the accuracy with which processes can be performed and the way that workflow can be controlled to smooth out fluctuations in demand. However unintegrated systems and a lack of IT skills to manage the process (and a limited budget to address this lack) will present obstacles that will need to be overcome if the implementation is to be successful. One of the benefits of the approach is reduction of staff costs on routine processes but this will be problematic if it is difficult to reduce the headcount.

Digital strategy – governance and elements of digital strategies

Chapter learning objectives

Lead	Component
F1: Describe the governance of digital transformation	(a) Describe the roles and responsibilities of the board and executive leadership in digital strategy
F3: Discuss the various elements of digital strategies	Discuss: (a) Economics of digitisation (b) Digital ecosystems (c) Digital consumption (d) Data and metrics (e) Leadership and culture

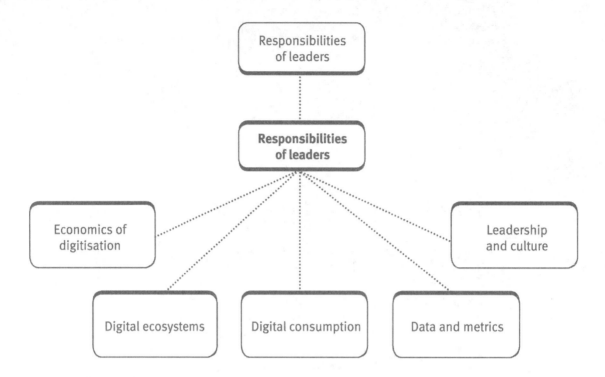

1 Introduction

In the previous chapter, we looked at modern digital technologies and the concept of digital disruption. In this chapter we will focus on the role of leadership in introducing and making best use of such technologies, and how digital transformation will affect the strategic thinking and control of the organisations that undergo such change.

2 The roles and responsibilities of the board and senior leadership

In order for an organisation to properly take advantage of a move to digital, or to survive digital disruption within its industry, the executive leadership team will need to demonstrate a number of abilities:

1 **Inspirational leadership** – digitisation will be an exercise in change management, but probably on a bigger and quicker scale than the organisation will typically be used to. The leadership team will need to energise the workforce and inspire confidence that digitisation is the right way forwards and is being carried out in the right way.

    The move to digital will only succeed if those at the top of the organisation take ownership and persuade others to commit to the change.

2 **Competitive edge** – not only will the leadership need to motivate others within the organisation to see the digital transformation as the right strategy; they will also have to persuade people to potentially change their mind-set. The need to adopt an inquisitive attitude, to be prepared to innovate and think outside the box, to experiment and to learn from failures may not be second nature to some, but is likely to be critical in transforming successfully to digital.

3   **Establishing a strategic direction** – this is probably something that the business has done for a long time, but a digital strategy may require it to be done in a different way. For example, the planning horizon may need to be shortened, or greater flexibility introduced – perhaps a move away from the rational model discussed in chapter 1 to a more emergent approach, which would enable the business to adapt as time passes.

4   **Influence external parties** – for example, providers of finance. Raising capital is likely to be necessary, but showing how that capital may be applied and the value that will result might be more problematic. Will investing in cloud technology deliver increased shareholder wealth? If so, how much? And when? There will be greater uncertainty over outcomes, and the leaders of the business will need to be persuasive and articulate a compelling value proposition.

5   **Collaboration** – as has already been mentioned earlier in this text, the organisation will need to see itself as part of a wider ecosystem if it is to deliver the requisite value. This will require careful thought on who to collaborate with and how each part of the ecosystem will contribute.

6   **Business judgement** – what sort of business model will the organisation need to put in place? It is probable that an altogether different model to what has worked in the past will be required.

7   **Execution** – having determined what technologies can help to drive the business forwards, thought must then be given to how these can be used most effectively by the people within the business. People and technology need to work in harmony to produce the desired outcomes.

    Careful thought must also be given to how the execution of the digital strategy and transformation is to be managed. For example, what sort of metrics (or KPIs) need to be put in place? What benchmarks should be adopted as a successful outcome?

8   **Building talent** – it will be critical to identify the skills that staff will need to demonstrate and to manage training/recruitment to ensure that the business has those skills. New roles are likely to be required, including at the most senior level – for example, perhaps a new board position of Chief Digital Officer.

Much of the above is discussed in more detail in the following sections.

Test your understanding 1

GHJ is a successful, long established business. It has a profitable product portfolio and a close relationship with its customers. Many of its shareholders have held their shares for many years and take a long-term view of their investment. One of GHJ's competitors recently approached the company with an opportunity to collaborate on a new digital product which, if successful, would revolutionise the business area in which it operates and earn profits for both companies. However sales of the new product would inevitably negatively impact its current product portfolio. The board has stated that to take up the offer the company would need to transform itself into a digital enterprise.

Which TWO of the following factors are MOST likely to be obstacles to the board accepting the opportunity and becoming a digital enterprise?

A   GHJ currently has a successful business model

B   The company has a close relationship with its customers

C   The current product portfolio may be negatively impacted

D   Shareholders currently take a long-term view of investment

E   The opportunity is being suggested by a competitor

3   Economics of digitisation

Organisations that want to become digital enterprises face two fundamental obstacles that need to be addressed: firstly, how to deal with the traditional business model that has served them so well for so long. It is being disrupted by digital innovation and no longer works the way that it used to. Secondly, a successful move to being a digital organisation will only work if that business is prepared to disrupt itself – does it have the stomach to do that?

The risk-averse business manager will naturally be alarmed at the prospect of damaging profitability, and will not therefore embrace a significant change to the business model. Critics would point out that such a leader is focussing purely on the present; they are not looking after shareholder value in the long term, which means looking to the future.

Illustration 1 – Amazon

Amazon has grown to become one of the world's most valuable companies through being prepared to disrupt itself on a number of occasions. Its first business model was based on selling books cheaply over the internet, and offering value that bricks and mortar retailers such as Waterstones and Borders could not match. But then it produced the Kindle, an e-reader which cannibalised sales of books in hard copy format.

The company moved from selling books to also selling DVDs, again challenging the market share enjoyed historically by organisations such as HMV. Amazon subsequently disrupted itself by launching Amazon Prime, a streaming service which made customers move away from buying hard copy product.

It is argued that Amazon's success is largely due to the vision of its founder Jeff Bezos, who has shown bold leadership and created an innovative culture at the company.

In looking at how to disrupt themselves, organisations should question the ways in which they can earn revenues. It used to be that businesses would see overall revenue as a very simple outcome: it is volume × price.

However, in the digital era the ability to generate revenue should be seen in a much broader context; in essence, there is more than 1 way to earn a living.

Key to recognising potential revenue opportunities is to make use of the wealth of data that the organisation has at its disposal i.e. to capitalise on its knowledge via Big Data analytics. Large organisations will have so much information available, both in a B2B and B2C capacity – the secret is to leverage that knowledge to the organisation's benefit. Furthermore, the cost of both storing and making use of such data is decreasing all the time, making such usage a more viable economic option.

In assessing the economics of digitisation, business leaders are encouraged to stop seeing revenue as being solely the preserve of selling a product or service; their horizons should be broadened by looking at how networks, sales channels and customer engagement can add value.

Nine revenue models have become evident from the possibilities that digital technology presents, some of which the organisation may already adopt, but others represent new opportunities:

- **Transaction** – a traditional approach, whereby goods are sold from one party to another.

- **Capacity leasing** – the organisation has a form of resource, such as machine time, asset availability or human time, and supplies such capacity to customers.

- **Licensing** – another traditional revenue source – instead of making a product itself, the organisation licences its technology, brand or intangible assets to another organisation for a defined period of time.

- **Subscription** – products or services are subscribed to and paid for in advance. This could be for a short or long period of time. For example, Netflix allows subscribers to cancel their payments at any point in time.

- **Commission** – revenue is earned through matching sellers to customers. For example, as well as selling its own products through its website, Amazon also allows third party retailers to market via the same platform, for a fee.

- **Advertising** – particularly for social media organisations, but not purely restricted to such businesses. For example, BT generates revenue through allowing advertisers to use its email platforms.

- **Trading** – it is possible to identify circumstances where the demand/ supply market forces are producing a sales value which is mispriced. Traders can use technology to identify opportunities to buy at a low price and sell when more realistic prices are in play.

- **Donations** – acts of philanthropy can result in intangible benefits to the donor.

- **Subsidies** – often found in public sector organisations, whereby subsidies are given to improve quality of service in areas which cannot be fully funded by traditional revenue models.

Illustration 2 – Michelin

Michelin has adapted its business model, from being a manufacturer and seller of tangible goods (tyres) to selling outcomes (a promise of performance that is backed by a guaranteed refund if not satisfied).

Michelin offers a package that is has branded EFFIFUEL, which includes sophisticated telematics, training in how to drive efficiently, and a tyre management system. It claims that purchasing such a service can save significant costs in operating trucks (fuel and replacing tyres) and also in terms of carbon dioxide emissions.

Test your understanding 2

BVF company is a broadcasting company.

It is introducing a new film and television streaming service with customers paying a monthly fee to access a wide range of programmes. Where possible, customers will also be offered the opportunity to buy the DVD accompanying a show for a small one-off sum. Demand for the service is expected to fluctuate so BVF will pay larger organisations to use their spare IT infrastructure as needed. BVF will offer other companies the chance to show short promotional videos at the start of streamed programming in return for a fee.

Based on the above information which of the following revenue models is BVF's move into digital technology exploiting?

Select ALL that apply.

A   Transactional

B   Capacity leasing

C   Subscription

D   Commission

E   Advertising

4   Digital ecosystems

In chapter 1 the term ecosystem was introduced, and it was identified that it relates to all the organisations that collectively work together – either through cooperation or competition – with a view to creating value. The real advantage of the ecosystem is that it is able to deliver greater value than the individual participants acting alone.

The need for the organisation to recognise that it is part of a broader ecosystem is even more apparent in a digital context. In order to keep up with the increasing demands of customers, organisations need to view themselves as part of a broader attempt to create value, otherwise the customer expectations are unlikely to be satisfied. This will inevitably mean that the business leader will need to consider how a participant in the ecosystem will impact on his/her own organisation's strategy. What is each organisation's function within the broader ecosystem?

For example, it may be that 1 participant is able to operate on a global scale, whilst other participants satisfy local demands. Or that, due to a lack of certain skills in-house, knowledge needs to be shared with other participants who can successfully fill that skills gap.

3 key questions need to be asked with regards to each participant that makes up the ecosystem, and thus how it might impact on any one organisation's strategy:

- **The precise role of the participant within the environment** – what is that participant bringing to the party? It may be cloud computing capacity. Possibly distribution capability. Possibly unique software skills. Access to certain markets, perhaps due to owning a particular licence to operate. It makes sense that, for the ecosystem to create the value that is possible, all necessary participants are present.

- **Each participant's reach through the environment** – this relates to the participant's ability to extend activity or interactions through the environment. For example, can the participant operate on a global or just a local level? Can it deal with both consumer (B2C) and industrial (B2B) markets?

- **The capability or key value proposition** – this is the range of activities that participants are able to pursue or undertake in the environment. What is the key value that each participant is able to deliver?

> **Illustration 3 – Nest**
>
> Nest is a US-based provider of home automation products, from thermostats that control the central heating system to surveillance cameras and smoke alarms. It has created a new technology platform that offers homeowners a unique experience because it has correctly brought in other companies such as Mercedes Benz and LG to bring capabilities that Nest itself does not possess.

5 Digital consumption

Organisations have always had to evolve to keep up with changing expectations of customers, very often driven by advances in technology.

For example, in the music industry the accepted offering for listening to music was, for many years, in vinyl and cassette format. This then changed in the 1980s to CD, before the advent of the internet enabled consumers to purchase online and download to mobile devices such as MP3 players. This then progressed further to streaming instead of outright purchase. Each successive development lead to a decline in demand for the previous format (although interestingly there has been a recent resurgence in demand for how it all started, as sales of vinyl have started to grow again!).

However, since the start of the new millennium, the rate of change has grown considerably, driven by 2 principal factors: organisations are adopting technologies that enable them to transform the experience that customers can enjoy; and the expectations of the customers themselves are changing at a much faster rate. This latter point is only likely to continue, as present and future consumers, who have been born and raised in such a digital world, embrace new technologies more quickly and expect that they will be able to benefit from improvements to their lives as a result, meaning that organisations will find it much more difficult to surprise them.

Organisations will therefore need to constantly reinvent what they offer to customers if they are to satisfy their rapidly changing expectations.

Drivers of the digital revolution

If organisations are to meet these ever-changing needs, it is important that they understand the key drivers behind such change. The following are identified as key factors:

- **Mobile and internet penetration** – the increasing rate of mobile phone ownership, combined with access to the internet (with mobile beginning to exceed broadband). It is estimated that by 2025 the number of smartphone subscriptions will reach 4 billion, with much of the growth coming from emerging economies.

- **Connected devices** – the number of connected devices are expected to grow from 2.5 billion in 2009 to 30 billion by 2020. This will help enable real-time customisation of products and services.

- **Data analytics and the cloud** – the increasing use of e-commerce platforms, social networks, apps etc. will result in increased need for automated data analytics.

- **User interfaces** – advances in how human beings interact with machines (e.g. through voice recognition or motion-tracking systems) means that carrying out tasks becomes quicker and more efficient for humans.

- **Global accessibility** – rising living standards in developing economies means that more and more people are gaining access to the internet and so increased connectivity.

- **Increasing urbanisation** – the growing percentage of people who live in urban as opposed to rural areas. The United Nations estimates that, from approximately 54% of the global population in 2014, this will grow to almost 60% by 2050.

In essence, more and more people are becoming connected to technology, enjoying the benefits that it delivers, and demanding that such benefits increase, not just within 1 industry but across industries – there is no reason to believe that advances in 1 area of business cannot be transferred to other areas.

Illustration 4 – Pager

Based in New York, Pager is a company that provides on-demand health care from local medical professionals via mobile-based services. Users can request services such as check-ups, arranging prescriptions and diagnosis of illnesses from the doctor of their choice within their local area. House calls are made within 2 hours of the service being requested.

In many respects, this is an example of how benefits can be transferred from 1 industry (such as Uber and transport requirements) to another (healthcare). It is therefore little surprise that Pager was founded by Oscar Salazar, a former Uber engineer.

What does the digital customer want?

According to the World Economic Forum/Accenture analysis, there are a number of factors that drive customer demands in the digital era. These include the following:

- **Contextualised interactions** – this is a rather complicated way of saying that customers expect a product or service that is tailored to their own specific needs. The video streaming service Netflix helps meets this demand by making recommendations on programmes that are likely to be of interest to the viewer based on historic patterns.

- **Seamless experience across channels** – from being made aware that a product or service exists, to doing the research about the product or service, to then taking the decision to purchase, customers expect a seamless service throughout the process. This can also be extended to how the customer pays and takes delivery of the goods.

- **Anytime, anywhere** – there is an expectation of being able to access real time information about a product or service. This does not just mean characteristics of the product; it also relates to inventory levels, how soon delivery will occur, the ability to track progress etc.

- **Great service (it doesn't matter who provides it)** – there is less instance these days of customers remaining loyal to a provider following an example of poor service. Customers are prepared to shop around for products or services if they have had a bad experience.

- **Self-service** – customers are prepared to invest more time and energy into getting exactly what they want. This doesn't simply mean customising the features of an existing product; it may mean developing new models that correspond exactly to their needs. Innovations such as 3D printing are an example of just how this is becoming possible.

- **Transparency** – the digital customer expects to have full transparency of information about a product or service before they commit to a purchase. This includes details such as precise features of the product, but also extends to how personal information is to be collected and used. Customers are protective of their personal data and want choice in deciding whether or not it is shared.

- **Peer review and advocacy** – there is greater instance these days of customers attaching more importance to independent reviews of products or services than to marketing information provided by the business or reviews from other organisations (such as trade journals). The purchase decision will be influenced by what fellow customers have said, meaning that a poor review can have a disastrous effect on future sales potential.

  For example, many customers on Amazon place great store by the reviews and star ratings attached to products that have been bought by other people. Similarly, the decision on which hotel to stay at or restaurant to eat at could well be determined by comments on sites such as Booking.com or TripAdvisor.

  It is also estimated that bad reviews are seen by twice as many people as good reviews.

Keeping ahead of customer expectations

The question must therefore be asked: given that customer demands are evolving at such a rapid pace, how can organisations adapt so that they keep up with, or preferably ahead of, those expectations? A seemingly successful offering today could rapidly fall out of favour and lead to a reversal of the organisation's competitive advantage.

This can be avoided via the following:

- **Design thinking** – instead of designing a single product or service that can be marketed to many customers, there should be a shift in mind-set to designing many experiences for one customer. This must be mixed with the ability to constantly learn and adapt as customer needs change.

- **Experiental pilots** – this refers to the need to monitor how customers behave and to gain an appreciation of their reaction to new experiences. Questions should be asked such as "How are the customers responding to a new technology in the way they engage with it? How are customers being influenced by others? What reactions, emotional and behavioural, are we seeing through the new customer experience?"

  The organisation should be prepared to continuously take products to a new level, through innovation and developing prototypes, to be able to gauge such reactions.

- **Prototyping** – instead of waiting until a new product has been perfected before bringing it to market, an organisation should recognise that speed to market is vital. So, the first generation of a product may be only about 80% ready, but it provides vital feedback in terms of customer reactions and what needs to be done with the second version.

- **Brand atomization** – organisations will need to design their offerings so that they can be more widely distributed and be part of the platform that is offered by other providers.

Test your understanding 3

In its attempts to keep ahead of customer expectations Geezer, a music streaming service, has allowed its technology to be compatible with many manufacturers of hardware, including Eros (which makes internet-connected audio systems), Singsam (a manufacturer of smart TVs), and the operating system of the world's leading computer software manufacturers.

This is an example of which **ONE** of the following?

A   Design thinking

B   Experiential pilots

C   Prototyping

D   Brand atomization

Test your understanding 4

QPO company supplies utilities to domestic customers. It has a wide range of services on offer.

The board of QPO company are discussing the importance of meeting the needs of its digital customers. The marketing director has explained that one factor driving digital demand is the need for contextualised interactions.

Which ONE of the following strategies would be most appropriate to provide customers with contextualised interactions?

A   Streamline the process of selecting, purchasing and receiving the services

B   Allow customers to select their own options to create a personalised bundle of services

C   Increase the quantity of information provided on each service and clarify how personal data will be used

D   Ensure customers can access their account and track the progress of any purchases at all time

Test your understanding 5

BNN company is a manufacturer of interactive video games. In order to maximise the player experience, teams of gamers are paid to play games during their 'beta' stage (before the design is finalised) and provide BNN with their feedback. The designers also work to ensure that when they are released the games can be played on multiple platforms to maximise sales.

Which ONE of the following techniques are being demonstrated by the design team at BNN?

A   Knowledge sharing

B   Design thinking

C   Brand atomisation

D   Experiential pilots

E   Journey management

6 Data and metrics

In chapter 8 the subject of metrics (or KPIs, to use an alternative phrase) was introduced, and it was identified that any organisation needs to adopt an appropriate mix of both financial and non-financial metrics as part of its strategic performance management system. This will be no different for a business in the digital era, and very careful thought must be given by management as to what measures should be put in place and how the necessary data relating to those measures can be captured.

A financial measure that has been given great importance historically has been Return on Investment (ROI). Digital transformation will represent a considerable investment, but few companies that have undergone such change have been able to quantify the ROI of their digital initiatives. It is therefore necessary to look for alternative measures, collectively referred to as **digital traction metrics**.

This will be particularly important if the organisation needs to attract investment from outside sources for the digital transformation to be possible. Such providers of capital are likely to be reassured that the long term prospects are attractive, as it has been proven that organisations with high digital traction are linked to high company valuation.

Digital traction metrics

Whilst they cannot give assurance about the ROI that an organisation is enjoying from its digital transformation, they do provide evidence as to how attractive the organisation's products or services are to customers. By looking at a combination of metrics in certain areas, focussing mainly on customer behaviour, the organisation can gauge both the appeal of its products or services, and how quickly they are likely to be adopted in the market.

Digital traction is a combination of metrics in 3 areas: **Scale, Active Usage, and Engagement**.

- **Scale** – this relates to the number of people who are showing an interest in the product or service. Typical metrics could include the number of visitors; unique users; the number of registered users; growth in registrations per month; or organic user acquisition.

- **Active usage** – this refers to the frequency with which a user interacts with the organisation. Appropriate metrics could include the number of active users; daily active users (DAU); monthly active users (MAU); conversion rate; abandon rates; the number of repeat users/customers.

- **Engagement** – these measures look at the degree to which the user has engaged with the organisation. Suitable metrics may include time spent on site; Net Promoter Score (NPS); customer satisfaction index; posts contributed; number of likes and shares; photos/videos shared/uploaded and views completed.

There should also be metrics that measure the financial impact of attracting and keeping customers, and assessing whether the organisation is being profitable in such dealings. Two metrics that help with this are:

- **Cost to acquire a typical customer (CAC)** – this can be calculated by looking at all expenditure on sales and marketing and dividing by the number of new customers won.

- **Lifetime value of a typical customer (LTV)** – this can be measured by multiplying the average monthly recurring revenue by the average customer lifetime.

It stands to reason that the LTV needs to be greater than the CAC for the organisation to be profitable. Success can be measured by how much LTV exceeds the CAC.

Such metrics can also be used to calculate ratios. 2 ratios that will give management valuable information are:

- **LTV:CAC** – as mentioned above, this gives insight into profitability and cash flow.

- **Months to recover CAC** – this can be calculated as CAC/average monthly recurring revenue, and is very similar to a payback period calculation.

As was examined in chapter 8, a suitable benchmark for digital metrics would need to be established taking specific industry circumstances into account.

For example, attracting one new customer per month might be deemed acceptable for a high value online company that deals in B2B services, but would not be particularly impressive for Facebook or Instagram.

Test your understanding 6

Sundog is an online greetings card company. It offers customers the opportunity to create customised greetings cards which can be sent either to the customer's home address or straight to the intended recipient. In measuring its digital traction, which **THREE** of the following would be classed as active usage metrics?

A   The number of customers purchasing from the site each day

B   The number of customers per day who have purchased from Sundog before

C   Feedback ratings from customers

D   The number of customers closing their accounts

E   The number of visitors to the website

Test your understanding 7

BSR company has recently expanded and has therefore launched a new website to promote and sell its new range of products. As the company uses a balanced scorecard approach to measure its performance, the board is meeting to discuss the new metrics it will need to include under each of the different perspectives.

One area of the customer perspective that the board wishes to measure is the extent of engagement with the organisation.

Which TWO of the following metrics would help the board to measure customer engagement with BSR?

A   Cost to acquire a typical customer (CAC)

B   Number of visitors to the site

C   Time spent on the site per visit

D   Net Promoter Score (NPS)

E   Number of daily active users (DAUs)

Test your understanding 8

MBP company operates in P-Land where the currency is the P$.

The board of MBP wishes to evaluate the ratio between the cost of acquiring a typical customer (CAC) and their lifetime value (LTV).

The following information is available:

Sales and marketing expenditure in the period   P$252,000

Number of new customers won in the period   500

Average monthly revenue per customer   P$8

Average customer lifetime   6 years

What is MBP's CAC:LTV ratio?

A   21:2

B   7:8

C   21:4

D   8:7

Test your understanding 9

VDS company wishes to gain some assurances about the success of their digital transformation strategy and plans to introduce a series of metrics to measure Digital Traction.

What are the THREE areas in which metrics will be needed to measure Digital Traction?

A Scale

B Size

C Engagement

D Active usage

E Data usage

7 Leadership and culture

Much has been discussed in the previous sections of this chapter about the benefit and impact of introducing digital strategies into an organisation, but there still remains the all-important question of how it can all be made possible. The business will need to ensure that it has staff with the right skills, that it can attract new recruits as necessary, that the appropriate leadership style is adopted, and that a digital culture is properly fostered.

These will now be looked at in turn.

Attracting and retaining talent in the digital age

With increasing levels of digitisation in the workplace, 2 features have become apparent with regards to employing staff.

1   There is much greater transparency about employment opportunities for those seeking a new challenge, with applicants becoming more and more informed thanks to increased levels of "inside information". This has come about because of the presence of agencies and peer reviews.

Illustration 5 – Glassdoor

One of the fastest growing jobs and recruiting sites in the world, Glassdoor keeps over 8 million reviews on more than 423,000 companies. Information such as CEO approval ratings, interview reviews and questions, office photos, benefits and salary reports etc. can be accessed. This is all provided by employees through a peer-to-peer network.

Businesses are realising that transparency needs to be encouraged, and that a mind-set of "we have nothing to hide" needs to be adopted. Research shows that fostering such a business culture actually results in a more productive workforce and lower levels of staff turnover.

2   The competition for digital talent is increasing; there is a global skills shortage in this area to cope with the increasing demand.

So what do organisations need to do to attract and retain the necessary talent? Firstly, they need to take great notice of what their staff are saying about their organisation, which can be done by monitoring social platforms such as Glassdoor, LinkedIn, and Twitter.

Secondly, they should look to introduce a referral programme. This means incentivising current staff to use such online networks to refer potential new employees; if employees are incentivised in the right sort of way to champion their employer's digital referral programme, attracting the right calibre staff becomes much easier.

Becoming an employer of choice

It stands to reason that the latest generation of employees, the so-called "millennials", should be the main target for organisations looking to embrace a digital strategy; after all, these are the people who have grown up in the digital era – they see digital as the norm, they have the necessary skills with digital technology, and they also understand what younger customers are looking for in products and services.

Millennials represent a generation that feels empowered to choose where and how they work, and employers must recognise this if they are to offer an attractive working proposition. Technology will be an important part of that proposition; the provision and use of technology is considered one of the most important factors in determining job satisfaction. However, it is not the only factor.

Illustration 6 – Zappos

Zappos is an online clothing retailer. It has a reputation for a strong corporate culture that employees identify with that makes them want to work for the company. This includes having a management structure that is task-orientated, rather than a more formal structure. Employees are encouraged to deal with customers in whatever way is felt appropriate, to use the Zappos Twitter account to air their thoughts, and to work wherever will let them be most creative, such as coffee bars and co-working spaces.

So how does an organisation become an employer of choice in the digital era? The World Economic Forum proposes the following:

- **Formulate a long-term working strategy for millennials** – identify the relevant positions that employees will occupy during their career with the company and then create suitable promotional opportunities.

- **Work with staff to formulate company values together** – this means listening to, and taking note of, the aspirations of those working for the business. Senior management should do this in person, not just as a communication sent company-wide.

- **Empower the workforce** – and give them incentives to perform e.g. via long term company share plans, project leadership responsibilities or training opportunities.

- **Build workspaces that attract digital talent** – this relates to the physical layout and appearance of the working environment. Flexibility and a dynamic appearance in the workplace inspires creativity and collaboration. Thought should also be given to allowing staff to work from home on occasions and flexible working hours.

- **Create policies that support collaboration and knowledge-sharing tools** – this can include encouraging staff to use platforms such as Facebook@work, Yammer or Sprinklr, or hardware preferences such as being to use your own laptop in the workplace.

Test your understanding 10

VMP company is expanding. The firm's future strategy is to fully embrace digital technology and it therefore needs a highly skilled digitally literate workforce. It operates a flat organisation structure. The board is meeting to explore the best ways to attract and retain employees.

The finance director believes that the company should set up a performance-based share option scheme. The human resources director recommends that VMP should expand opportunities for mobile working. The chief executive believes that to understand employee's aspirations a link to an on-line questionnaire should be sent to all employees for completion. The marketing director has suggested the creation of social work hubs within the building.

If the directors' suggestions are all put in place, which THREE of the following advantages are potential employees MOST likely to anticipate from working with VMP?

A   Identification of opportunities for progression through the organisation

B   Ability to help formulate company values

C   Incentives and rewards to work well

D   Flexible working

E   Opportunities for collaborative working

Creating a workforce with digital skills

In a recent survey conducted by PwC, almost three quarters of CEOs cited skills shortages as a threat to their businesses, and 81% claimed to be looking for a broader range of skills when recruiting. Digitisation is leading to new roles being created in companies, which demand different skills sets.

The table below shows roles that might now be relevant for certain aspects of an organisation:

Commercial	Technology	Web	Marketing	Facilitation	HR
E-business manager	Scrum master	Web project manager	Digital marketing professional	Service design thinker	Design learning manager
Digital account manager	Data scientist	Web designer	Digital copywriters	Content curator	Digital work experience officer
Digital product manager	Chief Data Officer (CDO)	Webmaster	Media acquisition manager	Editorial manager	Employer brand director
Fraud manager	Data protection officer	Developer	User experience designer	Chief Listening Officer	

In order to create a workforce with the right digital skills, organisations need to collaborate with educational establishments – universities, colleges, schools – with a long term view to giving students the right skills and confidence to be the employees of the future.

Illustration 7 – Lockheed Martin

The American aerospace and defence company Lockheed Martin has a programme whereby its engineers, scientists and IT professionals volunteer to meet with schoolchildren between the ages of 9 to 12 with a view to building their interest and confidence in science and technology. This is then sustained throughout school and college.

Organisations also need to focus on making in-house training a critical activity within their talent management programme. This will included the following:

- **Develop required competencies within the workforce** – this can be done by considering the skills that are currently needed and creating training strategies that are adapted to these. The organisation should look ahead and question where the high value work is likely to be in, say, 3 years' time compared to today, and train accordingly.

- **Mine your own organisation for hidden talent** – this will incorporate assessing employees' abilities and matching these to skills required.

- **Bring new skills into the organisation** – this can be done by either hiring new, digitally-competent staff, or running exchange programmes with other digital companies and sharing insights. Rotating staff internally to give them exposure to other aspects of the organisation is also common practice within tech giants such as Google and Amazon.

Bringing leadership to the digital age

In order for digitisation to work, leaders need to adapt. This may mean a different approach to establishing a corporate structure and also fostering an alternative culture in the workplace. Leaders need to show that they are forward-thinking and progressive, and not just rely on business practices that worked in years gone by.

A traditional approach to structure might be hierarchical and autocratic – roles and responsibilities are clearly defined and work on a top-down basis. In the digital age leaders need to accept that this traditional approach will not attract people of the right skills and will certainly not get the best out of them.

As Steve Jobs once commented: "We run Apple like a startup. We always let ideas win arguments, not hierarchies. Otherwise, your best employees won't stay. Collaboration, discipline and trust are vital".

It would therefore appear that flatter organisational structures are key to making digital work.

Furthermore, a culture of being more risk-tolerant is to be encouraged. Instead of focussing on the mistakes of employees, the organisation should be encouraged to accept failures and to persuade staff to take higher amounts of risk. This will necessarily mean changing the focus on how the organisation performs – it cannot restrict itself to just short term goals, with failure to hit annual targets being seen as career-threatening. Management need to take a longer view of performance, and instil a culture that promotes this.

According to the World Economic Forum, CEOs should fulfil six key roles in the digital age:

- **Creator of vision and mission** – the company's mission statement should be expanded to encompass a transformation purpose.

- **Strategic planner** – this is nothing new, but the focus will change. There should be a move from 5 year to 1 year planning cycles, driven by data and analysis. Greater focus should be on experimentation rather than long-term planning.

- **Driver of information-based business models** – find and develop new products that are (fully) data- and information-based for scalability.

- **Enabler of the shift to on-demand operating models** – the CEO should champion the benefit that can be gained from communities in the workplace, crowdsourcing and staff on demand.

- **Innovation promoter**

- **Operational excellence driver** – identify ways in which automation can be introduced into processes in all departments of the organisation.

Test your understanding 11

MBC company manufactures complex components for use in the aerospace industry. It works closely with its customers to develop new products and refine current ones in order to advance their goals as well as its own. Its mission statement is 'to build the best, to offer the closest partnerships, to always deliver'.

The company currently has a one-year planning cycle, which is regularly updated by reference to economic and competitor data as well as product design plans. MBC operates a just-in-time service and has set up customer service centres across international time zones so that customers can discuss their needs at all times. Back-office services are provided by a dedicated team of long-serving staff and production processes are fully automated.

The company has just approved a new digital transformation strategy. In order to decide what will be needed to oversee the process, MBC's CEO has been reviewing the 'roles for a digital age' suggested by the World Economic Forum (WEF).

According to the WEF, which TWO of the following actions does the CEO most need to take in order to oversee the desired digital transformation?

A   Drive organisational excellence

B   Change the strategic planning focus

C   Revise the mission

D   Shift to a an on-demand operating model

E   Promote innovation

Fostering a digital culture

Culture can be defined as the shared set of beliefs, values and mind-sets that guide a group's behaviours. Having the right sort of culture in place can give the organisation a sustainable competitive advantage, as competitors will find it very difficult to replicate. Mention has already been made in previous sections of this chapter about the need for a different sort of culture in the digital era, but how can this be created and adopted?

To answer this question, leaders must first recognise what factors distinguish a digital culture from others. These include:

- Having a strong mission statement and a clear sense of purpose

- Lean business structures, with small, cross-functional teams as opposed to individual divisions working as separate siloes

- A diverse workforce with good digital skills.

Leaders can then focus on four key areas in order to move towards a digital culture:

- **Communication** – communication by digital means needs to be encouraged. This should certainly not replace face to face conversations completely, but staff should be encouraged to communicate with each other in an honest and open style using all available digital channels – social media, blogs, forums, webcasts and videos, shared mailboxes etc.

- **Journey management** – the leadership team needs to be at the forefront of the cultural change. In order for this to take effect at the operational level, middle management need to be encouraged to think in different ways. Creativity needs to be released, and training should be provided so that middle managers recognise how to achieve this. Further support can come from implementing the right HR policies, rules etc.

- **Make changes visible** – visual aids such as diagrams and charts on office walls, highlighting the "journey" that the business is undertaking.

- **Continuous change monitoring** – using tools such as feedback surveys and performance monitoring to highlight gains made.

All of this can be accelerated through appointing to a senior position someone who is already well-versed in digital culture.

 Test your understanding 12

GHY company is determined to adapt its established approach to business to create a more progressive culture and facilitate flexibility in the digital age.

Which TWO of the following changes would be MOST likely to help GHY achieve this goal?

A   A more risk neutral approach

B   A more risk-averse approach

C   A more risk-seeking approach

D   A shorter-term view of success

E   A longer-term term view of success

8   Summary

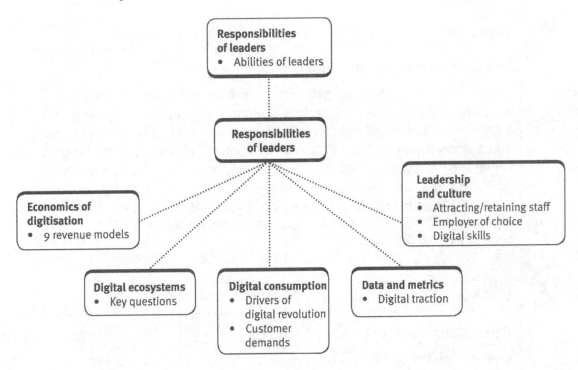

Test your understanding answers

Test your understanding 1

The correct answer is A and C

The new opportunity is an example of digital disruption. The two fundamental obstacles to the acceptance of digital disruption are that existing and successful business models will need to be changed and that a company's own sales will be disrupted. However shareholders with a long-term view and a close relationship with its customers should help GHJ to effect the change. The fact that the opportunity comes from a competitor need not present a major obstacle as working together will effectively strengthen the company against other competition in the market.

Test your understanding 2

The correct answer is A, B, C and E

The service being offered by BVF is a subscription service with customers offered the opportunity to enter into additional one-off transactions to purchase single DVDs. The utilisation of other company's infrastructure is known as capacity leasing, and the sale of promotional video space is a form of advertising. However BVF is not bringing together sellers and buyers for a commission.

Test your understanding 3

The correct answer is D

Allowing your design to be built into other manufacturers' platforms is brand atomization, by definition.

Test your understanding 4

The correct answer is B

To provide contextualised interactions means allowing customers to tailor their purchases to their own needs.

Test your understanding 5

The correct answer is C

Brand atomisation means designing products so that they can be more widely distributed and be used on platforms that are offered by other providers.

Experiential pilots involve monitoring the reaction of customers to new experiences.

Journey management refers to the role leadership must take in helping organisations move through a cultural change. Design thinking is a philosophy that focuses on maximising the number of experiences available to one customer rather than maximising the number of customers that might buy one experience. Knowledge sharing is a collaborative approach that is often taken by partner organisations working together to achieve a goal.

Test your understanding 6

The correct answer is A, B and D

Active usage refers to the frequency with which a user interacts with an organisation. This will therefore include the number of active users per day, the number of users who have purchased from the organisation before, and the number of users closing their accounts.

Test your understanding 7

The correct answer is C and D

To gauge customer engagement BSR needs to measure a customer's interaction with the organisation. Time spent on the site gives an indication of engagement. The NPS is completed by customers and specifically measures how willing they are to recommend an organisation's products.

CAC is a financial measure (often compared with the lifetime value of a customer (LTV)). Measuring visitors to the site can indicate the *scale* of customer interest, and DAUs can help to determine the level of *active usage*.

Test your understanding 8

The correct answer is B

CAC is expenditure on sales and marketing divided by the number of new customers won.

LTV is measured by multiplying the average recurring revenue by the average customer lifetime.

CAC = P$252,000/500 = P$504

LTV = P$8 × 12 months × 6 years = P$576

504:576 is equivalent to 7:8

Test your understanding 9

The correct answer is A, C and D

To measure the success of a digital transformation strategy, a company needs to measure Scale (the number of people who are showing an interest in the product or service), Active usage (the frequency with which a user interacts with the organisation) and Engagement (the degree to which the user has engaged with the organisation).

Test your understanding 10

The correct answer is C, D and E

A performance-based share option scheme should incentivise and reward great work, mobile working improves flexibility and social work hubs offer workers the opportunity to collaborate.

A flat organisation structure may not appear to offer many opportunities for promotion as there is little in the way of a hierarchy. To truly take part in formulating company values employees should be individually consulted by senior management rather than simply sent a generic email.

Test your understanding 11

The correct answer is A and C

The company will need to expand its mission statement to encompass a transformation purpose and should be looking for ways to automate back-office organisational processes as part of its drive for organisational excellence.

The company already has an appropriately short one-year planning cycle and operates an on-demand operating model allowing customers to drive their own services. The company also works with its customers to innovate to better achieve their goals.

Test your understanding 12

The correct answer is C and E

GHY will need to encourage a culture of risk tolerance and acceptance of the value of risk. Additionally it will need to look beyond annual targets towards longer term opportunities.

Index

Index